I0797886

Guns, Furs, and Gold

An American West History of Indigenous Peoples and Explorers

LARRY E. MORRIS

University of Nebraska Press
LINCOLN

Manufactured in the United States of America

The University of Nebraska Press is part of a land-grant institution with campuses and programs on the past, present, and future homelands of the Pawnee, Ponca, Otoe-Missouria, Omaha, Dakota, Lakota, Kaw, Cheyenne, and Arapaho Peoples, as well as those of the relocated Ho-Chunk, Sac and Fox, and Iowa Peoples.

For customers in the EU with safety/GPSR concerns, contact:
gpsr@mare-nostrum.co.uk
Mare Nostrum Group BV
Mauritskade 21D
1091 GC Amsterdam
The Netherlands

Library of Congress Control Number: 2025003243

Set in Arno Pro by Scribe Inc.

Dedicated to the memory of Lavina Fielding Anderson, 1944–2023

Friend, mentor, and scholar

CONTENTS

ILLUSTRATIONS

Following chapter 3

Figures

Maps

ACKNOWLEDGMENTS

Thanks to the Charles Redd Center for Western Studies at Brigham Young University, Provo, Utah, for funding research for this book. Thanks to the librarians and archivists at the following institutions for their help: Little Big Horn College, Crow Agency, Montana; the Missouri History Museum, St. Louis; the State Historical Society of Missouri and Western Manuscript Collection, the University of Missouri, Columbia; the Harold B. Lee Library, Brigham Young University; the Museum of the Mountain Man, Pinedale, Wyoming; the Filson Historical Society, Louisville; the Wisconsin Historical Society, Madison; the Oregon Historical Society, Portland; the Lewis and Clark Heritage Foundation Archives, Great Falls, Montana; the Montana Historical Society, Helena; and the Family History Library and Utah Historical Society, both in Salt Lake City.

Thanks to my family for their support—Isaac, Tahlia, Charles, Tiffani, Margo, Reagan, Courtney, Adam, Kinnell, Justin, Jen, Elliot, Liam, Anya, Lorraine, and especially Deborah and Whitney (expert editors, researchers, and proofreaders).

Thanks to my agent, Chris Rogers of the Dunow, Carlson & Lerner Literary Agency; my editor at the University of Nebraska Press, Clark Whitehorn; and Brianna Blackburn and her associates at Scribe Inc.

Thanks to the two eminent historians who inspired this book, both of whom I have had the pleasure of meeting: John Logan Allen and Gary Moulton. I also appreciate the scholarship of Henry Nash Smith, Bernard DeVoto, James P. Ronda, Stephen Aron, and David A. White.

I must also thank the usual suspects for their friendship and scholarship, some of whom are sadly no longer with us: Jay Buckley, Mark Kelly and Carol Kuhn, Jim Hardee, Clay Jenkinson, Ron Anglin, Clint Gilchrist, Jerry Enzler, William Foley, Adrian Heidenreich, Jim Holmberg, Ella Mae Howard, Lanny Jones, Barb Kubick, Clay J. Landry, Donna Masterson, Joe Mussulman, Don Peterson, and Brian Cannon.

Guns, Furs, and Gold

Prologue

"The Lewis and Clark expedition had its origins in the mind of Thomas Jefferson many years before a crowded keelboat was launched into the Missouri River," writes Gary Moulton, editor of the captains' journals. Captivated by books and maps—and without traveling west—Jefferson "understood the interior better than any other American of his generation."[1] Nothing reveals Jefferson's passion for the West like his long history of proposing expeditions to the region. Late in 1783, just three months after the Treaty of Paris ended the American Revolutionary War, Jefferson, then forty years old and serving as one of Virginia's delegates to the Congress of the Confederation, wrote to military hero George Rogers Clark (one of William Clark's elder brothers) and asked if he would like to lead an exploration of "the country from the Mississippi to California." Embroiled in personal financial problems, Clark politely declined, even though he found the prospect of "a tour to the west and North west of the Continent . . . Extreamly agreable." Clark advised against sending a large party of men because they would alarm the Indians: "Three or four young Men well qualified for the Task might perhaps compleat your wishes at a very Trifling Expence." Those men would have to learn "the Language of the distant Nations they pass through," and the expedition "would require four or five years."[2]

Three years later, while serving as U.S. ambassador to France, Jefferson met the American adventurer John Ledyard, "well known in the U.S. for energy of body & mind. He had accompanied Capt. [James] Cook in his voyage to the Pacific ocean, and distinguished himself on that voyage by his intrepidity. . . . His immediate object at Paris was to engage a mercantile company in the fur-trade of the West coast of America." When that venture failed, Jefferson wrote, "I then proposed to him to go by land to Kamschatka [the Kamchatka Peninsula, in the Russian Far East], cross in some of the Russian vessels to Nootka sound [on the west coast of present British Columbia's Vancouver Island], fall down into the latitude of the Missouri, and penetrate to and thro' that to the U.S." Although Ledyard "eagerly siesed the idea" and managed to travel within two hundred miles of Kamchatka, he was then arrested by Russian authorities, who deported him to Poland.[3] As Bernard DeVoto writes, Ledyard "came under the scrutiny of Russian fur traders who were developing the Aleutian field and at that moment were preparing to expand southward along the coast to California. They could not let him carry out his plan and they didn't."[4]

In 1793, almost ten years after approaching George Rogers Clark, Secretary of State Jefferson wrote to the French botanist and explorer André Michaux on behalf of the American Philosophical Society, offering to fund a journey to "the shortest & most convenient route of communication between the U.S. & the Pacific ocean . . . & to learn such particulars as can be obtained of the country through which it passes." Michaux was to reach the headwaters of the Missouri River and then find a river flowing to the Pacific—all while avoiding Spanish authorities. When Michaux reached Kentucky, however, the French ambassador ordered him to "relinquish the expedition."[5]

The patient Jefferson bided his time, however, and in the late 1790s—when he was vice president and in his mid-fifties—one favorable event after another fell into place, setting the stage for an expedition worthy of the vastness and mystery of the West, one that showed how ill-planned and untimely previous attempts had been. First, in 1798, came the posthumous publication of George Vancouver's monumental *A Voyage of Discovery to the North Pacific Ocean and round the World, 1791–1795*, invaluable for its detailed maps of the northwestern Pacific coast. (After departing London, sailing around Cape Horn, and wintering in the Hawaiian Islands, Vancouver reached North America about 110 miles north of present San Francisco and followed the coastline all the way to the Alaska Peninsula.)

Next, late in 1800, Jefferson was elected U.S. president. A year later, the preeminent explorer Alexander Mackenzie, the first European to cross North America north of Mexico, published *Voyages from Montreal . . . through the Continent of North America, to the Frozen and Pacific Oceans, in the Years 1789 and 1793.*[6] In 1802 the British cartographer and geographer Aaron Arrowsmith produced *A Map Exhibiting All the New Discoveries in the Interior Parts of North America.* With all this crucial information now available—and with Hudson's Bay Company and the North West Company both champing at the bit to found cross-continent fur-trade operations—Jefferson petitioned Congress in January 1803 to approve an exploration "to the Western ocean" focusing on "conferences with the natives on the subject of commercial intercourse."[7] Congress agreed a month later, and plans for the expedition were well underway by the time the Louisiana Purchase guaranteed—by pure happenstance—that Meriwether Lewis, William Clark, and their men could travel from St. Louis to the Rocky Mountains without trespassing on foreign territory.[8]

Over a twenty-year period, the persistent Jefferson thus set in motion the first interactions between American explorers and a host of western Indian nations, including those emphasized in this volume—the Crows, Arikaras, Cheyennes, and Arapahos. In his message to Congress, Jefferson became a prophet of sorts by stressing the importance of reaching the Pacific, meeting with Indigenous peoples, and conversing with them on trade—three key elements of the "opening" of the American West that began with the Louisiana Purchase and the Lewis and Clark Expedition (1803–6) and ended with the annexation of Texas, the Oregon Treaty, the Treaty of Guadalupe Hidalgo, and the California Gold Rush (1846–55).[9]

True, the Renaissance-man Jefferson instructed Lewis and Clark to investigate all kinds of topics, from latitude and longitude measurements; the courses of rivers; soil, plants, and animals; weather and climate; mineral productions, metals, limestone, and volcanic appearances, to the names and numbers of Indian nations; the extent of their territories; their language, traditions, and monuments; their occupations in agriculture, fishing, hunting, arts, and war; their food, clothing, and domestic accommodations; the diseases prevalent among them; and their laws, customs, and dispositions. All that notwithstanding, Jefferson clearly reiterated the key objective of the western excursion: "Explore the Missouri river, & such principal stream of it, as, by it's course and communication with the waters of the Pacific ocean, whether the Columbia, Oregan, Colorado or any other river may offer the most direct & practicable water communication across this continent for the purposes of commerce."[10] Like James Cook, Alexander Mackenzie, George Vancouver, and a long line of others, Lewis and Clark made their expedition not for the sake of exploration itself but for economic advantage, whether you call that commerce, trade, or filthy lucre. Discovery was always subordinate to business.

"Other Men, at Other Times, Had Used Different Words to Say the Same Thing"

The question is, If Jefferson inspired Lewis and Clark, who inspired Jefferson? That is not easy to answer because Jefferson was a remarkably well-read individual. Luckily, however, Moulton also offers valuable help on this issue. In his 1983 *Atlas of the Lewis & Clark Expedition* (volume 1 of *Journals*), Moulton writes that the expedition was "preeminently a geographic endeavor" and lists John Logan Allen—now emeritus professor of geography at the University of Wyoming and the University of Connecticut—as one who deserves "special mention" for his "interest, aid, and unfailing support" in deciding the arrangement and choice of maps for the volume. Moulton adds that the key source for his discussion of "Jeffersonian conceptions of the West" was Allen's "superb study" *Passage through the Garden: Lewis and Clark and the Image of the American Northwest,* released by the University of Illinois Press in 1975 and instantly hailed as one of the most important books ever published on the expedition.[11] Although *Image* filled "a long-felt need for a cartographic study of the expedition," writes Donald Jackson, it was much more than that: "The theme of the book is conceptual geography, those notions that men contrive from their superstitions, their folklore, or—more to our liking—their keenest observations of the natural world." The captains put the accumulated geographical knowledge and lore of the Northwest to the test as they sailed up the Missouri from St. Louis. "Was there a massive cordillera forming the backbone of the West, and did a great river system rise on either side of it and flow off to the eastern and western seas? Conventional wisdom said so, and it proved to be true," Jackson writes. Of course, "conventional wisdom also said that a short portage would take a traveler from the headwaters of that east-flowing river to those of a westering one, and thence to the Pacific and the wonders of the Orient. That bit of conceptual geography got trampled beneath the cold and bleeding feet of the explorers as they toiled for nine days across the Bitterroot. There was no easy passage through the garden."[12]

Just as Moulton relied on *Image* for a discussion of Jefferson's concept of the West, he turned to Bernard DeVoto's *The Course of Empire* (1952) as a "standard source of background" on Lewis and Clark.[13] The native Utahn DeVoto was a novelist, essayist, critic, and historian who received the Pulitzer Prize and Bancroft Prize for *Across the Wide Missouri*, a chronicle of the American fur trade in the 1830s. *Empire* is aptly described as a "sweeping narrative [that] traces North American expansion . . . from Balboa's route to the Pacific through the early days of the Lewis and Clark Expedition [and tells] the dramatic story of how the geography of North America both encouraged and limited continental expansion, and defined the political, imperial, and national borders of the American nation."[14]

Allen agreed with Moulton's opinion of DeVoto, writing in his preface to *Image*, "Perhaps the greatest contributor of all to this work has been a man I never had the pleasure of knowing—Bernard DeVoto [who died in 1955 at age fifty-eight]. Above all who have written about Lewis and Clark, he understood their role as accepters, modifiers, and shapers of geographical lore and images. His masterpiece, *Course of Empire*, has served as the major conceptual foundation upon which I have erected this book."[15] As a glance at Allen's bibliography shows, he also drew on a wealth of seventeenth-, eighteenth-, nineteenth-, and twentieth-century sources in producing his own masterpiece, but two in particular have proved invaluable for the present discussion: Henry Nash Smith's *Virgin Land: The American West as Symbol and Myth* (1950) and Loren Baritz's "The Idea of the West" (1961).

The works of Allen and DeVoto, supplemented by those of Smith and Baritz, offer a stunning background to Jefferson's twenty-year plan to explore the West. As Allen notes, "The key words in Jefferson's instructions were 'water communication across this continent for the purposes of commerce.' But although the phrasing was Jefferson's, the idea was not. Other men, at other times, had used different words to say the same thing and had called the water communication a Northwest Passage or a Passage to India."[16] The water communication could also have been called a southwest passage, a passage to the Indies or to China, a passage through the garden (as Allen titled his book), a passage to the West, or a passage to the East by way of the West, to mention a few.

Among them, these four historians offer bountiful evidence of the universality of Jefferson's idea. Take *Empire* as a prime example. Although Balboa is mentioned early on, the book actually begins in the eighth century, when "a mixed people whom history was to call the Moors crossed the Strait of Gibraltar from Africa." After a seven-hundred-year war between the people of the Iberian Peninsula and the Moors, an Italian navigator by the name of Cristoforo Colombo found himself recounting to the "most Christian, most exalted, most excellent and powerful Princes, King and Queen of the Spains and of the islands of the sea," how they had sent him "to the countries of India . . . to see what they were like" and ordered him "not to travel to the East, not to journey to the Indies by the land route that everyone had taken before . . . but instead to take a route to the West, which so far as anyone knows no man had ever attempted." For the next four hundred pages, DeVoto describes the course of the North American empire, from the likes of Hernán Cortés, Hernando de Soto, Jaques Cartier, and Jacques Marquette to Alexander Mackenzie, Robert Gray, David Thompson, George Vancouver, James Mackay, John Evans, and many others. The key theme? How trade prompted exploration and exploration in turn inspired theories of a passage to the Western Sea and attempts to find it. The final chapter of *Empire*, entitled "The Passage to India," begins at Great Falls in June of 1805, with the captains and their party gazing at the ominous beauty surrounding them: "The ranked ranges of mountains to the west, wearing midsummer stoles of snow, had to be crossed and they knew they had no forecast of what crossing them might involve." The chapter ends in December at the Pacific coast, with William Clark carving notice of his arrival—"by land from the U. States in 1804 & 1805"—into a big pine and noting in his journal that the Corps of Discovery had reached "the enterence of the Columbia River into the *Great South Sea* or Pacific Ocean." Yes, writes DeVoto, "the waves pounding the bar . . . were coming in from China . . . and India" and the kingdoms of "Prester John and the Grand Khan."[17]

Smith takes quite a different tack, starting rather than ending *Virgin Land* with Jefferson and Lewis and Clark. Still, he shares DeVoto's central concern, dividing his book into three sections and dubbing the first "Passage to India." Smith acknowledges, however, that although Lewis and Clark crossed the continent, carrying out and carefully recording the wide variety of investigations requested by Jefferson, they had not found a "practicable" water route from east to west. Indeed, none existed. In Lewis's confidential letter to Jefferson—written upon the corps' arrival in St. Louis—he candidly admitted that the advantages offered by the passage he and Clark had found "will never be found equal on an extensive scale to that by way of the Cape of good hope [the shipping route around the tip of Africa that enabled trade between India, Europe, and America]."[18] Despite that, writes Smith, "the idea of a passage to India, with its associated images of fabulous wealth, of ivory and apes and peacocks, led a vigorous existence on the level of imagination entirely apart from its practicability." So compelling was the image "that it remained for decades one of the ruling conceptions of American thought about the West. It was almost an obsession with Thomas Hart Benton . . . who during the thirty years following the death of Jefferson was the most conspicuous and best-informed champion of westward expansion in Congress." Benton's amazing career extended from the founding of the Santa Fe Trail to the zenith of the Rocky Mountain fur trade to the brink of the War between the States. "The trade of the Pacific Ocean, of the western coast of North America, and of Eastern Asia, will take its track; and not only for ourselves, but for posterity," Benton wrote in 1849. "That trade of India which has been shifting its channels from the time of the Phoenicians to the present, is destined to shift once more, and to realize the grand idea of Columbus. The American road to India will also become the European track to that region. The European merchant, as well as the American, will fly across our continent on a straight line to China."[19]

In 1871—thirteen years after Benton's death, two years after the completion of both the United States' transcontinental railroad and the Suez Canal, and one year after the death of ninety-eight-year-old Patrick Gass, the last surviving veteran of the Lewis and Clark Expedition—the great American poet Walt Whitman, who, according to Smith, "gave final imaginative expression to the theme of manifest destiny," composed a poem entitled "Passage to India." Whitman says it is an expression of "what, from the first, . . . more or less lurks in my writings, underneath every page, every line, every where."[20]

Early in the 2,273-word poem, Whitman praises the literal passage:

Our modern wonders, (the antique ponderous Seven outvied,)
In the Old World the east the Suez canal,
The New by its mighty railroad spann'd,
. . . .
Passage to India!
Lo, soul, seest thou not God's purpose from the first?
The earth to be spann'd, connected by network,
The races, neighbors, to marry and be given in marriage,
The oceans to be cross'd, the distant brought near,
The lands to be welded together.[21]

By the time Whitman concludes his opus, however, he is singing of the universal quest of the soul:

Passage to more than India!
. . . .
Passage, immediate passage! the blood burns in my veins!
Away O soul! hoist instantly the anchor!
Cut the hawsers—haul out—shake out every sail!
. . . .
Sail forth—steer for the deep waters only,
Reckless O soul, exploring, I with thee, and thou with me,
For we are bound where mariner has not yet dared to go,
And we will risk the ship, ourselves and all.
O my brave soul!
O farther farther sail!
O daring joy, but safe! are they not all the seas of God?
O farther, farther, farther sail![22]

"Westward the Course of Empire Takes Its Way"

"The importance of the Lewis and Clark expedition lay on the level of imagination," continues Smith. This was true for Benton and Whitman and also the explorers who followed in the wake of the captains. The expedition "gave tangible substance to what had been merely an idea, and established the image of a highway across the continent . . . firmly in the minds of Americans." Smith specifically mentions John Jacob Astor's "ambitious plan of establishing trade between the Columbia Valley and the Orient" and William Ashley's efforts to develop "an overland route through the Platte Valley and over South Pass."[23]

This study focuses on the interactions between explorers and American Indians, especially the Arikara, Crow, Arapaho, and Cheyenne nations. The explorers in question are Lewis and Clark, particularly the former, who never recovered from the emotional and physical ordeal he suffered in crossing from Great Falls to the Pacific; Thomas Fitzpatrick, Jedediah Smith, and Hugh Glass, Ashley men; and Edward Rose, an outlier who was both an Astorian and an Ashley man. As Allen, DeVoto, Smith, and Baritz make clear, one cannot understand the experience of these frontiersmen and how they dealt with Indigenous peoples without understanding Jefferson's vision and the myriad influences behind it.

Baritz asserts that a theme "constant in the human story [is] the yearning for a land . . . of peace, and of life eternal," a land that engaged poets and sailors and was often "located to the west of the man who wondered where it was" and was followed by "the concept of the destiny of nations . . . from Troy to Greece, Rome, and England . . . the notion that the secular sword must be taken by a nation to the west."[24]

The classical literature familiar to Jefferson abounded with allusions to the West, such as a 1728 poem by the Irish Anglo philosopher George Berkeley that prophesies,

> There shall be sung another golden age,
> The rise of empire and of arts,
> The good and great inspiring epic rage,
> The wisest heads and noblest hearts.

Not such as Europe breeds in her decay;
Such as she bred when fresh and young,
When heavenly flame did animate her clay,
By future poets shall be sung.
Westward the course of empire takes its way.[25]

Not surprisingly, Jefferson also studied the journals and memoirs of the adventurers who plunged into the wilderness, knowing they seldom, if ever, undertook their quests unless prompted by economic, religious, or patriotic motives. He took an interest in western geography at an early age and read such reports as Louis Armand de Lom d'Arce de Lahontan's *New Voyages to North America* (1703) and Robert Rogers's *Concise Account of North America* (1765). From 1784 to 1789, while serving as a diplomat in France, he bought some two thousand books. "In Europe I had purchased every thing I could lay my hands on . . . related to any part of America," he later wrote, "and particularly had a pretty full collection of the English, French & Spanish authors on the subject of Louisiana. The information . . . was entirely satisfactory, and I threw it into a shape which would easily take the form of a Memorial."[26]

French explorers made the first contributions to the late eighteenth-century knowledge—and folklore—of the trans-Mississippi region. For the ninety-year period from 1673, the year of the first European navigation of the Mississippi River, to 1763, when France was defeated in the French and Indian War, French reports laid the groundwork for a theme that proved so crucial to Jefferson as he planned an exploration of the West, a theme aptly identified by Henry Nash Smith: "When Lewis and Clark reached the shore of the Pacific . . . they reactivated the oldest of all ideas associated with America—that of a passage to India."[27]

1

"A Passage to India"

From Aristotle to Magellan

The motif of a passage to India has ancient origins. As John Logan Allen writes, "Classical antiquity bequeathed precious few geographical doctrines to the Middle Ages, but when the commercial desires of Renaissance Europe sought a short route to the silk and spices of the Orient, Strabo, Virgil, Senecca, Aristotle, and others were pressed into service, and their tales of the Elysian Fields and the Fortunate Isles and the other wonders to be found west from Europe assumed new importance."[1] The philosopher Aristotle (384–322 BC), like his mentor, Plato (428–348 BC), has had a huge influence and wrote, "The earth is spherical and . . . its periphery is not large. . . . For this reason those who imagine that the region around the Pillars of Hercules [the promontories on each side of the Strait of Gibraltar] joins on to the regions of India, and that in this way the ocean is one, are not . . . suggesting anything utterly incredible." Only the sea, he added, "prevents the earth from being inhabited all around."[2]

Strabo (ca. 64 BC–ca. AD 20), the Greek astronomer and geographer, called India "a nation greater . . . than any other [in the East],"[3] going on to quote a passage from the "father of geography," Eratosthenes (276–194 BC): "If the immensity of the Atlantic Sea did not prevent, we could sail from Iberia [the Spain/Portugal peninsula] to India along one and the same parallel."[4] None of this was news to Jefferson, who once wrote to a friend, "I read Greek, Latin, French, Italian, Spanish, and English of course, with something of it's radix the Anglo-Saxon."[5] Indeed, his incredible library held hundreds of books on both ancient and modern philosophy and geography and included these works by Aristotle and Strabo.

Not only was Eratosthenes one of the first to envision a western route to India; he was also the first "whose method for calculating the circumference of the Earth has been preserved," and "the value he obtained [was] reasonably close to the correct one."[6] Such interests portended the work of the astronomer Paolo dal Pozzo Toscanelli (1397–1482), who, in 1474, told King Afonso V of Portugal of "a shorter way to the places of the spices than that which you take by [Africa]."[7] Since the 1420s, the Portuguese had explored Africa's west coast, hoping to circumnavigate that continent to reach the "places of the spices," but the distances were so great—and currents so unpredictable—that progress was slow. By the time Toscanelli proposed his plan, Afonso's men had reached Ghana, but those navigators still had no idea how far south Africa extended—nor could they be certain that the Atlantic and Indian Oceans were connected.[8]

Aware of these conundrums, Toscanelli assured the king of a course from Lisbon to China, a 6,500-mile journey to the Canary Islands, then to the mythical island of Antillia, and finally to Japan and its palaces of solid gold. Although Afonso declined, Toscanelli held fast to his theory and sent copies of his letter and map to a navigator and explorer, and fellow Italian, who took up the cause of sailing west to Asia with a passion: Cristoforo Colombo—Cristóbal Colón in Spanish and Christopher Columbus in English—who called his project the "Enterprise of the Indies."

Columbus—a name and an image so enduring that in April 1805, as Meriwether Lewis sailed west with the corps, departing the Mandan and Hidatsa villages and venturing into largely unexplored country, he recorded the names of every individual in the company and then added, "Our vessels consisted of six small canoes, and two large perogues. This little fleet altho' not quite so rispectable as those of Columbus or Capt. Cook were still viewed by us with as much pleasure as those deservedly famed adventurers ever beheld theirs; and I dare say with quite as much anxiety for their safety and preservation."[9]

For Columbus and many others, such an enterprise involved spreading Christianity and finding gold but focused first on the spice trade: "Indian spice farming developed throughout the subcontinent some two thousand years before Christ. The earliest spice crops were cinnamon and black pepper; these became the basis for numerous trade relationships . . . and, eventually, among the world's most valuable commodities. At one point, in the 1300s, a pound of nutmeg in Europe was more valuable than gold."[10] The world's oldest recipes, recorded in cuneiform on Akkadian clay tablets, mention cumin, Persian shallot, and coriander.[11] A 1550 BC Egyptian medical document lists medical treatments using caraway, coriander, fennel, mint, and poppy. Around 1250 BC, when Moses anointed Aaron with oil, he was commanded to use "sweet cinnamon [and] . . . cassia."[12] About 580 BC, the Greek poet Sappho, beloved for her lyric verse, wrote of a wedding where "maidens sang" and the scents of "cassia and frankincense were mingled."[13] Spices have thus been used for everything from flavoring bland food to healing infirmities, conducting sacred rituals, and making perfumes: "Whether eastward-bound like Vasco da Gama or westward like Christopher Columbus and Ferdinand Magellan, the great Renaissance pioneers invariably sailed in search of spices."[14]

The quest for trade routes to India also had early origins. Phoenicia's King Hiram (r. 969–939 BC) and Israel's King Solomon became allies and "made a navy of ships . . . on the shore of the Red Sea. . . . And Hiram sent in the navy his servants . . . that had knowledge of the sea";[15] "The king's ships went to Tarshish . . . [and] every three years once came the ships of Tarshish bringing gold, and silver, ivory, and apes, and peacocks."[16] As one biblical commentary points out, "Gold, silver . . . ivory, apes, and peacocks . . . may be procured in India and in India alone."[17]

Jefferson's quest to hasten fur trade with Asia by finding a water route through North America was thus prefigured by Columbus's campaign to sail west to the spices and gold of the Indies, which was prefigured by Eratosthenes's lament that the immensity of the Atlantic closed off a watercourse to India, which was prefigured by Solomon's finding a passage to Tarshish. So it is hardly surprising that Herodotus's history—another volume in Jefferson's library—tells of the perennial predicament of European mariners: they could sail to Europe and northern Africa via the Mediterranean Sea but not from there to the Indian Ocean and share its gold, silver, cinnamon, cloves, ginger, nutmeg, pepper, sandalwood, frankincense, and myrrh.

Herodotus added that after canceling a project to dig a canal between the Red Sea and the Nile River, the Egyptian pharaoh Necho II (r. 610–595 BC) ordered a Phoenician fleet "to make for the [Strait of Gibraltar], and return to Egypt . . . by the Mediterranean. The Phoenicians took their departure from Egypt by way of the [Indian Ocean], and sailed into the southern ocean. When autumn came, they . . . [planted] corn, waited until the grain was fit to cut . . . and it was not till the third year that they . . . made good their voyage home." We thus have a description of circumnavigating Africa, something hardly novel to Herodotus, who added that the Carthaginians had also accomplished the task.[18]

Similar stories continued to circulate. Strabo noted that Posidonius, "in speaking of those who have sailed round Africa," told of Eudoxus of Cyzicus, "a learned man" who caught the attention of the Egyptian king Euergetes II. When a castaway from India was found "half dead" along the Red Sea, the Egyptians taught him Greek to hear his story. He then promised to show them "the route by sea to India. Eudoxus was of the number thus sent. He set sail with a good supply of presents, and brought back . . . aromatics and precious stones" only to see Euergetes take "possession of the whole treasure." Eudoxus carried on, however, and concluding "it was possible to circumnavigate Libya . . . he set out on his travels," passing through the Strait of Gibraltar to Cadiz, Spain. There he "gathered money sufficient to equip a great ship . . . [and] on board . . . he placed singing girls, physicians, and artisans of various kinds, and . . . was carried towards India." Although that journey ended in a shipwreck, Eudoxus survived, returned to Spain, and launched "two vessels, one . . . furnished with fifty oars . . . [placing] on board agricultural implements, seed, and builders, and hastened on the same voyage [to India]."[19]

Strabo, however, called the tale "Bergaean [fanciful] nonsense."[20] The question is, Why, then, did he recount it at all? Because, answers one scholar, "Eudoxus's African circumnavigation story was very popular at the turn of the Era." Indeed, the Roman historians Cornelius Nepos and Pliny the Elder wrote about Eudoxus, indicating he lived from about 145 to 80 BC.[21] One reason for Strabo's doubts, adds Luis A. Garcia Moreno, is that the account of Eudoxus blends "the exploratory trip [with] well-known elements of Hellenic mythology." Still, the independent references to Eudoxus from Strabo and Pliny weigh in favor of the reality of an original story.[22]

Those trying to sail to India from the Red Sea, however, faced a major hurdle, the yearly cycle of the monsoon: "The summer monsoon blows hard and wet out of the southwest. . . . By late August, the blustery squalls weaken into stiff breezes. . . . By September, the summer winds splutter and falter." Next, the winter monsoon brings "dry, balmy zephyrs from the northeast, as reliable . . . as any trade wind. With the right timing, outward or inward bound, ships were guaranteed a following wind in the starboard quarter."[23] The earliest document explaining how Greco-Roman sailors learned of the "right timing" is the tenth-century Greek *Periplus of the Erythraean Sea* (ostensibly based on a first-century original manuscript), in which an anonymous author writes, "Hippalos was the first navigator . . . [to discover] a route across the ocean. Since then . . . when the monsoon in the Indian Ocean appears to be south-west, it is called Hippalos."[24] Strabo himself witnessed how finding a "passage across" ignited the most fruitful trade era of the ancient world: "I was with [Aelius Gallus] at the time he was prefect of Egypt [26–24 BC] and accompanied him as far as . . . the frontiers of Ethiopia, and I found that about one hundred and twenty ships sail from Myos-hormos [a Red Sea port] to India."[25]

The irony is that Hippalos's monsoon breakthrough—which triggered Rome's long commerce with India—also brought an end to Eudoxus's other lofty mission: circumnavigating Africa. By the reign of Trajan (AD 98–117), the Roman Empire controlled the entire Mediterranean Sea and the Egyptian coast of the Red Sea. Although other powers held East Africa and the Arabian Peninsula, Rome had the status—and might—that allowed it safe and profitable access. The upshot was that Roman freighters with carrying capacities of up to five hundred tons sailed freely between Egypt and India and into the Persian Gulf. Goods from India or Sri Lanka went to Italy and other parts of Europe—making this the longest trade route of the ancient world.[26] Any notions of sailing around "Libya" vanished, not to see the light of day for 1,500 years.

The ancient Indian city of Muziris became the world's first major trading center, with an Indian poet describing it as "the city where the beautiful vessels, the masterpieces of the [westerners], stir white foam on the Periyar, river of Kerala, arriving with gold and departing with [black] pepper."[27] The *Periplus* affirmed the value of the spice that constituted three-fourths of westbound cargo: "Large [Roman] ships sail to these [Indian] ports on account of the large quantity of pepper . . . grown in quantity only in one place near these marts [ports]."[28]

"Sailing to Byzantium"

For more than a millennium, a powerful dominion centered on a small strip of land at the northwestern edge of Turkey wielded a huge impact on the trade, politics, and religion of the Eastern Roman Empire, often known by its capital city: Byzantium, built on the west side of a strait linking both the Mediterranean and Black Seas and thus Europe and Asia. So it was hardly by accident that in AD 330, the Roman emperor Constantine I—who had declared the toleration of Christianity—relocated the empire's capital to Byzantium, well known as a key trade hub. At Constantine's death, the city was renamed Constantinople (now Istanbul). It flourished as the wealthiest European city and the center of the eastern Christian church. With the decline of Rome, Byzantium overtook it as the West's key spice consumer. Using one major route, ships loaded with Indian Ocean spices ascended the Tigris River to Baghdad and transferred the cargo to caravans that carried it north to the eastern edge of the Black Sea. Merchant ships then took some of the imports to Constantinople and the remainder to Italy.[29]

Constantinople also became the main western terminus for the Silk Road, established by the second century BC, which involved overland trade routes stretching from China, India, and Arabia to Turkey, Greece, and Italy. Silk, jade, tea, and spices went west; horses, textiles, and glassware went east. A key route of the Silk Road was the four-thousand-mile-long path that originated in Xi'an, China, "followed the Great Wall westward, skirted the Taklamakan Desert, passed through the Ferghana Valley to the caravan cities of Samarkand and Bukhara [both in present Uzbekistan], and then [north] around the Caspian Sea to Turkey."[30]

The Byzantine Empire flourished and by AD 565 controlled the Mediterranean. Then came a seismic shift when the Prophet Muhammad—born to a family of merchants—and his army marched on the sacred site of Mecca and subdued it. Within a decade of Muhammad's death, the Rashidun Caliphate (AD 632–61) took control of the Levant (Israel, Jordan, Lebanon, and Syria), northern Egypt and Libya, and Iraq. The Persian Empire converted to Islam by 654, then parts of Turkey, Afghanistan, and Turkmenistan. By 850 the Umayyad Caliphate (661–750) and Abbasid Caliphate (750–1258) extended the Islamic domain to the Iberian Peninsula in the West; Pakistan and Kyrgyzstan in the East; and Uzbekistan and Kazakhstan in the North.

The Byzantine realm steadily decreased but in 850 still included Greece, most of Turkey, and parts of Italy. Constantinople, still a thriving cosmopolitan trading center—where one could see Christian churches, Jewish synagogues, and Muslim mosques—had used "Greek fire," a highly flammable mixture launched from the bows of Greek ships, to successfully defend the city from several Umayyad attacks. Although the rise of Islam largely cut Constantinople off from the spice route and the Silk Road, both sides trusted a group of Jewish merchants called the Radanites. A ninth-century Baghdad official wrote, "They journey from west to east, from east to west, partly on land, partly by sea," and take cloth, furs, and swords eastward and return with exotic spices. One commentator notes that such trade routes were possible "because of a series of Jewish communities along the way, from Spain at one end through, at the other, the . . . Jews of India and various settlements in China. . . . As a result, a Jewish trader from France, could . . . conduct business with a Jewish purveyor of goods in, say, Cairo or Baghdad."[31] The Byzantine emperor also maintained trade and diplomacy with the Indian subcontinent until at least AD 950. By the 1040s, however, the Islamic Seljuk Empire invaded Byzantine territory in central Turkey. Next came a series of pivotal episodes foreshadowing the Age of Discovery and the finding of two passages to India:

1054: The East-West Schism marked the final separation of the Eastern Orthodox Church and the Roman Catholic Church.

1071: At the Battle of Manzikert, Seljuk Turks defeated Byzantine forces and took Jerusalem.

1082: Byzantium granted Venice unrestricted trade access and exemption from customs tariffs in return for naval assistance in resisting Norman attacks.

1090: The Seljuk Empire, now extending eastward all the way to China, blocked all trade routes east of Constantinople.

1095: The Byzantine emperor Alexius I sent envoys to Pope Urban II requesting knights to help the Byzantine army repel Seljuk invasions.

Rather than sending a select group of mercenaries, however, Urban called on "all people of whatever rank, foot-soldiers and knights, poor and rich" to join the cause. Not only that, but this volunteer militia was commanded by Christ, said the pontiff, to make a pilgrimage to Jerusalem's "Holy Sepulchre [and] wrest that land from the wicked race," with the promise that "all who die by the way . . . or in battle against the pagans, shall have immediate remission of sins."[32] The congregation responded by shouting out a mantra and repeating it several times: "It is the will of God!" The pope's plea—and similar entreaties by his successors—led directly to the sacking of Constantinople, not by the Abbasid, Fatimid, Ayyubid, or any other Muslim empire, but by Christian "allies" supposedly on their way to the Holy Land.

"Deus le Volt!"

"The term *Crusades* . . . refers to a series of religious wars fought by Muslim and Christian armies between 1095 and 1291," write David M. Perry and Matthew Gebriele. Christians fought Muslims and also Jews and fellow Christians. Moreover, the "crusader states"—areas in the Levant conquered by the first crusaders—were diverse, with multiple forms of *Christianity*, *Islam*, and *Judaism* represented and several languages spoken.[33] It was no surprise that Alexius got more than he bargained for. While French and German believers prepared for the holy war, a throng of knights and peasants, the People's Crusade, arrived in Constantinople. Alexius tried to provide for the crowd and urged them to wait for the main force, but they were so impatient and unruly that they were soon ferried across the strait and were not far from Constantinople when, wrote Alexius's daughter Anna, "they fell foul of the Turkish ambuscades . . . and perished miserably. And such a large number of Franks and Normans were the victims of the Ishmaelite sword, that when they piled up the corpses of the slaughtered men . . . they formed, I say, not a very large hill . . . but a high mountain as it were, of very considerable depth and breadth—so great was the pyramid of bones."[34]

Undeterred, the well-organized troops of the First Crusade reached Constantinople in December 1096. The massive army, numbering perhaps four thousand mounted knights and twenty-five thousand infantry, presented Alexius with a host of new difficulties. He required leaders to pledge loyalty to him while in his kingdom. The leaders agreed and departed Constantinople in the spring of 1097. The crusaders soon attacked Antioch, a Byzantine trade center surrounded by mammoth walls. The Turks surrendered eight months later. In June 1099 Urban's warriors, now reduced by half, reached Jerusalem, soon catapulting boulders over the walls. On July 10 the crusaders wheeled siege towers to Jerusalem's walls and made an all-out attack. After five days of fierce fighting, with Muslim defenders even using Greek fire to defend their city, the Christians prevailed. Then came the slaughter of the Muslim and Jewish survivors—men, women, and children. "Everywhere lay fragments of human bodies," the Catholic historian William of Tyre (ca. AD 1130–86) wrote. "More dreadful . . . [than] the mutilated limbs strewn in all directions . . . was it to gaze upon the victors themselves, dripping with blood from head to foot." Still, William argued, "It was indeed the righteous judgment of God . . . that those who had profaned the sanctuary of the Lord . . . should [pour out] their own blood [to] purify the sacred precincts."[35]

The Second Crusade (1147–49) was an unsuccessful attempt to retake the city of Edessa, which had fallen to the Seljuk Turks in 1144. The Third Crusade (1189–92) was an unsuccessful attempt to retake Jerusalem from Saladin—founder of the Ayyubid dynasty—who had conquered it in 1187. In 1198 Pope Innocent III called for the Fourth Crusade (1202–4), another attempt to reconquer Jerusalem. The Franks offered to pay Venice merchants eighty-five thousand silver marks for provisions and ships to transport 33,500 soldiers and 4,500 horses to the Levant. When the Franks could not pay the full amount, the Venetian leader Dandolo agreed to forgive the debt if they helped capture and loot the Catholic city of Zara (in present Croatia), despite the protest of Innocent (who absolved the Franks but excommunicated the Venetians). When the crusaders ran low on funds in 1203, Alexius Angelus, a claimant to the Byzantine throne, arrived in Zara and promised the crusaders provisions, military cooperation, and two hundred thousand silver marks if they restored his father, Isaac II (imprisoned and near death), as emperor.

Innocent, who had already declined to help Alexius, ordered the crusaders to likewise reject his offer. Their task was to retake Jerusalem, and the 1182 Massacre of the Latins in Constantinople still loomed large in Venetian memory, making contact between the East and West that much more volatile. Although Maria of Antioch, widow of the Byzantine emperor Manuel I, had favored Venetian merchants, when the grandson of a former emperor staged a coup, he sent his army to incite the people against the Latins, or Roman Catholics: "The people needed no encouragement. With an enthusiasm fired by years of resentment, they set about the massacre of all the foreigners that they could find. . . . The slaughter was appalling . . . [and] some 4,000 westerners who had survived the massacre were . . . sold as slaves to the Turks."[36]

Little wonder that Innocent did not want his crusaders anywhere near Constantinople. Getting involved in Byzantine's tumultuous politics was unwise under any circumstance, but it was absolutely foolhardy when many Venetians were still agonizing over the loss of loved ones in the massacre only twenty years earlier. Again, however, the crusaders disobeyed the pope. As one scholar notes, "Over all prevailed the firm will of Dandolo and his unyielding determination to develop the trade activities of Venice" and take advantage of the "limitless wealth and brilliant future" of the eastern markets.[37]

The crusaders landed in Constantinople in June 1203. The emperor, Alexius III, fled, and Isaac II and Alexius IV were installed as co-emperors. They paid the crusaders half the debt and pleaded for more time, but the crusaders grew impatient. By late 1203 war broke out between the Byzantines and the crusaders.[38] Byzantine ships attacked Venetian galleys with Greek fire, but even that strategy failed to repel the crusaders, who, wrote the French knight Geoffrey of Villehardouin, "seized upon the fire ships, all burning as they were, with hooks . . . and set them into the current . . . it seemed as if the whole world were a-fire."[39]

At the same time, an insurrection among the Greeks simmered, and in January 1204 the son-in-law of a former emperor deposed Isaac and Alexius IV. He next disavowed the debt owed to the crusaders and ordered them to leave. No doubt fulfilling Innocent's worst fear, his Christian soldiers forgot Jerusalem and sacked Constantinople. "But with one consent all the most heinous sins . . . were committed by all with equal zeal," wrote a witness.

"In the alleys . . . in the temples, complaints, weeping, lamentations, grief, the groaning of men, the shrieks of women, wounds, rape, captivity, the separation of those most closely united. . . . All places . . . were filled full of all kinds of crimes. Oh, immortal God, how great the afflictions!"[40]

"The Book of the Marvels of the World"

In 1298 a Venetian merchant found himself a prisoner in Genoa. His cellmate was Rustichello da Pisa, author of an Arthurian romance. The two coauthored a book recounting the merchant's wanderings. Rustichello wrote, "Lords, emperors and . . . knights and townsfolk and all people who wish to know of . . . the diversities of diverse regions of the world, take this book and have it read to you," a tome that gave Europeans their first glimpse of life in Asia.[41] Although books were "published" only by tedious copying, the narrative found a wide audience and was known by such titles as *The Million* and *The Book of the Marvels of the World*, but the best-known title was *The Travels of Marco Polo*. Despite many of Columbus's biographers concluding *Travels* impacted his 1492 voyage, recent scholarship finds "good evidence that Columbus's first direct knowledge of [Polo's book] came well after his First Voyage."[42] Still, Marco was "the ghost hovering over Columbus's shoulder" via Toscanelli, whose 1474 letter not only proposed sailing west to the spice lands but also used "Marco-esque language" in telling of "a hundred great [Chinese] ships each year" loaded with pepper and Japan's palaces "covered with solid gold."[43]

Calling the incredible Marco Polo (1254–1324) a pivotal figure is a gross understatement. Just as he is tied to the Age of Discovery, his wayfaring is inexorably connected to the Fourth Crusade and the rise of the Mongol Empire. With the crusaders' 1204 victory, Venice took control of Constantinople's port, and Venetian trade—which had seen its ups and downs for centuries—hit its pinnacle. Thousands of Venetian merchants flocked to Byzantium, and by the 1250s Niccolò (Marco's father) and Maffeo Polo joined them, trading there and at the Black Sea port of Soldaia in everything from pepper and ginger to silk, dyes, cotton, timber, and fur.

By this time, the Mongol Empire had controlled Soldaia for more than a decade. Genghis Khan (1162–1227) rose to power in 1206, conquering Beijing nine years later and extending his kingdom from Korea to the Caspian Sea. By the 1250s, the Mongols had taken all of China, Iran, and Iraq, as well as eastern Europe, the largest contiguous land empire in history. "It was as if," writes one historian, "in the late nineteenth century, Geronimo at the head of his Apaches, had united the many Indian tribes, seized Washington, made an empire of all North America and claimed the world."[44] Although Mongol mounted troops "leveled cities," "tore down fortresses," and "massacred city dwellers and rural folk," the Polo brothers found the merciless horsemen replaced by pragmatic administrators content to allow Venetians to trade as they wished—as long as they paid their taxes.[45] In 1260, when the Polos had been away from Venice for seven years, they ventured to the trading city of Sarai, on Russia's lower Volga River. Here they met the governor, a grandson of Genghis Khan, who, according to Marco, "was delighted at [their] arrival . . . and treated them with great honour; so they presented to him the whole of the jewels that they had brought with them. The Prince was highly pleased with these, and accepted the offering most graciously, causing the Brothers to receive at least twice its value."[46]

And so began the Polos' fellowship with Mongol overlords, which proved invaluable when word came in 1261 that the Byzantines had reconquered Constantinople, killing or maiming Venice merchants who failed to escape, closing off any return to Venice via the Black Sea. The Polos transported their goods via caravan to the trade center of Bukhara, where they stayed until 1265, trading and learning Mongolian. When a Mongol ambassador going east stopped in Bukhara, he was astounded to learn of the presence of two European businessmen and said, "The Great Khan hath never seen any Latins, and he hath a great desire to do so. . . . Whilst in our company ye shall travel with perfect security, and need fear to be molested by nobody."[47]

In 1269, sixteen years after departing, the Polos returned to Venice. "Nicolas [Niccolò] found that his wife was dead," wrote Marco, "and that she had left behind her a son of fifteen years of age [Marco himself]."[48] Had the family given up hope of the brothers ever returning? When did Marco's mother die? Who took care of him afterward? We will never know, but Marco learned that the brothers accepted the ambassador's invitation to meet the Great Khan, Kublai, the most prominent grandson of Genghis Khan. He made them welcome and asked about their emperors and Catholicism, not surprising given that one of his wives was Nestorian Christian. Kublai then asked the brothers to have the pope send a hundred wise men to teach his people the Christian religion and the seven liberal arts: "Finally he charged the Envoys to bring back to him some Oil of the Lamp which burns on the Sepulchre of our Lord at Jerusalem."[49] Kublai also gave the Polos a gold tablet that enabled them to get supplies and escorts on their return journey. They reached a Mediterranean port three years later. "They could not always advance," noted Marco, "being stopped sometimes by snow or by heavy rains."[50] They next traveled to Acre, where they met Teobaldo Visconti, Pope Clement IV's apostolic legate, who told them Clement had died and advised them to wait until a new pope was named and then fulfill Kublai's charge and bring "great honour and advantage [to] the whole of Christendom."[51] The Polos then sailed to Venice, met Marco for the first time, and waited for notice of a new pope.

In 1271 the brothers concluded they had delayed long enough and—with seventeen-year-old Marco—sailed to the Levant, determined to return to China. At Acre they met again with Visconti, who approved their retrieving oil from Jerusalem's lamp of the Sepulchre, dangerous because the Muslims were wary of infidels.[52] The Polos headed east but had not gone far when they heard "that the Legate aforesaid was chosen Pope, taking the name Pope Gregory [X]" and wished to see them. They obeyed, and their old friend "received them with great honour . . . and gave them his blessing." The Polos and two friars departed late in 1271, but the group was again reduced to three when the friars heard rumors of a Muslim invasion and declined to continue.[53]

The return to China took three and a half years, wrote Marco, "owing to the bad weather and severe cold," false starts, and wars. From Acre, they traveled on horseback to the mountains of northwestern Turkey, then southwest to a trade center in Iran, where the inhabitants got their living by "weaving . . . valuable stuffs of silk and gold." They continued southwest, across a "very hot" plain to Hormuz, "a city of immense trade," where ships from India came "loaded with spicery and precious stones," but the Polos, well acquainted with Venice's masterful ships, found the watercraft to be "wretched affairs," concluding it was "a perilous business to go on a voyage in one of these ships" because of terrible storms in the Indian Ocean. Canceling their plans to sail to China, the Polos backtracked across the searing plain, then headed northeast.[54]

On the road to Iran's Kerman, wrote Marco, "you meet with some very fine plains, and . . . natural hot baths . . . where victual is cheap and abundant, with quantities of dates." Beyond Kerman, however, "you meet with no human habitation; it is all desert. . . . Even of wild beasts there are none." They finally found fresh water, then another desert "of surpassing aridity, which lasts for eight days . . . and what water there is bitter and bad, so that you have to carry both food and water." Continuing to northern Afghanistan, they finally found plains and valleys of "excellent grass pasture, and abundance of fruits." This was the Silk Road, and the great city of Balkh had been "greatly ravaged and destroyed" by the Mongols.[55]

The Polos rode through eastern Tajikistan and reached Kashgar, China, where the Muslim "merchants go forth about the world on trade journeys."[56] Next the travelers skirted the edge of the six-hundred-mile-long Taklamakan Desert, where both animals and plants were scarce. Most of the people they met were Muslim, but there were also Buddhists and Nestorian Christians. After another ten-day ride in which they found few human dwellings, the nomads reached the walled city of Sukchur, where "rhubarb is found in great abundance, and thither merchants come to buy it, and carry it thence all over the world." Then they saw "an enormous number" of statues of the Great Buddha, "both small and great . . . all highly polished, and then covered with gold."[57]

The Polos were about halfway between China's western border and Kublai's capital of Xanadu, a distance of 2,200 miles, when they met a band of mounted Mongols.[58] "When the Great Khan heard [the Polos] were on their way back," wrote Marco, "he sent people on a journey of full forty days to meet them; and on this journey, as on their former one, they were . . . supplied with all that they required." So for the last 1,100 miles of the Venice–Xanadu odyssey—a zigzagging path likely 7,000 miles long—the Polos and their armed escorts, all riding spectacular horses, traveled along Kublai's "pony-express" communication route, where, after each day's thirty-mile trip, they found warm meals, comfortable lodging, and fresh horses for the next day.

In the summer of 1275 they rode through the final stretch of gentle grassland and arrived at the Imperial Palace, where Kublai Khan was surrounded by an assembly of barons. "So they bent the knee before him," wrote Marco. "Then the Lord bade them stand up, and treated them with great honour . . . and asked many questions as to their welfare." The Polos presented the pope's letters and the oil from the Holy Sepulchre, which Kublai was "very glad" to receive. Then, "spying Marco," he asked who the young man was. "Sire," answered Niccolò, "'tis my son and your liegeman." The emperor smiled and said, "Welcome is he too."[59]

"As If Asking Help of the Father of Nature"

Europe memorialized Marco Polo as the ultimate traveler and confidant of the Great Khan, but what of his reputation, if any, on the American frontier? In 1879 the former trapper and prospector William Waldo answered that question by reflecting on his days with Kit Carson, William Ashley, and others, including Albert Pike, later a poet, journalist, and Confederate general. In 1832 Waldo and Pike trapped the Comanche country and were caught in a blizzard that froze several horses. Pike soon left and "after various adventures"—including trekking across Oklahoma—found his way to a fledgling settlement on the Arkansas River, where he was "unknown, without money, and almost without clothes . . . [but] found employment . . . at ten dollars a month and board . . . teaching a few children their A. B. C.'s amongst the rude, half civilized backwoodsmen." Families sat "till late hours of the night around their large log fires," mesmerized by Pike's "accounts of his . . . hair-breadth escapes from the Comanche." Pike never found more loyal friends "than these hardy mountaineers," wrote Waldo. "In their simple ignorance, they did not understand, whether this Marco Polo hailed from the country of the Great Mogul, Iceland, or Japan."[60] What better way to depict Pike, who trudged over Texas's rugged Caprock Canyon on his solitary six-hundred-mile excursion to Arkansas, than to envision him as the quintessential stranger in a strange land—Marco Polo.

When Marco, who married Donata Badoer and had four children after being released from Genoa, died in 1324—thirty years after Kublai's demise—the Mongol Empire was well into decline and the Ottoman well on the rise. The Chinese drove out the Mongols in 1368, the same time the Muslim Ottomans occupied much of Turkey. In 1422 the Ottomans laid siege to Constantinople, an attack barely withstood by the Byzantine Empire, and in 1444 they vanquished crusaders in Bulgaria. The final blow came in 1453, when the Ottomans, already in control of Greece, conquered Constantinople and permanently closed off trade to the East.

The fall of the Byzantine capital came amid another monumental confluence of circumstance. In 1420 Portugal's King John persuaded the pope to name his son Prince Henry the administrator of the Portuguese chapter of the Order of Christ, a powerful military and financial firm. The Order's treasury allowed Henry, a navigator in name only, to take up his passion: exploring Africa's west coast. He wanted to spread Christianity; search for Prester John, the (purely) legendary Christian monarch of the East; and find an ocean route to the Indies, but his immediate concern was finding Africa's rumored gold, which would enrich his country—and himself—while ruining Muslim middlemen. Henry's zeal only intensified in 1428 when a brother gave him a copy of Marco's *Travels*. His sailors reached Cape Bojador in 1434 and the Senegal River in 1445, but they did not discover the mother lode of gold. By this time Portuguese mariners had designed the caravel, a medium-sized ship equipped with lateen sails, able to sail into the wind, and perfect for entering African rivers. With Constantinople's sacking sounding a blaring reminder that a water route to the East had to be found, the Portuguese picked up the pace, reaching the Cape Verde Islands in 1456—one year after the publication of Gutenberg's Bible—and Sierra Leone in 1460, the year Henry died. Of all the expeditions sponsored by the prince, however, the most famous—or infamous—came in 1444. Although Henry's brother had granted him a monopoly over trade south of Cape Bojador, the goods brought back from Africa thus far, such as antelope skin, dates, and ostrich eggs, were interesting but hardly earthshaking (as spice or gold would be), and grumbling among the citizenry about the extravagant cost and meager return of the voyages reached Henry's ears: "The dissent was stilled by the arrival of a commodity nearly as valuable as gold: human beings."[61]

Indeed, Henry realized that slaves could be sold for gold and that Portugal's presence in western Africa allowed for easy slave raiding. Gomes Eanes de Zurara, a contemporary of Henry's, wrote that the prince launched his first slaving mission by sending a crew to a tranquil fishing village of about two hundred souls on the island of Arguin. "These blacks were Moors [Muslims] . . . who had become subject to all the other races," explained Zurara, "because of the curse which, after the Deluge, Noah laid upon his son Cain." As Henry's men approached the village under the cover of darkness, the leader reminded his fellows, "We have left our land to do service to God and to [Prince Henry] . . . it would be a matter of shame to turn back to Portugal without a worthy booty." The men agreed, and "they looked towards the settlement and saw that the Moors, with their women and children, were already coming as quickly as they could out of their dwellings, because they caught sight of their enemies." The crew responded with shouts of "St. James! St. George! Portugal!" and attacked, "killing and taking all they could."[62]

"Then might you see," continued Zurara, "mothers forsaking their children, and husbands their wives. . . . Some drowned themselves in the water; others thought to escape by hiding under their huts; others stowed their children among sea-weed, where our men found them afterwards, hoping they would thus escape notice." Henry's helpers thus "took captive of those Moors, what with men, women, and children, numbered 165, besides those that perished and were killed. And when the battle was over, all praised God for the great mercy that he had shewn them."[63]

Zurara witnessed the arrival of the human cargo in Portugal. Prince Henry was "mounted upon a powerful steed, and accompanied by his retinue, making distribution of his favours, as a man who sought to gain but small treasure from his share . . . and said he was well pleased." The sight of the enslaved Moors, however, made Zurara "weep in pity for their sufferings."[64] Zurara reported,

> Some kept their heads low and their faces bathed in tears, looking one upon another; others stood groaning . . . looking up to the height of heaven, fixing their eyes upon it, crying out loudly, as if asking help of the Father of Nature; others . . . [threw] themselves at full length upon the ground; others made their lamentations in the manner of a dirge . . . and though we could not understand . . . their language, the

> sound of it right well accorded with the measure of their sadness. But to increase their sufferings still more, there now arrived those who had charge of the division of the captives, and who to separate one from another . . . and then was it needful to part fathers from sons, husbands from wives, brothers from brothers. No respect was shown either to friends or relations, but each fell where his lot took him. . . . And who could finish that partition without very great toil? for as often as they had placed them in one part the sons, seeing their fathers in another, rose with great energy and rushed over to them; the mothers clasped their other children in their arms, and threw themselves flat on the ground with them; receiving blows with little pity for their own flesh, if only they might not be torn from them.[65]

Not that slavery was anything new. It was mentioned in Babylonian laws and accepted in Old Testament Israel, something not forgotten by its defenders. Muslim Arabs, Jewish Radanites, and Venetian Christians—including the Polos—all bought and sold children, women, and men. At the trading centers well known to Marco and his family, such as Constantinople, Hormuz, and Bukhara, human trafficking was a fact of life, with slaves—called "servants" by William Clark and his contemporaries—often mentioned alongside textiles, silk, horses, camels, furs, glassware, weapons, and of course, gold and spice.[66] Henry the Navigator, however, was not just another merchant—he founded the Atlantic slave trade, and by 1505 he and his successors exported between 140,000 and 170,000 slaves from Africa to Portugal or its island of Madeira. By 1888, when Brazil officially emancipated its slaves, approximately 12.5 million enslaved Africans had crossed to the Americas on some thirty-five thousand voyages.[67]

In 1470 Portuguese traders learned that native miners near Ghana's port of Elmina had struck a rich vein of gold—over the next decade, those traders made huge profits by concentrating on gold, slaves, malagueta pepper, and ivory. Elmina thus became the first permanent European settlement in western Africa, and in 1482 the Portuguese built Elmina Castle, now remembered as the last site thousands of enslaved Africans saw of their homeland, and for many the last site they saw at all, due to the high death rates in the dungeons.[68]

"Without the Slightest Pity"

Portuguese sailors crossed the equator in 1473 and Cape Cross in 1486, both historic but eclipsed when Bartolomeu Dias rounded the Cape of Good Hope in 1488, ending Columbus's hopes of sailing west with Portuguese help. In the meantime, German and Latin translations of *Travels* appeared—giving merchants Marco's list of trade goods: China's unlimited supplies of silk, pearls, coral, and amber; Cambodia's gold; Java's pepper, nutmeg, and cloves; Sri Lanka's rubies, sapphires, and garnets; and Malabar's pepper, ginger, cinnamon, sandalwood, and silver.

Not surprisingly, during Columbus's six years of convincing Spain's King Ferdinand and Queen Isabella to sponsor his enterprise, he, like Toscanelli, made "Marco-esque" references to China, Japan, and the Great Khan. Moreover, he again echoed Marco when he advised the Spanish monarchs of two cardinal reasons for a western venture: spreading Christianity and making a fortune in spice and gold.[69] Early in 1492, however, convinced all was lost, Columbus packed his mule and started down the road when a messenger overtook him and relayed Isabella's request to see him.[70] Within months, he set sail for the Indies. His flagship, the *Santa Maria*, was a carrack, *nau* in Portuguese, a large, three-masted vessel with a mix of square and lateen sails, perfect for long voyages and huge loads. The *Niña* and *Pinta* were caravels, and Columbus's use of both types set the pattern for the monumental voyages that followed.[71]

In 1494 Spain and Portugal signed the Treaty of Tordesillas, which was "an agreement . . . to divide the world between them into two spheres of influence. The imaginary dividing line [often called the line of demarcation] ran down the centre of the Atlantic Ocean, leaving the Americas to Spain and West Africa and anything beyond the Cape of Good Hope to Portugal."[72] Sanctioned by Pope Julius II in 1506, the treaty presumed that Indigenous peoples instantly became subjects of either country, an ethnocentric impulse that wreaked untold misery on "Indians" everywhere, from those met by Columbus in the Caribbean and Vasco da Gama in India itself to the Missouri River nations encountered by Jefferson's expeditioners. Portugal's Manuel I set the tone in 1497 when he commissioned Gama to "search for India," proclaim Christianity, and wrest "great wealth by force of arms from the hands of the infidels."[73] On July 8, after Gama and his crew were pardoned for future sins, they departed Lisbon in two carracks and a caravel, doubling the Cape of Good Hope and then reaching Mozambique in March 1498. In Kenya Gama met an Indian navigator who guided him across the Arabian Sea, completing the first documented circumnavigation of Africa. At Calicut he found the "spices, drugs, nutmeg, and . . . fine things of China, gold, amber, wax, ivory, fine and course cotton goods, both of silk and gold, cloth of gold . . . copper, quicksilver, vermilion, [and] coral."[74]

On October 5 Gama's ships fled under threat of attack, desperate to get home, but they were fighting the monsoon, and sailing across the Arabian Sea took three months. Scurvy soon hit. "All our people again suffered from their gums, which grew over their teeth, so that they could not eat," wrote one seaman. Thirty men died, the same number lost in a previous outbreak, leaving only seven or eight navigators per ship: "I assure you that if this state of affairs had continued for another fortnight, there would have been no men at all to navigate the ships . . . but it pleased God . . . to send us a wind which . . . carried us within sight of land."[75]

So many had perished that Gama ordered the *São Rafael* burned, leaving the *São Gabriel* and the caravel, *Berrio*. Along with concern for his men, Gama worried about returning to Portugal without the spices and gold he hoped to obtain—and saw in abundance at Calicut. In his western mindset, he had mistakenly assumed that the Indians would gladly halt trade with the infidel Muslims and fill his ships with costly wares in exchange for striped cloth, scarlet hoods, brass hand basins, sugar, and honey.[76] One misunderstanding followed another. When Indian sailors boarded Gama's ship and saw a painting of the Virgin Mary, they knelt and prayed, which the Portuguese interpreted as Christian discipleship but the Indians—actually Hindu—saw as respecting an object revered by the newcomers. Again, when the Indians chanted "Krishna! Krishna!" the Europeans heard "Christ! Christ!"[77] Nor did Indian merchants want to expel the Muslim traders they found honorable. Gama compounded things by misreading the intentions of the zamorin, the Hindu sovereign, who demanded gold and silver in return for spices and took offense when offered trinkets. The two wrangled back and forth, with the zamorin taking Gama hostage at one point and demanding to see the valuable goods supposedly hidden on the ship. As a violent conflict looked increasingly likely, Gama correctly concluded the Indians and Arabs had united against him and sailed for home.[78]

The ships landed in Portugal in the summer of 1499, receiving a heroes' welcome from a throng convinced all had vanished. Of the original 170 sailors, 55 survived, traveling some twenty-four thousand miles in their 732-day odyssey, by far the longest voyage in both distance and duration up to that time.[79] King Manuel honored Gama "as one who, by the discovery of the Indies had done so much for the glory of God, for the honour and profit of the king of Portugal."[80] Manuel also gave Gama the title *dom*—usually reserved for royalty—an estate, and an annual pension.

Six months later the king dispatched another fleet to India, expecting this one to return loaded to the hilt with spices, gold, and Calicut's other goods. Pedro Álvares Cabral commanded ten carracks and three caravels, between 1,200 and 1,500 men, and five priests: "Before [Cabral] attacked the Moors and idolaters of those parts with the . . . secular sword, he was to allow the priests . . . to declare to them the Gospel. . . . [But] should they . . . [not] accept this law of faith . . . [Cabral's party] should put them to fire and sword, and carry on fierce war against them."[81]

Cabral departed on March 9, 1500, following Gama's course but sailing even farther west, where he found the easternmost part of the Americas—Brazil, which appeared "pleasant and fertile, with extensive woods and many inhabitants . . . armed with bows and arrows, and all naked." Gama claimed the area for Manuel and sent a caravel to give him the news.[82] During the crew's Easter mass, "many of the natives gathered around . . . sounding cornets, horns, and other instruments." Cabral left two men to begin colonization. Three weeks later, as the fleet fought "high sea and heavy rain" followed by lulls, a "furious tempest . . . came on so suddenly that they had not time to furl their sails, and four ships were sunk with all their men," one of whom was Bartolomeu Dias, the discoverer of the Cape of Good Hope.[83]

The downsized but well-armed armada reached India in September and found a new zamorin eager to trade. Careful not to repeat Gama's blunder, Cabral humbly offered gifts adorned with gold, silver, and crimson velvet.

The zamorin was "much satisfied" and invited Cabral to establish a trading post—soon enclosed by ten-foot walls—"supplied with every kind of merchandise." Wasting no time in pitting Cabral against the "infidels," the zamorin asked Cabral to capture a large Moorish ship containing a "fine elephant" he wanted. Cabral asked the zamorin's sanction "to kill these people in case of resistance, which was accordingly granted." Cabral sent a caravel and "sixty fighting men, with orders to take this ship." Although the Moorish craft had a much larger crew, the caravel had superior firepower, and after many Moors were killed, the Moorish ship surrendered. Cabral then ordered the "ship to be delivered to the Zamorin, together with the seven elephants . . . which were worth in Calicut 30,000 crowns."[84]

Alarmed Arab merchants "procured an audience with the Zamorin," reminding him they had long been good trading partners, Portugal was five thousand leagues away, and the "great cost of their large ships with so many men and guns" meant they were making huge profits, bringing "great loss" to the zamorin. The strangers held the zamorin "in contempt" and would rob and plunder all merchant ships "to the ruin" of Calicut, a prescient prophecy because that is exactly what Gama did when he returned in 1502.[85] The warning struck a chord with the zamorin, who assured the Arabs "he would not forsake them" and tacitly approved as the Arabs loaded a ship with spices, contrary to the agreement with Cabral. When the latter learned of this, he sent his boats "to take possession of the Moorish ship." The Moors onshore "raised a great outcry against the Portuguese, incensing the people of the city to [complain] to the Zamorin . . . [who] gave them the license they required; on which they immediately armed themselves" and attacked Cabral's trading fort. Seventy Portuguese, including the friars, were inside. Four men were killed and several wounded: "The remainder mounted the wall to defend it by means of the crossbows, judging that the assailants were at least four thousand men." Although the Portuguese made a "valiant defence" and "killed great numbers of the assailants," the Arabs and Indians tore down the wall, and Cabral's men fled, hoping "to fight their way to the boats." Fifty of them were killed or taken prisoner, "twenty only escaping . . . most of whom were much wounded."[86]

Now allied with the Arabs, the zamorin took possession of all goods at the post and imprisoned the Portuguese captured onshore. Cabral and his officers responded by attacking ten large ships at anchor in the Calicut harbor: "It appeared that 600 Moors were slain in defending these ships. After every thing of value was taken from the Moorish ships, they were all burnt in sight of the city." Not pressing his luck, Cabral sailed south to three friendly ports where he traded and loaded his ships with spices. Then he followed Gama's advice and managed the monsoons by sailing west in January, losing more ships before reaching home in June 1501. Cabral thus completed what was now the longest voyage from Portugal and also the first to make a passage to India via four continents: Europe, South America, Africa, and Asia.[87]

King Manuel was pleased with the spices but apparently distressed that seven ships and hundreds of men had been lost, for when Manuel commissioned a new trading expedition in February 1502, the commander was the Admiral of India, Vasco da Gama, who put things straight by taking a stranglehold on trade through brute force. Nothing epitomized his truculence more than the sad tale told by the sixteenth-century Portuguese historian Gaspar Correia: "One day at dawn [along the Malabar coast] there came a large ship . . . with much wealth, and it fell in with [Gama's] caravels." The three hundred Muslims aboard were returning from a pilgrimage to Muhammad's birthplace, Mecca. The ship, *Mîrî*, offered no resistance, but when Gama learned the ship's owner was a wealthy Calicut merchant, he ordered his men to pillage it: "The crews went to do this in boats, and [carried] cargo to the ships, until the ship was empty." Gama then commanded his men to set fire to *Mîrî*. When the owner realized what was happening, he asked to be taken before the captain major, and when he boarded Gama's ship, he said, "Sir, command that we be put in irons, and carry us to Calicut, and if there they do not load your ships with pepper . . . then you may order us to be burned." Convinced the captain major was a knight, the owner appealed to Gama's sense of chivalry: "Consider that in war they pardon those who surrender, and since we did not fight, do you put in practice the virtue of knighthood?" Unfazed, Gama thundered, "Alive you shall be burned because you counselled the King of Calicut to kill and plunder the factor and Portuguese," even though there was no evidence the Muslim merchant had taken part in the assault on Cabral's traders.[88]

Gama's officers argued that "he ought not to choose to lose so great wealth as the Moor offered." Gama listened but was not convinced: "It is clear that if we now take this bribe, those who come here afterwards will pay it doubly. We should give a great account to God if we left such a charge upon them.... If I can do harm to ... [Calicut], I must." Of course, even that logic failed because the pilgrims had nothing to do with Calicut. Gama again ordered the ship burned. There were, however, Portuguese on the ship "looking for plunder ... [and] the Moors took up arms ... and set to fighting ... [making] a great resistance."[89] Maybe two days passed as Gama considered his options. Burning the ship was no simple task. He eventually commanded Stephen da Gama (no relation) and others to set fire to the vessel. They did so and got away safely, but the Moors put out the fires. Tomé Lopes, one of Gama's clerks, picked up the narrative:

> Night coming on, [Stephen da Gama] was obliged to desist without doing his work; but the General gave orders, that the vessel should be watched, that the passengers might not, by favor of the darkness, escape to land, which was near. All night long the poor unhappy Moors called on Muhammad to help them, but the dead can neither hear nor succor their votaries. In the morning, Stephen da Gama ... boarded the ship, and, [set] fire to it.... Many of the Moors, when they saw the flames ... leaped into the sea with hatchets in their hands, and swimming fought with their pursuers. Some even ... attacked, the boats, doing much hurt; however, most of them were at length slain, and all those drowned who remained in the ship, which soon after sunk. So that of three hundred persons, (among whom were thirty women,) not one escaped the fire, sword, or water.[90]

Portugal's false starts in empire building had ended: "Portuguese ships sailing into remote harbors for the first time would display the corpses of recent captives hanging from the yardarms to show that they meant business," a portrayal that fit Gama and his successors' vanquishing enemies and building forts throughout the area. Portugal monopolized the pepper trade by 1504 and took control of the Persian Gulf in 1507. When Muslim ships challenged European ascendancy in 1509, the Portuguese viceroy plundered their ports and routed their combined navy. The masters of the Indian Ocean then conquered part of Malaysia in 1511 and soon opened trade with Thailand, the Spice Islands, and China.[91]

"We Found, by a Miracle, a Strait"

After seventy years of striving to reach India by sailing around Africa, Portugal thus made such journeys commonplace, but what of Columbus's dream to find a passage by voyaging west? When the latter arrived at Cuba, four thousand miles from Lisbon, he thought it was Japan—actually 7,500 miles farther on. Even the best maps of the era still showed Cuba close to Japan. About this same time, Fernão de Magalhães, a young Portuguese sailor, made a name for himself, fighting Muslim forces in the Indian Ocean and once saving a fellow seaman's life. He showed a strong aptitude for navigation and by 1517 had three times proposed to King Manuel a voyage to the Spice Islands. The king rejected all three plans. Magalhães then followed the lead of Christopher Columbus, taking his case to Portugal's archrival—Spain—as well as adopting a Spanish version of his name, Fernando de Magallanes, Ferdinand Magellan in English.[92]

He arranged a meeting with King Charles I's ministers to discuss an expedition to the Indonesian archipelago of the Moluccas, the Spice Islands. From ancient times, these fertile, rain-forested, volcanic isles were virtually the sole source of nutmeg, cloves, and mace. The counselors had an immediate question: Would this excursion violate the line of demarcation defined in the Treaty of Tordesillas? Magellan assured his listeners that the Moluccas were clearly in Spanish territory.[93]

"Magellan had a well-painted globe in which the entire world was depicted," wrote one advisor, "and he said he intended to go by . . . the Rio de la Plata [a gulf between Uruguay and Argentina], and from thence to follow the coast until he hit the strait." Magellan thus confirmed that he would reach the Spice Islands by going west, and as the ministers knew, the Spanish explorer Vasco Núñez de Balboa had discovered a "South Sea" beyond an isthmus, and there were also reports that one could reach that sea by following a strait through

Tierra Firme, South America's mainland. This was an Age of Discovery mariner pitching a plan to reach Asia via a water passage through America, but it portended a similar scheme by a U.S. president almost three centuries later. The counselors were impressed, concluding Magellan "must have been a man of courage and valiant in his thoughts for undertaking great things."[94]

On March 22, 1518, Charles commissioned Magellan "to find in the domains that belong to us . . . islands, mainlands, [and] rich spices," taking care not to "encroach upon the . . . boundaries . . . of Portugal." The king named the fleet the Armada de Molucca, with the understanding that it would return by the same route, avoiding Portugal's claim to the Indian Ocean.[95] Partly due to a tight budget and partly to Magellan's gross underestimate of the distance involved, the crown offered just five ships, well used at that. Magellan was named the sole captain general when the armada and its 250-odd men departed Seville on August 10, 1519.

Three years and twenty-nine days later, on September 8, 1522, the weather-beaten *Victoria,* looking like it might disintegrate any second, inched its way toward Seville's harbor. "Of sixty men who composed our crew when we left [the Spice Islands]," wrote Antonio Pigafetta, the chronicler of the excursion, "we were reduced to only eighteen, and these for the most part sick." Despite that, a few able men announced their arrival by discharging the artillery, and when the word spread that this was one of Magellan's ships, onlookers gawked in astonishment. King Charles and his subjects had long been convinced that the captain general and the rest of his ships and men—as well as the spice they obtained—were forever lost. And while *Victoria*'s arrival thus came as a shock, the skeleton crew had one more thunderbolt in store. As Pigafetta said, "We had run more than fourteen thousand four hundred and sixty leagues, and we had completed going round the earth from East to West."[96]

Knowing his sailors would proclaim this achievement, *Victoria*'s captain had already dispatched a letter to Charles, telling him the armada had "found a Strait . . . through Your Majesty's mainland . . . [and arrived] at the [Moluccas] . . . and there we loaded the two ships with spicery." He added that his crew had "made a course around the entire rotundity of the world [via the Indian and Atlantic Oceans]."[97] Charles was delighted that *Victoria* returned with twenty-six tons of cloves—more than double the expense of the voyage—and believed that the circumnavigation of the earth gave Spain claim to the huge Pacific. The captain was designated as the first man to sail around the world. His name? Juan Sebastián del Cano, a veteran Basque seaman who was serving as master of one of the ships when the armada departed. In his letter to Charles, Cano wrote, "We lost by his death . . . Captain Ferdinand Magellan, with many others," offering no details at all.[98] Luckily, Pigafetta wrote a book describing what God permitted him "to see and suffer in the long and perilous navigation." One of Magellan's biographers calls Pigafetta's volume, now known as *Magellan's Voyage around the World*, "the most important account of distant lands to appear since *The Travels of Marco Polo*."[99]

Pigafetta found Magellan to be a "virtuous man," but it was clear from the start that "the masters and captains of the other ships . . . did not love him," apparently because of his being Portuguese and the others Spaniards or Castilians, "who for a long time have been in rivalry." This conflict became especially evident when Magellan's armada reached the Canary Islands in September of 1519, and he got word of two rumors—that the Spanish officers would kill him "if he annoyed them" and that the king of Portugal had sent two caravels to arrest him for treason. As a result, he changed his course but refused to tell the other captains why. Rather than sailing straight to Brazil, as expected, he navigated "by the coast of [Africa's] Guinea," enduring sixty days of "rains without wind."[100] Because of this delay, Magellan cut rations without consulting his officers, who were understandably frustrated. A mutiny looked more and more likely.

A respite of sorts occurred when the fleet reached Rio de Janeiro on December 13. Pigafetta noted that the inhabitants were not Christians and went "naked, both men and women." Indeed, naked women swam out to greet the ship, making themselves available for a price. "For a hatchet or for a knife," continued Pigafetta, the Indian men gave "one or two of their daughters as slaves"—sexual slaves, that is.[101] Nor did the religious Magellan object to the orgies that followed, even though the Bible prohibited such behavior, and King Charles had charged the captain general to never "have anyone [of his crew] touch a woman."[102]

The armada soon sailed south, and Magellan concluded they were now in Spanish territory, safely searching for the strait, but as the cold weather came on, officers and crew alike murmured about wintering in Rio, with its gentle climate and female friends. Magellan refused. After a six-day storm, the captain general cut rations again. The enraged captains argued that Charles "never intended" that they attempt what "nature itself opposed," but Magellan "had already made up his mind either to die or to complete his enterprise."[103]

The mutiny erupted on Easter Sunday, April 1, 1520. "The masters of [three] ships plotted treason against the captain-general," remembered Pigafetta.[104] The conspirators, however, knew little about naval tactics, and in Magellan they faced a veteran of maritime warfare in Africa, India, and Malaysia. He reacted swiftly, gaining the advantage when two of his men killed Mendoza, the captain of one of the ships, causing the crew to immediately pledge loyalty to the captain general. Now commanding three ships, Magellan blockaded the other two, and those captains—Quesada and Cartagena—soon surrendered. After a trial, the former was executed but the latter only jailed because of his political connections in Spain. Quesada's quartered body joined Mendoza's on display, a barbaric practice in modern eyes but not unusual in the 1500s. When Cartagena and a priest planned a second mutiny, Magellan marooned them on a small island, leaving them with their swords and a liberal supply of wine and biscuit. They were never heard from again.[105]

The ships spent the winter (June through August in South America) near Argentina's Port Saint Julian: "The days contracted to less than four hours of light and the snow line reached down the mountains, across the fields and swamps, eventually extending to the water's edge."[106] The men finally departed on August 24, searching for the elusive strait, now in four boats because one had been wrecked by a storm. A month later the armada entered what Magellan believed to be the strait that would take them to the Southern Ocean. They were well into the meandering labyrinth of a passage, with so many inlets and bays and dead ends that any captain could lose his way, when *San Antonio* failed to appear at an agreed meeting site, and the captain general ordered his ship, *Trinidad,* as well as *Concepción* and *Victoria* to conduct an extensive search. They found no sign of *San Antonio*. Magellan was worried about running out of food before reaching the Moluccas, but the men came first. The search continued for a week with no success. Magellan persisted. After further searches Magellan asked his astronomer/astrologer to divine an answer. The man concluded that *San Antonio*'s crew had mutinied against Captain Mesquita and departed for Spain—exactly what had happened, although neither Magellan nor the astrologer would ever know that for a fact. The fleet was now reduced to three carracks, and on November 21 Magellan, not at all certain when—or if—they would reach the southern sea, ordered the captains, pilots, masters, and mates of the armada to give him their "counsel . . . whether to go forward or to return [to Spain], each of you will give me your opinion . . . letting nothing prevent you from being entirely truthful."[107]

This was not the same commander who previously ruled by fiat. One officer's response indicated that Magellan had no qualms about his men speaking their mind: "I believe that Your Grace should . . . continue our explorations until the middle of January . . . at which time Your Grace will judge whether it will be appropriate to return to Spain."[108] On the morning of November 26 the crews of all three ships raised their flags, cheered, and fired their artillery as the squadron sailed west. "We found, by a miracle, a strait," wrote Pigafetta. "This strait is a hundred and ten leagues long, which are four hundred and forty miles, and . . . it is surrounded by very great and high mountains covered with snow. . . . The greater number of the sailors thought that there was no place by which to go out thence to enter into the peaceful sea [Pacific Ocean]. But the captain-general said that there was another strait for going out, and said that he knew it well, because he had seen it by a marine chart of the King of Portugal." On November 28, just two days after resuming the voyage, the little fleet "found the cape, and the sea great and wide." The ships spent thirty-eight days in the Strait of Magellan, "negotiating channels, bays, and glacier-fed fjords, past huge, snow-capped mountains and coarse, evergreen shores . . . a remarkable testament to [Magellan's] abilities as a navigator and strategist and to his crew's forbearance and skill."[109]

The men cheered and fired their guns again as they sailed north, but unimagined hardships lay ahead—not the moderate haul envisioned by Magellan and, before him, Columbus and Ptolemy (who underestimated the circumference of the planet by 28 percent), but a marathon voyage across the greatest expanse of water anywhere, predicted by Eratosthenes. "We came forth out of the said strait, and entered into the Pacific sea," wrote Pigafetta, "where we remained three months and twenty days [actually ninety-eight days] without taking in provisions or other refreshments, and we only ate old biscuit reduced to powder, and full of grubs, and stinking from the dirt which the rats had made on it when eating the good biscuit, and we drank water that was yellow and stinking. We also ate the ox hides . . . and rats which cost half-a-crown each."[110]

The ships crossed the equator on February 15, 1521, passing north of, but not seeing, the Marshall Islands.[111] On March 6 they sighted two islands, almost certainly Rota and Guam. "The captain-general wished to touch at the largest [island] . . . to get refreshments of provisions," but before that was possible, several islanders approached in "little boats," which the boatmen could change from stern to bow at will, "like dolphins bounding from wave to wave." Magellan's men thus saw both Polynesians and their outrigger canoes for the first time. Then, however, "the people of these islands entered into the ships and robbed us . . . [and] stole away . . . the skiff . . . at which he was much irritated." Like many subsequent explorers, including Lewis and Clark, Magellan was angry at "theft" by Indigenous peoples even though the explorers had invaded their territory without asking permission. Moreover, Magellan was so unforgiving that he made the first of several mistakes leading to his death. He "went on shore with forty armed men, burned forty or fifty houses . . . and killed seven men of the island."[112]

Magellan thus violated New Testament mandates, as well as King Charles's command not to harm Natives unless they attacked first, a bad omen for both his fleet and the islanders soon to see a steady influx of "colonization." Concluding he was north of the Spice Islands, Magellan sailed south to the Philippines, where his Malay slave, Enrique, was able to communicate with the Filipino leader Colambu. Colambu led the Europeans to a larger island, Cebu, and its king, Humabon, who converted to Christianity and pledged allegiance to Spain. Their subjects followed, as more than two thousand people accepted baptism. Then, once again disobeying Charles, Magellan demanded that local chiefs convert to Christianity and accept Humabon as their leader. Several chiefs refused, and Magellan punished one by burning his village.[113] He bragged that he could destroy the town with sixty men, but Humabon tried to persuade him otherwise. Convinced he was doing God's will, the captain general went ahead. At daylight on April 27 he and his men leaped from the ship into shallow water. "We were forty-nine in number, the other eleven [remaining in] the boats," wrote Pigafetta. "We found the islanders fifteen hundred in number . . . they came down upon us with terrible shouts. . . . Our musketeers and crossbow-men fired for half an hour . . . but did nothing, since the bullets and arrows, though they passed through their shields made of thin wood . . . yet did not stop them." The islanders jumped from side to side, "throwing arrows, javelins, spears hardened in fire, stones, and even mud, so that we could hardly defend ourselves." Magellan was wounded in the leg by a poisoned arrow, and "he gave orders to retreat by degrees; but almost all our men took to precipitate flight, so that there remained hardly six or eight of us with him." Magellan, Pigafetta, and their fellows retreated, now knee-deep in water, but the islanders knew who Magellan was and "aimed specially at him, and twice knocked the helmet off his head. He . . . like a good knight, remained at his post . . . [and] thus we fought, for more than an hour, until an Indian succeeded in thrusting a cane lance into the captain's face. He then . . . pierced the Indian's breast with his lance" but was unable to withdraw his sword: "The enemies seeing this all rushed against him, and one of them with a great sword . . . gave him a great blow to the left leg . . . then the Indians . . . ran him through with lances and scimetars . . . so that they deprived of life our mirror, light, comfort, and true guide."[114] "There was grandeur in Magellan's vision, however flawed his premises and selfish his motives," writes one historian.[115] Indeed, though Magellan's voyage and life were cut short, he proved himself to be an extraordinary navigator by being the first to find a course through America and across the vast Pacific.

2

"That Wretched Portion of Our Journey"

Meriwether Lewis and the Great Divide

On August 12, 1805, Meriwether Lewis and a few companions became the first U.S. citizens to cross the Continental Divide, fulfilling one of their fondest hopes but also bringing them face-to-face with a hostile new landscape. "West of the Continental Divide, Lewis and Clark found a confusing jumble of mountains and a complex network of streams, a discouraging perspective, given their primary goal," writes Vern Huser, author of *On the River with Lewis and Clark*. "They had anticipated a single river flowing directly west to the Pacific. They found rivers, but they didn't seem to go where the explorers wanted to go. . . . The rivers the Corps of Discovery knew back home in the eastern United States were tame compared to these western rivers."[1] Nothing illustrated the confusion and discouragement linked to this western geography more than Lewis's experience along the Montana/Idaho border, when he, George Drouillard, Hugh McNeal, and John Shields had the great pleasure of reaching the "most distant fountain of the waters of the mighty Missouri in surch of which we have spent so many toilsome days and wristless nights." The four men celebrated the occasion by drinking the "pure and ice cold water which issues from the base of a low mountain or hill." Then they "proceeded on to the top of the dividing ridge"—today's Lemhi Pass—and descended the steep mountain about three-quarters of a mile "to a handsome bold running Creek of cold Clear water," where Lewis celebrated again and "first tasted the water of the great Columbia river."[2]

All this was worthy of commemoration because the quartet of explorers had apparently completed a crucial step in fulfilling Thomas Jefferson's instructions to explore "the portage between the heads of the Missouri & of the water offering the best communication with the Pacific ocean" and find "the most direct & practicable water communication across this continent for the purposes of commerce."[3] But there was a problem—Lewis and the others had ascended the "dividing ridge" expecting to be close to the Pacific; instead, they found "immence ranges of high mountains still to the West of us with their tops partially covered with snow."[4] Not only that, but Cameahwait, the Shoshone chief they met the next day, told them that the "handsome bold running Creek" they had found was part of a river, now known as the Lemhi, that "discharged itself into another doubly as large . . . and that the river was confined between inacessable mountains, was very rapid and rocky insomuch that it was impossible for us to pass either by land or water down this river to the great lake where the white men lived."[5] Clark soon confirmed that the turbulent river, the Salmon, was indeed impassable and therefore provided no passage to the Pacific: "The hope of an easy portage between the Northwest's great arterials vanished in the reality of the Bitterroot mountains and the gorge-sluicing tributaries of the Columbia. . . . Any lingering optimism had to be cast aside."[6]

Lewis and Clark thus found themselves in a quandary because Jefferson "had studied the geographical lore of the Northwest thoroughly and had extracted from it a proposal to establish a Passage to India," which theorized that the explorers would proceed to the head of the Missouri River "until they located a portage over a height-of-land. From here they would pass over a divide into the navigable waters of westward-flowing streams and then down to the Pacific." This simple idea was reinforced by all of Jefferson's study of the geography of North America.[7] Yes, Lewis and the others easily walked from a rivulet of the Atlantic to one of the Pacific, and if the waters of the Columbia were as navigable as those of the Missouri—which carried them from St. Louis to southwestern Montana—they could have reached the coast in a month, but Jefferson and all the "experts" who preceded him were mistaken. There was no "height-of-land" where the sources of the key rivers were in close proximity, and there was no easy portage across the Continental Divide—quite the opposite. Instead, Lewis and Clark obtained horses from the Shoshone Indians and headed back north, back into Montana and its Bitterroot Range, where they scaled "high rugged hills" in a September hailstorm and later "descended a Mountain nearly as steep as the Roof of a house." Almost every day, morning rain turned to afternoon snow, with no game in sight, and the mountains were so rocky and steep that the horses were in constant "danger of Slipping to Ther certain destruction."[8] After getting lifesaving help from the Salish Indians, they continued north, following the Bitterroot River downstream, and on September 9, 1805, twelve miles south-southwest of present Missoula, Montana, they found a "fine . . . clear running stream . . . about 20 yards wide" that Lewis found quite appealing. "I determined to halt the next day rest our horses and take some [celestial] Observations," he wrote. "We called this Creek *Travellers rest*," now called Lolo Creek.[9]

Lewis knew that without the horses, the entire party could have perished in the most rugged and treacherous wilderness they had yet seen on the expedition, but he also knew that their guide, an elderly Shoshone man they called Old Toby, was just as crucial. When he and Clark pleaded for a "pilot" to show them the way, Cameahwait assured them that the old fellow knew the country to the north better than anyone else in the tribe. Even though they were now more than 160 miles from the Shoshone village, they still depended on Old Toby, and he offered additional advice as Lewis and all the others took a well-deserved interlude along the trickling stream. "Our guide informes that we should leave the [Bitterroot] river at this place," wrote Lewis, adding that Old Toby did not know where the Bitterroot "discharged itself into the columbia river [and] . . . that it continues it's course along the mountains to the N., as far as he knew it and that not very distant from where we then were it formed a junction" with a large westbound river that the captains dubbed Clark's River. Old Toby then surprised the captains by announcing that Clark's River—now known as the Clark Fork River—took its rise from the mountains near the Missouri River to the east and that if a party ascended Clark's River through an extensive valley, they could reach the river's source and then cross the Continental Divide to a point "about 30 miles above the *gates of the rocky mountain*" and thus "pass to the missouri from hence by that rout in four days."[10]

"*Four days*!" bellows Stephen E. Ambrose. "It had taken the expedition fifty-three days to travel from the Gates of the Rocky Mountains [about twenty miles north of the future site of Helena, Montana] to its present location.

Whatever emotions Lewis felt when he learned that the party might have saved seven weeks he kept it to himself."[11]

Despite this discouraging news, Old Toby's recommendation that the corps stop descending the Bitterroot River proved accurate, something confirmed the next day when John Colter befriended three Nez Perce Indians and brought them to camp. One of them, Lewis wrote, "agreed to continue with us as a guide, and to introduce us to his relations whom he informed us were numerous and resided in the plain below the mountains on the columbia river, from whence he said the water was good and capable of being navigated to the sea."[12]

"The Dissolution of Meriwether Lewis"

So the corps went west with new hope, soon finding the Lochsa River and being warmly welcomed by the Nez Perce nation, who fed them and helped them prepare to descend the Clearwater, Snake, and Columbia Rivers to the coast. For the present, however, they still had another Rocky Mountain pass—and another crossing of the Montana/Idaho border—ahead of them. Sergeant Patrick Gass, initially calling the peaks to the west "large" and "very steep," soon said they "made the travelling fatiguing and uncomfortable," finally calling them "the most terrible mountains I ever beheld."[13] On September 14 the rain turned to hail and the hail to snow. Old Toby got lost and led them down a road "excessively bad & Thickly Strowed with falling timber . . . Steep & Stoney." Men and horses grew "much fatigued" and desperate for food, but the hunters found no game, and Indian horses had eaten all the grass: "We were compelled to kill a Colt . . . to eat . . . and named the South fork Colt killed Creek." On September 16 the snow started before dawn and continued all day. Clark went ahead on foot but "found great difficuelty in keeping" the trail because of the deep snow, "passing emince Dificulet Knobs Stones much falling timber and emencely Steep," and concluding "I have been wet and as cold in every part as I ever was in my life."[14] Still, Clark retained his endless optimism.

Not so with Lewis. In a landmark essay entitled "The Columbia Country and the Dissolution of Meriwether Lewis," David L. Nicandri suggests, "The first cracks in Lewis's psyche"—which eventually led to his suicide at an obscure Tennessee inn three years after his return to civilization—"occurred in the Pacific Northwest. From his first few days west of the Continental Divide in the summer of 1805 until he re-crossed the Bitterroot Mountains in June 1806, Meriwether Lewis was confounded by the country drained by the Great River of the West."[15] In a summary of the expedition likely written to William Henry Harrison, Lewis revealed just how deeply the nerve-racking experience of crossing the Bitterroot Range affected him: "I have not leisure at this moment to state all those difficulties which we encountered in our Passage over these Mountains—suffice it to say we suffered everything Cold, Hunger & Fatigue could impart, or the Keenest Anxiety excited for the fate of Expedition in which our whole Souls were embarked."[16]

On Monday, October 7, 1805, eight weeks to the day since Lewis quenched his thirst with the "pure and ice cold water" of a Missouri stream, crossed the Continental Divide, and "first tasted the water of the great Columbia river," he, Clark, and the others finally set out on a watercourse for the Pacific Ocean, with no one in the party doubting that this had been by far the most trying period of the excursion. Nor were the next two months getting off to a good start. "I continuu verry unwell but obliged to attend every thing," Clark wrote that day.[17] Lewis was apparently so sick that he had not made a journal entry for the past two weeks. "During our residence at this compound we were all Sick," he later reported. "For my own part I suffered a severe Indisposition for 10 or 12 days, thus sick feeble & emaciated, we commenced & continued the operation of building four large Pirogues & a small Canoe."[18] Lewis had a simple and reasonable explanation for the ill health of the corps: they were famished when they reached the Nez Perce village, and although their new friends supplied them with an abundance of dried Salmon and roots, the radical change in diet had severe but predictable results.

The eight-week delay in transitioning from Atlantic to Pacific waters was disheartening and cast an irreversible pall over Lewis, but ironically, the Corps of Discovery, with invaluable help from the Shoshone, Salish, and Nez Perce nations, had fulfilled Jefferson's instructions the best they could by finding the one and only reasonable passage between the Missouri and the Columbia. Jefferson's assumption that the latter had several tributaries in the vicinity of the sources of the former was correct, but he could not foresee the effect the unforgiving western landscape had on the course of rivers. The Snake River was the key tributary of the Columbia, but as the Astorians would discover, the upper Snake (unexplored by Lewis and Clark) did not offer navigable access to the Columbia because of the deep gorge along the Idaho/Oregon border called Hell's Canyon. As for the Salmon River, the key tributary of the Snake, Clark himself confirmed that it was impassable. Then there was the fork of the Columbia that completely bypassed the Snake—the Clark Fork / Pend Oreille River, but even the experienced navigator David Thompson waved the white flag when trying to reach the Columbia from Metaline Falls. That left one option, the same option recommended by Old Toby and the Nez Perce—the Clearwater, which flowed into the Snake above both Hell's Canyon and the mouth of the Salmon. But even passing from the Dearborn River to Travelers' Rest and then to the Clearwater would have required advance planning and packhorses to carry food, supplies, and equipment over a long haul. And while the corps successfully reached the coast from the Clearwater River, they frequently fought rapids, chutes, and falls.[19] The upshot? Whether called the Passage to India, the Northwest Passage, or something else, Jefferson's "direct and practicable water route for the purposes of commerce" was nowhere to be found.[20] Did that reign in the passion to go west? Not at all. The quest for furs, land, personal or religious freedom, and especially gold kept migrants hurrying west throughout the antebellum period.

Making good time in their pirogues and single canoe, the corps reached the confluence of the Snake and Columbia Rivers on October 16, the Great Falls of the Columbia (Celilo Falls) on October 23, and the Great Rapids (Cascades of the Columbia) on October 30. The most memorable day of the voyage came on November 7, one month to the day after the explorers launched their boats into the Clearwater. "Great joy in camp we are in View of the Ocian," Clark wrote. "This great Pacific Octean which we been So long anxious to See. and the roreing or noise made by the waves brakeing on the rockey Shores (as I suppose) may be heard distictly."[21] On November 24 the captains asked the group, including York (Clark's slave) and Sacagawea (the Indian wife of interpreter Toussaint Charbonneau), to vote on where to spend the winter. In December the men built Fort Clatsop, where they would spend the next three and a half months, but we don't know how Lewis felt about any of these happenings because he had not, with two minor exceptions, updated his journal since September 22. What we do know is that the winter and spring spent on the coast was full of boredom, sickness, and constant rain that often spoiled the elk, fish, and roots they did not enjoy that much in the first place. "Relations with the local Indians were not as satisfactory as they had been at Fort Mandan. The captains found many of the natives' customs and attitudes repugnant," writes Gary Moulton. "Although the Indians never manifested real hostility, the commanders took strict security measures to insure the safety of the party."[22] Although Lewis was silent, Clark told the story of the first two months on the coast:

> A Tremendous wind from the S. W. about 3 oClock this morning with Lightineng and hard claps of thunder . . . all wet and Cold our bedding also wet.
>
> The wind increased to a Storm . . . and blew with violence throwing the water of the river with emence waves out of its banks almost over whelming us in water, O! how horriable is the day.
>
> We Could find no deer, Several hunters attempted to penetrate the thick woods to the main South Side without Suckcess . . . we have nothing to eate but a little Pounded fish which we purchased . . . the robes of our Selves and men are all rotten from being Continually wet.
>
> I Sunk into the mud and water up to my hips without finding any bottom on the trale of those Elk.
>
> The flees were So troublesom that I Slept but little.
>
> Some rain and hail last night and this morning it rained hard untill 10 oClock . . . 3 Indians came with Lickorish Sackocomie berries & mats to Sell, for which they asked Such high prices that we did not purchase any of them,—Those people ask double & tribble the value of everry thing they have to Sel.

> Our Store of Meat entirely Spoiled, we are obliged to make use of it as we have nothing else except a little pounded fish.[23]

"A Canoe Which Belonged to the Clatsop Indians"

Lewis resumed writing in his journal on January 1, 1806, returning to his regular and detailed entries, not mentioning his failure to write for more than three months but making his homesickness—and perhaps his fragile mental state—clear by noting, "Our repast of this day . . . consisted principally in the anticipation of the 1st day of January 1807, when in the bosom of our friends we hope to participate in the mirth and hilarity of the day, and when with the zest given by the recollection of the present, we shall completely, both *mentally* and corporally, enjoy the repast which the hand of civilization has prepared for us."[24] His subsequent entries frequently provide detailed descriptions—and impressive sketches—of everything from Indian fishhooks, arrows, swords, bludgeons, canoes, paddles, and head-flattening methods to pine cones, evergreen shrub and fern leaves, condors, white gulls, and white salmon trout. Despite that favorable sign, however, Lewis was more like an inmate biding his time than a man who had found his mental and emotional bearings. When he was just a few weeks away from the Pacific, he would reflect on his time there as "having been so long imprisoned in mountains and those almost impenetrably thick forrests of the seacoast."[25] Indeed, the corps' four-month sojourn—was it only four months?—ended on quite a sour note, a fitting portent of Lewis's final months as Thomas Jefferson's trailblazer. "Drewyer [Drouillard] was taken last night with a violent pain in his side," Lewis wrote on March 18 as the group prepared to head east. "Several of the men are complaining of being unwell. it is truly unfortunate that they should be sick at the moment of our departure." A few days later, things looked just as glum: "It continues to rain in Such a manner that there is no possibility of getting our canoes completed. . . . The hunters all returned except Colter, unsuccessfull. We determined to set out tomorrow at all events."[26] Set out they did on March 23, paddling upstream against the Columbia's powerful current. Sergeant John Ordway described the woeful conclusion to the Oregon interlude: "4 men went over to the prarie near the coast to take a canoe which belongd to the Clotsop Indians, as we are in want of it. . . . The others took the canoe near the fort and concealed it, as the chief of the Clotsops is now here."[27] The phrase "take a canoe" was Ordway's careful way of saying *steal a canoe*. In his instructions to Lewis, Jefferson had stressed the necessity that the Indians "will find in us faithful friends and protectors."[28] Now, however, as James P. Ronda laments, "The captains were abandoning a two-year tradition of never stealing from the Indians. The essential honesty that distinguished Lewis and Clark from explorers like Hernando DeSoto and Francisco Pizzaro"—a list that could include Christopher Columbus, Vasco da Gama, and a host of others—"had been tarnished. . . . It had been one thing to trick Cameahwait into thinking that Clark's party was close at hand when the fate of the expedition hung in the balance at Shoshoni Cove. . . . It was another thing to cheat Coboway [the Clatsop chief]—a man Lewis described as 'friendly and decent,' 'kind and hospitable'—and not even feel a pang of conscience . . . [in a] singular betrayal of friendship."[29]

Unfortunately, the corps' theft of a Clatsop canoe set the tone for Lewis's treatment of Indians over the next month, a period Nicandri puts in sharp focus: "Surely Lewis's behavior on the Columbia in April 1806 represents a man stressed to the limit and seemingly just short of a nervous breakdown. It is here that we find the onset of a troubled trajectory that terminated at Grinder's Stand"—where Lewis took his own life with a pair of pistols—"just over three years later."[30] On April 11, for instance, at the Cascades, which Clark called the "Great Rapids of the Columbia," the water was now an amazing twenty feet higher than it had been five months earlier. During the portage, two "illy disposed" Natives attempted to take a dog John Shields had bought from other Indians and "pushed him out of the road." When Shields drew a large knife, his assailants "instantly fled through the woods." Next came an offense that Lewis predictably considered a cardinal sin: "Three of this same tribe of villains . . . stole my dog this evening, and took him towards their village."[31] Lewis's pet was a male Newfoundland dog named Seaman, a companion that was with him as early as September 1803. Lewis soon learned of Seaman's theft and "sent three men in pursuit of the theives with orders if they made the least resistance or difficulty in surrendering the dog to fire on them; they overtook these fellows or reather came within sight of them at the distance of about 2 miles; the indians discovering the party in pursuit of them left the dog and fled." Canine lovers empathize entirely with Lewis's rage—never steal someone's dog. For that very reason, however, it's a mystery how Lewis could (understandably) be so upset at Seaman's temporary loss but shrug his shoulders at stealing an Indian ally's canoe when he himself acknowledged that the coastal people looked on their finely crafted and indispensable canoes with the same kind of affection he had for his dog. All that notwithstanding, Lewis gave no sign of contemplating such complexities. "We ordered the centinel to keep [the Indians] out of camp," he wrote, "and informed them by signs that if they made any further attempts to steal our property or insulted our men we should put them to instant death."[32]

Instant death? For insulting the captains or their men or even attempting to steal something? That did not sound like the Lewis who had dealt successfully with one Indigenous nation after another for almost two years. One would hope that such a drastic threat would turn out to be rare hyperbole ignited by the stealing of Seaman, but Lewis's erratic behavior continued. Going upstream on the powerful Columbia got harder and more dangerous. At The Dalles, Lewis managed a portage while Clark went upstream to negotiate for horses so the group could go overland. "The long narrows are much more formidable than they were when we decended them last fall," wrote Lewis. "There would be no possibility of [passing] either up or down them in any vessel." When Alexander Willard "was negligent in his attention to his horse and suffered it to ramble off," Lewis confessed that he found the situation "truly provoking" and reprimanded Willard "more severely . . . than had been usual with me."[33]

Lewis's nerves were just as frayed the next day. He characterized the local Indians as "poor, dirty, proud, haughty, inhospitable, parsimonious and faithless in every rispect, nothing but our numbers I believe prevents their attempting to murder us at this moment. . . . I ordered the indians from our camp this evening and informed them that if I caught them attempting to perloin any article from us I would beat them severely. . . . I directed the party to examine their arms and be on their guard."[34] Lewis soon backed up his threats of violence. On the morning of April 21, when a corps tomahawk came up missing, Lewis "surched many of [the Indians] but could not find it." Apparently hitting his limit, he "ordered all the spare poles, paddles and the balance of our canoe put on the fire as the morning was cold and also that *not a particle should be left for the benefit of the indians*."[35] As Nicandri so aptly says, "It is not hard to discern from this scene, one of Lewis's own self-incriminating construction, which of these motives—warmth or spite—was primary. The scene worsened. Seeing this wasteful destruction taking place, one Indian attempted to retrieve an oarlock from the bonfire, an act the obstreperous Lewis characterized as 'stealing.'"[36] A surprisingly candid Lewis wrote that he gave the Indian "several severe blows and mad[e] the men kick him out of camp. I now informed the indians that I would shoot the first of them that attempted to steal an article from us. that we were not afraid to fight them, that I had it in my power at that moment to kill them all and set fire to their houses, but it was not my wish to treat them with severity provided that they would let my property alone."[37]

Sergeant Gass also recorded Lewis's appalling response to the Indian's harmless attempt to get the oarlock: "While we were making preparations to start, an Indian stole some iron articles from among the men's hands; which so irritated Captain Lewis, that he struck him; which was the first act of the kind, that had happened during the expedition."[38] Although Gass failed to mention Lewis's already discarding the item by throwing it in the fire, he still offered a valid criticism of Lewis—something he and the other journal keepers, including Clark, almost never did—by acknowledging that this was the first time he had seen Lewis strike an Indian.

"Here Was Winter with All Its Rigors"

As regrettable as Lewis's assault on the hapless Indian was, the corps was now on its way home—just five months from St. Louis, and one has to wonder how Lewis would have fared if he and Clark had simply stayed together for the rest of the journey, but as early as March 1806 the captains planned on splitting up after crossing the Bitterroot Mountains. "We shall be necessarily dividied into three or four parties on our return in order to accomplish the objects we have in view," Lewis wrote.[39] He and Clark had three key reasons for splitting up: to confirm if Old Toby's description of a pass over the Continental Divide (roughly halfway between present Missoula and

Hardy, Montana) was accurate, to check the latitude of the northernmost reaches of Marias River (which they had explored in early June 1805 before deciding—correctly—to take the southern, or main, fork of the Missouri to the Rocky Mountains), and to explore the Yellowstone River to its confluence with the Missouri. Even Lewis's liberal estimate of splitting into three or four groups was not quite right—there were eventually five, putting each band in extreme danger of Indian attacks or some other catastrophe. Through both skill and luck, the five parties successfully reunited with no loss of life.

So with plans of dividing into separate troops already in place, the expedition crossed to the north side of the Columbia and transitioned from navigating canoes to riding on horseback, rapidly increasing their eastward progress: "They made twenty miles the first day, twenty-eight the second, then thirty-one, much better mileage than they'd been making on the river."[40] They entered Idaho just two weeks later, soon meeting Nez Perce friends from their stay the previous autumn. The captains held several councils with various chiefs and obtained most of the horses they had left in Nez Perce care the previous October. It was quickly evident, however, that the snow was too deep to cross the Bitterroot Range, so the corps established a camp on the north bank of the Clearwater River, near present Kamiah, Idaho, that offered access to hunting grounds, a pasture for the horses, and of course, fish and water. The captains, who called the Nez Perces the *Chopunnish* nation, dubbed their new dwelling place Camp Chopunnish. Clark served as the physician, making many notes similar to the following:

> An old man and a woman arrived the man with Sore eyes, and the woman with a gripeing and rhmatic effections. I gave the woman a dose of creme of tarter and flour of Sulphur, the man some eye water.
>
> About 11 oClock 4 men and 8 Women Came to our Camp . . . those Men applied for Eye water and the Women had a Variety of Complaints tho' the most general Complaint was the Rhumitism, pains in the back and the Sore eyes, they also brought fowd. a very young Child whome they Said had been very Sick—. I administered eye water to all, two of the women I gave a carthartic, one whose Spirets were very low and much hiped I gave 30 drops of [Laudanum], and to the others I had

their backs hips legs thighs & arms well rubed with *Volitile leniment* all of those pore people thought themselves much benifited by what had been done for them.[41]

The month with the Nez Perces—which included a warm camaraderie between explorers and Indians as they ate side by side, passed pipes to each other, danced together to Pierre Cruzatte's fiddling, and competed in horse races (won by the Indians) and shooting contests (won by soldiers, particularly Lewis)—served as a hiatus, giving Lewis a chance to get back to his pre-crossing-the-divide self, but that did not happen. In early June, as the time approached to cross the Bitterroots, he revealed his dread, writing that the corps was preparing "in the most ample manner in our power to meet that wretched portion of our journy, the Rocky Mountain, where hungar and cold in their most rigorous forms assail the waried traveller; not any of us have yet forgotten our sufferings in those mountains in September last, and I think it probable we never shall."[42] Despite that feeling—or maybe because of it—Lewis was overly eager to get going. He had asked the Nez Perces for guides, and one of the chiefs assured him two young men who knew the way across the mountains and to the falls of the Missouri would soon overtake the expedition. "Our party seem much elated with the idea of moving on towards their friends and country," he wrote on June 9. The next day, around 11 a.m., "we set out with the party each man being well mounted and a light load on a second horse," along with several extra horses.[43] Sacagawea was mounted as well, with her sixteen-month-old son Jean Baptiste, now called Pomp, strapped to her back.

Three days passed with no sign of the guides. Despite that, Lewis was determined to go ahead: "From hence to traveller' rest we shall make a forsed march." At the same time, he acknowledged feeling "apprehensive that the snow and the want of food for our horses will prove a serious embarrassment to us as at least four days journey of our rout in these mountains lies over hights and along a ledge of mountains never intirely destitute of snow."[44]

The corps proceeded on, making twenty-two miles the next day and coming upon "handsom meadows of fine grass." While the horses grazed in "a handsome little glade," Lewis, a botanist at heart, relished the spring weather, noting, "The dogtooth violet is just in blume, the honeysuckle, huckburry, and a small species of white maple are beginning to put forth their leaves." As they rode to a higher elevation, the spring day vanished: "The snow has increased in quantity so much that the greater part of our rout this evening was over the snow which has become sufficiently firm to bear our horshes, otherwise it would have been impossible for us to proceed as it lay in immence masses in some places 8 or ten feet deep."[45]

The next morning, June 17, "we collected our horses and set out early," Lewis wrote. "We found it difficult and dangerous. . . . We ascended about 3 miles when we found ourselves invelloped in snow from 12 to 15 feet deep even on the south sides of the hills. . . . Here was winter with all it's rigors; the air was cold, my hands and feet were benumbed." Lewis's quarrel and bafflement with the northwestern landscape thus continued right to the end of his time west of the divide. In his haste to return to the Missouri country, he had led the party right back into another Bitterroot trap. He had no illusions otherwise: "If we proceeded and should get bewildered in these mountains the certainty was that we should loose all our horses and consequently our baggage instruments perhaps our papers and thus eminently wrisk the loss of the discoveries which we had already made if we should be so fortunate as to escape with life." He and Clark talked things over, conceiving "it madness in this stage of the expeditin to proceed without guide who could certainly conduct us to [Travelers' Rest]. . . . We therefore came to the resolution to return with our horses while they were yet strong and in good order and indeavour to keep them so untill we could procure an indian to conduct us ove the snowey mountains." This was the first time the expedition had been "compelled to retreat or make a retrograde march."[46]

"We therefore hung up our loading on poles, tied to and extended between trees," wrote Sergeant Gass, "covered it all with deer skins, and turned back melancholy and disappointed."[47] The group's "loading" included the roots the Nez Perces had given them as a food supply and the corps' "instruments" and "papers," presumably referring to the scientific implements Lewis used to make celestial observations and the journals of Lewis, Clark, Ordway, Gass, and Joseph Whitehouse. The journals, of course, were the group's most valuable possessions, and leaving them behind was hazardous, to put it mildly.

Lewis's belief that they were "safer here than to wrisk them on horseback over the roads and creeks which we had passed" reveals how short-sighted his impulse to depart without pilots had been.[48]

The next morning, the captains sent Drouillard and George Shannon back to the Nez Perces "to procure a [guide] at all events and rejoin us as soon as possible," adding, "We sent by them a rifle which we offered as a reward to any of them who would engage to conduct us to travellers' rest."[49] Just as Lewis's striking an Indian and ordering a retreat were both "firsts" on the excursion, offering a rifle for Indian help was also unparalleled—and certainly never mentioned as an option in trading for a canoe. Moreover, the rifles carried by Lewis, Clark, and their men made for prime trading currency because they were much more accurate than the smooth-bored "trade guns" that Canadian trappers had distributed to many Indian nations, a reality not gone unnoticed by the Nez Perces when Lewis proved himself to be an excellent shot using an excellent firearm.[50]

The main group slowly retreated for the next few days, growing increasingly nervous when they did not see Drouillard or Shannon or Nez Perce guides. The situation looked more and more perilous. "We have determined to wrisk a passage," Lewis wrote. "Capt. C. or myself shall take four of our most expert woodsmen with three or four of our best horses and proceed two days in advance taking a plentiful supply of provision." These men would attempt to find the trail to Travelers' Rest by looking for "the marks which the baggage of the indians has made in many places on the sides of the trees" by rubbing against the trunks and also by the Indians' blazing the trail with tomahawks. "After proceeding two days . . . two of these men would be sent back to the main party" to let them know whether to go ahead or wait for further word from the scouts. If the scouting party could not find the trail after making their best effort, they would "then return to the main party . . . and attempt a passage over these mountains through the country of the Shoshones further to the South by way of the main S. Westerly fork of Lewis's river [the upper Snake River] and Madison or Gallatin's rivers, where from the information of the [Nez Perces] there is passage which at this time of year is not obstructed by snow."[51]

The captains were thus contemplating a variety of high-risk ventures, all abounding with crucial—and unanswered—questions. Luckily, the next day they met "two indians who were on their way over the mountain; they had brought with them the three horses and the mule that had left us. . . . As well as we could understand the indians they informed us that they had seen Drewyer and Shannon and that they would not return untill the expiration of two days." With new hope, the captains shelved their tentative plans and returned to the site of their encampment a week earlier, where they "anxiously await[ed] the return of Drewyer and Shannon." The next day brought more good news: "All hands who could hunt were sent out; the result of this days performance was greater than we had even hoped for. we killed eight deer and three bear."[52]

On June 23 Lewis wrote, "Apprehensive from Drewyer's delay that he had met with some difficultly in procuring a guide, and also that the two indians who had promised to wait two nights for us would set out today, we thought it most advisable to dispatch Frazier [Robert Frazer] and Wiser [Peter Weiser] to them this morning with a vew if possible to detain them a day or two longer." The two privates left and had not returned by afternoon, but Lewis was not worried because he had instructed them to accompany the two Indians to Travelers' Rest if necessary. Around 4 p.m. all worries vanished when Drouillard and Shannon rode into camp with Whitehouse (sent on an errand the previous day) and "three indians who had consented to accompany us to the falls of the Missouri for the compensation of two guns. . . . These are all young men of good character and much respected by their nation." Hugely relieved, Lewis added, "We directed the horses to be brought near camp this evening and secured in such manner that they may [be] readily obtained in the morning . . . to make an early start if possible."[53]

What could be better? He was about to get clear of the Columbia country once and for all. The corps and their guides set out early the next day as planned, meeting Frazer and Weiser and the two Indians later that day. "We had fine grass for our horses this evening," Lewis said. At nightfall, the guides set "fir trees on fire" by igniting "a great number of dry lims . . . [that created] a very suddon and immence blaze from bottom to top of thos tall trees. they are a beautiful object in this situation at night. this exhibition reminded me of a display of fireworks. the natives told us that their object in setting those trees on fire was to bring fair weather for our journey."[54] Two days later the group reached the spot where they had stored their invaluable journals and other materials: "Here we necessarily halted about 2 hours to arrange our baggage and prepare our loads . . . [and] made a haisty meal of boiled venison." Then, at the Indians' encouragement, they resumed their march in order to reach grass for the horses before stopping for the night: "Accordingly we set out with our guides who lead us over and along the steep sides of tremendous mountains entirely covered with snow except about the roots of the trees." Late that evening, "much to the satisfaction of ourselves and the comfort of our horses," wrote Lewis, "we arrived at the desired spot and encamped on the steep side of a mountain convenient to a good spring." The young guides had proved their worth beyond any doubt—just as they predicted, the site also included an "abundance of fine grass" for the horses.[55]

Lewis's appreciation for the Nez Perce guides only escalated the next day. Reaching an elevated point the captains recognized from their desperate westbound trek nine months earlier, the party found a conic mound of stones eight feet high. Indians had previously constructed it, placing a fifteen-foot pole at the summit. The Nez Perces and Lewis and Clark smoked a pipe to honor the site: "From this place we had an extensive view of these stupendous mountains principally covered with snow like that on which we stood; we were entirely surrounded by those mountains from which to one unacquainted with them it would have seemed impossible ever to have escaped; in short without the assistance of our guides I doubt much whether we who had once passed them could find our way to Travellers rest in their present situation."[56]

Two days later they reached another familiar site, the "warm springs," now known as Lolo Hot Springs. "The prinsipal spring is about the temperature of the warmest baths used at the hot springs in Virginia," Lewis wrote. "In this bath . . . I bathed and remained in 19 minutes, it was with difficulty I could remain thus long and it caused a profuse sweat." Then Lewis watched as the men and Indians amused themselves: "The indians after remaining in the hot bath as long as they could bear it ran and plunged themselves into the creek the water of which is now as cold as ice can make it; after remaining here a few minutes they returned again to the warm bath, repeating this transition several times but always ending with the warm bath."[57]

On June 30 they drew near to Travelers' Rest: "In descending the creek this morning on the steep side of a high hill my horse sliped with both his hinder feet out of the road and fell, I also fell off backwards and slid near 40 feet down the hill before I could stop myself such was the steepness of the declivity; the horse was near falling on me in the first instance but fortunately recovers and we both escaped unhirt." If the tumble left Lewis unsettled, that soon faded because a little before sunset, they arrived at their old encampment along the pleasant stream that flowed into Clark's River. Deer were plentiful, so there would be no lack of food while they and their horses finally rested: "Our horses have stood the journey supprisingly well, most of them are yet in fine order, and only want a few days rest to restore them perfectly."[58]

"I Hoped This Separation Was Only Momentary"

On July 3, at Travelers' Rest, Lewis and Clark split the Corps of Discovery into two groups: "The proposed rendezvous at the Missouri-Yellowstone junction was a full five hundred miles east of Travelers' Rest, as the crow flies. Clark's proposed route would cover nearly a thousand miles, Lewis's nearly eight hundred."[59] Clark wrote that his group of twenty-two included "interpreter Shabono [Toussaint Charbonneau] & wife [Sacagawea] & child [Jean Baptiste Charbonneau] (as an interpreter & interpretess for the Crow Inds and the latter for the Shoshoni) with 50 horses."[60] As noted, Clark was on his way to explore the Yellowstone River, and his mention that Charbonneau was coming as an interpreter for the Crow Indians was hardly incidental—he fully expected to meet that nation on the Yellowstone. During the 1804–5 winter at Fort Mandan, the captains had continually queried the Mandans and Hidatsas about the Indigenous nations, rivers, and mountains to the west. In talks with the Hidatsas, who ranged considerably farther west than the Mandans, Clark learned that "the Big bellies [Hidatsas]" and the "ravin [Crow] Indians Speake nearly the Same language and the presumption is that they were origionally the Same nation"—important because Charbonneau spoke Hidatsa. Clark wrote, "The Ravin Indians 'have 400 Lodges & about 1200 men, & follow the Buffalow, or hunt for their Subsistance in the plains & on the Court noi [Black Hills] & Rock Mountains, & are at war with the Sioux Snake Indians.[']"[61]

The captains also gathered the following information from Hidatsas, other Indian nations, or Missouri River fur traders (who likely got their knowledge of the Crows from other Indians): The Crows do not cultivate the soil but live by hunting. Their country is full of animals or game of every kind, especially beaver. "Their country is fertile, and well watered, and in most parts well timbered." They trade "horses, mules, leather lodges, and many articles of Indian apparel" to their allies, the Mandans and Hidatsas, and receive in return "guns, ammunition, axes, kettles, awls, and other European manufactures," some of which they trade to the Shoshone Indians for Spanish bridle bits and blankets. The number of souls in the Crow nation is 5,000 or 3,500. They are at defensive war with the Sioux and Assiniboine nations. They reside mainly on the Yellowstone River, a short distance above its mouth and near the mouth of the Bighorn River. They can provide horses, deer meat, buffalo robes, dressed buffalo skins, and beaver, fox, and otter pelts for trade. The mouth of the Yellowstone was "mutually advantageous to form the principal establishment in order to Supply the Several nations with Merchindize."[62]

The captains' obtaining this kind of data before entering Crow country or even meeting any Crow people reveals the encyclopedic knowledge that the Native nations had about one another and the geography and topography of neighboring lands.[63] Whether Lewis and Clark were planning routes, drawing maps, searching for food, wintering in a subzero climate, or fighting for survival—twice—in the Bitterroot Mountains, they and their party relied tremendously on the help of Indians.

Thomas Jefferson's profound influence on the captains is evident in the information they compiled on the Crow nation. Ethnographic facts were important, but commercial details were even more so. Months before they saw the Yellowstone River, Clark and Lewis reached a preliminary conclusion that the mouth of that river would be an ideal site for a U.S. trading post. Clark's plan to explore the Yellowstone, therefore, had a strong economic objective, like the expedition itself. As for reaching and exploring the upper Yellowstone, while still at Fort Mandan, Lewis—again relying on "Indian information"—wrote, "The yellow Stone river is navigable at all seasons of the year, for boats or perogues to the foot of the Rocky Mountains, near which place, it is said to be not more than 20 miles distant from the most southernly of the three forks of the Missouri, which last is also navigable to this point." Just twenty miles from one of the forks of the Missouri to the Yellowstone River? If true, this was crucial intelligence because, as Lewis wrote, the Yellowstone "waters one of the fairest portions of Louisiana, a country not yet hunted, and abounding in animals of the fur kind . . . [a waterway] affording to our citizens the benefit of a most lucrative fur trade . . . [that] might be made to hold in check the views of the British [North] West Company on the fur-trade of the upper part of the Missouri, which we believe it is their intention to panopolize if in their power."[64]

Given the strategic importance of the Yellowstone River, exploring it was mandatory to meet Jefferson's directives. At the same time, Lewis believed it just as important to explore Marias River, which the corps had first seen on June 3, 1805, two months after departing Fort Mandan. "We . . . formed a camp on the point formed by the junction of the two large rivers," he wrote. "An interesting question was now to be determined; which of these rivers was the Missouri." Most of the group, including the expert boatman Cruzatte, thought the northern branch was the Missouri, but after much discussion and a brief reconnaissance of each fork, the captains correctly concluded they should take the south branch, the true Missouri. Lewis nevertheless took a special interest in the north fork, naming it Marias River, after his cousin, Maria Wood: "It is a noble river; one destined to become in my opinion an object of contention between the two great powers of America and Great Britin with rispect to the adjustment of the Nor westwardly boundary of the former; and that *it will become one of the most interesting branches of the Missouri in a commercial point of view*."[65] By referring to the issues of the northwestern border between Britain and the United States and the commercial value of Marias River, Lewis apparently made up his mind at that instant to explore it on the return journey if at all possible, a plan he carried out one year and one month after first seeing Marias River.

"We saddled our horses and set out," wrote Lewis. "I took leave of my worthy friend and companion Capt. Clark and the party that accompanied him. I could not avoid feeling much concern on this occasion although I hoped this seperation was only momentary."[66] Lewis was accompanied by Sergeant Gass, Drouillard, brothers Joseph and Reubin Field, Frazer, Silas Goodrich, McNeal, Thompson, William Werner, and five Nez Perce Indians whose names were not recorded. Mounted on horseback, Lewis and his men went north along the Bitterroot River to the mouth of the Clark Fork River (near present Missoula, Montana). They then ascended the Clark Fork to the east, staying to the left, or north, when they found a key fork, thus following the Blackfoot River (not the main Clark Fork, which meanders to the southeast) along a route similar to that now taken by Montana Highway 200. About seventeen miles northeast of present Lincoln, they followed a well-worn Indian trail over the Continental Divide, making an easy crossing at present Lewis and Clark Pass (elevation 6,424 feet). Ten miles farther on, they found the Dearborn River, with the trip from Travelers' Rest to the Dearborn taking five days, once again proving Old Toby's incredible geographical knowledge of the area.

Lewis and his companions were finally back on the Atlantic side of the divide, where they had spent all their lives except the previous eleven wearisome months. "R. Fields killed a fine buck," Lewis wrote on July 8. "We halted and dined. . . . We saw a great number of deer goats and wolves as we passed through the plains this morning . . . much rejoiced at finding ourselves in the plains of the Missouri which abound with game." The good fortune continued as the party saw "several gangs of Elk" and "vast heards of buffaloe in the evening below us on the river." They feasted on "very fat buffaloe" and took as much of the meat as they could carry on their horses.[67] These were the first buffalo they had killed in a year. On July 11 they came in sight of the White Bear Islands, south of present Great Falls, Montana, where they had camped and cached quite a variety of items in June of 1805 after completing their portage of the Great Falls. "The missouri bottoms on both sides of the river were crouded with buffaloe," Lewis wrote. "I sincerely belief that there were not less than 10 thousand buffaloe within a circle of 2 miles arround that place." Not that all was perfect—the mosquitoes were "extreemly troublesom," the bearskins and plants Lewis had left in the cache were all destroyed because of rising water, "the stoper had come out of a phial of laudinum and the contents had run in the drawer and distroyed a gret part of my medicine," and ten horses turned up missing, presumably stolen by Indians, and Lewis sent Drouillard to search for them.[68]

Luckily, the "carriage wheels" cached after the 1805 portage were in good condition. The men not going up Marias River with Lewis would now use those wheels for another portage, which would be completed when several members of Clark's party arrived from Three Forks in canoes. "Waited very impatiently for the return of Drewyer," Lewis wrote on July 13. "He did not arrive." When another day passed with no sign of Drouillard, Lewis tried to accept the possibility "that a whitebear [grizzly] had killed him" and that Lewis "should have to set out tomorrow in surch of [Drouillard]." If any accident had separated Drouillard from his horse, Lewis added, "the chances in favour of his being killed [by a grizzly] would be as 9 to 10. . . . These bear are a most tremendous animal; it seems that the hand of providence has been most wonderfully in our favor with rispect to them, or some of us would long since have fallen a sacrifice to their farosity." On the afternoon of July 15, however, Drouillard made it back to camp, reporting that "after a diligent surch of 2 days he had discovered where the horses had passed Dearborn's river at which place there were 15 [Indian] lodges that had been abandoned." Although there was no hope of retrieving the horses, Drouillard's safe return had relieved Lewis "from great anxiety"—he "felt so perfectly satisfied" that Drouillard had returned safely that he "thought but little of the horses." Still, the loss of the horses had a serious consequence: instead of taking six men with him to the Marias, Lewis could only take three. There were just ten horses remaining; Lewis left the "two best" and "two worst" with the men making the portage—Gass, Frazer, Goodrich, McNeal, Thompson, and Werner—and took six with him, Drouillard, and the Field brothers so they could have two spare horses to relieve those they rode.[69]

The mosquito misery did not let up. "The musquetoes continue to infest us in such a manner that we can scarcely exist," Lewis wrote. "My dog even howls with the torture he experiences from them." But Lewis also had a portent nagging at him: "There seems to be a sertain fatality attached to the neighborhood of these falls, for there is always a chapter of accedents prepared for us during our residence at them."[70]

"We collected our horses, of which Capt. Lewis took six . . . and then started to go up Maria's river, with only three hunters," Sergeant Gass wrote on July 16. "Capt. Lewis . . . gave orders that we should wait at the mouth of Maria's river to the 1st of Sept., at which time, should he not arrive, we were to proceed on and join Capt. Clarke at the mouth of the Yellow-stone river, and then to return home: but informed us, that should his life and health be preserved, he would meet us at the mouth of Maria's river on the 5th of August."[71]

"The Indian Woman Has Been of Great Service to Me as a Pilot"

"Our Course this evening was nearly South," Clark wrote on July 3, "making a total of 36 miles today. we encamped on the N. Side of a large Creek where we found tolerable food for our hourses." The next day the group continued their way south, ascending the Bitterroot River. At midday Clark observed "the tracks of two men" he presumed to be Shoshones but saw no Indians: "This being the day of the decleration of Independence of the United States and a Day commonly Scelebrated by my Country, I had every disposition to Scelebrate this day and therefore halted early and partook of a Sumptious Dinner of a fat Saddle of Venison."[72]

The next day Clark saw "fresh Sign of 2 horses and a fire burning on the side of the road" and presumed that "those indians are spies from the Shoshones." Late that afternoon, "we . . . Crossed the Mountain into the vally where we first met with the flatheads [Salish]."[73] "Some frost this morning," Clark wrote the next day, July 6. "The last night was so cold that I could not sleep." After collecting the horses that strayed during the night, the group proceeded on, soon going east of the road they had traveled with Old Toby ten months earlier and, about ten miles southeast of present Sula, Montana, passing "over a dividing mountain [Gibbons Pass, elevation 6,946 feet] which Seperates the waters of the Missouri from those of [the Bitterroot] river."[74] A few hours later, Clark wrote, "we . . . entered an extensive open Leavel plain in which the Indian trail Scattered in Such a manner that we Could not pursue it." How could they find their way without Old Toby? Fortunately, they had another Shoshone Indian with them—Sacagawea. "The Indian woman wife to Shabano [Charbonneau] informed me that she had been in this plain frequently and knew it well," Clark wrote.[75] At Sacagawea's direction, they followed the Big Hole River south to the site of present Jackson, Montana, then east across Big Hole Pass, and then southeast to Divide Creek, which led them to the present site of the ghost town of Bannack. They next descended Grasshopper Creek and Horse Prairie Creek to the forks of the Beaverhead River and reached Camp Fortunate, where they had camped on August 17, 1805, and cached their canoes and other items. Several of the men were frenzied to open the cache, but not to get to the boats or other practical objects: "Most of the Party with me being Chewers of Tobacco become So impatient to be chewing it that they Scercely gave themselves time to take their Saddles off their horses befofre they were off to the deposit." Clark gave each man who used tobacco "about two feet off a part of a [roll]." Also a "chewer of tobacco," Clark kept one-third of what remained for himself and put the rest "in a box to Send down with the most of the articles which had been left at this place, by the Canoes to Capt. Lewis."[76]

As for the canoes, Clark found them "all Safe except one of the largest which had a large hoe in one Side & Split in bow." The men repaired that one, washed all the canoes, and put them out to dry. On the cold morning of July 10—water left in a basin was covered with a thick layer of ice—Clark had "all the Canoes put into the water and every article which was intended to be Sent down put on board, and the horses collected and packed with what fiew articles I intend taking with me to the River Rochejhone [Yellowstone River]." They set out after breakfast, with one group on horseback and the other in canoes, descending the Beaverhead River, which flows into the Jefferson, reversing the route they had taken from Three Forks the previous August. Just as Lewis had done—two days earlier and two hundred miles to the north-northeast—Clark gloried to be back on the Atlantic side of the Continental Divide: "We . . . proceeded on Down Jeffersons river . . . into that butifull and extensive Vally open and fertile which we Call the beaver head Vally which is the Indian name." There were innumerable beaver and otter on the many creeks joining the river, great numbers of deer in the bushes along the river bottom, and antelope and bighorn sheep feeding on the higher parts of the valley.[77]

"Set out early this morning and proceeded on very well to the enterance of Madicines [Madison] river at our old Encampment of the 27th July last," Clark wrote on July 13 at the confluence of the Jefferson and Madison Rivers, two miles northeast of present Three Forks, Montana. "I found Sergt. Pryor and party with the horses, they had arrived at this place one hour before us." Clark had all the horses driven across the Madison River and then across a short plain to the Gallatin River, which flowed in from the east, and let the horses feed near the mouth of the Gallatin. Then Clark "had all the baggage of the land party taken out of the Canoes and after dinner the 6 Canoes and the party of 10 men under the direction of Segt. Ordway Set out." Sergeant Ordway and his crew were on their way down the Missouri to meet Sergeant Gass and the five men with him at the White Bear Islands. Clark gave them instructions and also gave them a letter for Lewis. Clark's party rode four miles east and "encamped on the bank of Gallitines River which is a butifull navigable Stream. . . . The indian woman who has been of great Service to me as a pilot through this Country recommends a gap in the mountain more South which I shall cross."[78] The gap in question was Bozeman Pass, now traversed by Interstate 90.

At 2 p.m. on July 15 Clark and his party reached the Yellowstone River, near present Livingston, Montana. With Sacagawea's help, they had traveled from Gibbons Pass to the Yellowstone as efficiently as possible. In the process, they confirmed what other helpers, the Hidatsas, told them at Fort Mandan—that the Yellowstone was "not more than 20 miles distant from the most southernly of the three forks of the Missouri." Clark no doubt had that statistic in mind when he wrote, "The Distance from the three forks of the Easterly fork of Galletines river . . . to the river Rochejhone is 18 miles on an excellent high dry firm road."[79]

"I Left the Medal about the Neck of the Dead Man"

As Clay Jenkinson, the author of *The Character of Meriwether Lewis: Explorer in the Wilderness,* writes, Lewis "made his excursion to the upper waters of the Marias River (July 16–28) to determine if its sources were located somewhere in today's Alberta, because the Louisiana Purchase Treaty entitled the United States to all the lands watered by the Missouri River and its tributaries. A tributary with a source deep in the Canadian north would drive back the border and change the course of American history"—and would certainly please President Jefferson.[80] Lewis's plans were quite specific—to "ascend Maria's river with a view to explore the country and ascertain whether any branch of that river lies as far north as Latd. 50 and again return and join the party who are to descend the Missouri, at the entrance of Maria's river."[81]

Such details raise the obvious question: What northern boundary did the French Republic and the United States of America agree to when they signed the Louisiana Purchase Treaty in 1803? The answer: "Louisiana's boundaries were vague, even in the treaty."[82] Indeed, the treaty made no mention at all of any boundaries or borders—nor did it reference any rivers, lakes, or oceans. The next question: What was Jefferson's understanding? The answer: he was not certain, but his estimate that the purchase contained "500 millions of acres" proved to be amazingly close to the 529,402,880 officially determined in 1819.[83] Nor is it surprising that Jefferson did his best to determine the exact boundaries of Louisiana. He specifically asked several citizens of New Orleans "best qualified" to answer "questions on boundaries" and William C. C. Clairborne, governor of the Mississippi Territory. Clairborne answered that he had "not been able to obtain any satisfactory information" on the western boundaries of Louisiana, and two other correspondents who offered valuable geographical insights about Lower Louisiana reported that "almost nothing is known" about the area north and west of St. Louis.[84]

Lewis had high hopes of claiming new territory for the United States as he, Drouillard, and the Field brothers made their way north, through "wide and level plains which have somewhat the appearance of an ocean, not a treee nor a shrub to be seen . . . like a well shaved bowlinggreen, in which immence and numerous herds of buffaloe were seen feeding." The men camped near the Teton River and dined on buffalo "hump and tongue which furnish ample rations for four men one day." Despite this paradisiacal setting, Lewis was nervous. They saw a wounded and bleeding buffalo and concluded Indians had been running the herd: "The blackfoot indians rove through this quarter of the country and as they are a vicious lawless and reather an abandoned set of wretches I wish to avoid an interview with them if possible."[85]

The quartet reached Marias River early on the evening of July 18: "We killed a couple of buffaloe in the bottom of this river and encamped on it's west side in a grove of cottonwood. . . . I keep a strict lookout every night, I take my tour of watch with the men."[86] The next few days they ascended Marias to the northwest, the buffalo becoming more scarce each day. At midafternoon on July 21 they "struck a northern branch of Marias river about 30 yds. wide." This was Cut Bank Creek: "Being convinced that this stream came from the montains I determined to pursue it as it will lead me to the most northern point to which the waters of Maria's river extend which *I now fear will not be as far north as I wished and expected.*" They followed Cut Bank Creek north-northwest about thirteen miles until darkness fell, making twenty-eight miles for the day. Finding no timber, they made a fire of buffalo dung: "Our provision is nearly out, we wounded a buffaloe this evening but could not get him." They camped on the west side of the creek, about a mile southwest of present Cut Bank, Montana.[87]

The next day they made another twenty-eight miles, stopping "in a beautifull and extensive bottom of the river about 10 miles below the foot of the rocky mountains where this river enters them." The plain on which they had halted was "very high," and as Lewis gazed out at the Continental Divide along the eastern edge of present Glacier National Park, he reached a significantly disappointing conclusion: "I thought it unnecessary to proceed further. . . . I now have lost all hope of the waters of this river ever extending to N Latitude 50° though I still hope and think it more than probable that . . . [the] milk river extend[s] as far north as latd. 50°." Lewis nevertheless decided to stay at this camp for two reasons—first, to "rest ourselves and our horses," and second, to "take the necessary observations," as instructed by Jefferson.[88]

On July 23 Drouillard found "an indian camp of eleven leather lodges which appeared to have been abandoned about 10 days." Lewis believed the Indians to be somewhere on the main branch of Marias River and decided not to "strike that river on my return untill about the mouth of the North branch," the junction of Cut Bank Creek and Two Medicine River.[89] The next day clouds and rain prevented Lewis from completing the observations he wished to take: "I determined to remain another day in the hope of it's being fair." Food was running low; Drouillard and the Fields were convinced "it was useless to hunt within 6 or 8 miles of this place." Not only that, but the cold, wind, and rain rendered their situation "extreemly unpleasant." The bad weather did not let up: "I did not see the sun through the whole course of the day," Lewis wrote on July 25. "I shall . . . [leave this place] with much reluctance without having obtained the necessary data to establish it's longitude—as if the fates were against me my chronometer from some unknown cause stoped today." But there was also good luck, at least for the moment—they found several Indian wintering camps and considered themselves "extreemly fortunate in not having met with these people."[90]

Rain was falling on the morning of July 26, but the clouds seemed to be thinning, so Lewis waited, hoping the sky would clear: "Finding the contrary result I had the horses caught and we set out biding a lasting adieu to this place which I now call camp disappointment." They took their route through the open plains, soon striking Willow Creek and seven miles later Two Medicine River. When they stopped to eat and let the horses graze, they found "some indian lodges which appeared to have been inhabited last winter." They rode on. Early in the evening, Lewis and the Fields ascended a high plain while Drouillard continued along the river: "I had scarcely ascended the hills before I discovered to my left at the distance of a mile an assembleage of about 30 horses, I halted and used my spye glass by the help of which I discovered several indians . . . who appeared to be looking down towards the river I presumed at Drewyer. . . . This was a very unpleasant sight, however I resolved to make the best of our situation and to approach them in a friendly manner." Running would invite the Indians' pursuit, Lewis reasoned, and would put Drouillard—still unaware of the Indians—in grave danger.[91]

After a series of nerve-racking attempts to keep the peace—during which one Indian charged toward Lewis on his horse, as if to count coup, but halted when the latter calmly held out his hand—Lewis gave a medal, a flag, and a handkerchief to three of the Indians. Although Lewis concluded these eight men were "Minnetares," they were actually Piegan Blackfeet. "I told them that I was glad to see them and had a great deel to say to them," he wrote. With Drouillard interpreting via sign language, Lewis "had much conversation with these people. . . . I found them extreemly fond of smoking and plyed them with the pipe untill late at night." Then, the man who had been so apprehensive about encountering the "vicious" Blackfeet and kept a "strict watch" each night, somehow became nonchalant at the worst possible time. He accepted the Indians' invitation to camp with them and failed to have at least two of his party awake and alert throughout the night, which could have prevented the violence that followed: "I took the first watch tonight and set up untill half after eleven; the indians by this time were all asleep, I roused up R. Fields and laid down myself; I directed Fields to watch the movements of the indians and if any of them left the camp to awake us all as I apprehended they would attampt to seal [steal] our horses." Not a word—nor a thought, it seems—about the rifles he and the others carried, weapons much more accurate than the Indians' trade muskets and therefore coveted by the Blackfeet more than horses: "This being done I fell into a profound sleep and did not wake untill the noise of the men and indians awoke me a little after light in the morning."[92]

The "noise" was a scuffle between Drouillard and an Indian trying to take his gun. Then Lewis realized his gun and at least one of the Fields' were missing. Part of the outcome was perfectly predictable—two Blackfeet suffered fatal wounds in the melee that followed, causing the six survivors to scatter. The surprising result was that Lewis, Drouillard, and the Fields all escaped without injury, even though Lewis, "being bearheaded," "felt the wind" of one bullet fired at him. Lewis then left "the medal about the neck" of one of the dead Indians, "that they might be informed who we were." Next, "having no doubt" that a "large party" of Indians would pursue them, the four explorers fled, pushing their horses "as hard as they could bear," taking to the "open plains," riding hard till dark, and making an incredible eighty-eight miles before stopping to rest themselves and their horses. Each man was able to switch mounts when needed because they took fifteen of the Indians' horses with them. Two hours later they "again set out by moon light," covering another twenty miles before sleeping. They left at daylight, even though all four complained of being "so soar" from the previous day's ride that they "could scarcely stand." They debated which route to take to the Missouri River, but Lewis insisted they head for the mouth of Marias

River, where he had promised to meet the canoe party—now consisting of the men Clark had sent from Three Forks as well as those Lewis had left at the White Bear Islands. Lewis told Drouillard and the Fields that they had to risk their lives and warn the boatmen before the Blackfeet took them by surprise. They rode another twenty miles, and then, wrote Lewis, "we heared the report of several rifles very distinctly on the river to our right, we quickly repared to this joyfull sound and on arriving at the bank of the river had the unspeakable satisfaction to see our canoes coming down."[93]

Sergeant Ordway, a passenger in one of the canoes, described meeting Lewis and the others in what some must have considered a miraculous coincidence: "About 9 A.M. we discovred on a high bank a head Capt. Lewis & the three men who went with him on horse back coming towards us on N. Side we came too Shore and fired the Swivell to Salute him & party . . . and were rejoiced to See them &c. Capt. Lewis took us all by the hand."[94] As for the fatal conflict with the young Piegans, "It was Lewis's fault. He was the one who had dreamed up this exploration, the one who had decided to make it with a party of four only, the one who had delayed two full days even though he knew that every additional hour in Blackfoot country raised the risks of an unwelcome encounter."[95]

The remarkable and sad postscript is that three of the four escapees from Blackfeet country would perish from gunshot wounds in less than four years—Joseph Field and George Drouillard, both at the hands of Indians, both on the Lewis and Clark trail, and Meriwether Lewis, by his own hand in Tennessee, on a wilderness path called the Natchez Trace.

"All in Good Health, except Captain Lewis"

The men got back to normal business the next day, with most of them descending the Missouri in the white pirogue and five small canoes: "I placed the two Fieldses and Colter and Collins in the two smallest canoes . . . with orderes to hunt, and kill meat for the party and obtain as many Elkskins as are necessary to cover our canoes and furnish us with shelters from the rain." The hunting was good—on July 31 they saw a "large herd of Elk . . . killed 15 and took their skins." To a man, the group was "anxious to get on" and "plyed their oars faithfully," making about seven miles an hour on the river.[96]

"We are all extreemly anxious to reach the entrance of the Yellowstone river where we expect to join Capt. Clark and party," Lewis wrote on August 2.[97]

On August 3 John Collins and Colter boarded a canoe and left camp early to hunt. Lewis and his band passed the canoe later that day, "hailed [Colter and Collins] but received no answer [and] proceeded," assuming the two would catch up later. Making good time on a swift portion of the Missouri, Lewis estimated that his group traveled about seventy-three miles, seeing buffalo, "a great number of Elk, deer, wolves, some bear, beaver, geese . . . ducks . . . [and] a number of bald Eagles." Lewis also noted, however, that there was no sign of Collins and Colter.[98] Nor did he see them the next day. He delayed on August 5, waiting for the two to arrive. When that did not happen, he concluded they must have passed him during the night, so he stayed on the river much later than normal to catch them. Still no luck. August 7 dawned "cold and extreemly unpleasant" after a hard rain fell all night. Still, the group "set out early resolving to reach the Yellowstone river" that very day, even though he estimated that it was eighty-three miles away, not an easy trip under the best of conditions.[99] Lewis had good reason to be especially cautious because Willard had nearly drowned on August 4 when he and Sergeant Ordway hit a sawyer. Lewis, however, was more anxious than ever to reach what he called "this long wished for spot." He certainly hoped to meet Clark, but there was no way of knowing what kind of scrapes the latter may have encountered—or even if he and his group were still alive. The high-strung Lewis was thus in a fragile state, questioning what possibly had become of Collins and Colter and trying to muster hope that he would find Clark and all his party at the confluence.

He had another concern weighing on his mind. Because Marias River had not offered the northernmost point he sought, he was determined to take careful latitude readings beyond the mouth of the Yellowstone River. From traveling that region in 1805, he knew the Missouri zigzagged to the north until it reached its confluence with the White Earth River and then flowed south. Since he and Clark would unite by that point, he would have the time he needed to make his astronomical observations and accurately measure latitude to a fraction of a degree.

Luckily, the Missouri's current was even more rapid than the day before: "The men plyed their oars faithfully and we went at a good rate. . . . At 4 P.M. [on August 7] we arrived at the entrance of the Yellowstone river."[100] What he found was not at all what he expected: "Capt. Clark had been encamped at this place and was gone from appearances had left it about 7 or 8 days." What? Clark had arrived but had not waited for Lewis? That made no sense at all: "I found a paper on a pole at the point which merely contained my name in the hand wrighting of Capt. C. we also found the remnant of a note which had been attached to a peace of Elk's horns in the camp; from this fragment I learned that game was scarce at the point and musquetoes troublesome which were the reasons given for his going on; I also learnt that he intended halting a few miles below where he intended waiting my arrival." Lewis then wrote a note to Collins and Colter, wrapped it in leather, and placed it on a pole, "ordering them to come on without loss of time; . . . this being done I instantly reimbarked and descended the river in hope of reaching Capt. C's camp before night." Already exhausted by their long trip, the men staggered back in their canoes, going about seven miles before they saw a recently abandoned campsite: "From these circumstances we [concluded] that Capt. C's camp could not be distant and pursued our rout untill dark with the hope of reaching his camp in this however we were disappointed and night coming on compellled us to encamp on the N. E. shore."[101]

Why would Clark leave the confluence in the first place, and why would he then double down by breaking his pledge to wait "a few miles below"? Nor did Clark's "reasons" of scarce game or troublesome mosquitoes sound convincing. When the corps first landed at the confluence in late April 1805, they found "the whol face of the country was covered with herds of Buffaloe, Elk & Antelopes" and "abundant" deer.[102] Worse yet was the mention of mosquitoes. Yes, the corps had battled the pests constantly, but that was a fact of life on the river, except in freezing weather. Lewis responded cynically to that defense when he wrote, "We found the Musquetoes extreemly troublesome but in this rispect there is but little choise of camps from hence down to St. Louis."[103]

What an incredible contrast to what Lewis experienced almost sixteen months earlier, when he and four others reached the mouth of the Yellowstone ahead of the rest of the corps. "I ascended the hills from whence I had a most pleaseing view of the country," he wrote, "perticularly of the wide and fertile vallies formed by the missouri and the yellowstone rivers, which occasionally unmasked by the woods on their borders disclose their meanderings for many miles in their passage through these delightful tracts of country."[104]

Now, however, as Jenkinson observes, "William Clark set off a chain of events that would alter the nature of the Lewis and Clark Expedition and cast a shadow over Lewis's return from the wilderness."[105] Lewis—already worried about Colter and Collins, his celestial observations, and getting down the Missouri before the ice set in—was now disquieted by Clark's mysterious behavior. On August 8 his mood swung from one extreme to the other. Convinced that "Capt. Clark could be at no great distance below," he set out early, traveling at a good rate until 10 a.m., when hope faded: "Not finding Capt. Clark I knew not what calculation to make with rispect to his halting and therefore determined to proceed as tho' he was not before me and leave the rest to the chapter of accedents." *As tho' he was not before me?* What could that possibly mean? He knew for certain that Clark was before him, and the sooner they reunited the better. Nor was Lewis a man to leave his fate to *accidents*. He had every reason to be frustrated with Clark's failure to wait for him—at least twice now—but the only solution was to chase his friend down the river. Instead, Lewis "determined to halt at this place untill the perogue and canoe could be repared and the men dress skins and make themselves the necessary cloathing."[106] This was not the rational, pre-Continental-Divide Lewis but the troubled soul still suffering the "psychological toll exacted by the harsh geographic extremes of the Columbia country."[107]

By January 18, 1803, when President Thomas Jefferson requested an appropriation of $2,500 from Congress "for the purpose of extending the external commerce of the U.S.," he had already selected "an intelligent officer . . . fit for the enterprize and willing to undertake it"—his twenty-nine-year-old personal secretary, Captain Meriwether Lewis. From the start, Lewis was the solitary head of the effort to "explore the whole line" of Missouri River commerce, "have conferences with the natives," and "return with the information acquired in the course of two summers."[108] True, six months later, William Clark gladly accepted his old friend Lewis's invitation to participate in the expedition's "fatietues . . . dangers and . . . honors,"[109] but by then Lewis had made all kinds of arrangements and purchases and had been tutored by experts in everything from anatomy and medicine to astronomy and cartography to botany and zoology. He was ready to proceed whether Clark signed on for the entire trip, part of it, or none at all. Lewis was the one who would report to Jefferson. When the corps departed Fort Mandan in April 1805, it was Lewis who thought of his legacy, concluding that "the picture which now presented itself to me was a most pleasing, one. Entertaing now as I do, the most confident hope of succeading in a voyage which had formed a da[r]ling project of mine for the last ten years <of my life>, I could but esteem this moment of my <our> departure as among the most happy of my life." Nor was he exaggerating when he said he had dreamed of such an opportunity for a decade—it had actually been thirteen years since eighteen-year-old Lewis volunteered to lead an expedition to the Pacific.[110]

Few admirals have shared their command with an ensign the way Lewis shared his with Clark—in their case, captain and second lieutenant—but it was the Lewis Expedition, for all intents and purposes, and no shock that Lewis was the first to see the confluence of the Missouri and the Yellowstone, first to gaze upon the spectacular Great Falls, first to drink from the waters of the Columbia, and first to walk the Pacific shore. Now he found himself in a spot where, whether he privately acknowledged it or not, he had made one bad decision after another—stealing the canoe, striking the Indian reaching for the oar in the fire, threatening to kill or burn the lodges of Indians who offended him, trying to cross the Bitterroots without a guide, venturing into Blackfeet territory with just three companions, and failing to keep a careful watch while camped with the Piegans. On top of that, not only had he not been first to reach the rendezvous site; his junior officer had not waited for him or even stopped where he promised—because of *mosquitoes*. As Jenkinson says, Lewis's "behavior and his mindset were erratic, irrational, contradictory, manic, and confused. . . . Nonplussed . . . he was off his center of gravity . . . making decisions based on pride and ego." The upshot? Lewis made another flawed decision—staying put to dress skins and make minor repairs to the boats rather than finding Clark as fast as possible: "Three days later, this kind of erratic logic would nearly cost him his life."[111]

So Lewis relaxed. Sunday, August 9, "proved fair and favourable for our purposes," he wrote; the group stayed put. "The men were engaged dressing skins and making themselves cloathes except R & J. Fields, whom I sent... in surch of Capt. C. and to hunt." When the Field brothers returned, they said "they saw no appearance of Capt. Clark or party." But something else worried Lewis: "Colter and Collins have not yet overtaken us I fear some missfortune has happened them for their previous fidelity and orderly deportment induces me to believe that they would not thus intentionally delay."[112] Lewis thus faced the real possibility that he would never see the two men again. They might have hit a sawyer in the river and drowned; they might have been killed or taken prisoner by Indians.

On August 10 there was still no sign of Colter and Collins or Clark. Although the men had the pirogue and canoe repaired by 2 p.m., they did not get underway for another three hours, making six or seven miles before stopping for the day: "The musquetoes more than usually troublesome this evening."[113] On August 11, after three leisurely days, the impulsive Lewis was suddenly in a hurry, making sure the party set out early, "it being my wish to arrive at the birnt hills by noon in order to take the latitude of that place as it is the most northern point of the Missouri." He told the men he was "anxious to get forward" and "requested that they would exert themselves to reach the place in time." What? Why was he mentioning this for the first time? Had he waited to dress elk skins and repair the boats, he easily could have reached the Birnt Hills the previous night, with ample time to ready his scientific tools and select the best site for observations, which he needed to take just before, precisely at, and just after meridian—noon—when the sun would be directly overhead. Apparently from studying Clark's latest maps at Fort Clatsop, Lewis had concluded—correctly, as it turned out—that Birnt Hills was the northernmost point of the main fork of the Missouri, crucial information for Jefferson and his successors as they claimed as much fur-trading territory as possible for the United States.[114] Given his failure to get good readings of Marias River at Camp Disappointment, Lewis likely wanted to compensate for that as much as possible by getting accurate information on the main fork. That all made sense. What made no sense was his announcing it so late in the day. Still, the men rowed hard and "proceeded rapidly." Why, then, would Lewis take time for anything other than making the noon deadline? But he did, shooting a buffalo swimming in the river around 9 a.m., "leaving the small canoes to dress it." Not long after that, they saw a large grizzly bear and tried to kill it, but it took wind of them and fled. Then the small canoes overtook Lewis and told him the meat of the buffalo was unfit for use. Next, they saw a large herd of elk on the north shore, and Lewis directed the men in the small canoes to hunt. All this took time, a few minutes here, ten minutes there, in fair weather, the sun rising in the sky: "When I arrived [at Birnt Hills] it was about 20 minutes after noon and of course the observation for the [sun's] meridian Altitude was lost."[115]

The lost observation was probably as predictable as the young Piegan Indians' grabbing a rifle at the first opportunity. "Off his center of gravity," Lewis made another grave judgment—he went hunting with Cruzatte, just the two of them, "on a thick willow bar," something that would not have happened with Clark on the scene. By Lewis's own admission, we know that he was dressed in brown leather and could have been mistaken for an elk by Cruzatte, who could not see very well, and that the two of them took different routes through the thick willows—"an accident waiting to happen," as one commentator so aptly puts it.[116]

"I was in the act of firing on an Elk . . . when a ball stuck my left thye about an inch below my hip joint, missing the bone," Lewis wrote. "The stroke was very severe." He called out to Cruzatte, "Damn you, you have shot me!" but hearing no reply, he concluded they had been ambushed by Indians.[117] Despite a serious wound—and his fragile state of mind—Lewis kept his cool, more concerned about Cruzatte and the others than himself:

> I thought best to make good my retreat . . . calling out as I ran for the first hundred paces as loud as I could to Cruzatte to make his retreat. . . . I called the men to their arms to which they flew in an instant, I told them I was wounded but I hoped not mortally . . . and directed them to follow me that I would return & give battle and relieve Cruzatte if possible who I feared had fallen into their hands; the men followed me as they were bid and I returned about a hundred paces when my wounds become so painfull and my thye so stiff that . . . I was compelled

> to halt and ordered the men to proceed and if they found themselves overpowered by numbers to retreat in order keeping up a fire. I now got back to the perogue as well as I could and prepared my self with a pistol my rifle and air-gun being determined . . . to sell my life as deerly as possible.[118]

The character of Meriwether Lewis? Like Lord Jim, we are fated never to see him clearly, but in this moment of both decline and crisis, Jefferson's phrase "of courage undaunted" fits him well.

Lewis waited "in this state of anxiety and suspense" for about twenty minutes, "when the party returned . . . and reported that there were no indians nor the appearance of any. . . . I asked [Cruzatte] whether he did not hear me when I called to him so frequently which he absolutely denied," but Cruzatte "was anxious to conceal his knowledge of having [shot me]" and dropped the matter. Still, Lewis had no doubt that the private had accidentally shot him: "The ball had lodged in my breeches which I knew to be the ball of the short rifles such that he had"—a .54 caliber Model 1803 rifle. Lewis was lucky, to put it mildly. He had been shot at close range by a powerful weapon without suffering artery or bone damage—otherwise, he was almost certainly doomed. With Sergeant Patrick Gass's assistance, Lewis gave himself first aid, "introducing tents of patent lint into the ball holes" and then "proceeded on," going farther downriver before camping: "As it was painfull to me to be removed I slept on board the perogue; the pain I experienced excited a high fever and I had a very uncomfortable night."[119]

To no one's surprise, Lewis did not pause for convalescence the next day. "Captain Lewis is in good spirits, but his wound stiff and sore," wrote Gass.[120] "We set out early and proceeded with all possible expedition," added Lewis, "being anxious to overtake Capt. Clark who from the appearance of his camps could be at no great distance before me." He said nothing about waiting till noon to attempt an observation, which was out of the question, the opportunity now gone as each bend of the river took them farther southeast. Around 8 a.m. a man called out that there was a camp on shore he believed to be of white men: "I directed the perogue and canoes to come too at this place and found it to be the camp of two hunters from the Illinois by the name of

Joseph Dickson and Forest Hancock . . . [who] informed me that Capt. C. had passed them about noon the day before." These were the first Europeans the group had seen since leaving Fort Mandan in April 1805. Dickson and Hancock paddled up the Missouri in August 1804, just three months after Lewis and Clark, possibly wintering near present Sioux City, Iowa. In 1805 they met and worked with Charles Courtin, a French Canadian trader who had been active in the Great Lakes fur trade, and spent the winter in South Dakota's Teton Sioux country. They also told Lewis "they had been robed by the indians and [Dickson] wounded by the Tetons of the birnt woods [Brulé Sioux Indians], that they had hitherto been unsuccessfull in their voyage having as yet caught but little beaver, but were determined to proceed." Lewis, likely reclining on a buffalo robe, gave the trappers a file and "a couple of pounds of powder with some lead . . . articles which they assured me they were in great want of." Lewis gave the two "a short discription of the Missouri, a list of distances to the most conspicuous streams . . . on the river . . . and pointed out . . . the places where the beaver most abounded."[121]

In the midst of this fascinating dialogue, someone announced that Collins and Colter, missing for nine days, were paddling their way down the Missouri. "The two men with the small canoe, who had been some time absent, came down and joined at the place where we met with the two strangers," wrote Gass.[122] It was too bad that neither Colter nor Collins left a record of that incredible morning. We'll never know which news they learned first—the interesting presence of two Illinois trappers or the shock of a seriously wounded Captain Lewis. Regardless, no one was happier to see them than Lewis. "They were well no accident having happened," he wrote. "They informed me that after proceeding the first day and not overtaking us that they had concluded that we were behind and had delayed several days in waiting for us and had thus been unable to join us untill the present moment."[123] Sergeant John Ordway answered any questions about how Collins and Colter fared: "They had killed 6 buffaloe 13 deer 5 Elk & 31 beaver," a report that left its imprint on Dickson and Hancock, who figured prominently in Colter's future. For the time being, however, the two decided "to go back to the Mandans in hopes to git a frenchman or Some body to go with [them] to the head of the river." So Lewis's party, now joined by Collins and Colter in one canoe and Dickson and Hancock in another, proceeded on.[124]

There was another reunion an hour or two later. "At meridian Capt Lewis hove in Sight," Clark wrote, with rich but unintended irony, "with the party which went by way of the Missouri as well as that which accompanied him from Travellers rest on Clarks river."[125] The immediate concern was whether everyone in the other group had survived. Ordway answered in the affirmative: "Capt. Clark and party all alive and all well. . . . We fired the blunderbusses and Small arms being rejoiced to meet all together again." Gass expressed a similar sentiment: "We . . . overtook Captain Clarke and his party . . . and now, (thanks to God) we are all together again in good health, except Captain Lewis, and his wound is not serious."[126]

Lewis, of course, insisted his injury was minor, but it wasn't. Positive reports on his recovery were frequently followed by the opposite. "Capt. Lewis fainted as Capt. Clark was dressing his wound," Ordway said on August 14.[127] Five days later Clark wrote that Lewis's wounds were healing fast but told a different story on August 28: "Capt. Lewis had a bad nights rest and is not very well this morning." Two weeks after that, Lewis had "entirely recovered," able to "walk and even run," but "the parts are yet tender."[128]

So it was that Lewis completed his "darling project" not as a triumphant Columbus or Captain Cook but as an invalid. Virtually all mentions of him in the journals after he was shot deal with his recovery. There were detailed descriptions of friendly encounters with the Mandans and Arikaras; a rebuke of the Teton Sioux; sending men out to hunt; the false alarm of an attack; farewells to Colter and Charbonneau, Sacagawea, and Pomp; and frequent meetings with westbound trappers, but the commander handling all this business was William Clark, who was his usual pragmatic, reliable self. Nothing is known of Lewis's perspective because after August 12, 1806, the day the captains finally reunited, he never wrote in his journal again.

3

"He Draws a Line from His Heart to His Mouth"

Eagle Feather, Emissary of the Arikaras

On October 8, 1805, the same day that a canoe full of Lewis and Clark's men—"Several of which Could not Swim"—escaped drowning on the raging Clearwater River, James Wilkinson, the governor of Upper Louisiana stationed in St. Louis, wrote to Secretary of War Henry Dearborn informing him that "the Riccari & Otto' Chiefs have been dangerously ill & remain so feeble, as not to be able to accompany the deputation Destined to the City of Washington, and have become impatient to be returned to their respective Nations." The safe return of these chiefs to their homelands was "deemed an Object of great Magnitude," wrote Wilkinson, crucial to future negotiations with Missouri River Indians. Wilkinson therefore planned to dispatch two officers and thirty men, properly equipped and supplied, to safely escort the Oto chiefs to their towns near Nebraska's Platte River and the Arikara chief to his village on the Missouri.[1]

The name of the Arikara chief was Eagle Feather, or Too Né. Lewis and Clark first met him a year earlier, on October 9, 1804. The next day, Clark wrote, "We Delivered a Similar Speech to those delivered the Ottoes and Sioux."[2] Lewis then read a standard speech, which was translated by Joseph Gravelines, a French Canadian interpreter who had lived among the Arikaras for several years:

> *Children.* Convene from among you the old men of experience; the men, on the wisdom of whose judgement you are willing to risk the future happiness of your nations; and the warriors, to the strength of whose arms you have been taught to look for protection in the days of danger. . . .

Children. Commissioned and sent by the great Chief of the Seventeen great nations of America, we have come to inform you . . . that a great council was lately held between this great chief of the Seventeen great nations of America, and your old fathers the french and Spaniards. . . . It was agreed that all the white men of Louisiana . . . are bound to obey the commands of their great Chief the President who is now your only great father. . . .

Children. From what has been said, you will readily perceive, that the great chief of the Seventeen great nations of America, has become your only father . . . the only friend to whom you can now look for protection, or from whom you can ask favors, or receive good councils, and he will take care that you shall have no just cause to regret this change; he will serve you, & not deceive you.

Children. The great chief . . . has sent us out to clear the road, remove every obstruction, and to make it the road of peace between himself and his red children residing there; to enquire into the Nature of their wants, and on our return to inform Him of them, in order that he may make the necessary arrangements for their relief. . . .

Children. The road in which your great father and friend, has commanded us to tell you and your nation that you must walk in order to enjoy the benefit of his friendship, is, that you are to live in peace with all the *white men*, for they are his children; neither wage war against the *red men* your neighbours, for they are equally his children and he is bound to protect them. Injure not the persons of any traders who may come among you, neither destroy nor take their property from them by force. . . .

Children. Do these things which your great father advises and be happy. Avoid the councils of bad birds; turn your heel from them as you would from the precipice of an high rock . . . lest by one false step you should bring upon your nation the displeasure of your great father, the great chief of the Seventeen great nations . . . who could consume you as the fire consumes the grass of the plains. . . .

Children. If you open your ears to the councils of your great father . . . & strictly pursue the advice which he has now given . . . he will as soon as possible after our return, send a store of goods . . . to trade with you for your pelteries and furs; these goods will be furnished you annually in a regular manner. . . .

Children. If your great Chief wishes to see your great father and speak with him, he can readily do so. . . .

Children. We hope that the great Spirit will open your ears to our councils, and dispose your minds to their observance. Follow these councils, and dispose your minds to their observance. Follow these councils and you will have nothing to fear, because the great Spirit will smile upon your nation, and in future ages will make you to outnumber the trees of the forest.[3]

What were the Arikaras or any other Indian nation to make of the proclamation that they had somehow been conquered—without a fight or even a warning—by an unnamed great chief who was suddenly their only great father, a parent who would consume them like wildfire if they made one false step? As Robert J. Miller has written, from the fifteenth century on, when European countries set out to colonize the New World, they acted under widely accepted international law eventually known as the Doctrine of Discovery: "The Doctrine provided . . . that newly arrived Europeans immediately and automatically acquired property rights in native lands and gained governmental, political, and commercial rights over the inhabitants without the knowledge or consent of the indigenous peoples."[4] Lewis and Clark thus emulated the examples of Christopher Columbus, Vasco da Gama, and Ferdinand Magellan. True, Jefferson treated Indigenous peoples with much more compassion than fifteenth- and sixteenth-century explorers, and his push westward lacked the religious bigotry of the Portuguese and Spanish, but he nevertheless was determined to impose western *values* on the Indian nations. Moreover, just as the fifteenth- and sixteenth-century "discoverers" had the line of demarcation, American and British explorers had the 49th parallel. The Portuguese and Spanish came looking for spices; the Americans and British for fur.

After concluding his speech, Lewis wasted no time demonstrating the military might of the seventeen great nations—shooting his air gun, "which astonished them," and having one of the men fire three rounds from the swivel cannon on the keelboat. Then the gifts were brought out: medals, American flags, red coats, cocked hats, and feathers for the chiefs; vermilion paint for the warriors; and needles for the women, followed by cloth, razors, combs, beads, scissors, knives, and tomahawks.[5]

One gift was not appreciated: whiskey. According to Nicholas Biddle, the first editor of the captains' journals, who had consulted extensively with Clark, the chiefs declined alcohol "with this sensible remark, that, they were surprised that their father should present to them a liquor which would make them fools."[6] What did catch the Arikaras' attention was York, the first African American they had ever seen. "The Inds. much astonished at my black Servent, who made him Self more turrible in their view than I wished him to Doe," wrote Clark.[7]

Chief Grey Eyes was traveling at the time and did not meet Lewis and Clark until their return journey in 1806. As for the three chiefs who received medals in 1804, Chief Crow Going Across and Chief Hay both said they were glad to see the captains and offered them gifts but declined going to Washington. Eagle Feather, however, said he would visit his "grandfather" even though that meant passing the Sioux, who did not have good hearts. He wished "to return quicke for fear of my people being uneasy," adding, "My Children are Small & perhaps will be uneasy [until] I return safe." He hoped he could bring his people knives, powder, and balls when he returned: "I must go, I also wish to go, perhaps I may when I return make my people glad."[8]

Eagle Feather accompanied the captains to the Mandan villages at the mouth of Knife River (near present Stanton, North Dakota) and was instrumental in conducting a successful peace council with Mandan and Hidatsa chiefs. He returned to his home early in November 1804. In April 1805, as Lewis, Clark, and most of their party started up the Missouri, Eagle Feather bade farewell to his family and friends and boarded a keelboat with Corporal Richard Warfington, eight other expedition soldiers, trader Pierre-Antoine Tabeau and a few of his men, and Gravelines, who would pilot the boat and also serve as Eagle Feather's personal escort to Washington.[9] Warfington carried letters and maps from the captains addressed to Thomas Jefferson, William Henry Harrison, and others. Warfington and his men had also loaded the boat with provisions and supplies for the journey and artifacts for Jefferson to keep or distribute as he wished—everything from antelope skins and skeletons to specimens of earths, salts, minerals, and several dozen plants; a Mandan bow with a quiver of arrows; several buffalo robes, including one "painted by a Mandan man representing a battle which was faught 8 years since"; a large pair of elk horns; and a live prairie dog.[10] Lewis and Clark, as well as Eagle Feather and Gravelines, were worried that the group might have trouble getting through Sioux country, so Warfington and the others were well armed and prepared to defend themselves, but they apparently passed without incident, although Warfington left no specific record. As the contingent descended the river, Ponca, Omaha, Oto, and Missouri chiefs joined them. Warfington and his party reached St. Louis on May 20.

The various chiefs spent the summer of 1805 in St. Louis. As Wilkinson noted in his letter to Dearborn, however, Eagle Feather and the Oto chiefs could not travel to Washington because of illness, and they departed St. Louis with a group of soldiers on October 20 on their way to the chiefs' homelands. Two days later, the other chiefs—escorted by Lewis's good friend Captain Amos Stoddard and others—left for Washington. Then came another wrinkle in Eagle Feather's venture east: the party was turned back by hostile Kansas Indians about twenty leagues below the mouth of the Kansas River (at present Kansas City, Kansas) and had to return to St. Louis.[11] Writing to Jefferson this time, Wilkinson reported that he had assigned Lieutenant Eli B. Clemson to escort Eagle Feather, who had apparently recovered from his illness and was accompanied by Gravelines, to Washington. Pierre Chouteau also joined the group, along with other Indian delegates, and they departed St. Louis on December 23.

Wilkinson had clearly spent a good deal of time with Gravelines and Eagle Feather, for he had high praise for the latter. "I think you may be able to derive a fund of correct Information from this Chief, relative to the region Watered by the South Western Branches of the Missouri & its Inhabitants," Wilkinson advised Jefferson. "I understand Him to be a great traveller, a warrior & Geographer, and He is certainly a *learned* Savage, because He not only speaks Eleven different Languages, but is Master of the *Language* of Arms, Hands & Fingers, the only practicable mode of Communication (he informs me), at the Annual Grand Councils of twelve or fifteen Nations of his Acquaintance." Wilkinson further suggested that because of Eagle Feather's vast experience and knowledge of and influence with Indian nations of the upper Missouri, he could have value as "an important Instrument of Humanity & of policy." Then he should "be returned as early as possible . . . & sent up to his Nation, by a Military Escort loaded with presents."[12]

By February 1806 Eagle Feather and Gravelines reached Washington, where they met Thomas Jefferson, and the chief served as an interpreter for several representatives of Missouri River Indian nations. At the end of that month, playwright and artist William Dunlap, New York senator Samuel Latham Mitchill, and New York representative Gurdon Mumford visited Eagle Feather and Gravelines at their boardinghouse. "The great man was seated cross-legg'd on a matress scraping & cutting Guinea-hen feathers & did not deign to raise his eyes to us," wrote Dunlap. "His dress was a second hand blue military coat, without facings, but with two large gold epaulets, a flannel shirt, dirty light colored pantaloons & shoes covered with mud of many days standing. He had rings in his ears & a blue cotton handkerchief, tied about his head in the French manner with a buckle disposed in the front." Gravelines, who spoke to the three guests in French, told Eagle Feather that the Americans wanted to talk to him because they had "heard that he was a learned traveller." The chief continued "cutting & trimming feathers, occasionally whistling in a whispering key as he attended to his work, & without once looking at us or appearing to hear the interpreter."[13]

The three visitors waited patiently: "By & by the old man smiled & . . . now very deliberately put away his knife & work & began to prepare some tobacco for smoking. . . . At length having prepared his pipe, lighted it, placed a chair in the middle of room & seated himself, the chief appeared for the first time to notice us. Still he spoke not, but pulled . . . out of a pouch . . . some papers & presented one of them to Mitchill who read it aloud." It was a certificate and recommendation signed by Lewis and Clark. Mitchill returned the paper. Eagle Feather then shook hands with all three men and "presented 3 pieces of paper, which joined lengthwise, presented a map of his rout, of his country, the course of the Missouri, the relative situations of a great many Indian nations, & Captain Lewis's encampment."[14] Eagle

Feather then spoke in sign language as he referred to the map, with occasional explanations from Gravelines, allowing Dunlap, Mitchill, and Mumford to "perfectly understand him." Pointing to a spot on the map, Eagle Feather said, "Here is my country." He also identified neighboring tribes, "marking by signs their distinguishing characteristics." The sign for entering a village was raising the left hand, arching it, and then passing the right hand with the fingers pointing under the arch. Eagle Feather signified his crossing a river by the action of rowing. Through additional signs, "he marked the whole of his route, ending it by a rude figure signifying the presidents house in Washington: beyond which he had drawn a gun, a sword, powder, ball & tobacco as the presents he expected." Perhaps most memorable were Eagle Feather's signs for speaking truth and the contrary: for truth, "he draws a line with his finger from his heart to his mouth & thence straight to the . . . spectator; for falsehood the line comes crooked from any part of the Abdomen & on issuing from the lips, splits, diverges & crosses in every direction." After a pretty long interview, Dunlap concluded, "We shook hands & parted, much pleased with the novelty of the exhibition & the animation & intellince of [Eagle Feather]."[15]

Lewis and Clark had had the opportunity to hear such a fascinating discourse, but their Eurocentrism cut that chance short. "This Chief tells me of a number of their Treditions about Turtles, Snakes, &. and the power of a perticiler rock or Cave on the next river which informs of everr thing none of those I think worth while mentioning," Clark wrote in 1804.[16]

Eagle Feather's amazing work of cartography revealed that he had traveled as far south as Santa Fe, New Mexico, and as far north as Fort Assiniboine, a trading post in Canada. Along with details on the Arikaras, the map offered information on many other Indian nations, including the Sioux, Pawnees, Missourias, Omahas, Cheyennes, Kiowas, Kiowa Apaches, Mandans, Hidatsas, Crows, Assiniboines, Crees, Atsinas, and Blackfeet.[17] The "map distilled a lifetime of diplomacy in an expansive and complicated landscape," notes one scholar: "While William Clark was mapping the . . . West, Too Né asserted an alternative indigenous geography in which Native borders replaced American boundary lines, the landscape itself held spiritual meaning, and political influence emanated not from Washington but from the upper Missouri

River. . . . Too Né confirmed the length of Arikara territorial claims and identified the American explorers as recent additions to a landscape with a much older history."[18]

On Monday, April 9, from his office at the War Department, Henry Dearborn wrote a letter to Wilkinson: "Sir, The Missouri and Mississippi Indian Chiefs, will leave this place tomorrow for Pittsburg, from whence they will descend the [Ohio] River & proceed to St. Louis. Several have died; but what is more especially to be regretted is the death of the very respectable & amiable Ricara Chief, which happened on the 7th Instant."[19] Less than six weeks after his delightful conversation with Dunlap and the others, Eagle Feather was dead.

Dearborn instructed Wilkinson to send Gravelines and a Pawnee Indian who spoke the Arikara language "in a light boat, with a sober, discreet Sergeant & four faithful sober soldiers, up to the Ricara Nation, as soon as you can make the necessary arrangements." Dearborn said he would send the possessions of "the Old Chief," to be given to his favorite son, and advised sending $300 worth of factory goods to the family, nine muskets for his sons, and one hundred pounds of powder and balls to other Arikara chiefs. He indicated that Gravelines would soon be on his way to St. Louis, in time to reach the Arikara villages by autumn.[20]

Dearborn apparently told Jefferson in person of Eagle Feather's death. On April 11 the president penned this epistle:

> My friends & children of the Ricara nation
>
> It gave me a great pleasure to see your beloved chief arrive here on a visit to his white brothers of the United States of America. I took him by the hand with affection, I considered him as bringing to me the assurances of your friendship and that you were willing to become of one family with us. Wishing to see as much as he could of his new brethren he consented to go towards the sea as far as Baltimore & Philadelphia. He found nothing but kindness & good will wherever he passed. On his return to this place he was taken sick; every thing we could do to help him was done; but it pleased the great Spirit to take him from us. We buried him among our own deceased friends and relatives, we

shed many tears over his grave, and we now mingle our afflictions with yours on the loss of this beloved chief. But death must happen to all men; and his time was come.[21]

"The Chief Who Went Down Last Summer"

Lewis, Clark, and their men, now accompanied by the Mandan chief Sheheke and his wife Yellow Corn and son White Painted House—but no longer attended by John Colter, Toussaint Charbonneau, Sacagawea, and Pomp—rose early on August 21, 1806, a little more than four months after Eagle Feather's death. The mosquitoes were "very troublesom," just as they were the night before. Although Lewis was doing reasonably well, it had just been ten days since Pierre Cruzatte accidentally shot him, and he could not yet walk unassisted. He tried to get as comfortable as possible lying in the bottom of one of the boats. At 8 a.m. the party met three French trappers paddling upstream. Two of them—likely François Rivet and an employee of Gravelines by the name of Grenier—had wintered with them at the Mandan villages in 1804. Clark talked with them and was told that seven hundred Sioux had passed the Arikara villages and were on their way to attack the Mandans and Hidatsas. The three also said "they were informed that the . . . Ricara Chief who went to the United States last Spring [1805] died on his return at Smoe place near the Sieoux river."[22]

Clark did not say whether the trappers offered any details or if he even asked, but after talking to them for an hour and giving them some powder and balls, he "proceeded on." Two hours later the group came in view of the upper Arikara villages, saluting the Indians by firing their guns. The Arikaras returned the fire. Clark and the others were "met by the most of the men womaen and children of each village," who "all appeared anxious to take [them] by the hand and much rejoiced to see [them] return." Clark soon met for the first time Grey Eyes, "a man of about 32 years of age . . . intreduced . . . as 1st Chief of the nation." Clark urged Grey Eyes and the other chiefs to make peace with the Mandans and Hidatsas. Sheheke spoke "at some length . . . informing them of his wish to be on the most friendly termes." Giving a "very animated Speach," Grey Eyes said that he wanted to follow Clark's advice, that some of his young men unwilling to follow council had been driven out of the villages, that the Sioux were the cause of the misunderstanding, and "that Several of the chiefs wished to accompany [Lewis and Clark] down to See their great father, but wished to see the Chief who went down last Sumer return first."[23]

The expedition party stayed two days with the Arikaras. Sheheke was generally well received, but the presence of the Mandan chief and his family was a constant reminder of all the skirmishes fought with the Mandans and Hidatsas over the decades, even though there had been periods of calm.[24] When the Arikara chief One Arm spoke to Sheheke in a loud and threatening tone, Clark was alarmed for his safety and warned the Arikaras that the Mandan chief was under his protection and that he and his men "should all die to a man" to protect him. Fortunately, One Arm had a change of heart and invited Clark and Sheheke to his house; after "takeing a very Serimonious Smoke," One Arm said he had opened his ears to Clark's words and that Sheheke was as safe as if in his own village. After that, Grey Eyes invited Clark and Sheheke—who "stuck close to me," wrote Clark—to his lodge for "a Supper of boiled young Corn, beens & quashes . . . & informed me he had always had his ears open to what we had Said. . . . [He] gave a pipe with great form and every thing appeared to be made up."[25]

The next morning, however, the interpreter, Joseph Garreau, told Clark that he had just talked to the Arikara chiefs and warriors, and they had no intention of visiting Washington until the return of the chief who went down last spring. Then the chiefs themselves informed Clark "that they must trade with the Sieoux one more time to get guns and powder," something he could not give or promise them. The only good news that day was that Lewis had walked a little for the first time. On August 23 the corps said their goodbyes and "set out very early." In all his talks with the Arikaras, Clark had said nothing at all about the unconfirmed rumor of Eagle Feather's death.[26]

Three weeks later, on September 12, a few miles north of present St. Joseph, Missouri, the captains and their party set out at sunrise and "proceeded on very well," soon meeting trappers in pirogues heading upriver. One of those nomads, who had accompanied the expedition to the Mandan villages in 1804, said Mr. Robert McClellan was just a few miles below. Over the past few weeks Clark and Lewis, now recovered and able to walk and even run, had met one band of hopeful traders after another plying their oars, but meeting McClellan was different. He was an old army friend of Clark's, and according to Washington Irving, "M'Lellan was a remarkable man. He had been a partisan under General Wayne, in his Indian wars, where he had distinguished himself by his fiery spirit and reckless daring, and marvelous stories were told of his exploits. His appearance answered to his character. His frame was meagre, but muscular; showing strength, activity, and iron firmness. His eyes were dark, deep-set, and piercing. He was restless, fearless, but of impetuous and sometimes ungovernable temper."[27]

Sergeant Ordway wrote that McClellan commanded a large keelboat, "well loaded down with Marchandizes," with twelve hands manning the oars. McClellan told Lewis, Clark, and their men of the widespread concern for them by many Americans who had heard two different rumors: "that we were all killed" and "that the Spanyards had us in the mines &C." McClellan was therefore "rejoiced to see" the captains, and to celebrate the occasion, he "gave our officers wine and the party as much whiskey as we all could drink."[28]

Along with this royal welcome came a surprise: accompanying McClellan were two men well known to Clark and Lewis—Joseph Gravelines and Pierre Dorion Sr., a fifty-something-year-old trader and interpreter who had assisted the captains in the summer of 1804. "We examined the instructions of those interpreters," wrote Clark, "and found that Gravelin was ordered to the Ricaras with a Speach from the president of the U. States to that nation and some presents which had been given the Ricara Cheif who had visited the U. States and unfortunately died at the City of Washington.... [Gravelines] was instructed to ... make every enquirey after Capt Lewis my self and the party." Dorion had also been told to seek information on Lewis and Clark. A fluent speaker of Sioux languages, he was to use his influence with the Teton Sioux, or Lakotas, to help Gravelines pass safely through their territory.[29]

Ordway added that Dorion was also escorting several Omaha and Yankton Sioux Indians from St. Louis back to their homelands in Nebraska and southeastern South Dakota, respectively, and that McClellan planned on wintering in that area. This meant, of course, that Gravelines and Dorion could not reach the Arikara villages until the spring of 1807 at the earliest. As noted, Dearborn had instructed Wilkinson to have five soldiers escort

Gravelines to the Arikara villages in time to reach their destination by the autumn of 1806. The record is silent on why neither of those plans developed. Nor did Clark or Ordway say if McClellan planned on taking the two interpreters all the way to the Arikara villages.

"No Other Liar but Their Father"

McClellan and a number of other traders likely spent the winter of 1806–7 in southeastern South Dakota at the mouth of the James River, near present Yankton.[30] From that location, on April 5, 1807, McClellan wrote a historic two-page dispatch that depicts the context and alludes to the key players in the intricate drama surrounding the Arikaras that unfolded that remarkable summer of 1807. The letter ended up in Clark's hands because the addressee, Lewis, the newly named governor of the Louisiana Territory, had not arrived from the east—and would not do so until March of 1808.

McClellan announced that the Indians "in this quarter" were all peaceable, a good reason why other traders had also wintered there and no doubt traded with the Indians. Furthermore, the Omaha and Yankton Indians who set out with him the previous summer had arrived safely at their villages, except for one chronically ill Omaha chief who died on the way. McClellan also made it clear that he was returning to St. Louis as soon as possible to obtain trade goods and would then "visit the upper parts of the Missouri," Next, indicating that Dorion was no longer with him, McClellan wrote, "I have Learned from the Sioux Nation that Mr. P. Dorion delivered the Speech sent by Government To the [Lakota] chiefs who would give no answer [but] have said the[y] would lay on the banks of the Missouri this summer for the purpose of stopping boats should any attempt to pas[s]."[31] When and how did Dorion arrange to give his speech to the Lakotas, who were considerably farther up the Missouri (near its Big Bend) than McClellan's camp? That question remains unanswered.

The next question, of course, was what had become of Gravelines and the presents he carried for the Arikaras. McClellan's letter made no mention of him but nevertheless offered an important clue. Speaking of how he had been instructed by the government—probably meaning James Wilkinson—to examine the "licenses of the Traydors in this Nation," he wrote, "There is also a Certain Mr. Corta a Kenedian who obtained Licenses to Traide with the Sioux & Poncaws [Poncas] for the year 1806 Proceeds On a voige this Spring up the Missouri Expecting to Reach the falls before he stops." This was Charles Courtin, called "Mr. Coutau" by Clark, the trader who spent time in Sioux country with Joseph Dickson and Forrest Hancock in 1805 and met Lewis and Clark as he again ascended the Missouri—with a crew and a large keelboat—on September 14, 1806, the day after the captains parted with McClellan, Dorion, and Gravelines. Not missing a beat, McClellan added, "Should Goverment think proper to send the Mandaine Chiefe to his Respective hoame I will with Pleasure take him under my charge as there will be but little danger to feare. I shall have two boats well Mand and armed."[32] McClellan's urgency to return to St. Louis and again ascend the Missouri as soon as possible and his offers to check trading licenses or take Sheheke home all reflect his ambition to outdo a competitor he looked on with contempt: Manuel Lisa.

Precisely when Dorion, Gravelines, and McClellan parted ways is not known, but by the time the latter drafted his letter to Lewis, Dorion was preparing to escort fifteen Sioux chiefs to St. Louis, apparently catching a ride with one of the keelboat commanders who wintered nearby. Dorion's party reached St. Louis around May 15. As for Gravelines, he became a passenger on the keelboat of fellow French Canadian Courtin, who had agreed to stop at the Arikara villages on his way to the Great Falls of the Missouri.

With Lewis and Clark's much-talked-about return in September of 1806 and their boast that the Missouri River and its branches from the Cheyenne River upward "abound more in beaver and Common Otter, than any other streams on earth," it was no wonder that a host of traders, *engagés*, trappers, hunters, blacksmiths, gunsmiths, interpreters, cooks, clerks, vagabonds, and impostors fixed their gaze on the upper Missouri the next spring, dreaming of the enormous amount of money to be made in the fur trade.[33] McClellan himself, deep in debt in St. Louis, was quite hopeful of striking it rich, but his letter to Lewis—with its mentions of Dorion, Courtin, and Sheheke—portended something darker, bringing the focus back into the real world, where the wilderness was full of hazards and interactions with Native nations were inevitably fraught with misinterpretations, misunderstandings, and broken promises. While some St. Louis businessmen made a profit and some Indian tribes enjoyed relative peace that memorable summer of 1807, the Arikara nation and several parties headed their way felt the impact of Eagle Feather's death in very personal terms and saw what it meant for the European Americans to presume the American Indians were their "children."

Courtin, his crew, and Gravelines led the pack. They had left their Yankton Sioux winter camp sometime in April, apprehensive about getting through Lakota country safely and even more so about telling the Arikaras of the passing of their beloved chief. Next came Manuel Lisa, commanding two keelboats, fifty men, and $16,000 worth of trading goods, having departed St. Louis around the first of May. Lisa's chief lieutenant was George Drouillard, and five other expedition veterans were also onboard: Pierre Cruzatte, Jean Baptiste Lepage, John Potts, Peter Weiser, and Richard Windsor. Lisa was headed for the section of the Yellowstone River explored by Clark in 1806. On May 14, at the mouth of the Osage River, east of present Jefferson City, Missouri, Lisa hired another hand: Edward Rose, a boatman and brawler from Louisville, Kentucky, known as Nez Coupé, or Cut Nose, because of the scar on his nose reportedly left by the jaws of a ferocious opponent.

A combined group of forty or fifty soldiers, hunters, traders, and boatmen, under the command of expedition veteran Ensign Nathaniel Pryor and recent West Point graduate Auguste Pierre Chouteau, was two or three weeks behind Lisa. Expedition veterans George Gibson and George Shannon were among the group, and quite likely Joseph Field, as well as interpreters Pierre Dorion and René Jusseaume (also spelled *Jessaume*), who had lived among the Mandans for fifteen years before assisting Lewis and Clark in 1804. The orders from Henry Dearborn: safely return the Mandan chief Sheheke and his wife and son to their home. Bringing up the rear were Robert McClellan and his new partner, Ramsay Crooks—quite likely one of the "two young Scotch gentlemen" who, on September 20, 1806, gave Lewis and Clark "a very agreeable supper" and a tent to sleep in—commanding eighty men and two keelboats and determined to reach the upper Missouri before wintering.[34]

On June 22 Charles Courtin wrote a detailed letter to Lewis reporting on his and Gravelines's encounter with the Arikaras: "On the 3rd Instant, Mr. Joseph Graveline Inerpreter for the United States arrived at the Ricaras

Village in the Boat belonging to Mr. Charles Courtin who made all the necessary expences to go to the upper Missouri." Courtin and his men then helped Gravelines unload the muskets, powder, balls, and trade goods sent for Eagle Feather's family and the other chiefs. Considering his task completed, Courtin said he and his crew would continue up the Missouri, but a chief named Left Handed convinced Courtin and Gravelines to come to his lodge. They had barely reached the lodge when Left Handed warned Courtin "that it was absolutely necessary for him to unload his Boat quickly because the Indians would plunder it." Soon after that, one of Courtin's men ran into the lodge and told him "that the Indians were unloading his Boat and taking away the Merchandize." Courtin rushed to the keelboat only to find that other than a few remaining items, "the whole was lost."[35]

"On the day following," continued Courtin, "Mr. Graveline convened the Indians in order to deliver them the speech of their father [Thomas Jefferson] which was read by Mr. Courtin and translated by Mr. Garout [interpreter Joseph Garreau, who had apparently remained with the Arikaras since seeing Lewis and Clark the previous August]." The innocent bystander Courtin, who had taken the place of a military escort out of the goodness of his heart, now found himself in the impossible spot of announcing the worst possible news to the Arikaras. Would they kill the messenger? Gravelines tried to soften the tension by presenting the muskets to Eagle Feather's sons, the one hundred pounds of ammunition to the chiefs, and the goods—likely including white and red glass beads, calico shirts, blankets, copper kettles, silk handkerchiefs, and thimbles, needles, and thread—to the wives and children. Unimpressed, an Arikara chief proclaimed that "there was no other liar but their father, and that . . . they had resolved to do the same as the Sioux in stopping and plundering all and every boats that would ascend as far as their villages and that they would also kill all those who would oppose their designs because the Americans were uncapable of revenging themselves."[36]

Eagle Feather's people were understandably hurt and resentful over his death, but there were also other forces at work: "Arikara hostility toward the white intruders may have manifested their unhappiness over the changing trading patterns in the Upper Missouri country, particularly their gradual displacement as the principal intermediaries in Indian trading operations within the region." In addition, "agents of the British-controlled Canadian fur houses took advantage of the Ree disaffection to urge them to resist American advances into the coveted trade zone."[37]

Courtin wrote his letter almost three weeks after his and Gravelines's arrival. The latter was obviously released soon thereafter because he reached St. Louis by August 1 with the letter in hand. Dorion would have passed the flotillas of both Pryor and Lisa on his way to St. Louis, but there is no record of any meetings with them. Courtin said nothing about Dorion's release in the letter; nor did he know how long the Arikaras, whom he called "that brute but coward nation," would hold him. He concluded his plea for help by hoping "that a convoy of one hundred men will asend here in order to prove them that their father is not a liar."[38]

"The Bank Was Crowded with Six Hundred and Fifty Indians, All Armed"

Toward the end of June, about a week after Courtin wrote his letter, Lisa and his crew came upon a massive river flowing in from the west with "great velocity," dumping huge amounts of sand into the tamer Missouri. This was the mouth of "the Great River Platte," south of present Omaha, Nebraska. The Lewis and Clark veterans knew this spot well, likely telling Lisa the deer hunting was good. He decided it was a good place to camp. The next morning someone spotted something coming downstream on the Missouri, a speck that gradually came into focus—a lone voyager paddling a small canoe. A man on the shore welcomed the visitor with a rifle shot—then one of the expedition men recognized him: John Colter.[39]

It had been ten months since Colter paddled north with Dickson and Hancock—nothing had been heard from them since. The irony was this: the first to give an account of Colter's companions was none other than Charles Courtin, of course familiar with both men. A week and a half after he and Gravelines endured the Arikaras' "welcome," he watched as Dickson came ashore in a fur-laden canoe, barely escaping when Arikaras tried to steal the fur and then fired at him. A week later, Hancock arrived, not loaded down with furs, bringing a message from the Mandans that invited the Arikaras "to come and Smock with them." Courtin's letter, however, said nothing about Colter, who likely passed the Arikaras' villages a few days before Dickson.[40]

The best evidence indicates that Dickson split from Colter and Hancock not long after they reached the Bighorn River country and that the latter two themselves soon went their separate ways. Colter then made a monumental marathon journey into what is now Yellowstone Park, an area not seen by Lewis and Clark. What Colter told Lisa's party about all this is not known—no one was keeping a careful record the way the captains and their sergeants did. What we do know is that Lisa offered Colter a job and that Colter said yes, abandoning, for the second time in a year, a return to European civilization for the lure of the trapping life.[41]

Lisa reached the Arikaras' towns around early August. Henry Brackenridge wrote, "Two or three hundred warriors were drawn up and on [Lisa's] approach, such as had fire arms discharged a volley before the boat, to indicate the place where he should land. He accordingly put to shore, but made it known, that no one of them was to enter his boat; while the chiefs appointed warriors to stand guard and keep off the crowd." What some considered Lisa's arrogance served him well in this moment—when an Indian rushed forward and slit open bags of corn offered for trade by Arikara women, Lisa "instantly called his men to arms, pointed a couple of swivels which were fixed on his boats, and made every preparation for defence." Then the chiefs came to him and "according to their custom, stroked him on the shoulders," begging him not to be angry and assuring him that the Indian who offended him was a bad man.[42]

At least that was Brackenridge's secondhand account, based on his interview with Lisa in 1811. A Mandan woman held hostage by the Arikaras, who was an eyewitness of the event, told quite a different story, claiming that Lisa informed the Arikara chiefs that Pryor's two boats would soon be coming with trade goods and that the Mandan chief would be with them. On hearing this, the Arikara chiefs "pillaged [Lisa] of about half his goods, and suffered him to pass on, determining to kill [Lisa] on his return, and to lose no time in preparing to murder the Mandane and his Escort as soon as [they] should arrive."[43] The actual event likely included elements of both stories, but there is no doubt that one hunter and trapper in the group was paying close attention to the manners and language of the Arikaras—Edward Rose, who would spend most of his future as a member of an exploring or trading expedition or as a resident, or chief, of an Indian town, either Crow or Arikara.

Pryor himself heard the Mandan woman's report via Jusseaume's translation, and his experience with the Arikaras lends credence to her narrative. He, Chouteau, and their men, with Sheheke and his wife and son, reached the Arikaras' villages about five weeks after Lisa, on September 9 at 9 a.m. The crowd that gathered on the shore seemed friendly at first, but then Dorion learned from Sioux visitors that the Arikaras and Mandans were at war and that two of the former had recently been killed, the last news a Mandan chief's escort wanted to hear. Pryor immediately secured Sheheke and his family in the cabin of his keelboat, with soldiers standing guard and with all the men "prepared for action." Within minutes, "the bank was crowded with about six hundred and fifty Indians, all of them were armed with guns," wrote Pryor, "and many of them with additional warlike weapons."[44]

Chief Grey Eyes approached and gave Pryor a letter from Courtin and said "that [Grey Eyes] alone had been friendly to that unfortunate Trader, who owed his safety and ultimate release to his friendly offices." Even while Pryor and Grey Eyes were talking, Arikara warriors "were observed checking their bullets and driving away their women and children." Despite that, Pryor did his best to keep the peace, over the next few hours reminding them he had been sent by the great father and thanking them for their kindness to Lewis and Clark. He presented a medal to Grey Eyes and thanked him for his friendship. Every attempt at peace failed, however, and when Grey Eyes threw his medal on the ground, an Indian struck a boatman with the butt of his rifle: "The Indians now raised a general Whoop, and as they retired to the willows, fired on the men, on the Beach, as well as on both Boats in the same instant." Pryor's men returned fire with a "well directed volley of Swivels, Blunderbusses and small arms."[45]

The battle raged for fifteen or twenty minutes, but Pryor was so badly outnumbered that he ordered a retreat. His soldiers managed to launch their boat into the current, but when Chouteau's boat got stuck on a sandbar, his crew was "obliged to drag the Barge while exposed to the continual fire of the enemy." They finally got the keelboat free, surmounting "difficulties which had nearly proven fatal to the whole party." The Mandan woman told Pryor that Lisa "had given the Ricaras, through *compulsion* . . . a number of guns and a considerable quantity of powder and ball."[46] The assault on Pryor's party thus prefigured that on William Ashley's sixteen years later, with men under fire from their own nation's arms and ammunition, even worse in the latter instance because Ashley himself was the provider.

Three traders died in the fight, and another perished from his wounds nine days later. Six others suffered serious wounds but recovered. Jusseaume was "badly wounded in the thigh and shoulder."[47] One of those killed was quite likely Lewis and Clark veteran Joseph Field, which would make him the first expedition veteran to die after the expedition.[48] Two other Lewis and Clark veterans were wounded—George Gibson and George Shannon. The former mended, but Shannon almost died. When the group finally reached Fort Bellefontaine, near St. Louis, a doctor amputated Shannon's leg above the knee. The Mandan chief Sheheke and his wife and son escaped without injury, and Pryor saw them safely to the fort.

In reporting the catastrophe to William Clark, Pryor wrote that if he were asked how many men "would be necessary to escort this unhappy chief [Sheheke] to his nation," he would be compelled to say that "a force of less than 400 men ought not to attempt such an enterprize" and that "even one thousand men might fail in the attempt."[49]

"The Chiefs of the Sioux and Mandan Have United for Your Pardon"

As for Crooks and McClellan, an 1819 account said they and their eighty men, two keelboats, and any number of canoes and pirogues were north of present Omaha, Nebraska, when they met Pryor's "boat sent by the United States to carry back the Mandan chief brought into this country by Captains Lewis and Clarke."[50] Pryor's news of Arikara hostility "discouraged Messrs. [McClellan] and Crooks, and they thought it prudent to decline going on." Determined to try again the next spring, the partners therefore navigated downstream to the mouth of the Nodaway River, not far from where McClellan had met Lewis and Clark in 1806. Taking advantage of the abundant red and white oak trees, they "constructed comfortable quarters, the house having three rooms."[51]

In July 1808, ten months after Pryor's—and Sheheke's—retreat back to St. Charles, an impatient Thomas Jefferson wrote to Lewis, "The misfortune which attended the effort to send the Mandane chief home became known to us before you had reached St. Louis. We took no step on the occasion, counting on receiving your advice . . . knowing that your knowledge of the whole subject & presence on the spot would enable you to judge better than we could what ought to be done." Confident that he would soon hear from Lewis, Jefferson waited, but no word came: "The present letter however is written to put an end at length to this mutual silence, and to ask from you a communication of what you think best to be done to get the chief and his family back. We consider the good faith, & the reputation of the nation as pledged to accomplish this." Before concluding the letter and wishing Lewis "every blessing of life & health" and saluting him "with constant affection & respect," Jefferson mentioned two other subjects: first, "a Mr. Astor" was forming "a powerful company" to take up "the Indian commerce on a large scale," and second, Jefferson had heard nothing on Lewis's writing the history of the expedition and hoped "the first part will not be delayed much longer."[52]

Lewis's long decline that began when he crossed the Continental Divide in 1805 had hardly abated—no document illustrates that quite like this one. His failures in keeping in touch with Jefferson (as well as several other friends and associates), acting promptly to return Sheheke to the Mandan villages, and writing his history—not even beginning "the first part"—were only part of the picture. He had also inexplicably tarried in the east for a year after being named governor and was unsuccessful in finding a wife. Clark, by contrast, had quickly taken up his duties as brigadier general of the militia and principal Indian agent for most of the nations west of the Mississippi, marrying Julia Hancock in January 1808. When Lewis finally reached St. Louis, he found one thorny problem after another: territorial secretary Frederick Bates resentful of his absence and eager to undermine him at every opportunity, French settlers and American newcomers bickering over confusing land titles, white squatters and hunters trespassing on Indian land, traders stirring up trouble, British attempts to turn Indians against the United States, and the ramifications of Aaron Burr and James Wilkinson's treasonous activities (although Wilkinson's role was unknown to American officials until 1854).[53]

Although Jefferson wrote additional letters to Lewis, there is no evidence that Lewis ever replied. In fact, Lewis wrote his last known letter to Jefferson on June 27, 1807.[54] The two friends apparently saw each other for the last time in Albemarle County (where Lewis was born and his mother still lived) in September 1807.[55] Other than that, "the eight months between Lewis's departure from Philadelphia [August 1807] and his arrival in St. Louis [March 1808] were a lost period in his life. . . . He makes no appearance in Jefferson's extensive, often chatty correspondence. William Clark made no mention of him."[56] By the time Lewis put plans in place to finally return the Mandan chief to his motherland, however, Jefferson was about to leave office. In February 1809, in a move that would be illegal in the twenty-first century (and was certainly objectionable in the nineteenth because of a blatant conflict of interest), "His Excellency Meriwether Lewis, Governor of the . . . Territory of Louisiana," agreed to pay the Missouri Fur Company, a firm that included his brother and his best friend, $7,000 to escort Sheheke and his family back to their North Dakota home—the same job McClellan had applied for in the spring of 1807. Although the contract identified the mission's purpose as the "safe conveyance and delivery of the Mandan Chief, his Wife, and child, to the Mandan Nation," there was no doubt that this well-financed voyage up the Missouri would give Pierre Chouteau, commander of the detachment, and his partners in the company an unparalleled opportunity to make crucial trade treaties with Indians, both en route and at the final destination of the Mandan and Hidatsa villages. Making no effort to keep this benefit a secret, the agreement specifically pledged that Lewis would not "authorize any other person or persons to ascend the Missouri any higher . . . than the Mouth of the River La Platte, for the purpose of Trading with the Indians," nor "permit any party accompanying the said detachment or any other party, to ascend the River, go before or in advance of the said detachment by said Choteau from the mouth of the said River La Platte, to the Mandan village."[57] Not only would the Missouri Fur Company be well paid—to put it mildly—for the mission; it was virtually assured first trading rights with the Omaha, Yankton Sioux, Lakota, Mandan, and Hidatsa nations.[58]

In an August 24, 1808, letter to Lewis, Jefferson said he considered "a severe punishment of the Ricaras indispensable" but did not specify how to do that.[59] In his instructions to Pierre Chouteau, Lewis repeated those very words, adding quite specific details: "You will demand of [the Arikaras] the unconditional surrender of those individuals among them, who killed any Person in their attack on the Party under the command of Ensign Prior; if they cannot ascertain the particular individuals who killed our citizens on that occasion they will in that case be required to deliver an equivalent number with those murdered, from among such of their nation as were most active in stimulating them to the Commission of those murders; these murderers, when Delivered will be shot in presence of the nation." As if those consequences were not severe enough, Lewis advised Chouteau or his Indian allies to "exterpate" or "distroy" the Arikaras if they did not make peace.[60] These mentions of genocide reveal an ugly side of Lewis's character, first seen in his 1806 threats to burn the lodges or even kill Columbia River Indians for minor offenses. Always an enigma, however, Lewis had hardly selected a man known for similar harsh attitudes to lead the mission—quite the opposite. Fifty-one-year-old Pierre Chouteau was considered "a brave and daring man of unsurpassed skill for maintaining peace with, and among, Indian tribes." Pierre and his older brother, Auguste, had been raised "to be equally at home in the drawing room and the Indian lodge. . . . Despite the trappings of French style and sophistication, the brothers had been students of Indians and Indian ways since their adolescent years."[61]

On leaving St. Louis, Lewis and Clark had gone to great lengths to equip and feed about fifty soldiers and boatmen. Chouteau, Lisa, and their partners, by contrast, had to provide for approximately 350 men—including forty of whom had to be expert American riflemen with at least fifty rifles and "a sufficient quantity of good Amunition." The multitude would go upriver in thirteen keelboats and an armada of canoes and pirogues. The endless list of supplies included everything from rope, spades, axes, gun slings, paddles, chains, boat hooks, and knives to awls, iron spoons, portable soup, lamps and wicks, calomel, lancets, and ointment. There were also gifts for Indians: glass beads, needles and thread, spun tobacco, red silk handkerchiefs, and fishing hooks. It was no surprise that a list of partial expenses showed $6,171.14 worth of goods purchased from a single company.[62]

Chouteau wrote that his attempt to recruit a large force of Sioux allies, as Lewis suggested, failed when the Sioux themselves "said one tribe ought not to countenance any attempt to distroy another." Chouteau then tried to convince some of the chiefs to accompany him and "succeeded in procuring six of the principal chiefs." The throng of traders, trappers, marksmen, boatmen, and one Mandan family reached the Arikara settlement on September 12, 1809. "On approaching their village we took precautions against an attack," wrote Thomas James, one of Lisa's men. "A guard marched along the shore, opposite to the boats, well armed. My crew composed a part of this force. When within a half mile of the village we drew up the cannon and prepared to encamp. The whole village came out in a body, as it seemed, to [meet] us. They had not come far toward us when an old chief rode out at full speed and with violent gestures and exclamations . . . motioned back his countrymen . . . [supposing] we were about to inflict a proper punishment for the attack on Capt. Prior's troops . . . the year before."[63]

Then something remarkable happened, a rare, if not unique, event in the history of the Plains Indians: two Native nations often in conflict themselves united as intermediaries to save a third nation from war and possible annihilation. "Eighteen or twenty of the Chiefs and principal men of the mandan nation," wrote Chouteau, had somehow learned that the armada escorting Sheheke and his family was on its way. "Fearing that another attack might be made on the party who were bringing their chief," these Mandans "had been waiting the arrival of the detachment several days. . . . Those [Mandan] chiefs with the chiefs of the sioux who had accompanied us, then demanded the pardon of the ricaras."[64]

Chouteau gave no assurances but told the Mandan and Sioux emissaries that he wanted to hold a council with the Arikara chiefs, several of whom "dare not come" because they feared an attack. The next day Chouteau managed to meet with eight Arikara chiefs: "I told them that their Great father the president of the United States had sent me to conduct the mandan chief to his village a second time. The first time you Permitted Yourselves to fire upon the colours of your father, and to attack his men. I have orders to destroy your nation, but the chiefs of the sioux and mandan nations have United together and interceded for your pardon. At their particular request, I shall

Ground my arms, untill new orders can be received from your Great father who alone can pardon or destroy." Chouteau then told the Arikara chiefs they could call back their wives and children who had fled. He sent for Sheheke, who was brought from the safety of a keelboat cabin and presented to the Arikaras, who took him by the hand, saying they had fired on him the first time because "the death of their Chief in the United States had been the Cause of Great dissatisfaction." The Mandan chief "might with Great safety now pass in their Villages without fearing any thing."[65]

The Sioux and Mandan chiefs thus convinced Chouteau to wisely set aside Lewis's draconian measures, allowing for a peaceful resolution worthy of the noble Eagle Feather. On September 24, after a three-year absence, Sheheke, Yellow Corn, and White Painted House were joyfully received by their friends and relatives. The contingent that safely delivered Sheheke's family then split into at least three groups: one to trade at the Mandan and Hidatsa villages; a second—which included the likes of Pierre Menard, Andrew Henry, Reuben Lewis, George Drouillard, John Colter, and Edward Rose—to ascend the Missouri and then the Yellowstone, eventually crossing to build a fort at Three Forks; and a third, which included Lisa and Chouteau and many of their men, as well as Charbonneau and Sacagawea, to descend the Missouri. The latter group reached St. Louis on November 20, but there was little chance to announce the successful return of the Mandan chief. "But what was my surprise since I arrived here three days ago," Chouteau wrote in a letter. "I learned of the tragic and untimely death of Gov. Lewis."[66]

Fig. 1. Thomas Jefferson, from life, ca. 1791–92, by Charles Willson Peale. Courtesy of the National Gallery of Art, Washington.

Fig. 2. Meriwether Lewis, from life, 1807, by Charles Willson Peale. Courtesy of the National Gallery of Art, Washington.

Fig. 3. William Clark, from life, 1807–8, by Charles Willson Peale. Courtesy of the National Gallery of Art, Washington.

Fig. 4. Arikara village, by Charles Catlin, 1866. Courtesy of the Missouri History Museum, St. Louis.

Fig. 5. Manuel Lisa. Courtesy of the Missouri History Museum, St. Louis.

Fig. 6. Henry Leavenworth. Courtesy of the Missouri History Museum, St. Louis.

Fig. 7. Stán-au-pat, Bloody Hand, chief of the Arikara tribe, 1832, by George Catlin. Courtesy of the Smithsonian American Art Museum. Gift of Mrs. Joseph Harrison Jr.

Fig. 8. Kah-béck-a, the Twin, wife of Bloody Hand, 1832, by George Catlin. Courtesy of the Smithsonian American Art Museum. Gift of Mrs. Joseph Harrison Jr.

Fig. 9. Crow lodge of twenty-five buffalo skins, 1832–33, by George Catlin. Courtesy of the Smithsonian American Art Museum. Gift of Mrs. Joseph Harrison Jr.

Fig. 10. Distinguished Crow Indians, 1861/69, by George Catlin. Courtesy of the National Gallery of Art, Paul Mello Collection.

Fig. 11. Jedediah Smith. From the interior of Morgan, *Jedediah Smith*.

Fig. 12. Thomas Fitzpatrick. Painting by Waldo Love, based on a photograph. Courtesy of History Colorado, Denver.

Fig. 13. Cheyenne village, 1861/69, by George Catlin. Courtesy of the National Gallery of Art, Paul Mello Collection.

Fig. 14. An Arapaho chief, his wife, and a warrior, 1861/69, by George Catlin. Courtesy of the National Gallery of Art, Paul Mello Collection.

Fig. 15. Two Arapaho warriors and a woman, by George Catlin. Courtesy of the National Gallery of Art, Paul Mello Collection.

Fig. 16. Fort Laramie, by William Henry Jackson. Scotts Bluff National Monument. Courtesy of the National Gallery of Art, Washington.

Fig. 17. Sutler's Store, Fort Laramie National Historic Site, 1877. Library of Congress, HABS WYO,8-FOLA,2-1.

Fig. 18. Father Pierre Jean DeSmet, SJ, ca. 1865–71, photo by John A. Scholten. Courtesy of the Missouri History Museum, St. Louis.

Fig. 19. Crazy Bull and Friday. Courtesy of History Colorado, Denver.

Fig. 20. Camp Weld Conference. The peace conference was held in late September 1864, just two months before the Sand Creek Massacre. Front row, kneeling, left to right: Major Edward W. Wynkoop and Lieutenant Silas Soule. Seated, left to right: Neva (Arapaho), Bull Bear (Cheyenne), Black Kettle (Cheyenne), One Eye (Cheyenne), and unidentified. Standing, left to right: two unidentified men, John Smith (interpreter), White Wolf (Kiowa?), Bosse (Cheyenne), and last two men unidentified. Courtesy of History Colorado, Denver.

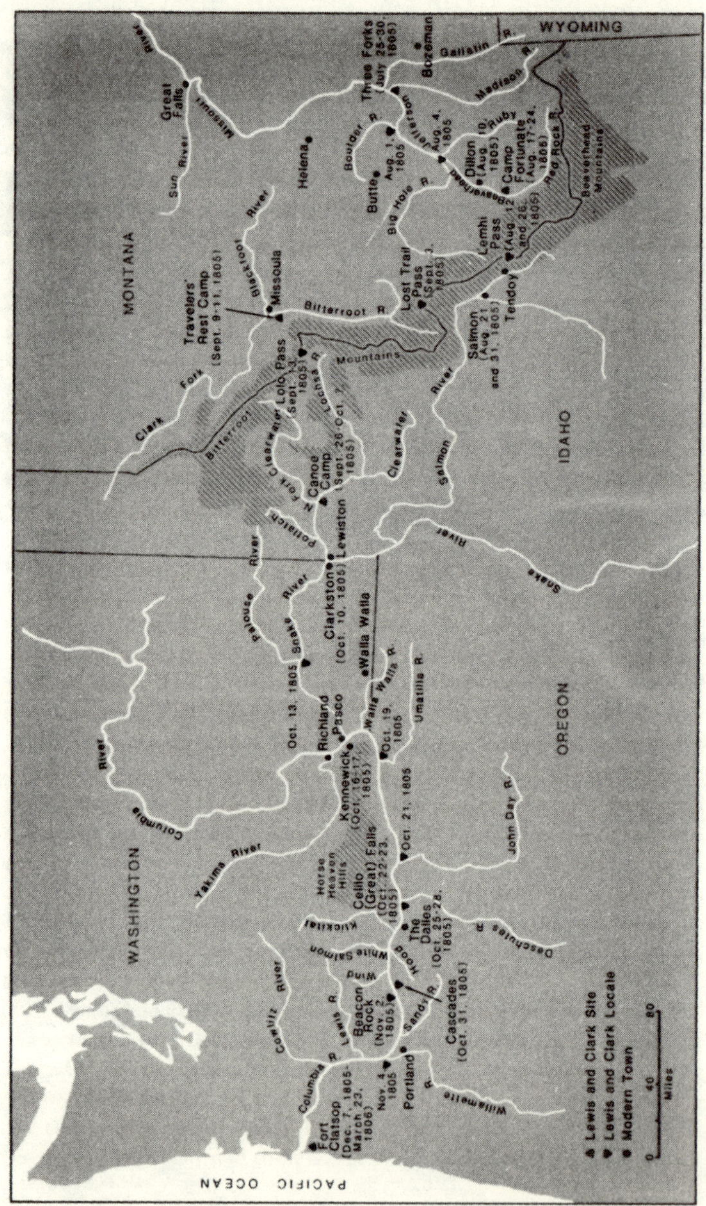

Map 1. Route of the expedition, July 28–November 1, 1805. Lewis crossed the Continental Divide at Lemhi Pass on August 12. The perilous journey to the Pacific coast took a huge emotional and psychological toll on Lewis. From Moulton, *Journals*, 5:6.

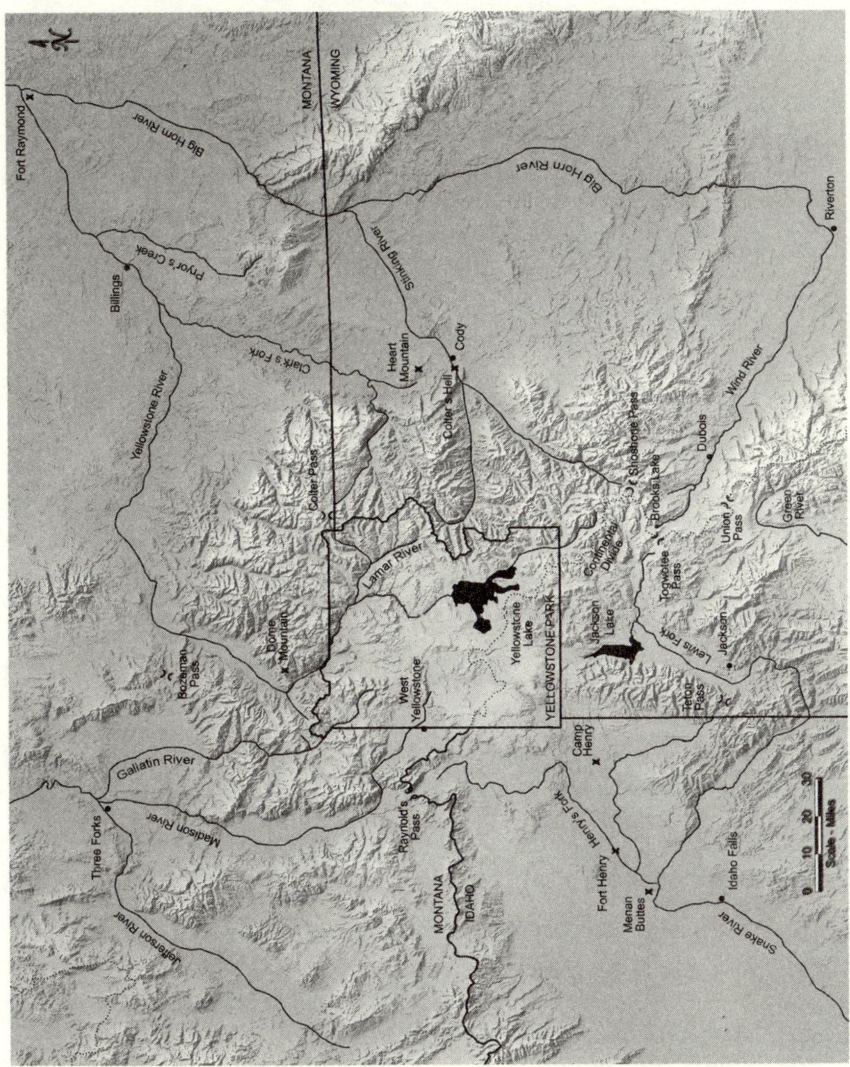

Map 2. Key rivers of the Rocky Mountain fur trade. As the map shows, several key tributaries of both the east-flowing Yellowstone River and the west-flowing Snake River originate in northwestern Wyoming near the Continental Divide. Created by Clint Gilchrist.

4

"Mr. Rose Came Running into Camp"

The Arikara War

Amid lightning and thunder and driving wind and rain, a frontiersman galloped through the darkness, down the long sandy shore of the Missouri River, fleeing two Arikara Indian villages. Although the running man had cheated death more than once, he took nothing for granted. When another lightning bolt lit up his fellow hunters encamped on the sandbar—and beyond them two keelboats anchored in the narrow channel of the river—he sprinted harder and shouted out a warning.

"Our Interpreter Mr [Edward] Rose . . . came running into camp & informed us that one of our men [Aaron Stephens] was killed in the village and war was declared in earnest," storied mountain man James Clyman recalled decades later.[1]

It was just after midnight on June 2, 1823, near present Mobridge, South Dakota. Clyman and the three dozen other men on shore, tasked with tending a herd of horses purchased the previous day from the Indians, had long given up any hope of sleep. They knew Rose, a skilled, forty-something backwoodsman, for his "reckless bravery" and "strong and vigorous constitution"—his frantic retreat from the towns convinced them an attack was indeed imminent.[2] The men checked their rifles and hoped for the best, but those who feared the gale was a portent of a hail of musket fire from the Arikaras were not mistaken.

This was hardly the scene the men envisioned a few months earlier when they responded to an advertisement in a St. Louis newspaper:

> *For the Rocky Mountains.*
>
> THE subscribers wish to engage One Hundred MEN, to ascend the Missouri river to the *Rocky Mountains*, there to be employed as

> Hunters. As a compensation to each man, fit for such business, *two hundred dollars per annum* will be given for his services, as aforesaid. For particulars apply to J V GARNER or W H ASHLEY at St. Louis. The expedition will set out from St. Louis on or before the 1st day of March next.
>
> Jan 15
>
> *Ashley & Henry*[3]

The annual wage of $200 was extraordinary for the time. Most of Lewis and Clark's men, by contrast, were paid about $60 a year. The key was that these "hunters" would actually be trapping beaver, and beaver pelts were the most valuable raw material of the profitable fur trade, in huge demand by eastern and European companies "not for the dark brown fur but for the barbed, fibrous underhair [used] to make felting material for hats."[4] William Henry Ashley (ca. 1778–1838)—the lieutenant governor of Missouri, brigadier general in the state militia, and partner with Andrew Henry in a well-funded trapping operation—thus had little trouble filling his quota, just as he and Henry had a year earlier.[5]

Rivers were the key to the fur trade, and St. Louis was situated on the west bank of the body of water recognized for almost three hundred years—ever since Hernando de Soto dubbed it Rio del Espiritu Santo (River of the Holy Spirit)—as the key waterway in the New World, the Mississippi. Not only that, but St. Louis was also just south of the mouth of the river Lewis and Clark followed west to the Rockies in 1804 and 1805—the Wide Missouri. What better spot to recruit "hunters" than St. Louis? Although the beaver pelt business, which flourished immediately after Lewis and Clark, faltered with the War of 1812 and its economic backlash, Ashley and Henry and their competitors—John Jacob Astor and Ramsay Crooks, Joshua Pilcher and Edward Hempstead, and Bartholomew Berthold, Bernard Pratte, and Pierre Chouteau Jr.—believed the time was right to make a fortune in fur, fueling the enthusiasm of the young men who slapped one another on the back, roared with delight, and fired guns as they headed up the Missouri, dreaming of all they could do with $200. But now, with Rose sounding the alarm, the men concentrated on one thing: surviving.

"My party consisted of ninety men," wrote Ashley, "forty of whom were selected to accompany me to the Yellow Stone river by land, and were encamped on the sand beach in charge of the horses."[6] The fifty others were hands on Ashley's two keelboats, his flagship *Rocky Mountains* and the *Yellowstone Packet*.

Rose, who battled Blackfeet Indians in 1810 with Lewis and Clark veterans John Colter and George Drouillard, took a skiff to the *Rocky Mountains*, where he warned Ashley, in the latter's words, "that the Indians had killed one of my men Aaron Stephens and in all probability would attack the boats in a few minutes."[7] Despite this warning from Rose, who had lived among the Arikaras for years, knew them well, and spoke their language, Ashley inexplicably decided to wait until daybreak to deal with the crisis. Nor was this the first warning Ashley disregarded. The previous day, a boatman wrote, "One of the friendly Indians informed us of their intention to attack us before our departure; if they did not, we might calculate on their attacking us when separated; he advised Ashley to swim the horses that night across the river."[8]

A St. Louis Indian agent who later talked with Ashley confirmed this report, although Ashley himself did not mention it. "In the course of the evening [before the attack]," wrote the agent, "Gen. Ashley was notified, by a chief, of the intention of the villages to attack him that night, or very early the next morning, and advised him to take his horses [to] the opposite bank of the river." Ashley, however, believed "it was the intention of this chief to steal the horses, by his urging him to remove them across the river, as small parties of Indians were occasionally seen on the opposite side."[9]

Regardless, Stephens's murder gave Ashley every reason to get his men out of harm's way immediately. Even if there were small groups of Indians on the other side of the river, the two sides would be equally vulnerable if a skirmish broke out, but the hunters stranded on the sandbar were virtually defenseless if the hundreds of well-armed Arikaras attacked from their well-picketed lodges situated on a bluff forty feet above the open beach. Ashley had other reasons to be especially cautious in Arikara territory—he knew of the 1807 attack on Nathaniel Pryor's party, as well as the Arikaras' plundering trading houses in Sioux country in 1820. Ironically, upon his arrival, Ashley had negotiated with Arikara chiefs to buy horses. The chiefs eventually agreed, "but the onley article of Trade they wanted was ammunition." The upshot? Ashley obtained nineteen or twenty horses but at the cost of "a fine supply of Powder and ball," which was now about to be used against him and his hunters.[10]

Clyman, who fought Shawnees in the War of 1812 and had more combat experience than "General" Ashley, had no illusions, reporting that the group had no military organization or discipline. "Several advised to cross over the river at once," he added, "but Gnl. Ashley our imployer Thought best to wait till morning and go into the village and demand the body of our comrade and his Murderer[.] Ashley being the most interested his advice prevailed."[11] As a partner in the company, of course, Ashley was "the most interested" party, the one with the money and the authority, whose "advice" predictably carried the day, but it was also true that Ashley's cabin on the cannon- and blunderbuss-armed *Rocky Mountains* was vastly safer than the hunters' sandbar. "We laid on our arms e[x]pecting an attact as their was a continual Hubbub in the village," Clyman said.[12]

"The Attack Terminated with Great Loss on My Part"

A few minutes after dawn, a chorus of Arikara voices called out to their friend Rose, urging him "to take care of himself, before they fired on Genl. Ashley's party."[13] Then the maelstrom erupted:

> The Indians commenced a heavy and well directed fire.[14]

> We had little else to do than to Stand on a bear sand barr and be shot at, at long range Their being seven or Eight hundred guns in village.[15]

> They immediately commenced firing upon us. The men on the beach were drawn up in front of the boats, their horses forming a breastwork. So severe was the fire, that in a few minutes all the horses were either killed or wounded, and many of the men.[16]

A deafening fusillade of shots rained down from the villages, striking the water, the sand, the bleating horses, and the screaming, moaning men, the air thick with the smoke and smell of gunpowder and the stench of burning horseflesh. "Never did men in my opinion act with more coolness and bravery than the most of those exposed on the sand bar," wrote Ashley.[17]

Edward Rose had surprised no one by shunning the sanctuary of the keelboat to take a stand with his comrades. He had, wrote an army officer who knew him well, "at the very commencement, taken his station behind a small bunch of willows, from which, detached and alone, he fired as often as an Indian showed himself at the narrow spaces between the pickets that surrounded the villages." Rose reportedly gave no thought to his own safety, firing so single-mindedly that it was only after someone called him from a boat that he realized he was "the sole occupant of the bar," soon plunging into the river and swimming for the boats "amid the pattering of a shower of balls on the water around him," reaching a boat with rifle in hand, "the last man who did so."[18]

Not surprisingly, another secondhand source bestowed the "last man on the bar" honor to a different Ashley man, with an 1832 obituary for Jedediah Smith announcing, "He was exact in his requisitions of duty, determined and persevering, always confident of success. When his party was in danger, Mr. Smith was always among the foremost to meet it, and the last to fly; those who saw him on shore, at the Ricacaree fight, in 1823, can attest to the truth of this assertion."[19]

Regardless of who fled the sandbar last—no eyewitness ever said—praise for the men's courage continued over subsequent decades. In his reminiscence, an Ashley man who in 1831 heard firsthand accounts of the "battle of the Rickarees on the Missouri" remembered, "At the attack . . . after the land body in charge of the animals were mostly killed,—[William Lewis] Sublette and [David E.] Jackson, after fighting bravely around the animals, until all were either killed or dispersed, fought their way through the crowded ranks of Indians, leaped into the river, and under a hail storm of arrows and balls, swam to the boats."[20]

Although Ashley, realizing that every man on the sandbar was about to perish, ordered the steersmen of both keelboats to weigh their anchors and lay their boats to shore, the pilots were so panic-stricken they couldn't move. Nor would the oarsmen on either keelboat lift a hand to help. "No prayers or threats had the [slightest effect]," wrote Clyman, "the Boats men being completely Parylized."[21] Ashley continued pleading, however, and finally convinced a crew member to man a skiff and row to shore.

Three witnesses offered accounts of what they experienced. Clyman, the only one of the three to have been on the sandbar itself (and also the last to record his narrative), said several men were wounded when the first skiff was brought ashore: "All rushed for the Skiff and came near sinking it but it went the boat full of men." Despite the heavy gunfire, the skiffs took several loads of men to board the boats. Then, with "the shot coming thicker and faster one of the skiffs . . . was let go the men clambering on Board let the skiff float off in their great eagerness to conceal themselves from the rapid fire of the enemy."[22]

Ashley wrote that two skiffs "were taken a shore for the embarkation of the men, but (I suppose) from a predetermination of the men on the beach not to give way to the Indians . . . not more than five of them made use of the large skiff." When those men reached the keelboat, Ashley ordered it back to the sandbar, "but unfortunately one of the men that worked it was shot down and by some means the skiff set adrift. By this time the most of the horses were killed or wounded and about half the men."[23]

"Both skiffs were manned," wrote a boatman, "but they had not advanced a rod from the boat before those at the oars were shot down; finding all lost, those on the beach attempted to swim to the boats; some who could not, fell alive in the hands of the Indians; many who attempted to swim, were, by the violence of the current, driven below the boats and drowned."[24]

Of course, each man's witnessing the chaotic chain of events from a different vantage point explains some of the disparities in their accounts, but the clashing interpretations are ultimately a good reminder that observers often perceive or remember incidents differently.

Regardless, Clyman offered an unparalleled and stirring account of the Arikara raid in a narrative completed in 1871, eleven years before he died at age eighty-nine: "I seeing no hopes of Skiffs or boats comeing ashore left my hiding place behind a dead hors, ran up stream a short distance to get the advantage of the current and concieving myself to be a tolerable strong swimmer stuck the muzzle of my rifle in [my] belt, the lock ove my head with all my clothes on but not having made sufficien calculation for the strong current was carried passed the boat within a few feet of the same."[25]

Thomas Eddie, a hunter aboard the keelboat, saw Clyman struggling for help and held out a pole but couldn't reach him because of the constant gunfire from the Indians. Clyman's greatest obstacle was his rifle: "In my attempt to draw it over my head it sliped down the lock ketching in my belt[,] comeing to the surface to breathe I found it hindred worse than it did at first[,] making one more effort I turned the lock side ways and it sliped through which gave me some relief but still finding myself to much encumbred I next unbucled my belt and let go my Pistols. . . . I next let go my Ball Pouch and finally one Sleeve of my Hunting shirt which was buckskin and held an immence weight of water."[26]

As a gasping Clyman surfaced, he heard a voice say, "Hold on Clyman I will soon relieve you." It was fellow hunter Reed Gibson, who had swam downstream to the skiff abandoned by the others. Clyman was so exhausted that Gibson had to help him into the skiff. Finally catching his breath, Clyman rose to take the remaining oar, but Gibson called, "Oh, god I am shot" and fell forward in the boat. Clyman encouraged his friend, saying, "Perhaps not fatally give a few more pulls and we will be out of reach." Gibson rose and rowed several more strokes before complaining of feeling faint and falling forward again. Clyman took Gibson's place in the stern, rowed to the east shore, hauled the boat up on the bank, and told Gibson to stay in the skiff while he went to higher ground to see if they were still in danger, but he saw several Indians swimming across the river, some of them quite close.[27]

Clyman told Gibson the Arikaras were coming, but Gibson merely said, "Save yourself Clyman and pay no attention to me as I am a dead man and they can get nothing of me but my Scalp." Clyman's first idea was to get in the skiff, meet the Indians in the water, "and brain them with the oar. But on second look I concluded there ware to many of them and they ware too near the shore." Then he looked for a place to hide, "but there being onley a scant row of brush along the shore I concluded to take to the open Prairie and run for life." By this time, Gibson had managed to scramble up the bank and stood by Clyman's side. "Run Clyman," he said, "but if you escape write to my friends in Virginia and tell them what has become of me."[28]

Gibson straggled into the brush to hide, and Clyman ran for the open prairie:

> Looking back I saw three Indians mount the bank being intirely divested of garments excepting a belt aroun the waist containing a Knife and Tomahawk and Bows and arrows in their [hands] they made but little halt and started after me one to the right the other to the left while the third took direct after me I took direct for the rising ground I think about three miles of[f] there being no chanc for dodging the ground being smooth and level but haveing the start of some 20 or 30 rods we had appearantle an even race for about an hour when I began to have the palpitation of the heart and I found my man was gaining on me.[29]

Luckily, Clyman hid in a hole surrounded by weeds and grass, and his closest pursuer ran by without seeing him. Staying on low ground, Clyman made his way to a steep ravine. After climbing to the top of the ridge, he finally stopped wheezing, estimating he was at least a quarter mile from the Arikaras: "When I gained this elevation I turned around [and saw] the three standing near together I made them a low bow with both my hand and thanked god for my present Safety and diliveranc."[30]

Eager to get as far away as possible from the Indians, Clyman ran southward, over smooth rolling ground: "But what ware my reflection being at least Three Hundred miles from any assistanc unarmed and u[n]provided with any sort of means of pecureing a subsistance not even a pocket Knife I began to feel after passing So many dangers that my pro[s]pects were still very slim." Mounting a spot of high ground, Clyman saw the Missouri ahead and a grove of trees: "Being verry thirsty I made for the water intending to take a good rest in the timber I took one drink of water and setting down on a drift log a few minuits I chanced to look [at] the [river] and here came the boats floating down the stream the [men] watcing along the shores saw me about as soon as I saw them." One of the keelboats landed and picked Clyman up. He asked about Gibson and learned the wounded man was already onboard: "I immediately wen[t] to the cabin where he lay but he did not recognize me being in the agonies of Death the shot having passed through his bowels[.] I could not refrain from weeping over him who lost his lifee but saved mine he did not live but an hour or so and we buried him that evening. . . . Before leaving the grave of my friend Gibson that [day and] before I had an oppertunity of writeing to his friends I forgot his post office and so have never writen."[31]

In a makeshift funeral service, Ashley and his men buried Gibson, other victims, and a man by the name of John S. Gardner. Although a hunter named Hugh Glass was wounded himself, he composed a letter to Gardner's parents:

> Dr Sir,
>
> My painful duty it is to tell you of the death of yr Son wh befell at the hands of the indians 2nd June in the early morning. He lived a little while after he was shot and asked me to inform you of his sad fate[.] We brought him to the ship where he soon died. Mr Smith a young man of our company made a powerful prayr wh moved us all greatly and I am persuaded John died in peace. His body we buried with others near this camp and marked the grave with a log. His things we will send to you. The savages are greatly treacherous. we traded with them as friends but after a great storm of rain and thunder they came at us before light and many were hurt. I myself was hit in the leg. Master Ashley is bound to stay in these parts till the traitors are rightly punished.
>
> Y^r^ Obt Svt
> Hugh Glass[32]

Ashley made serious errors in dealing with the Arikaras but was also a victim of the convergence of four unrelated events: an Arikara raid of a Missouri Fur Company post (weeks before Ashley's arrival) in which the son of Chief Grey Eyes, a friend of Lewis and Clark, was killed; a dispatch from Henry asking Ashley to buy horses from Indians at the next opportunity; the violent storm that delayed Ashley's departure; and hunter Aaron Stephens's disobeying orders by venturing into the Arikara villages in search of female companionship.[33]

By June 4, two days after the attack, Ashley moved his keelboats twenty-five miles downstream, where he wrote a letter to the Indian agent—and nephew of William Clark—Benjamin O'Fallon and commanding officer Colonel Henry Leavenworth, both stationed at Fort Atkinson (east of present Fort Calhoun, Nebraska), the westernmost outpost of the U.S. Army, which housed 350 soldiers. "On the morning of the 2d Inst I was attacked by the Ricaree Indians," Ashley wrote, "which terminated with great loss on my part."[34]

Ashley listed his killed and wounded men as shown in table 1.

As Dale Morgan points out, the casualties among Ashley's hunters have been unfailingly misstated, "even in the sources." Ashley wrote two letters on June 4 and one on June 7, giving different lists each time. Moreover, in his second June 4 report, he added, "Another of the wounded men has since died, making in all 14 dead," but the June 7 letter lists the same thirteen fatalities included in both June 4 letters. Nor did Ashley ever identify the wounded man who subsequently died. O'Fallon, however, gave an updated number in a letter addressed to William Clark on July 3, 1823: "Another of Gen. Ashley's wounded men is dead, making 15 men killed, by the A'Rickarees." The total number of wounded was nine.[35]

Ashley, of course, also had to get word of the attack to Henry, then camped at the confluence of the Missouri and Yellowstone Rivers. William Waldo, an 1831 Ashley man, wrote that when Ashley called for volunteers "to undertake this long, hazardous, and desolate journey . . . an inexperienced and beardless youth stepped forward and offered himself for the enterprise. Genl. Ashley was charmed with his intrepidity, and accepted his offer, but induced a Canadian Frenchman of great experience to accompany him. This youth was Jedediah Smith. After many miraculous escapes, he reached the Yellowstone and found the company, which hastened to re-enforce Ashley."[36] Smith's volunteering did not come out of the blue because he had just arrived from Henry's camp on May 30, bringing the latter's request for more horses. And while Waldo may have embellished his secondhand account, Smith—who signed with Ashley in 1822—had clearly earned the respect of both partners by this time.

In the letter to O'Fallon and Leavenworth, carried by an aide descending the Missouri on the *Yellowstone Packet*, Ashley said he was not sure how many Indians were killed but likely not more than seven or eight. "I

Table 1. W. H. Ashley's list of killed and wounded men

KILLED	WOUNDED
John Matthews	John Larrison
John Collins	Joseph Monso
Benjamin F. Sneed	Reed Gibson "(since dead)"
Thully Piper	Joseph Thompson
James M'Daniel	Robert Tucker
Joseph S. Gardner	James Davis
George Flages	Aaron Ricketts
David Howard	Jacob Miller
Aaron Stephens	August Dufren
James Penn Jr.	Hugh Glass
John Miller	Daniel M'Clain
Elliss Ogle	Willis "(black man)"

Source: William H. Ashley to a gentleman in Franklin, Missouri, June 7, 1823, in Morgan, *West of William H. Ashley*, 30. Ashley recorded three lists, which include several inconsistencies among them (27–30).

have thought proper to communicate this affair as early as an opportunity offered," he continued, "believing that you would feel disposed to make those people account to the government for the outrage committed. Should that be the case and a force sent for that purpose in a short time, you will oblige me much if you will send me an express . . . that I may meet and cooperate with you."[37]

Ashley also warned that making the Arikaras account for their outrage would not be easy. The Indian towns lay on high ground, picketed by well-entrenched timber six to eight inches thick and twelve to fifteen feet high. About three-fourths of the six hundred warriors were armed with "London Fuzils"—shoulder firearms commonly called Northwest or Indian trade guns—and the others were armed with bows and arrows and tomahawks.[38] Leavenworth's armed forces, Ashley advised, would require at least one six-pound cannon to attack the towns effectively. Ashley told O'Fallon and Leavenworth that he had sent an express to Henry and expected to hear back from him in twelve or fifteen days. He also asked them to care for the five wounded men aboard the *Yellowstone Packet*, not mentioning that thirty-eight boatmen had deserted and were desperate to get back to St. Louis as fast as possible.

"Mother Corn Led the People to the Missouri River"

Edward Rose, who first saw the Arikara villages in 1807 and spent a good deal of time there over the next fifteen years, was the only member of Ashley's party well acquainted with Arikara culture. The others had little or no idea of the Arikaras' rich history.

The Arikara villages' site on the Missouri River offered excellent opportunities for trade but also made them vulnerable to attacks from other Indian nations either up- or downstream. By 1800 those neighbors wanted guns, ammunition, and manufactured goods in addition to corn, beans, and squash, causing the Arikaras to become increasingly dependent on European American traders, a double-edged sword because the whites shaped commerce to their advantage and wanted to dictate intertribal relations.

Depopulation and divided loyalties made it difficult for various factions of the tribe to peacefully coexist, greatly complicating relations with European American traders. One trader in 1804 said there were forty-two chiefs in the two villages, so it's no surprise that Ashley got different signals from different chiefs. "There was no such thing as *the* Arikara in 1823," writes one scholar, "but rather a number of once politically autonomous groups who, through the events of history, were found in two villages."[39]

The Arikaras, also known as Ricaras, Arickarees, and Rees, settled along the Missouri as early as AD 1300, about the same time Marco Polo, already renowned for his amazing travels from Venice to China, was marrying and having children. Arikara women tended massive cornfields, providing a harvest surplus that became the core of tribal affluence and trade with other Indian nations. Little wonder that Lakota winter counts used the symbol of an ear of corn to represent the Arikaras and their Pawnee relatives: "By the mid-eighteenth century, the Mandans, Hidatsas, and Arikaras had made their villages into a great . . . exchange center for European goods and Plains produce as well and for guns and horses in particular." They obtained manufactured goods directly from French or British traders in the northeast or by way of Cree and Assiniboine middleman, from the west came horses and plains products, and more horses and Spanish and Pueblo goods came from the southwest. Assiniboines, Crees, Ojibwes, Crows, Blackfeet, Flatheads, Nez Perces, Shoshones, Cheyennes, Arapahos, Kiowas, Kiowa Apaches, Pawnees, Poncas, and a variety of Sioux bands all made trips to the upper Missouri Indian towns.[40]

In 1781 a catastrophic smallpox epidemic struck the Arikara nation (as well as several other Missouri River Indians). Fourteen years later Jean Baptiste Truteau reported, "In ancient times the Ricara nation was very large; it counted thirty-two populated villages, now depopulated and almost entirely destroyed by the smallpox. . . . A few families only, from each of the villages escaped; these united and formed the two villages now here."[41]

In the first third of the nineteenth century, the Arikara people manufactured sophisticated pendants (a piece of jewelry hanging from a chain worn around the neck), which were often buried with loved ones. The Arikaras "produced these pendants by first grinding blue-glass beads to form a powder. They then moistened the powder to form a paste and shaped and fired the paste to the desired form on a copper plate."[42]

The Arikaras had a rich oral folklore tradition, passing from one generation to another such tales as "The Holy Boy Who Stopped Animals from Killing Humans," "The Young Woman Who Married the Moon," "The Young Man Who Did Not Believe in Ghosts," and "The Singing Coyote."[43] No narrative was more important than the creation story; drawing on several Arikara oral histories, Mark van de Logt, author of *Between the Floods: A History of the Arikaras*, offers this interpretation:

> In the beginning, "the Great Chief Above" created "the stars, the earth, and the four corners of the universe." Chief next created a race of giants, but they rebelled against him. He punished them by turning them into mountains. Chief next formed smaller beings, but when they mocked him he drowned them in a great flood. After the waters receded, Chief formed the first man and woman and all the animals, who lived with him in the sky. He then told Thunder to take all living things to earth, but when "Thunder's lighting bolt struck the earth, it pressed too deeply into

the soil. . . . Thunder cried out in sadness, and ever since one can hear his cry whenever lighting strikes." The people, still not fully developed, now dwelled under the earth's surface. They longed to be brought into the light, and Chief answered their prayers by sending them Mother Corn. After guiding the people to the earth's surface, Mother Corn led them on a long, dangerous journey, where they were saved from disaster first by a kingfisher, then an owl, and finally a loon. Each time, some of the people stayed behind, turning into the creatures that inhabited those places. "Finally, Mother Corn led the people to the Missouri River. The people saw that it was wonderful and called it the Mysterious River or Sacred River. Here they settled, and Mother Corn gave them corn and other crops to grow. 'You shall have my corn to plant that you will grow and multiply,' she said. She also taught the people how to hunt buffalo, cook meat, and prepare the skins" and how to perform sacred offerings of smoke, corn, and meat.[44]

"The Most Disagreeable Place Short of the Bottomless Pit"

On June 18, the same day the *Yellowstone Packet* reached Fort Atkinson, Colonel Leavenworth sent a dispatch to General Henry Atkinson in St. Louis, reporting the Arikara attack and his plans to go to Ashley's aid "tomorrow or the next day. We shall take two six pounders and small swivels, and, perhaps a howitzer. My party will be about 200 strong in rank and file." If necessary, he believed he could raise a considerable auxiliary force among the Sioux: "We go to secure the lives and property of our citizens, and to chastise and correct those who have committed outrages upon them. It will be our endeavor to do this as peaceably as the nature of the circumstances . . . will admit."[45]

Leavenworth thus declared the first U.S. war west of the Mississippi. Recently appointed commanding officer at Fort Atkinson, Leavenworth was "caught in an ambiguous Indian policy: as commander, he had to protect American fur traders while, simultaneously, being ordered to 'gain the confidence and friendship of all the Indian tribes.'"[46] Nor did he have firsthand experience or a detailed knowledge of the Arikaras. He was so new in his post that Ashley did not know his name, so it was no surprise that Leavenworth relied heavily on O'Fallon, U.S. Indian agent for the upper

Missouri nations, who received Ashley's letter and told the colonel of the assault. Given Leavenworth's inexperience, O'Fallon was likely the one who recommended involving the Sioux, a serious mistake.

Prior to 1822 the last trade activity between the Arikaras and U.S. merchants occurred in 1812 and 1813. Manuel Lisa and a contingent of trappers arrived in August of 1812 and by November completed building a fort on a bluff twelve miles north of the Arikara towns (just south of the North Dakota / South Dakota border). They called it Fort Manuel, and it offered trading opportunities to a host of Indian nations, including the Cheyennes, Hidatsas, Mandans, Arikaras, and Sioux. The trouble was, James Madison had declared war against Great Britain in June 1812: "The effect of the war on the Northern Plains was to throw the fur trade into chaos. The British had come to the Plains before the Americans and had built personal and commercial relationships with the various bands. In the late summer of 1812, they carried the flag to their friends, using their contacts to encourage Indian attacks on men from the United States."[47] The Hidatsas and Sioux, both friendly to the British, responded, with Hidatsa warriors killing one of Lisa's trappers in September and another in October and Sioux murdering three in November and one in December.[48] Skirmishes even broke out between the Mandans (who favored the United States) and their longtime allies, the Hidatsas. Fearing the Sioux—who passed through Arikara territory whenever they journeyed north from their homeland near the Big Bend of the Missouri River—groups of Arikaras frequently sought shelter at Fort Manuel. A key reason for Lakota opposition to Fort Manuel was likely their desire to prevent the Arikaras from obtaining guns from the Americans. By the spring of 1813 Lisa had seen enough. He left by March and the rest of his men by May, after burning the fort to the ground. Lisa's departure, the war, American trappers' fear of being robbed by Canadian traders or Indians, and the financial panic of 1819 all combined to isolate the Arikaras for nine years, leaving them dependent on the more powerful Sioux for firearms and ammunition.[49] The sincere but naive Leavenworth could hardly expect to deal "peaceably" with the Arikaras if he were accompanied by warriors of the neighboring nation they resented so deeply.

O'Fallon was enraged and had no interest in a peaceful resolution, writing to his uncle, William Clark, superintendent of Indian Affairs, "Those inhuman monsters will most probably be made to atone for what they have done by a great effusion of their blood."[50] Although O'Fallon made no plans to accompany Leavenworth, he made sure that Missouri Fur Company head and Indian subagent Joshua Pilcher did so. Pilcher relished the assignment. He had gone up the Missouri to the Mandan villages that same year, reporting that the Arikaras, friendly on his outbound trip, had "attempted . . . to rob . . . and committed violence" on one of his men on the return journey. Sharing O'Fallon's view that strong punitive action against the Rees was required, Pilcher wrote that "a decisive blow is indispensable for the safety of every white man on the river above the Council Bluffs."[51] Neither O'Fallon nor Pilcher had any awareness of the nuances of Arikara culture or sympathy for that nation's exasperation at "enterprising young men" continually trespassing their territory on the way to provide valuable trade goods, including firearms and powder, to possible enemies—the kinds of misunderstandings that were the rule rather than the exception in the fur trade. Although Leavenworth initially considered Pilcher an ally, the latter's arrogance and resolve to punish the Arikaras would prove disastrous.

Leavenworth and his 230 men departed Fort Atkinson on June 22, 1823, with three keelboats transporting provisions, supplies, and two six-pounders and some of the men, with the rest of the regiment going overland. "The river being very high, the navigation was exceedingly difficult and hazardous," wrote Leavenworth. The men pulling the boats with cordelles "were obliged to be continually in the mud and water. . . . The river bottoms were so much inundated that those [soldiers marching by land] were frequently compelled to swim and wade through the water waist deep." Pilcher and his sixty traders, carrying supplies and Leavenworth's five-and-one-half-inch howitzer in their boats, caught up with the main party on June 27. A week later, about 130 miles above Fort Atkinson, one of the boats hit a sawyer, broke into two pieces, and sunk. "We unfortunately lost fifty-seven muskets and bayonets," wrote Leavenworth. "What was still worse, we found on mustering the crew that we had lost one sergeant and six men. For their names and description I beg leave to refer you to the Company reports."[52]

Leavenworth reached Fort Recovery (also called Cedar Fort) on July 19 and stayed there for three days to refit and reorganize his company. If he had earlier been skeptical of joining forces with the Sioux, that was no longer so. "We found here a small band of the Sioux Indians called Yanktons and also a small number of the Teton band of the same nation," he wrote. "They were anxious to join us against the Aricaras. I told them that we had men enough, but as those bad Indians were enemies to them as well as to us I was willing they should join us and help to punish them." On July 28 Leavenworth and his men "came to where two bands of the Sioux Indians . . . had pitched their lodges, about two hundred in number." He held a council with them, and when Pilcher told them the object of the expedition, "they cheerfully consented and appeared anxious to join" with the soldiers and traders.[53]

Two days later Leavenworth reached Ashley's camp, at the mouth of the Teton River, at present Fort Pierre, South Dakota, in the heart of Sioux country. By this time Andrew Henry, Jedediah Smith, and others had arrived from Henry's camp at the mouth of the Yellowstone. "Genl. Ashley here made a tender of his services and those of his party amounting to eighty men," wrote Leavenworth. "They were divided into two companies. Genl. Ashley nominated his officers and their appointments were confirmed in orders."[54] They were confirmed as shown in table 2.

Leavenworth, who died in 1834 at age fifty, would never realize that in the standard procedure of reporting details of a military campaign to his superior officer—General Atkinson—he thus created the first list of a historic band of frontiersmen known as "Ashley men," who played key roles in the exploration of the West and both peaceful and hostile encounters with scores of Indian nations, from Lisa's first trapping venture in 1807 to the Powder River Expedition in 1865.

The appointments of Ashley's hunters were "nominal," with the understanding that Ashley's hunters pledged to obey Leavenworth's orders even though they were not technically enlisted in the army. Ashley himself already had military status as a brigadier general in the Missouri state militia. The services of Pilcher and forty of his traders were also accepted. Pilcher was given the nominal rank of major and "was assigned to the command of the Indians."[55]

Table 2. W. H. Ashley's officer nominations

Jedediah Smith	for	Captain
Hiram Scott	"	Captain
Hiram Allen	"	Lieut.
George C. Jackson	"	Lieut.
Charles Cunningham	"	Ensign
Edward Rose	"	Ensign
Fleming	"	Surgeon
T. Fitzpatrick	"	Quarter Master
William Sublett	"	Sergeant major

Source: Cited in Morgan, *West of William H. Ashley*, 52.

Putting Pilcher in command of the Sioux was another mistake. Their number continued to increase, and by August 7 the army was accompanied by "an Indian force of 750 men," most of them mounted and about a third of them armed with guns. Leavenworth soon had "much reason to be displeased" with the interpreter employed by Pilcher: "He no doubt did all in his power to increase the influence and importance of that [Missouri Fur] Company, not only at the expense of other traders but also at that of our expedition."[56]

On August 8 they camped about fifteen miles from the Arikara towns, moving forward again the next morning. "During the day we continually received the most strange and contradictory accounts from our Indians," recalled Leavenworth. "It appeared that there were several Sioux living with the Aricaras and who had intermarried with them. They were sent for, to come out and see their friends who were coming as the Sioux said to smoke and make peace with the Aricaras. Some said the Aricara villages were strongly fortified and furnished with ditches as deep as a man's chin when standing in them." Others thought the Arikaras believed the Sioux were coming to make peace and had taken down their fortifications. There were also rumors that many of the Sioux would join the Arikaras if the battle turned in their favor: "Nothing appeared certain but that the Arikaras were still in their villages. These contradictory stories . . . had the effect to create suspicions of [the] fidelity [of the Sioux]."[57]

After Leavenworth crossed the Grand River, six miles from the Arikara villages, he ordered a small band of Sioux to go ahead, prevent the Rees from escaping, and defend themselves if attacked. Not long afterward, wrote Clyman, a large force of Indians galloped ahead of the foot soldiers: "Being generally mounted they out went us although we ware put to the double Quick and when we arived the plain was covered with Indians which looked more like a swarm [of] bees than a battle field they going in all possible directions the Rees having mounted and met the Sioux a half mile from their pickets But as soon as we came in sight the Rees retreated into their village. . . . Quite a number of dead Indians streued over the plain."[58]

Leavenworth formed his line, sending Ashley and his mountain men to the right, several infantry companies to the center, and a company of riflemen to the left. They advanced to within three or four hundred yards of the villages but could not shoot because the Sioux were ahead of them. They therefore held their fire, waiting for the artillery to arrive on the river, but the boats were held up by strong winds. "It was said that the Sioux had killed ten of the Aricaras," wrote Leavenworth. "We saw three or four with their heads—arms—hands—feet and legs cut off. Several Sioux were dragging about in great triumph the hands, feet, legs, or arms of the slain Aricaras by means of a long string or cord."[59]

The artillery boats arrived just before sundown, too late to attack because "it would have the effect to drive the Indians away under cover of night. Arrangements were made to commence the attack on the morning of [August 10]."[60] Like the soldiers, Jedediah Smith and the other Ashley men had not eaten since morning. As they tried to settle in for the night, they must have reflected on the sleepless night nine weeks earlier when they waited in the gale for the inevitable attack. In a dramatic swap of roles, they were now in a position of strength, backed up by two hundred soldiers and three times as many Sioux, but sleep was once again out of the question. Clyman described the nightmarish scene: "We had a lively picture of pandimonium the wa[i]ling of squaws and children the Screams and yelling of men the firering of guns the awful howling of dogs the neighing and braying of hosses and mules with the hooting of owls of which thy [were] a number all intermingled with the stench of dead men and horses made the place the most disagreeable that immagginnation could fix Short of the bottomless pit."[61]

When dawn finally came, Leavenworth focused on the lower town, which had led the June 2 assault. "The troops having obtained their respective stations, the attack was commenced by Lt. Morris with his Artillery," wrote Leavenworth. "His first shot killed their celebrated and mischievous Chief called Grey Eyes and the second cut away the staff of their Medicine flag."[62] Grey Eyes's death demoralized his people, but they did not give up. "While the warriors looked about for leadership, the bombardment continued," notes van de Logt. "The grapeshot-filled bombs caused much destruction. Some Arikara warriors earned war honors by running up to the shells to defuse them before they could explode. . . . The warriors took up positions at various locations to prevent a direct assault on the palisade. The women, meanwhile, gathered food and supplies from caches in event of a retreat."[63]

Leavenworth next turned his attention to the upper village, but the artillery squad was "so near the town or village and so much elevated above it, that many of [the cannon] shots passed entirely over and lodged in the river." Even after the men adjusted the six-pounder's sights, however, the bombardment was ineffective. Not impressed, the Sioux meandered off to the Arikaras' fields to feast on ripening corn, pumpkins, and squash. When it became evident that the artillery would not drive the Arikaras from their villages, Leavenworth made "a more close examination of their defences." One of Pilcher's traders, Angus McDonald, who had considerable experience with the Arikaras, advised that "the defences were so strong and those Indians so confident in their own strength, that in case we made a charge or assault upon the villages 'Even every Squaw would count her coup,' by which I supposed he means that every Squaw would kill a man." Leavenworth considered his options, deciding on "making an assault upon an acute angle of the upper town, which I could approach within 100 steps under cover of a hill." He told Ashley to prepare to advance and ordered another company to bring axes to cut down the pickets. "But when all other things were ready I was mortified exceedingly to learn from Mr. Pilcher that no assistance could be obtained from the Sioux in consequence of their being so deeply engaged in gathering corn," Leavenworth wrote. Not only that, but he was worried that some of the Sioux, seeing his troops now outnumbered, would join the Arikaras. He therefore "gave up the idea of making a charge."[64]

One of Leavenworth's junior officers, Captain Bennet Riley, was not happy with the change in plans, with Clyman reporting he "became allmost furious and swore that he demande the priviledge stating that they had been laying at garison at Council Bluffs for 8 or 10 years doeing nothing but eating pumpkins and now a small chance for promotion occurred and it was denied him and might not occurr again for the next 10 yeares."[65]

Colonel Leavenworth had other things on his mind—provisions were short, so he gave permission for the senior officers to march their men as soon as possible to the Arikaras' fields and provide themselves with "refreshment," as the Sioux had done. Along with making sure the men were fed, Leavenworth wanted to keep the Arikaras from escaping so he could take control of their villages the next day. He was conversing with Ashley when he "heard and saw a Sioux and an Aricara holding a conversation on the plain in front of the villages." He sent for Pilcher, told him about the parley, and asked him "to go and see to it." Pilcher moved off in that direction with his interpreter. "On casting my eye upon the hills in our rear," said Leavenworth, "I discovered that they were covered with the retreating Sioux and soon had reason to know they were all going off. I immediately mounted my horse and went after Mr. Pilcher to be present at the parley with the Sioux and Aricara." After some preliminary negotiation, the Arikara stepped forward. Leavenworth told the interpreter to ask what he wanted: "I was told that . . . the Aricaras wished us to have pity upon their women and children and not to fire upon them any more. That we had killed the man who had done all the mischief and who had caused both us and themselves so much trouble. He wished we would permit the Chiefs to come out and speak to us and make peace, it was the wish of the whole nation for we had killed a great many of their people and of their horses."[66]

This was just what Leavenworth had hoped for—the chance to deal with the situation "as peaceably as the nature of the circumstances" would allow. He was also beginning to understand that the Arikaras had several chiefs who were not united in the decision to attack Ashley's men. As for the disappearance of the Sioux, their absence could well improve the odds of a peace treaty. The same was true for Grey Eyes's death. Through Pilcher's interpreter, Leavenworth told the Arikara to inform the chiefs that "if they were sincerely disposed for peace," he expected them to come out immediately and discuss the terms of peace. He, Pilcher, and the interpreter then returned to a keelboat anchored in the Missouri. They had not waited long when ten or twelve Arikaras cautiously approached the boats: "I invited the Senior Officer of my command . . . and Mr. Pilcher to go with me and meet them. We did so. They appeared very much terrified."[67]

These chiefs repeated what the other Arikaras had said and added, "Do with us as you please, but do not fire any more guns at us. We are all in tears." Leavenworth told them they had to make up for the losses of General Ashley, behave in the future, and turn over five of their principal men as security or hostages. Leavenworth warned the chiefs that they had "seen but a small specimen" of the power of the United States, and if they behaved badly, "they might expect to be more severely punished than they ever yet had been."[68]

The chiefs agreed to the terms. Considering his small force, "the strange and unaccountable conduct of the Sioux" and the probability of their joining with the Arikaras, the importance of saving the United States "the expense and trouble of a long Indian war, and the importance of securing the Indian trade," Leavenworth thought it prudent to accept the terms. The peace pipe was therefore brought forth—"it passed round very well, untill it came to Mr. Pilcher, he refused to smoke. He also refused to shake hands with the Indians, but got up and walked back and forth with much agitation." Not surprisingly, Pilcher's response had "a very unfavorable effect upon the Indians, especially as his Interpreter (one Collin Campbell) had told the Indians, that Mr. Pilcher was the principal, or first chief of our Expedition."[69]

Had Pilcher been a genuine rather than nominal major, he would have been a prime candidate for a court-martial. Not given that option, Leavenworth did his best to keep the calm—something that soon looked impossible. As the group, which now included Leavenworth and his staff, the Arikara hostages and chiefs, and Pilcher and Campbell, walked toward the boats, Campbell continued with his threats, "continually [keeping] his thumb on the cock of his rifle." Then they passed "the body of one of the Aricaras who had been killed by the Sioux and most shockingly mangled and stuck full of arrows." Fearing they were about to be killed, the chiefs refused to move. "I endeavored to convince them, that they should not be hurt, if they would go with us, but all was in vain," wrote Leavenworth. Then the whites fired at least three shots, "all fired in very quick succession, and [just] as quickly returned by the Indians." Incredibly, no one was hurt. "The Indians returned to their villages and we to our camp," Leavenworth recounted.[70]

The next day, August 11, Little Soldier, now considered the "first chief" of the Arikaras, came out to talk to Leavenworth, asking why the whites had fired on them so soon after smoking the peace pipe. "I told him that it had been done contrary to my orders," said Leavenworth. Little Soldier asked if the "other chief," meaning Pilcher, would make peace. Leavenworth said Pilcher would do so because the colonel was the authority, and Pilcher had vowed to obey him. Little Soldier said he would try to get the other chiefs to come out and smoke the pipe. He also asked Leavenworth if he and some of his men could come into the villages to ease the people's fears.[71]

Responding to that request, the colonel turned to one of the Ashley men destined for renown. "Previous to this, I had not found any one willing to go into the villages except a man by the name of Rose, who held the nominal rank of Ensign in Genl. Ashley's volunteers," wrote Leavenworth. "He appeared to be a brave and enterprising man and was well acquainted with those Indians. He had resided for about three years with them. Understood their language and they were much attached with them. . . . He was perfectly willing to go into their villages and did go in, several times. He fully confirmed everything the Indians told us. He said they had been severely whipped and were the most humble beings on earth, but they were so much afraid of us, that they dare not come into our camp."[72]

Following Rose's lead, two of Leavenworth's men also visited the village and confirmed what Little Soldier and Edward Rose had said, adding, "On parting with him, he shook us by the hand and said, he had understood that we were hungry and requested us to send some of our small boats opposite the village and he would have them loaded with such articles as we required, for our subsistence." Later that afternoon, Leavenworth drafted a peace treaty, which "every Chief or principal man of both villages . . . except one who had always been considered as the first soldier of the late Chief Grey Eyes" signed in the presence of Leavenworth and his officers. The substance of the treaty was that the Arikaras would make restitution to Ashley for his lost property, no longer obstruct the navigation of the Missouri, and "treat the Americans as friends wherever they might meet them."[73]

With the treaty signed, the Arikaras came out and buried their dead, freely interacted with Leavenworth's men, and supplied them "with plenty of corn and other vegetables." The soldiers asked if they could "make them some compensation . . . [and] they replied that if [Leavenworth's men] were pleased to give their women any trifles," they might do so.[74]

The situation thus looked quite favorable on the night of August 11, despite the stench of unburied bodies: "In the morning, it became necessary to see that our new friends fulfilled their stipulations as to Genl. Ashley, and they were called upon to do so. They delivered to the Genl. three rifles, one horse and sixteen buffalo robes and said it was all they could do for him. They were told that it was not enough, and that they must go back to their villages and tell their people to come forward and renumerate Genl. Ashley or that we should again attack them."[75]

The chiefs said they would do so and returned to the villages accompanied by Rose, who soon reported that Little Soldier and the other chiefs "expressed much mortification" over Pilcher and his traders' unwillingness to shake hands with any of the chiefs and their appearing "to think that they were not bound by [the treaty]." The Sioux had taken many of the Arikaras' horses, and the bombings had killed most of the others. They did not want to give their remaining horses to Ashley for fear that they would need them to escape an attack: "Mr. Rose informed me that their women were packing up evidently for the purpose of going off. He said they had again become exceedingly alarmed. The least unusual noise in our camp . . . terrified them greatly." Not long after that, Little Soldier himself came to Leavenworth's boat, saying it was impossible to do anything more for Ashley. The people of the upper village felt it was unfair for them to "pay for the mischief which the Chief Grey Eyes of the lower village had done, and that . . . it was very difficult for him to prevent them from running away from the villages." Little Soldier also said he had always been a friend of the Americans, that he had warned Ashley of the attack—as Ashley himself and one of his boatmen both reported without identifying the chief—and that he had nevertheless lost a son in the fight with Ashley's men.[76]

Leavenworth summed up the conundrum: "On me lay the responsibility of decision." He pondered both the practical and ethical implications of his decision. Pilcher and all his traders had "thrown their whole weight against the treaty," and Leavenworth's men were also "anxious to charge upon the towns." His reputation and the honor of the expedition seemed to require an attack, but he also thought that "sound policy and the interest of my Country required that I should not." His force was small, and ammunition and provisions were running low. Even if an assault succeeded, it would do little more than kill a few more Indians and drive the rest to be "left in the Country in a confirmed state of hostility to every white man." For his part, Leavenworth was confident that the Arikaras had been sufficiently humbled: "I also felt satisfied that the blood of our Countrymen had been avenged and I also felt an unwillingness to re-commence hostilities on account of the articles of property. It was the principle."[77]

Little Soldier asked if an attack could be postponed until the next morning so he could bring out his family. Leavenworth asked the opinions of Major Abram R. Wooley, General Ashley, and Pilcher.[78] Wooley wanted to attack immediately, but Ashley and Pilcher favored a postponement. Leavenworth agreed and directed the troops to be dismissed. Then he asked Little Soldier to make one more effort to save his people. More important than property was their assurance that they would behave well in the future. Little Soldier and Rose then went back to the village. Not long afterward, the two returned with a few more buffalo robes, saying "they had taken these off their backs" and could do no more. They begged for pity: "Mr. Rose now informed me that the Indians were in great distress and alarm and that there was no doubt that they would leave their villages in the course of the night. I told him to go immediately to the village and tell the Little Soldier that we had concluded to be satisfied, and that we were so. We would not attack them."[79]

Rose carried this message to the Arikaras. However, wrote Leavenworth, "early on the morning of the 13th we discovered that the Indians had abandoned their villages and gone off during the night."[80] All the Arikaras had left behind was a few dozen dogs, a rooster, and a lone human: "We placed the mother of the late chief, Grey Eyes, (an aged and infirm woman, whom they left in their flight) in one of the principal lodges of the lower village, gave her plenty of provisions and water, and left her in the quiet possession of the towns."[81] Leavenworth did not say how the Arikaras were able to flee the villages without being noticed by soldiers or traders despite Rose's unambiguous warning: "Arikara oral tradition states that while the town was surrounded by the troops, a mysterious dog appeared to help the people. In a remarkable parallel to the Arikara creation account, the dog showed the Arikaras how to change themselves into animals and directed them to go through a hole in the ground to elude the troops."[82]

There is little doubt that Pilcher and Campbell's hostility had convinced the Arikaras they would be attacked even though Leavenworth promised otherwise. Desperate to resolve the situation, Leavenworth asked Andrew Henry, previously named an Indian subagent, to send men to find the Arikaras. Henry tasked Toussaint Charbonneau, interpreter for Lewis and Clark and so-called husband of Sacagawea, to lead the group and give the Arikaras this message:

> Ricaras
>
> You see the pipe of peace which you gave to me in the hands of Mr. [Toussaint] Charbonnau and the flag of the United States. These will convince you that my heart is not bad—your Villages are in my possession. Come back and take them in peace and you will find evry thing as you left them, you shall not be hurt if you do not obstruct the road or molest the Traders—If you do not come back there are some bad men and bad Indians who will burn your Villages. Come back and come quickly. Be assured that what I say is the truth.[83]

Charbonneau returned with no luck and no chance to deliver Leavenworth's heartfelt note. The next day there was still no sign of the Arikaras. Leavenworth had no choice but to pack up and leave. Around 10 p.m. he and his staff finally boarded a keelboat headed for Fort Atkinson. "Before we were out of sight of the towns, we had the mortification to discover them to be on fire," he remembered. "There is no doubt but that they have been consumed to ashes, nor is there any doubt but that they were set on fire by one [Angus] M'Donald, a partner, and one [William] Gordon, a clerk of the Missouri Fur Company." Leavenworth's prophecy that the villages would be burned had been fulfilled in short order. If that had not happened, Leavenworth argued, "there is no room to doubt, but that the Ricara Indians would, in future, have behaved as well towards our countrymen as any other Indians on the river. It is now my deliberate opinion, that those Indians will be excited to further hostilities."[84]

Leavenworth and Pilcher carried on a bitter correspondence over the next several months, with several of their missives published in newspapers. "You came to restore peace and tranquility to the country, & leave an impression which would insure its continuance," Pilcher wrote to the colonel. "Your operations have been such as to produce the contrary effect, and to impress the Indian tribes, with the greatest possible contempt for the American character. You came (to use your own language) to 'open and make good this great road of the upper Missouri River'; instead of which you have, by the imbecility of your conduct and operations, created and left impassable barriers."[85] O'Fallon similarly criticized Leavenworth, although Ashley remained silent. While tempering their comments somewhat, historians such as Hiram M. Chittenden, Dale Morgan, and LeRoy R. Hafen have also criticized Leavenworth for his failure to act decisively. While it's true that Leavenworth frequently changed his mind, it should also be pointed out that he often did so based on new information and that he recognized the multitude of both moral and practical problems of punishing the entire Arikara nation. His final decision—not to attack the defeated and meek Arikaras—did not please Pilcher and Campbell, who wanted genocide, but it was ethically sound. Despite anything else, it is to Leavenworth's lasting credit that his "expedition to the Arikaras" has never been included in the list of massacres identified by such names as Bad Axe, Horseshoe Bend, and Wounded Knee.

"The Beginning and the End of the World for Missouri River Peoples"

With the "Arikara campaign" ended, Ashley, Henry, and their men—honorably discharged from the U.S. Army (not true of Pilcher and his traders)—dropped down the Missouri to Fort Kiowa, also called Fort Lookout, near present Chamberlain, South Dakota, where the company's goods were stored. Still smarting from the Arikara attack that killed fifteen and wounded nine—one of the worst calamities in the history of the fur trade—the partners counted their financial losses: $2,265 from the June disaster, $420 from horses stolen by the Sioux, and $1,540 from the assault on Henry's men on the upper Missouri. Though offering little in the way consolation, the other firms also faced hard times: the Missouri Fur Company had abandoned its Mandan trading post, and the Immell-Jones massacre had driven it from the Yellowstone; the French Fur Company looked unlikely to go beyond Fort Kiowa; and the Columbia Fur Company had reached the Mandans from the Mississippi, but the post was garrisoned by only seven men. Whatever it was worth, Ashley and Henry essentially had the upper Missouri trade to themselves, and they were determined to carry on.[86]

The hunters who survived the carnage that June morning had also made it through the Arikara War, and they would play prominent roles in the history of the West, ushering in what one historian calls the "era of discovery . . . personified by the work of Ashley men . . . [who] discovered or rediscovered, among other sites, the South Pass, the Great Salt Lake, and overland routes to California and Oregon."[87] Indeed, the band stranded on that sandbar was arguably the most notable collection of mountaineers ever involved in a single chapter of the fur trade:

Edward Rose (ca. 1780–?): son of a white father and Black Cherokee mother; explorer, hunter, scout, guide, and interpreter fluent in both the Crow and Arikara tongues; the only person who journeyed with Lisa to the Bighorn River in 1807, Henry to Three Forks in 1810, and the westbound Astorians in 1811.

Jedediah Smith (1799–1831): explorer extraordinaire; the first to reach California from the east, first to trek from San Diego to the Columbia

River; devout shunner of the carnal life but also a sometimes duplicitous negotiator; rediscoverer of South Pass, the gateway for a quarter-million nomads headed to Oregon, Utah, or California.

Thomas Fitzpatrick (1799–1854): Irish immigrant; coleader with Smith of the brigade that crossed South Pass in 1824; guided the first two wagon caravans to reach Oregon; valuable scout for General Kearny both before and during the Mexican War; prominent Indian agent who played a key role in negotiating the Fort Laramie Treaty of 1851.

James Clyman (1792–1881): soldier, trapper, trailblazer, pioneer, farmer, and diarist; met Washington as a boy; served with Lincoln in the Black Hawk War; life spanned the era of western expansion; author of a homespun reminiscence revealing a delightful personality and an astute sense of history.[88]

Hugh Glass (1783–1833): Pawnee Indian adoptee and alleged pirate who was wounded by the Arikaras but still wrote a poignant letter informing an elderly couple of their son's death; a western icon due to his incredible survival after a grizzly bear mauling—depicted in the movies *Man in the Wilderness* and *The Revenant*.[89]

William Lewis Sublette (1799–1845): fur trader, pathfinder, entrepreneur, banker, investor, and politician; revolutionized western immigration by taking the first mule-drawn wagons across South Pass and along the Santa Fe Trail; survived several near brushes with death to become one of the most successful fur merchants.[90]

David E. Jackson (1788–1837): married with children when he enlisted with Ashley; partnered with Smith and Sublette in a fur-trading concern; uncle of Stonewall Jackson; died of typhoid fever at age forty-nine; memorialized by Jackson Lake and Jackson Hole.

Hiram Scott (1805–28): voyaged up the Missouri in 1822 with Smith and a host of others; like Smith, became one of Ashley's most trusted lieutenants; "showed much promise as fur trader and leader of men, but was cut off in the prime of life by an unidentified illness or accident which led to his tragic death on the Platte River Road."[91]

Thomas Eddie (1799–1891): ran away from his Scotland home at sixteen and made his way to the United States; risked his life during the Arikara attack to save Clyman from drowning; recovered from a thigh wound inflicted by Blackfeet Indians after Sublette cut the bullet out with his knife; the last known survivor of "Ashley's hundred."

Although relegated to footnote status by some, the "Arikara War" was a powerful portent of things to come, a watershed encounter highlighting perennial misunderstandings between Indians and European Americans. Ashley's trappers could not fathom an Arikara culture that reverenced Mother Corn. Intertribal commerce and warfare were also key parts of the story, as well as the "pox" transmitted by interlopers. Moreover, the conflict ushered in the fur-trade rendezvous era and opened the way for a flood of missionaries, homesteaders, and gold seekers storming westward—over Indian lands—in the 1830s, '40s, and '50s. As one historian has written, "Contact established by Lewis and Clark was both the beginning and the end of the world for upper Missouri River peoples."[92]

5

"Captain Smith Had Crossed the Mountains"

The Discovery and Rediscovery of South Pass

"On July 18, 1811," wrote Wilson Price Hunt, "Messrs. Hunt, Mackenzie, Crooks, Miller, McClellan and Reed, who were accompanied by fifty-six men, one woman and two children, and had gone by water from Saint Louis to the Aricaras' village on the Missouri, left there with eighty-two horses laden with merchandise, equipment, food and animal traps. All traveled on foot except the company's partners and the woman or squaw."[1]

Hunt, Donald Mackenzie, Ramsay Crooks, Joseph Miller, Robert McClellan, and John Reed were all known as Astorians, after their employer, John Jacob Astor. The woman was Marie Dorion, an Iowa Indian probably about twenty years old, the wife of Pierre Dorion Jr., hired by Hunt as an interpreter, hunter, and scout. The children were Marie and Pierre's sons, about four and two years old. Hunt's group, like Lewis and Clark's, thus included one family. As for Hunt's destination, although dozens of exploring and trading expeditions had ventured west since Lewis and Clark's departure in 1804, none had gone beyond the Rocky Mountains. Hunt's band intended to make their own "passage to India" by crossing to the Pacific, building a trading post there, and carrying on fur trade with both China and London. In addition, as Hunt noted, these Overland Astorians went west from the Arikara towns, blazing a new trail to the Columbia River. Although not listed in Hunt's introduction, his group included another person of particular note: Edward Rose.

"Two Expeditions Devised by Mr. Astor, One by Sea, the Other by Land"

Astor, the same man Jefferson mentioned in his July 1808 letter to Lewis, immigrated to the United States in 1784 at age twenty-one, quickly getting involved in the fur trade and soon on his way to becoming the wealthiest man in America. As Jefferson said, he was the founder of powerful companies empowered to carry on Indian commerce on a large scale—the American Fur Company in 1808 and the Pacific Fur Company in 1810. For the latter firm, Astor furnished an advance of $400,000 and agreed to bear all losses for the first five years. He received fifty shares in the company, with the other fifty distributed among his partners, most of whom signed contracts with Astor in New York on June 23, 1810.[2]

Hunt, Mackenzie, and Crooks received five shares each; Miller and McClellan two and a half shares each. Hunt, the lone American partner to receive five shares, arrived in St. Louis in 1804 and entered the retail business with John Hankinson. As a "chief agent" for Astor, he took command of the Overland Astorians. Miller, born in Pennsylvania, served in the U.S. Army from 1799 to 1805, becoming acquainted with Crooks and McClellan by 1809. John Reed, quite likely the same man who met Lewis and Clark with Crooks on September 20, 1806, was the clerk who went overland with Hunt and kept a detailed financial record of the journey, which included an inventory of the crew's purchases from the company store—everything from buffalo robes to knives, blankets, blades, leggings, and hooks and fishing line, but the most common article bought, by far, was tobacco, with tobacco pipes, two bits each, taking second place.[3]

Crooks's and McClellan's efforts to trade on the upper Missouri had been continually thwarted—in 1807 by Nathaniel Pryor's defeat by the Arikaras and in 1808 by stiff competition from Manuel Lisa and the Robidoux family and the 1807 U.S. Embargo Act, which closed off exports to Canada and severely restricted imports. On February 17, 1809, the two officially announced that their partnership "is this day disolved by mutal consent."[4] Still, in the summer of 1809, Crooks, McClellan, and Miller went up the river—contrary to Lewis's edict that the Missouri Company men escorting Sheheke had a trade monopoly on the upper Missouri—only to be blocked by the Lakotas, who nearly attacked them. That same year, however, when their prospects could not have looked bleaker, Crooks got word, apparently from Hunt, of the "electrifying news" that he, McClellan, and Miller had been invited to join Astor's new company. Not only did this development resurrect Crooks's and McClellan's trading hopes; it offered an incredible opportunity for them to compete with or even surpass their chief rival—Lisa.[5]

Anyone concluding that the successful efforts of Alexander Mackenzie and later Lewis and Clark to cross to the Pacific made sailing around the tip of South America obsolete was in for a surprise, for Astor was an entrepreneur of vast imagination. While Hunt and Donald Mackenzie were recruiting men and buying supplies for their cross-country trek, Astor was paying $37,860 for *Tonquin*, "a ship of 300 tons mounting twelve guns and mustering a crew of twenty-one men." As Washington Irving—who conducted extensive interviews with Astor and several of his men and drew on a wealth of original documents in writing *Astoria*—said, "In prosecuting his great scheme of commerce and colonization, two expeditions were devised by Mr. Astor, one by sea, the other by land. The former was to carry out the people, stores, ammunition, and merchandise, requisite for establishing a fortified trading post at the mouth of the Columbia River. The latter, conducted by Mr. Hunt, was to proceed up the Missouri, and across the Rocky Mountains, to the same point; exploring a line of communication across the continent, and noting the places where interior trading posts might be established."[6]

On September 6, 1810, the crew, the four partners (Duncan McDougall, Alexander McKay, and David and Robert Stuart), eleven clerks, thirteen boatmen, and five mechanics boarded *Tonquin*. "It set sail," remembered one passenger, "and a fresh breeze springing up, soon wafted her to a distance from the busy shores of New York."[7] The captain, Jonathan Thorn, would enter Cape Horn by following the passage taken around 1579 by Sir Francis Drake, the first captain of a ship to circumnavigate the globe. (Whether Thorn had a map depicting the Strait of Magellan or even knew about it is not clear.[8]) Thorn then planned to sail over a huge stretch of the Pacific Ocean to the Sandwich Islands, pick up men and goods, and end the journey at the mouth of the Columbia River, which he did. While Irving praised Thorn as a brave, honorable man well qualified for the mission, historian Edgeley W. Todd, editor of the 1964 edition of Irving's *Astoria*, argues the opposite: "The evidence shows that Thorn was a martinet of the worst sort, ill disposed to accommodate himself to the civilians on his ship, and heedless to the point of sadism concerning the safety of the men, eight of whom lost their lives because of his despotic sense of duty at the mouth of the Columbia. The loss of his entire crew resulted later from his lack of judgment in handling Indians and his refusal to heed the advice of his officers."[9]

Six days after *Tonquin* departed New York, William Clark wrote a letter to Secretary of War William Eustis stating that "Mr Hunt & McKinzey are in this place [St. Louis], prepareing to proceed up the Missouri and prosue my trail to the Columbia. I am not fully in possession of the objects of this expedition but prosume you are, would be very glad to be informed."[10] Although he did not know the details of Hunt's project, Clark was correct that the Overland Astorians planned to follow his and Lewis's path. In a letter to Albert Gallatin written in May 1810, Astor said he had "made arrangements to send a party of good men up the Missurie for the purpose of exploring the country . . . to ascertain whether it afords furrs suficient to carry on an extensive trade," adding that the group planned "to cross the Rockey mountains to columbia's river where it is hoped they will meet" the men who sailed on *Tonquin*.[11] Neither Clark nor Hunt left any record of the two discussing a route to the Pacific, but Hunt noted in his record of the westbound journey that he did have a copy of Clark's 1810 map of the West.[12] By the end of July, however, Hunt had second thoughts about following the Missouri all the way to its source at Three Forks because Pierre Menard, recently returned from that location, reported that early in May, George Drouillard and two companions had been "attacked by a party [of Blackfeet Indians] in ambush . . . [and] literally cut to pieces."[13]

"All Agreed Lewis and Clark's Route Was Far from Being the Best"

In August 1809 a Scottish English botanist by the name of John Bradbury visited Thomas Jefferson, a private citizen since James Madison took office as president in March, at Monticello and spent ten days there. The Renaissance-man Jefferson was curious about everything under the sun, of course, but botany was high on his list, and he and Bradbury spent many hours talking and touring Jefferson's unparalleled gardens. Knowing that Bradbury would soon leave for St. Louis, intending to make it his primary residence while he explored upper Louisiana and the Illinois Territory "for the purpose of discovering and collecting subjects in natural history, either new or valuable," Jefferson asked him to deliver a letter to Governor Lewis, who, as evidenced by frequent descriptions of plants in his expedition journals, had a passion for botany himself. Jefferson had no doubt that Lewis would also have fascinating talks with Bradbury, whom he called "a botanist of the first order" and "a man of entire worth & correct conduct."[14]

By the time Bradbury arrived in St. Louis in December, however, he learned that Lewis had died in Tennessee in October. Lewis thus never read Jefferson's last letter to him, which included these affectionate lines: "Your friends here are well, & have been long in expectation of seeing you. I shall hope in that case to possess a due portion of you at Monticello."[15] Bradbury carried on with his plans, making frequent solo excursions to the wilderness and usually staying within eighty or a hundred miles of St. Louis.[16] When he visited William Clark in 1810, he was surprised that his host was "more intelligent in Natural History than from his few opportunities of intercourse might be expected."[17]

Late that same year, Bradbury heard that a group of men had arrived from Canada and that they intended "to ascend the Missouri, on their way to the Pacific Ocean, by the same route that Lewis and Clarke had followed, by descending the Columbia River." Bradbury soon became acquainted with the "principals of this party, in whom the manners and accomplishment of gentlemen were united with the hardihood and capability of suffering, necessary to the backwoodsman." When Wilson Price Hunt learned of Bradbury's botanical quest, he, "in a very friendly and pressing manner," invited the latter to accompany the group up the "River Missouri, as far as might be agreeable" to him. Bradbury gladly accepted the invitation, "to which an acquaintance with Messrs. Ramsey Crooks and Donald M'Kenzie . . . was no small inducement."[18] Bradbury, also a writer with an engaging, informative style, kept a daily diary of the journey—the perfect supplement to John Reed's financial record.

On March 14, 1811, Bradbury was onboard as Hunt's "boat with ten oars" departed St. Charles, "the Canadians measuring the strokes of their oars by songs, which were generally responsive betwixt the oarsmen at the bow and those at the stern." Three days into the voyage, they stopped at a French village called La Charette (also called St. Johns). "Mr. Hunt pointed out to me an old man standing on the bank," wrote Bradbury, "who, he informed me, was Daniel Boone, the discoverer of Kentucky. . . . I went ashore to speak to him, and . . . remained for some time in conversation with him. He informed me, that he was eighty-four years of age; that he had spent a considerable portion of his time alone in the back woods, and had lately returned from his spring hunt, with nearly sixty beaver skins."[19]

As incredible as it seems, the next day, March 18, Bradbury had a conversation with another iconic American frontiersman: John Colter. This was actually their second meeting—in May 1810, when Colter returned from his six-year sojourn in the wilderness, Bradbury interviewed him, recording the first detailed account of Colter's Run, a dramatic escape from Blackfeet Indians. This time Colter stayed with Hunt's party for "some miles," quite possibly giving them the details of the Blackfeet attacks at Three Forks and discouraging them from following Lewis and Clark's original trail. Bradbury wrote that Colter "seemed to have a great inclination to accompany the expedition; but having been lately married, he reluctantly took leave of us."[20]

Hunt's party reached Fort Osage on April 8. "We were saluted with a volley as we passed to the landing place," wrote Bradbury. The first person he met at the fort was Crooks, who had come down the river with a keelboat and crew from the mouth of the Nodaway River, his and McClellan's old home, where many of the Canadians recruited by Crooks and Mackenzie had spent the winter with McClellan. Bradbury and Crooks immediately struck up a friendship, likely reminiscing about friends or relatives in Scotland. The group spent three days at the fort and then reached the wintering site on April 17. "We again embarked in four boats," noted Bradbury. "Our party amounted to nearly sixty persons: forty were Canadian boatmen, such as are employed by the North West Company, and are termed in Canada *Engagés* or Voyageurs. Our boats were all furnished with masts and sails"—one of which featured two swivel howitzers—"and as the wind blew pretty strong from the southeast, we availed ourselves of it during the greater part of the day."[21]

On May 24, while Hunt was camped near a Ponca Indian village, two Missouri Fur Company men arrived on foot with a letter from Manuel Lisa, who was on his way up the Missouri to trade with Indians and also to investigate the whereabouts of Missouri Fur Company partner Andrew Henry, who had crossed the Rockies after being attacked at Three Forks and had not been heard from since. "It appeared that [Lisa] had been apprised of the hostile intentions of the Sioux," wrote Bradbury, "and the purport of the letter was to prevail on Mr. Hunt to wait for him, that they might, for mutual safety, travel together on that part of the river which those blood thirsty savages frequent."[22] The irony was rich—in 1807 Pryor had asked Lisa to wait for him so the combined party could show strength and discourage an Arikara attack. Instead, Lisa hurried, making sure he stayed ahead of Pryor—and, according to the Mandan woman, put Pryor in peril by announcing the latter would soon reach the Arikara villages with Sheheke in tow. Not only that, but Crooks and McClellan were also convinced that in 1809, as Sheheke was finally being returned to his home, Lisa encouraged the Sioux to stop Crooks and McClellan from going farther. Now the proud Lisa, who left St. Louis three weeks after Hunt, was begging his competitors to wait for him for "mutual safety," of all things.

By a strange coincidence, Lisa also had a guest aboard, a neutral observer who was the only person keeping a record of the voyage. In Lisa's case it was a writer and lawyer by the name of Henry Marie Brackenridge, only twenty-five years old and thus eighteen years younger than Bradbury. The two well-educated men already knew each other and got along well. Like his counterpart, Brackenridge was meeting individuals who would make it into the history books. Early in his chronicle, for example, he noted that Sacagawea was aboard Lisa's keelboat, as well as her husband, Charbonneau, once again working as an interpreter.[23]

Before seeing the letter from Lisa, Bradbury gave no indication that Hunt was even aware of Lisa's plans, but it was a different story with Brackenridge, who noted that Lisa constantly asked both traders and Indians if and when they had seen Hunt's group, carefully keeping track of how many days he was behind. He kept his men rowing furiously. "Lisa himself seized the helm," wrote Brackenridge, "and gave the song, and at the close of every stanza, made the woods ring with his shouts of encouragement. The whole was intermixed, with short and pithy addresses to their fears, their hopes, or their ambition." By April 26 Lisa had gained three or four days on Hunt. Brackenridge was well aware, however, that "there existed a reciprocal jealousy and distrust" between Lisa and Hunt and that the latter "might suppose, that if Lisa overtook him, he would use his superior skill in the navigation of the river, to pass by him, and (from the supposition that Hunt was about to compete with him in the Indian trade) induce the Sioux tribes, through whose territory we had to pass . . . to stop him, and perhaps pillage him." Able to see both sides, Brackenridge also recognized that Lisa had strong reasons to believe Hunt, encouraged by Crooks and McClellan, would thwart Lisa's attempts to ascend the Missouri.[24]

Pushing the men to the limit, Lisa gained several more days by May 4. Sitting by the fire that night, however, Brackenridge overheard some of the boatmen expressing their resentment, saying it was impossible for them "to persevere any longer in this unceasing toil, this over-strained exertion which wears us down. We are not permitted a moment's repose; scarcely is time allowed us to eat, or to smoke our pipes. We can stand it no longer, human nature cannot bear it; our bourgeois has no pity on us." Brackenridge gently suggested that they were approaching open country, where they would be carried by the wind, that Lisa wanted to get them through safely: "The admonitions had some effect, but were not sufficient to quell entirely the prevailing discontent."[25]

As for the two men who delivered Lisa's letter to Hunt and talked with him on May 24, they obtained a canoe from the Poncas and departed that same day. Although Bradbury learned of the contents of the letter, he apparently did not hear the private conversation between Hunt and the Missouri Fur Company messengers. So after describing the delivery of the letter, Bradbury next wrote, "It was judged expedient to trade with the [Ponca] Indians for some jerked buffalo meat, and more than 1000 lbs. was obtained for as much tobacco as cost two dollars. About noon we set out."[26] All this seemed innocent enough, but Brackenridge's narrative fills in the blanks.

"At daylight," he wrote on May 26, "discovered a canoe descending with two men, who prove to be those sent by us, to Hunt." Brackenridge had earlier identified one of these men as Charbonneau. "They bring us the pleasing information, that Hunt, in consequence of our request, has agreed to wait for us, at the Poncas village," Brackenridge recounted.[27] Not true. As verified by Bradbury, the minute Charbonneau and his companion left Hunt's camp, the latter traded for a thousand pounds of jerked meat, allowing his band to travel faster. In addition, he packed up and left the Ponca village in the middle of the day, when he typically would have stayed till the next day, if not longer. The race was on.

Lisa reached the Ponca village three days later, but Hunt was nowhere to be found. Then two deserters from Hunt's party, on their way back to St. Louis, stopped and told the group that Hunt had sent "a feigned answer [to Lisa] in order to conceal his real design, which was to make all possible haste to keep out of [Lisa's] reach"—a crucial detail not reported by Bradbury, of course. Lisa now drove his crew even harder. "Determining to strain every nerve, in order to overtake Hunt," wrote Brackenridge, "we resolved to run the risk of sailing after night. We continued underway until eleven o'clock," despite the risk of "running aground, and being detained several days." They rested for two hours, then boarded the boat again, sailing until the moon disappeared, when they stopped at an island and found evidence that Hunt had camped there "but a few days" earlier. They "continued under sail until eleven at night, having in little better than twenty-four hours, made seventy-five miles"—an unheard-of distance in going upstream on the Missouri.[28]

Meanwhile, on May 26, the same day Charbonneau told Lisa that Hunt would wait for him, Hunt's group saw two canoes coming downstream. "A gun was discharged," wrote Bradbury, "when they discovered us, and crossed over. We found them to be three men belonging to Kentucky." Their names were John Hoback, Jacob Reznor, and Edward Robinson: "They had been several years hunting on and beyond the Rocky Mountains, until they *imagined* they were tired of the hunting life; and having families and good plantations in Kentucky, were returning to them; but on seeing us, families, plantations, and all vanished; they agreed to join us, and turned their canoes adrift."[29] The Kentucky trio had gone up the Missouri with Lisa in

1807, meaning they were present when Rose joined the group at the mouth of the Osage River and Colter at the mouth of the Platte. They were still on the upper Missouri when Chouteau, Lisa, Henry, and the other Missouri Fur Company partners returned Sheheke to his home in 1809; they went with Henry to Three Forks, surviving the Blackfeet attack in the spring of 1810 that sent Drouillard to his eternal home and Colter to his earthly one. Next, as they explained to Hunt, they trekked beyond the Rockies with Henry, crossing the Continental Divide and building a rude fort on a tributary of the Snake River soon known as Henrys Fork, not far from present St. Anthony, Idaho. In the past several weeks, the three Kentuckians had somehow made it all the way back to the Missouri River.

Just a few days earlier, two other trappers—Ben Jones and Alexander Carson, also likely with Henry at Three Forks—had joined Hunt. "As we had now in our party five men who had traversed the Rocky Mountains in various directions," wrote Bradbury, "the best possible route in which to cross them became a subject of anxious enquiry. They all agreed that the route followed by Lewis and Clarke was very far from being the best, and that to the southward, where the head waters of the Platte and Roche Jaune [Yellowstone] rivers rise, they had discovered a route much less difficult." With this information in hand, Hunt and the other partners "now concluded that it would be more adviseable to abandon the Missouri at the Aricara Town."[30] Hoback, Reznor, and Robinson would be the primary pilots because they had successfully returned on their own from the Snake River country.[31]

On May 31, after two Indians on a bluff called out to the boat, Hunt took Dorion with him to talk to them. Dorion was known for his temper and his drinking, but he was a good man in a fix, especially with Sioux Indians because his mother was Yankton, and he was fluent in their language and well versed in their traditions. He and Hunt soon returned with bad news, however. Several hundred Sioux Indians—of both the Yankton and Lakota nations—had blocked the river because they were at war with the Arikaras, Mandans, and Hidatsas and would not allow trade goods, especially guns, to be delivered to their enemies. What a change from two years earlier, when the Mandans and Sioux had united to save the Arikaras. The Sioux were now "all armed and painted for war. Their arms consisted chiefly of bows and arrows, but a few had short carbines." Hunt weighed his options. He now had sixty men, all armed with rifles or trade guns, backed up by three cannons. There were so many Indians guarding the river that sneaking past them in the dark was out of the question. "Our alternative, therefore," wrote Bradbury, "was, as we supposed, either to fight them or return [to St. Louis]." A return to St. Louis, of course, would put Astor's entire mission in serious jeopardy: "The former was immediately decided on, and we landed nearly opposite to the main body." Hunt called his men to arms. Then he ordered the cannons loaded with powder only and fired to convince the Indians he was well prepared for battle: "The Indians now seemed to be in confusion, and when we rose up to fire, they spread their buffaloe robes before them, and moved them from side to side." At that sight, Dorion called out for no one to fire, "as the action indicated, on [the Indians'] part, a wish to avoid engagement and to come to a parley. Hunt instantly agreed and requested Mackenzie, Crooks, McClellan, and Miller—along with the indispensable Dorion—join him in smoking the calumet with the Sioux chiefs."[32]

When the ceremony ended, Hunt rose and spoke in French, Dorion's other native tongue. Dorion translated as Hunt assured the Sioux that the object of his voyage was not to trade, "that several of our brothers [the partners who sailed on *Tonquin*] had gone to the great salt lake in the west [Pacific Ocean], whom we had not seen for eleven moons; that we . . . [were] on our way to see our brothers . . . that we would rather die than not go to them." To show his goodwill, Hunt had fifteen "carrottes" of tobacco and another fifteen of corn brought from the boat and laid near the great chief, who accepted the gifts and even advised Hunt to camp on the opposite side of the river to avoid overzealous Indians.[33]

The Astorians were thus able to continue up the river but had not gone far when they saw "with horror" a war party of about three hundred Mandans, Hidatsas, and Arikaras, all painted with black and white stripes and carrying arms and shields. Luckily, Hunt's anxiety was changed to surprise as the Indians threw down their arms and plunged into the water to greet him and his men, deciding on the spot to accompany Hunt to the Arikara villages, where they expected to obtain guns and ammunition from him before attacking the Sioux. Hunt camped with the warriors and shared his food with them but put off their requests for arms, saying that would happen when he reached the Arikara towns. On June 3, however, an Arikara chief overtook Hunt's boat on horseback and said "his people were not satisfied to go home without some proof of their having seen the white men. Mr. Hunt could not now resist, and gave him a cask of powder, a bag of balls, and three dozen knives, with which [the chief] was much pleased."[34]

While this was happening, another Indian ran up and said there was a boat approaching on the river. Hunt concluded it must be Lisa; he was right. Neither Brackenridge nor Bradbury described the meeting between Hunt and Lisa, but several in Hunt's party believed Lisa, who had more oarsmen, would now try to reach the Arikaras first and turn them against Hunt. "Independent of this feeling," said Bradbury, "it had required all the address of Mr. Hunt to prevent Mr. M'Clellan or Mr. Crooks from calling [Lisa] to account for instigating the Sioux to treat them ill the preceding year."[35] Brackenridge agreed, writing that McClellan had vowed to shoot Lisa on sight if he fell in with him in Indian Country and that it was through Hunt that McClellan "was induced not to put his threat in execution."[36] There was also a long-running feud between Lisa and his erstwhile interpreter Dorion, with Brackenridge and Bradbury barely preventing a duel between the two—although Lisa had nothing but a knife and Dorion a pair of pistols.[37] For the next few days the two groups kept the peace simply by staying apart.

On June 12, however, two Arikara chiefs, accompanied by none other than Joseph Gravelines, visited the Astorians and Missouri Fur Company traders on Lisa's boat, with the Astorians still quite suspicious of Lisa. The chiefs sent a pipe around, and one of them said he was happy the Americans had come to his village. Then came a pleasant surprise:

> Lisa . . . observed that he was come to trade amongst [the Arikaras] and the Mandans, but that these persons, (pointing to Hunt and his comrades,) were going on a long journey to the great Salt lake, to the west, and he hoped would meet with favourable treatment; and that any injury offered them, he would consider as done to himself; that although distinct parties, yet as to the safety of either, they

> were but one. This candid and frank declaration, at once removed all suspicion from the minds of the others, who had become seriously apprehensive that Lisa, finding himself amongst a people who were perfectly at his disposal, might betray them.[38]

Lisa further lessened any doubts about his sincerity by offering to buy Hunt's boats and providing much-needed horses from Fort Mandan as part of the deal. The Arikara chief Left Handed even ordered his men to guard the boats of both groups to prevent pilfering, after which Lisa and Hunt both presented him with gifts.

Over the years, the Arikara nation was best remembered for the attacks of 1807 and 1823, but it should also be memorialized for the fruitful peace talks of 1809 and 1811.

"A Natural Born Indian"

As Hunt's party prepared to go overland to the west, some of the men worried about venturing into unknown country; neither Lewis and Clark nor any of the explorers or traders who followed them had left the Missouri River this far south. "Their apprehensions were aggravated by some of Lisa's followers, who, not being engaged in the expedition, took a mischievous pleasure in exaggerating its dangers," wrote Irving. "They painted in strong colors, to the poor Canadian voyageurs, the risk they would run of perishing with hunger and thirst; of being cut off by war parties of the Sioux . . . of having their horses stolen by the . . . Crows, who infested the skirts of the Rocky Mountains" and "were noted for daring and excursive habits, and great dexterity in horse stealing."[39]

Indeed, Lewis and Clark veterans signed on with Lisa in 1807 and afterward likely passed down stories of the Crows' "dexterity," telling how Clark, expecting to meet the Crow nation on the Yellowstone River, prepared a speech to deliver to them and saw smoke presumably coming from their camps but never actually saw them. Sergeant Pryor, Hugh Hall, George Shannon, and Richard Windsor, tasked by Clark to take a herd of about twenty-five horses to the Mandan villages, had a different experience. On July 24, 1806, near present Hardin, Montana, they found a good grazing spot for the horses and decided to stop for the night. "In the morning [Pryor] could see no horses," wrote Clark. "In [looking] about their Camp they discovered Several tracks within 100 paces of their Camp, which they pursued [and] found where [the Indians] had Caught and drove off all the horses." Pryor and the others tracked the missing horses and their new drovers for ten miles but found "there was not the Smallest Chance of overtakeing them." So they did what they had to do—"returned to their Camp and packed up their baggage on their backs and Steared a N. E. course to the River Rochejhone . . . killed a Buffalow Bull and made a Canoe [hemispherical bullboat] in the form and shape of the mandans," catching up with Clark two weeks later.[40] This was definitely Crow territory, and concluding that nation captured the horses was a reasonable, though not proven, conclusion.

Six years later—and three hundred miles to the southwest—Crooks and McClellan had a remarkably similar experience. Like Pryor's group, they were not harmed, but the difference was this: Crooks and McClellan watched as their mounts were taken by Indians who "were beyond all doubt of the Absaroka nation."[41]

Continuing his commentary on the Crow Indians, Irving wrote,

> [Hunt] considered himself fortunate in having met with a man who might be of great use to him in any intercourse he might have with the tribe. This was a wandering individual named Edward Rose, whom he had picked up somewhere on the Missouri—one of those anomalous beings found on the frontier, who seems to have neither kin nor country. He had lived some time among the Crows, so as to become acquainted with their language and customs; and was, withal, a dogged, sullen, silent fellow, with a sinister aspect, and more of the savage than the civilized man in his appearance.[42]

Irving never met Rose, but his characterization of the "sullen, silent fellow" had a lasting influence on subsequent historians, several of whom echoed his description. Hiram M. Chittenden, however, rejected that trend, writing, "It is apparent . . . that Rose bore a bad reputation, but the singular thing is that everything definite that is known of him is entirely to his credit."[43]

The intriguing and controversial Rose first turned up in Reed's account book on June 13, 1811, the day after Hunt, Lisa, and the Arikara chief Left Handed held their cordial council. Over the next month, as Rose and all the others prepared for the westward journey, they bought items on credit from the company store, some for personal use and some, as Todd puts it, "to procure the favors of Indian women." Take this sample of Rose's purchases: one yard of green cloth, $5.00; one-half yard of blue cloth, $2.00; one yard of blue flannel, $2.00; three and one-third pounds of balls, $1.75; one and one-half pounds of powder, $2.25; four scalping knives, $2.00; one-half pound of white beads, $2.00; one axe, $5.00; a coffee kettle, $6.00; a handkerchief, $2.00; a quarter pound of blue beads, $1.00; six pipes, $1.50; one carrot of tobacco, $3.00; two dozen brass rings, $1.00; three fathoms of gartering, $1.50; and a bridle, $2.00.[44]

As for Rose's whereabouts the last three and a half years, his friend Captain Reuben Holmes wrote that during Lisa's trip up the Missouri in 1807, he had noted Rose's "reckless bravery, . . . strong and vigorous constitution, his tact and facility in overcoming sudden difficulties and dangers, his untiring perseverance, and the faculty of 'turning his hand to every thing.'" After reaching the mouth of the Bighorn River and building Fort Raymond there, Lisa sent Colter, Drouillard, and Peter Weiser out to invite the Crow Indians to trade, predictable because all three were well experienced in dealing with Indians. He was also impressed enough with two novice traders, Jean Baptiste Champlain and Rose, that he also sent them as emissaries to the Crows. Champlain accompanied Weiser, but as far as is known, the other three went by themselves, all "supplied with such articles of trade as were considered best calculated to promote the interests of the expedition."[45]

There were Crow villages throughout the area, especially on the Yellowstone River and its tributaries—including Clark's Fork, the Bighorn, the Little Bighorn, Tongue River, and Powder River.[46] Which direction Rose went is unknown, but he was soon learning the Crow language "with considerable facility" and engaging in their pursuits. The Crows were pleasantly surprised when they found that Rose "could run a buffalo or a Black-foot as well as they could." With a little paint, the black-haired Rose looked like "a natural born Indian."[47] He grew accustomed to sleeping in one of the large Crow lodges, typically twenty-five feet high, covered with fourteen or fifteen buffalo hides, and capable of accommodating thirty or forty people.[48]

Rose gave away all his trade goods, not asking anything in return, staying with his new friends as winter turned to spring. In the summer of 1808 the men Lisa sent out to the Crow nation had all returned—except Rose. Perhaps Lisa believed him killed or lost, but neither he nor any of his band kept a record. In July, after collecting the proceeds of trapping and hunting excursions, especially beaver pelts, as well as trade items obtained from the Crows, Lisa loaded up his keelboat and prepared to return to St. Louis. He and Drouillard and several others were about to leave when Rose, wearing Crow attire of buckskin shirt, leggings, and moccasins—and probably initially mistaken for an Indian—finally appeared. Lisa dispensed with formalities and demanded to know what had become of the beaver pelts Rose should have obtained for his trade goods. Rose, alone in the fort's counting room with Lisa, had no satisfactory answer. Lisa likely reminded him that the trade goods, guns, powder, and balls he departed with nine months earlier had been worth almost $2,000. "During the dispute," wrote Holmes, "Rose sprang, like a tiger, upon his disputant, and overpowering him before he had noticed such an intention, would probably have killed him, had not the noise of the scuffle brought a man, by the name of Potts [Lewis and Clark veteran John Potts] . . . to the relief of Mr. Lisa. His coming saved Mr. L., but he suffered severely by the interference."[49]

As Potts tried to defend himself, "Rose saw the boat about moving slowly from the shore, as she swung around into the current; infuriated with passion, and almost blind with rage, he ran to a swivel pointed towards the river, and quickly directing its line of fire, 'touched it off' with his pipe." Balls from the swivel gun struck the cargo box of the boat but missed the men aboard. Rose tried recharging the swivel "but was prevented from completing his object by the intervention of about fifteen men, who could barely restrain the effects of his ungovernable passion." Not surprisingly, Rose soon returned to his Crow friends, staying again for several months. In the summer of 1809 he "was found at the Aricara village by Mr. Henry, and taken by him to the mountains, in the capacity of a Crow interpreter and trader."[50] Henry, of course, was part of the group escorting Sheheke to his village. Whether Rose and Lisa had any contact is not known, but as one of Henry's partners, Lisa certainly learned of Rose's hiring and apparently did not object. Indeed, Lisa, who was constantly suing debtors, never did so with Rose, even hiring him again in 1812. There is no record of the two arguing after 1808.

Rose was thus with Henry at Three Forks when the Blackfeet attacked, killing Drouillard and several others. He watched as Colter threw his hat on the ground, announcing that in his earlier escape, he had promised God never to return: "Now, if God will only forgive me this time and let me off I *will* leave the country . . . and be d——d if I ever come into it again."[51] Declining the chance to join Henry's group crossing the Continental Divide, Rose traveled into Crow country with Champlain, Ezekiel Williams, and others. "One of Captain Williams's men, whose name was Rose," wrote David H. Coyner in his 1847 book *The Lost Trappers*, "expressed his intention to abandon his party and remain among the Crows. It appears that whilst the men were in the Crow village, Rose was not able to resist the charms of a certain Crow beauty, whom he afterwards selected as his wife and with whom he lived for several years."[52] This secondhand account agrees with what Holmes heard from Rose himself—that after serving under Henry, "he again joined the Crows . . . he . . . exchanged a favorite rifle and accoutrements for a wife, and slung a bow and quiver to his back."[53] Although Rose may have lived with his Crow wife for several years, they were not consecutive years—ten months after leaving Champlain and Williams, he was back with the Arikaras, where he signed on with Hunt.

"The Crow Chief Sent Rose to Place Us on the Right Road"

"On the 17th [of July] I took my leave of my worthy friends, Messrs. Hunt, Crooks, and M'Kenzie, whose kindness and attention to me had been such as to render the parting painful," wrote Bradbury. "I am happy in having this opportunity of testifying my gratitude and respect for them: throughout the voyage, every indulgence was given me." Lisa had loaded two six-man canoes with skins and furs, and Bradbury and Brackenridge were two of the twelve men returning to St. Louis: "Mr. Hunt caused the men to draw up in a line, and give three cheers, which we returned; and we soon lost sight of them."[54]

Hunt's party left the next day, a week later making camp on a tributary of the Grand River: "They had traveled 67 miles, bearing a little more toward the west in the prairies where the grass was knee-deep the horses could graze to their satisfaction. The country was bare. Only a few cottonwoods grew along the rivers." Hunt visited a Cheyenne camp nearby, in present Corson County, South Dakota, buying thirty-six horses at a better price than he had paid the Arikaras: "The camp was in the middle of the prairie near a little stream. The Indians used buffalo chips as fuel. Their tents are made of the skins of this animal well-prepared, carefully sewn together and supported by poles which are joined at the top; they can hold fifty people. These Indians are honest and cleanly; they hunt bison; they raise many horses which every year they exchange at the Aricaras' village for corn, beans, squashes and merchandise. They had a dozen beaver pelts, but they do not seem to know how to trap these animals."[55]

After stopping for several days to let sick members recover, Hunt's party continued west and slightly south and crossed a range of mountains—today's Slim Buttes in Harding County—"irksome because of steepness and the great number of stones." By August 13 they reached northeastern Wyoming's Little Missouri River, "300 feet wide, swift, muddy and filled with eddies." Four days later, in the southern edge of the Powder River Range, they found the country "extremely rugged." They saw several bighorn sheep "running and jumping on the edge of precipices." In the mountains the weather was "cold and disagreeable." A stream froze on the night of August 21, "the ice being as thick as a dollar." Just a few days later, in a dry ravine, "the great heat, the bad road and the lack of water caused much suffering; several persons were on the verge of losing courage. A dog of Mr. Mackenzie died of fatigue."[56]

By the end of August, the Astorians reached the Bighorn Range. Several days earlier, they had first seen the highest mountain in the range—13,171-foot Cloud Peak (twenty-five miles west of present Buffalo, Wyoming)—and camped at its foot: "On the evening of the 30th, two Absarokas came to our camp. The next morning, more of them arrived. They were all on horseback. Even the children do not go afoot. These Indians are such good horsemen that they climb and descend the mountains and rocks as though they were galloping in a riding school. We followed them to their camp, which was near a clear stream on the side of the mountain." The chief greeted Hunt and the other partners in a friendly way and showed them a good spot for their camp: "I made him a present of tobacco, knives and various trinkets for his men," said Hunt, "and I gave him for himself a piece of scarlet cloth, some powder, bullets, and other things."[57]

As the one man in the group known to be a fluent speaker of the Crow language, Rose likely assisted in communicating with the chief. The Astorians and Crows spent the next day trading, and Hunt increased his number of horses to 121—"most of them well-behaved and capable of crossing the mountains." On September 2 and 3 Hunt's group tried to "get out of the precipices and arid mountains" but found it necessary to "retrace the path and to regain the banks of the small stream." At this point, Hunt's narrative makes an interesting detour and mentions Rose for the first time: "We had in our party a hunter by the name of *Rose*; he was a very bad fellow full of daring. We had been warned that he had planned to desert us as soon as we should be near the Absarokas, take with him as many of our men as he could seduce, and steal our horses. Wherefore, we kept close watch during the night." Fearing that Rose's purported plans would "cripple" the expedition, Hunt "resolved to forestall him." On September 2 a different band of Crows visited Hunt, who consequently suggested to Rose "that he remain with these indians, offering him half of his year's wages, a horse, three beaver-traps and some other things. He accepted these terms, and immediately quitted his confederates, who, no longer having a leader, continued the journey. Accordingly, Rose went to join the first Absarokas that we had met."[58]

This passage from Hunt's "journal" is full of unanswered questions: If Rose were simply a hunter known as a "bad fellow," why did Hunt, who had plenty of hunters, hire him in the first place? Who warned Hunt of Rose's scheme? Who were the men who planned to desert with Rose, and what attraction did the Bighorn wilderness—so far from employment, friends, or family—possibly hold for them?[59] Irving goes so far as to claim that "M'Lellan, with his usual *tranchant* ['sharp'] mode of dealing out justice, resolved to shoot the desperado on the spot in case of any outbreak," a detail not mentioned by Hunt.[60] All this looks like a case, as mentioned by Chittenden, of negative judgments being made about Rose without solid evidence.

Whatever Rose's true character—always a mystery because the man himself left no record and we are left to second- or thirdhand sources that frequently disagree—Hunt was now rid of him. Or was he? The Crow chief, said Hunt, "knowing that we had taken the wrong road, sent Rose on the 4th [of September] to tell us this and to place us on the right road which crossed the mountains and which was shorter and better." Hunt's last reference to Rose was thus nothing but positive, even though the former said nothing about changing his opinion. "We soon met the Absarokas," he continued, "who were going the same way as we; this gave me a chance to admire the activeness of those indians on horseback. It was really unbelievable. There was among others, a child tied to a two-year-old colt. He held the reins in one hand and frequently plied his whip. I inquired his age"—with Rose interpreting?—"they told me that he had seen two winters. He did not talk as yet."[61]

"A Bleak and Barren Country"

With help from Rose and his Crow friends, Hunt's Astorians found their way out of the Bighorn Mountains by late August 1811. Hoback, Reznor, and Robinson then guided them to the Wind River—actually the upper Bighorn River—and then, on September 15, to Union Pass (thirteen miles west-southwest of present Dubois, Wyoming), where they crossed the Continental Divide, their party still intact. Their next objective: reach the mouth of the Columbia River, where the partners sailing on *Tonquin* had hopefully already built a trading post.

As shown, Lewis and Clark's journey from Lemhi Pass to the Pacific took a huge emotional and psychological toll on Lewis, but none of the corps died or suffered lasting injuries. Even after delays and backtracking, they arrived at the coast three months after reaching a tributary of the Columbia River. Hunt's quest would be radically and tragically different.

Several men, including the three Kentuckians, kept their horses and stayed near the Wyoming/Idaho border to trap, but Hunt continued west to the fork of the Snake River, where Henry's men spent the previous winter. The Astorians were busy building dugout canoes for a week, and on October 19, after leaving almost all their remaining horses in the care of two Shoshone Indians, they embarked in fifteen canoes. The weather had turned cold—it snowed the entire day. Nine days later, near present Burley, Idaho, wrote Irving, the river grew "rough and impetuous . . . chafed and broken by numerous rapids." Canadian voyager Antoine Clappine was the steersman of the second canoe swept into the whitewater; Crooks one of the other four passengers. The canoe crashed into a boulder, split, and overturned. Crooks and another man "were thrown amidst roaring breakers and whirling current, but succeeded, by strong swimming, to reach the shore." Clappine and two others clung to the fragment of a boat, but it struck another boulder "and swinging round, flung poor Clappine off into the raging stream, which swept him away, and he perished," the first fatality among the Overland Astorians.[62]

Other canoes had also overturned, with the men surviving but many goods lost. An inventory found that the group had just five days' worth of food left. Hunt scouted the river for thirty-five miles, finding it "full of rapids and intersected by falls from ten to forty feet high," with "precipitous banks everywhere."[63] Crooks and five others started hiking upstream along the Snake, hoping to return with the horses. Hunt sent out other scouting missions, but none of those that returned found possible passages or Indians who could help. The days passed, with Hunt and the others hoping for good news from Crooks. He and his companions finally appeared, but not on horseback, "completely disheartened by this retrograde march through a bleak and barren country," soon realizing that it would be impossible to reach Henry's Fort and return before winter.[64] Hunt and the other partners now had no choice but to proceed on foot in uncharted territory with no way of knowing how far they were from the mouth of the Columbia. That was probably a good thing—they were one thousand miles away.

On November 9, although the three bands of scouts led by McClellan, Mackenzie, and Reed had not returned from their scouting pursuits, Hunt and Crooks divided the remaining party into two groups. Hunt took his people along the north bank of the Snake and Crooks on the south. Both parties were soon on the verge of starvation, with Crooks suffering from a chronic illness. By December 10 Hunt's group had just one horse left. It belonged to the interpreter and hunter Dorion, who had bought it from Indians by selling a buffalo robe. "Killing it [for food] was suggested," wrote Hunt. "Dorion would not consent, and Hunt did not argue since the poor beast was only skin and bones."[65] Luckily, they soon met Shoshone Indians who sold them five horses. Hunt had one killed and prepared to send some meat across the Snake to Crooks's party, who had not eaten for three days. Using a newly constructed canoe, one of Hunt's men made it across the river and delivered the meat. He was about to return when a boatman by the name of Baptiste Provost forced his way into the boat, insisting he was so hungry that he could not wait for the meat to be cooked. As the two men drew near the shore and "beheld meat roasting before the fire, [Provost] jumped up, shouted, clapped his hands, and danced in a delirium of joy." The result was predictable—he swamped the canoe, and "the poor wretch was swept away by the current and drowned." The other man barely escaped drowning before struggling to the shore.[66]

On December 30, near present North Powder, Oregon, Marie Dorion gave birth to a baby. Hunt did not say whether the child was a boy or girl but did comment that because "the fortitude and good conduct of the poor woman had gained for her the good-will of the party, her situation caused concern and perplexity." Dorion stayed with his family but rejoined Hunt the next day: "His wife was on horseback with her newborn infant in her arms; another, aged two years, wrapped in a blanket, was slung at her side." The infant died one week later.[67]

"A Shorter Trace to the South"

The exploring detachments of McClellan, Mackenzie, and Reed somehow "came together fortuitously among the Snake River Mountains," making a group of eleven men. They followed the same "rugged defile"—today's Hell's Canyon—later found impassable by Hunt and Crooks because of deep snow: "Its banks were so high and precipitous, that there was rarely any place where the travellers could get down to drink of its waters." When a severe blizzard halted further progress forward or back, they cowered in the half shelter of a rocky overhang and prepared for the inevitable. "At this critical juncture," McClellan saw a bighorn sheep "sheltering itself under a shelving rock." More capable of responding than any of his companions, McClellan "scrambled up the hill with utmost silence, and at length arrived, unperceived, within a proper distance. Here, leveling his rife, he took so sure an aim, that the bighorn fell dead on the spot." Consumed slowly over several days, the bighorn saved the men's lives. Three weeks later they made it out of the canyon, fell in with friendly Indians—almost certainly Nez Perces—and "procured two canoes, in which they dropped down the [lower Snake River] to its confluence with the Columbia, and then down that river to Astoria, where they arrived haggard and emaciated, and perfectly in rags."[68] These eleven were the first overlanders to reach Astoria, doing so at 5 p.m. on January 18, 1812.

Hunt, who backtracked after being blocked by Hell's Canyon and crossed the Snake, also received invaluable help from Indigenous peoples, a large encampment of Cayuse and Tushepaw Indians he met near present Pendleton, Oregon, on January 8. They fed his party and sold them horses, a joyous occasion dampened by the disappearance of a voyager named Michael Carriere, who was never heard from again even though Hunt's men searched for him. Hunt reached the Columbia on January 21, eventually trading horses for boats. On the morning of February 15, Hunt wrote, "The fog was so thick that we could see only the lowlands and some small islands." Luckily, the fog disappeared in the afternoon: "I found that we were navigating along a large bay, and shortly afterward I saw the fort of Astoria on the southerly bank. I had the pleasure there of again meeting Messrs. Mackenzie and McClellan, who had arrived more than a month before, after having suffered incredible hardships."[69]

Two men were missing: Crooks and a friend he had worked with for four years, John Day, who stayed behind in Idaho when Crooks was too sick to travel. As spring came on, many of those at Astoria concluded the two would never be seen again. They were mistaken. Crooks later told the story of how he and Day spent the winter in the mountains, "subsisting sometimes on beaver and horse meat, and their skins, and at others on . . . finding roots." Toward the last of March, the two, finding the snow sufficiently diminished, undertook, from Indian information, to cross the last ridge, which they happily effected and reached the banks of Columbia by the middle of April. Not long after that, however, they were robbed by Indians, who, as Crooks put it, "stripped us of our clothes, ammunition, knives, and everything else, leaving us as naked as the day we were born." Then the Indians ignored them as they walked away. Four days later, "without fire, food, or clothing," their feet "severely cut and bleeding," they made it back to an Umatilla Indian village whose chief previously helped them and now offered them sustenance, clothing, and rest. That was when McClellan, Reed, Astor partner Robert Stuart, and several others came down the Columbia from Fort Okanogan in a boat loaded with 2,500 beaver pelts. Crooks and Day joined them and reached Astoria on May 12.[70]

Within weeks, Crooks and McClellan—both of whom had obviously endured extreme privation and suffering and were now enjoying the comfort and safety of the fort—announced, to the astonishment of their fellow traders, that they were giving up their partnerships and returning overland to St. Louis with Robert Stuart and a few others tasked with delivering dispatches to Astor in New York. Were Crooks's feet even healed by that time? Neither man ever recorded the reasons behind their decision. The party of seven left Fort Astoria on June 29 in two canoes, changing to horses where the Columbia turned to the north. On August 15, along southwestern Idaho's Boise River, they met one of the Indians who guided Hunt near the Idaho/Wyoming border the previous October. The Indian, whose name was not recorded, told them that some of the trappers left behind had been robbed by Crow Indians. He also said, "There is a shorter trace to the South than that by which Mr. Hunt had traversed the [Rocky] Mountains," and he knew the route well.[71] Stuart hired him on the spot, and although his time as a guide was short, he gave the group crucial information for avoiding the rugged country of Union Pass, where they had crossed the Continental Divide on their way west.

Just a few days later, along the Snake River near present Grand View, Idaho, in another remarkable coincidence, Stuart's group met Hoback, Reznor, and Robinson, as well as Astor partner Joseph Miller, who had stayed behind to trap with the trio of Kentuckians. The four men had enjoyed great success in trapping beaver but had also been robbed by Indians more than once. Their pilgrimage had certainly been every bit as harrowing as that of Crooks and McClellan, so it was no surprise that all four agreed to travel to St. Louis with Stuart's party. In late August, however, when the group reached the site where Clappine had drowned—and also where Hunt had cached some goods, arms, ammunition, and traps—the triumvirate of nomads changed their minds again. Stuart gave them everything he could spare and wished them the best, but they would never see Kentucky again. Miller, however, wanted to return to St. Louis and guided the group to the Bear River in southeastern Wyoming. On the morning of September 19, near present Alpine, Wyoming, they barely had time to grab their guns when "two Indians at full gallop passed 300 yards to one side of our station driving off [*by their yells*] every horse we had [*notwithstanding their being tethered & hobbled*], towards them."[72] Joining William Clark, Andrew Henry, and many others, Stuart and his companions had lost their mounts to the unparalleled horsemen of the Rockies—the Crow Indians.

Over the next month, the eastbound Astorians endured the most grueling part of their trek, building rafts and descending the Snake River back into Idaho, where they found game—but also evidence of Blackfeet Indians—and prepared to go east over the mountains as soon as possible. The flighty McClellan refused to follow the same path and hiked off on his own. Crooks came down with a violent fever, and some of the men wanted to go on without him to save their own lives. Stuart refused. Early in October, when they were almost out of food, Ben Jones killed five elk. In "piercingly cold" weather the men carried Crooks "six miles south . . . to where the dead animals lay and encamped in the vicinity." They luckily crossed the Teton Range where there was little snow and then followed a tributary of the Snake—now called the Hoback River—to the southeast, keeping in that direction rather than going north toward 9,212-foot Union Pass. They found McClellan "lying on a parcel of straw . . . worn to a perfect skeleton," saying he might as well die there as anywhere else. Stuart prevailed on McClellan to continue, and the group passed the future site of Pinedale, Wyoming, again running out of food. McClellan solved that problem by shooting a buffalo. On October 21 Stuart wrote, "The cold continued and was accompanied by Snow soon after we left the drain which compelled us to encamp at the end of 15 miles E N E on the side of a Hill . . . where we found a sufficiency of dry Aspen for firewood, but not a drop of water." The next day they set out early, making five miles before they "found a small stream of water and breakfasted." Ten more miles took them to "the head drains of a watercourse *running East*." Five miles farther on, they "at last found a little water oozing out of the earth, it was of a whiteish colour and possessed *a great similarity of taste to the muddy waters of the Missouri*."[73]

The seven eastbound Astorians had discovered South Pass.

"He and the Bear Met Face to Face"

Robert Stuart, Ramsay Crooks, Robert McClellan, Joseph Miller, Ben Johnson, André Vallé, and François Le Clerc (also spelled *Le Clairc* or *Le Claire*) arrived in St. Louis at sunset on April 30, 1813. The *Missouri Gazette* announced their arrival on May 8 and published a detailed account of their adventures on May 15, making it clear—to careful readers—that Stuart and his fellows had crossed the Continental Divide by pursuing "their rout towards the Rocky mountains at the head waters of the Colorado or Spanish river [Green River, which flows into the Colorado, which in turn flows into the Pacific Ocean via the Gulf of California], and stood their course. E.S.E. until they struck the head waters [Sweetwater River] of the great river Platte, which they undeviatingly followed to its mouth [at the Missouri River]."[74]

A few years earlier this would have been earthshaking news, but not now. War with Great Britain had been declared days before the seven sailed from Fort Astoria, and they had learned at Fort Osage "that the upper Great Lakes area was entirely in British hands and that Indians from as far away as the Missouri River were flocking toward Prairie du Chien and Green Bay to . . . join the fight against the Americans."[75]

In October 1813, six months after Stuart reached St. Louis, a group of North West Company traders arrived at Fort Astoria with an offer to buy the fort and all its assets. They made a simple argument to Astor's partners: "Why risk death and destruction at the hands of the Royal Navy when lives and investments could be saved by selling at a fair price?"[76] The papers were signed on October 13, and Fort Astoria was renamed Fort George. Astor got the news in New York six months later. He was not happy. In November 1814 a New York newspaper ran the simple announcement "The firm of the Pacific Fur Company is dissolved."[77] Any conclusions that Astor himself had gone out of business, however, were premature. In 1811 he and agents of the North West Company had formed the South West Company, referring to the southwestern portion of the Great Lakes area, especially the south shore of Lake Superior and the headwaters of the Mississippi River. Agreements made between Britain and the United States when the War of 1812 ended early in 1815 helped Astor strengthen his hold on the South West Company, and he took full control of the firm in 1817, with Ramsay Crooks and Robert Stuart as two of his key agents.

Still, the sale of Astoria had given the North West Company a virtual monopoly in the Pacific Northwest, and in 1818 the former Astorian Donald Mackenzie led a band of beaver hunters into the Snake River territory. Over the next three years they "trapped almost the whole of the Snake Country . . . giving to most of the tributaries of the Snake the names they have borne ever since (among others the Malheur, Owyhee, Bruneau, Raft, and Portneuf)," ranging as far south as the Bear River and coming within a day's trek of discovering the Great Salt Lake.[78]

About this same time, such traders as Manuel Lisa, Joshua Pilcher, the Chouteau family, the Robidoux brothers, the Pratte brothers, Louis Vasquez, and Joseph Brazeau were making small profits trading among the Osage, Omaha, Iowa, Kansas, Oto, Pawnee, and Yankton Sioux nations, with virtually all that commerce taking place near or below the Platte River.[79] Even the 1819–20 Yellowstone Expedition of Colonel Henry Atkinson and Major Stephen Harriman Long, which intended to build a fort at the mouth of the Yellowstone River, did not reach the upper Missouri.

Ashley and Henry thus set their sights high in 1822 when they made the first significant U.S. trading voyage to the Mandans and to the mouth of the Yellowstone in more than a decade. No one was thinking of trying to cross the Great Divide. The picture was quite positive until the attack on Ashley's hunters. "By fall [1823]," writes Will Bagley, "it looked like the firm of Ashley & Henry was headed for utter financial ruin. Ironically, the ambush at the Arikara villages set in motion events that led to the practical rediscovery of South Pass," opening the way for explorers, traders, trappers, pioneer families, schoolmarms, store owners, missionaries, blacksmiths, mercantile owners, and of course, gold seekers and soldiers.[80]

Not that Ashley and Henry's men set out to discover or "rediscover" anything—they were just trying to help the company recover from the Arikara attack and the time spent serving with the Missouri Legion. By early September, Clyman remembered, Henry and his men, "furnished [with] a few horses onley enough to pack their baggage," headed "back to the mouth of the yellow Stone." A few weeks later, Jedediah Smith and Thomas Fitzpatrick led a group of sixteen men, including Clyman, Rose, Bill Sublette, and Thomas Eddie, who, "having bought a few horses and borrowed a few more," "proceded westward over a dry rolling highland."[81] Their destination was the Spanish River, said to be prime beaver territory, but they were leaving late in the season—it would not be easy to cross the plains, the Badlands, and the Rockies before winter.

The fascinating prelude to the revival of a critical westward route was that in each of the two expeditions, a man who had survived the Arikara onslaught was attacked and seriously injured by a grizzly, often called a "white bear" by the frontiersmen. The victim of the first mauling was Hugh Glass, the man who wrote the kind letter to John S. Gardner's parents despite being wounded himself. Although neither Glass nor any of his companions left a detailed account of the incident, a Philadelphia newspaper described it in 1825, saying that Glass was with Henry, and "their route lay up the Grand River, and through a prairie country, occasionally interspersed with thickets of brush-wood, dwarf-plum trees, and other shrubs." The newspaper continued,

> The rifle of Hugh Glass being esteemed as among the most unerring, he was on one occasion detached for supplies. He was a short distance in advance of the party, and forcing his way through a thicket, when a white bear that had imbedded herself in the sand, arose within three yards of him, and before he could "set his triggers," or turn to retreat, he was seized by the throat, and raised from the ground. Casting him again upon the earth, his grim adversary tore out a mouthful of the cannibal food which had excited her appetite, and retired to submit the sample to her yearling cubs, which were near at hand.[82]

Glass tried to escape, "but the bear immediately returned with a reinforcement, and seized him again at the shoulder; she also lacerated his left arm very much, and inflicted a severe wound on the back of his head. . . . Meantime, the main body of trappers having arrived, advanced to the relief of Glass, and delivered seven or eight shots with such unerring aim as to terminate hostilities, by despatching the bear"—and her cubs—"as she stood over her victim."[83]

Glass had suffered several grave wounds: "His whole body was bruised and mangled, and he lay weltering in his blood, in exquisite torment. To procure surgical aid, now so desirable, was impossible; and to remove the sufferer was equally so. The safety of the whole party—being now in the country of hostile Indians—depended on the celerity of their movements. . . . Under these circumstances, Major Henry, by offering an extravagant reward, induced two of his party to remain with the wounded man until he should expire, or until he could so far recover as to bear removal to some of the trading establishments in that country." The two trappers stayed with Glass for five days. Then, believing "his recovery no longer possible, they cruelly abandoned him, taking with them his rifle, shot-pouch, &c. and leaving him no means of either making fire or procuring food." When they overtook Henry and the others, they reported that Glass had died, and they had given him the best burial possible, producing "his effects in confirmation of their assertions."[84]

But Glass was still alive, barely. He crawled to a spring a few yards away, drank the water, and "subsisted upon cherries that hung over the spring," gradually regaining his strength enough to start crawling eastward. At first he had nothing but berries to eat, but "he had, however, the good fortune one day to be 'in at the death of a buffaloe calf,' which was overtaken and slain by a pack of wolves. He permitted the assailants to carry on the war until no signs of life remained in their victim, and then interfered and took possession of the 'fatted calf;' but as he had no means of striking fire, we may infer that he did not make a very prodigal use of the veal thus obtained." Somehow, with "indefatigable industry," Glass made it back to Fort Kiowa, which he could have done by following the Grand River back to the Missouri and the Missouri to the fort. The story of his survival is now the stuff of legend—often liberally embellished—and is probably the best-known episode involving any of the multitude of Ashley men.[85]

One of the men who abandoned Glass is believed to be John S. Fitzgerald, who enlisted in the U.S. Army at Fort Atkinson in 1824 and went up the Missouri with the Atkinson-O'Fallon Expedition in 1825.[86] Several historians have claimed the second man was young Jim Bridger, but Bridger's biographer Jerry Enzler argues convincingly that there is insufficient evidence to support such a conclusion.[87]

The second grizzly attack happened several weeks after and some three hundred miles to the southwest of the first, near the headwaters of the south fork of the Cheyenne River, in present Converse County, Wyoming. The victim was one of the commanders of the contingent, Jedediah Smith. The men were all on foot, in single file, with each of them leading two packhorses through thick underbrush, when "a large Grssely came down the valley," wrote Clyman. "Capt. Smith being in the advance he ran to the open ground and as he immerged from the thicket he and the bear met face to face." The bear sprung, seized Smith by the head, and threw him "sprawling on the earth." Then the behemoth thrashed at Smith's torso, at least partially protected by his ammunition pouch and his butcher knife, both promptly destroyed. Smith's companions presumably shot the bear at that point, but Clyman skipped over that detail, simply reporting the grizzly broke several of Smith's ribs and cut his head badly. The worried men turned one to another, not sure what to do: "I asked the Capt what was best." Despite his injuries, Smith kept his wits about him, telling one or two of the men to get water. "If you have a needle and thread," he said to Clyman, "git it out and sew up my wounds around my head." Those wounds were bleeding badly, but Clyman also stayed calm: "I got a pair of scissors and cut off his hair and then began my first Job of d[r]essing wounds upon examination I [found] the bear had taken nearly all his head in his capcious mouth close to his left eye on one side and clos to his right ear on the other and laid the skull bare to near the crown of his head leaving a white streak where his teeth passed." One of Smith's ears was torn from his head to the outer rim. Clyman stitched all the wounds the best he could but told Smith he could do nothing about the ear almost ripped from the head. "O you must try to stich up some way or other," Smith pleaded. "Then I put in my needle stiching it through and through and over and over laying the lacerated parts togather as nice as I could with my hands," remembered Clyman.[88]

Water was found a mile away, and with the captain somehow "able to mount his horse and ride," the group made camp near the water, pitching their only tent to allow Smith to be "as comfortable as circumstances would permit." Clyman's medical handiwork had stopped the bleeding, probably saving the captain's life, but the scars left by the grizzly, especially a missing eyebrow and mangled ear, were permanent, and Smith always wore his hair long, covering his ears, afterward. He rested in his tent as the men brought food and water. After ten or twelve days he was ready to go west again, the emotional scars no doubt permanent as well.[89]

Clyman offered the final word: "This gave us a lisson on the charcter of the grissly Baare which we did not forget."[90]

"There Is No Country like the Crow Country"

"As winter was rapidly approaching we began to make easy travel west ward and Struck the trail of [Cheyenne] Indians," wrote Clyman. "The next day we came to their village [and] traded . . . a few horses with them."[91] This brief but friendly encounter with the Cheyennes was reminiscent of how the westbound Astorians, twelve years earlier and farther east, were also well received by that nation. Lewis and Clark met Cheyennes at the Arikara villages and knew them to be congenial trading partners who sometimes stayed for months among the Arikaras and brought with them "shirts of antelope skin, ornamented and worked with different colored quills of the porcupine," particularly valued by their Arikara allies.[92] The Cheyennes spoke a language of the Algonquian family and during the seventeenth century were driven from the Great Lakes region to Minnesota and North Dakota. By 1790 they migrated to the Black Hills area of South Dakota, where they obtained many horses and gave up farming to become skilled buffalo hunters, something encouraged by their prophet Sweet Medicine, who was given four medicine arrows by sacred persons—two for killing buffalo and two for killing enemies. Sweet Medicine also predicted the coming of the white man and gave the Cheyenne nation its code of sacred laws.[93]

After leaving the Cheyennes, the men descended a ridge and "came to the waters of Powder River Running West and North," the country mountainous and rocky. They were hoping to see Edward Rose, called a "half Breed" by Clyman, because the very day of the "Baare" attack, Rose, "who spoke the Crow tongue," "was dispatched ahead to find the Crows and try to induce some of them to come to our assistance." Now, with Smith slowly getting back to half normal, the hopes of meeting Rose were soon realized: "Rose with 15 or 16 Crow Indians came to our camp as soon as we raised a fire in the evening."[94] Rose and his Crow friends had been watching Smith and Fitzpatrick's group for two days, making sure there were no Cheyennes with them because the Crows and Cheyennes were at war. Despite their small population, the Cheyennes were becoming a powerful military force on the Central Great Plains.[95]

"The Crows brought us several spare Horses," Clyman continued, "which relieved our Broke down animals and gave us a chance to ride." The Crows wanted to return to their village faster than Smith was inclined to go, so he showed his trust by "giving them what they could pack" and "sending Rose with them." Smith and Fitzpatrick's men followed at their "own gait stoping and Traping for beaver occasionly Crossing several steep and high ridges which in any other country would be called mountains." The nights "war frosty but the days ware generally warm and pleasant." Then they hit the Owl Creek Mountains, where they found no game, the "meals being few and far betwen." The weather grew "cold and blustry"; the "Strong north winds prevailed continually," leaving both men and horses "completely exhausted." Clyman felt the Wind River was "well named." Finally, north of 13,754-foot Fremont Peak, near present Dubois, Wyoming, they reached the Crow encampment, where they halted for the winter of 1823–24.[96]

The party spent about ten amiable weeks with the Crows, getting a glimpse of the life Rose knew so well, witnessing and then taking part in several "grand" buffalo hunts. The "whole grown male population" turned out, "taking rank along each side of a narrow vally those on fleetest horses taking a circuit and getting behind a large herd of Bufflo drove them pell mell down the vally those Stationed on the sides falling in as they passed they run down the Buffaloe so that [the] old and slow could even catch them and even men on foot Killed them with Bow and Arrow the Squaws old men and children following and Buchering and secureing meat and skins as fast as possible."[97]

Smith, Fitzpatrick, Clyman, and the others likely heard the kind of speech about the wonderful Crow country attributed to the prominent Crow chief

Sore Belly (also called *Arapooash* or *Arapooish*), who spent most of his time north of the Yellowstone River. In his vision quest in Montana's Crazy Mountains, the young Sore Belly "was suddenly confronted by a terrifying thunderbird, a spirit creature who spouted lightning and made a terrible roar," but rather than harming Sore Belly, the thunderbird became his guardian spirit, allowing him to manipulate the weather and see the future. Sore Belly subsequently captured "large herds of horses from neighboring tribes" and "urged his followers to trade for guns and ammunition first and to shun less practical items."[98]

The notable trader Robert Campbell recorded Sore Belly's discourse:

> The Crow country is a good country. The Great Spirit has put it exactly in the right place; while you are in it you fare well; whenever you go out of it, whichever way you travel, you fare worse. . . . When the summer heats scorch the prairies, you can draw up under the mountains, where the air is sweet and cool, the grass fresh. . . . When winter comes on, you can take shelter in the woody bottoms along the rivers; there you will find buffalo meat for yourselves, and cotton-wood bark for your horses: or you may winter in the Wind River valley, where there is salt weed in abundance. The Crow country is exactly in the right place. Everything good is to be found there. There is no country like the Crow country.[99]

Rose, for one, needed no convincing. For the umpteenth time, he left his St. Louis associates—did he have any compadres in that group?—to be with Crow friends, perhaps finding his way back to his wife and children's village. The pattern came full circle, however, in June 1825, when references to "Rose, a half Indian" and "Rose, the interpreter" showed up in the official journal of the Atkinson-O'Fallon Expedition sent to make peace with Missouri River nations.[100]

"At the time we ware [at the Crow encampment]," wrote Clyman, "at least one third of the warriors ware out in war parties in different directions they being in a state of warfare with all the neighbouring tribes." Rose may well have joined one of the war parties because there was no mention of him in February when the Ashley men tried to cross Union Pass—used by Hunt's westbound party in 1811—but found the snow much too deep.[101] Luckily, before Rose's departure, he had acted as interpreter as a Crow chief told Fitzpatrick of a pass in the Wind River Mountains, "through which he could easily take his whole band upon streams on the other side. [The chief] also represented beaver so abundant upon these rivers that traps were unnecessary to catch them—they could club as many as they desired."[102]

With Rose gone, however, getting specific "information about the country west of [the Crows] . . . seemed impossible," said Clyman. "I spread out a buffalo robe and covered it with sand, and made it in heaps to represent the different mountains . . . and from our sand map with the help of the Crows, finally got the idea that we could go to the Green River, called by them Seeds-ka-day. We undertook it in February."[103] Smith, Fitzpatrick, and the others thus learned that they could follow the Popo Agie River (the south fork of the Wind River) to a wide gap lying between the east-flowing Sweetwater River (a tributary of the North Platte) and the south-flowing Big Sandy River (a tributary of the Green, or Spanish, River). Making the journey in Wyoming's long winter was much easier said than done. Clyman's stream-of-consciousness narrative includes one amazing detail after another:

> Our horses being too poor to run we made an effort [to hunt] by crawling over ice and snow.
>
> The North wind arose and grew stronger and stronger and a cold frosty snow commenced falling.
>
> Our hands became exposed to the air they became so numb that we could not hold thee flint and Steel.
>
> The wind arose to a hericane direct from the north and we . . . [held] on to our blankets and robes to keep them from flying away.
>
> Sublett beat me in reloading and . . . [shot the buffalo] Just as the company came in sight on a hight of land when they all raised a Shout of Delight . . . not having tasted food for four days.

Some of the men were so hungry they ate the buffalo meat raw: "We . . . traveled on untill in the afternoon in hopes of finding water but did not succed but finding large clumps of sage brush we camped all eaving & part of the night." Firewood but no water—the exact situation described by Stuart in 1812. And, again like Stuart's company, Smith and Fitzpatrick's men realized after the fact that they were on the other side of the Continental Divide because they paid attention to the water flow—when they finally found water, that is. "Continuing on," wrote Clyman, "we found we had crossed the main ridge [South Pass] of the Rocky mountain."[104]

With both the Astor men going east and the Ashley men going west, there was no dramatic scaling and descending of a majestic summit. So-called South Pass was hardly a pass at all—rather, as Jedediah Smith's biographer Barton H. Barbour puts it, "a twenty-mile wide swath of unimpressive highland," but nevertheless "a discovery of major significance," precisely because it was so undramatic and "provided an easy traverse" of the plain that "formed the crucial link that later enabled thousands of ox- and horse-drawn wagons to cross the continent. . . . More than a quarter-million emigrants followed the trail across South Pass into the Far West until 1869, when the transcontinental railroad rendered it obsolete."[105]

Three months after the crossing, in June 1824, a St. Louis newspaper announced that a "Mr. Vasques"—actually Louis Vasquez—had returned from the upper Missouri with the news that three of Major Henry's men—"More, Chapman, and Glass"—had been killed by Arikara Indians. Glass, of course, was very much alive. The short article closed with one other bit of news from Vasquez: "Captain Smith, with some of the party, had crossed the Mountains," the first notice of the rediscovery of South Pass.[106]

Upon his arrival in St. Louis, Vasquez had met first with William Ashley, who had parted with Henry nine months earlier and "suffered through the winter and spring of 1824 without a hint of the fate of his enterprise," finding it "neither necessary nor possible to prepare a spring expedition to supply his partner and employees, because he did not know where they were, he could not depend on safe passage past the Missouri River tribes, and he possessed no further assurance of success which would induce his creditors to extend their commitments yet another time."[107] The mixed news from Vasquez was not encouraging enough for Ashley to organize a return mission in June, but all that changed by around September 21, when he "received a letter from Fitzpatrick, relating to him the discovery of South Pass, their successes in trapping on the newly found streams, and their disasters. In that letter, the Major [Fitzpatrick] stated that the new route would easily admit of the passage of wagons."[108]

Ashley acted immediately, getting funding from a sponsor, obtaining a trading license from William Clark, recruiting and supplying twenty-five men, and buying enough horses and pack mules to make the journey overland. He made good time, reaching Nebraska's Fort Atkinson around October 20.[109] A hard winter and the theft of seventeen horses—by Crow raiders, of course—kept Ashley from reaching the Green River until mid-April, when he divided the company into four separate trapping parties. Then "Ashley almost incidentally set the foundation for the most dazzling institution of the fur trade."[110] He told the leaders of each band of traders "that I would decend the [Green] River . . . about one hundred miles below; there deposite a part of my mechandize, and make such Marks as would designate it as a place of General Rendezvous for the men in my service . . . and where they were all directed to assemble on or before the 10th July following."[111]

The rediscovery of South Pass thus ignited the heyday of the Rocky Mountain fur trade—the rendezvous system, with gatherings of company trappers, free trappers, and Indians being held every year from 1825 to 1840. Most assemblages were held in western or central Wyoming but some in both northeastern Utah and southeastern Idaho: "The trappers left their camps each summer to trade at the annual rendezvous. After the isolation of winters spent setting up new camps and falls and springs spent setting traps and following the beaver, the men were delighted to tear loose and spend money on goods brought by pack trains from St. Louis. At the carnival-like rendezvous they picked up letters from home, newspapers, and news from the men of the freight caravans."[112]

6

"A Young Arapaho Indian Named Friday"

Encounters with Fitzpatrick and the Elusive Edward Rose

In late September 1831, at Walnut Creek on the Arkansas River, about 250 miles from the settlements in western Missouri, a twenty-three-year-old man by the name of Austin Smith wrote a letter: "My Dear Father, It is painful at all times to communicate the death of a friend, but when it falls to the lot of a son to communicate to a father the death of a Brother it is more so—Your son Jedediah was killed on the Semerone [Cimarron River] on the 27th of May on his way to Santa fé by the Curmanch [Comanche] Indians."[1]

Austin and his brother Peter were members of the same caravan as Jedediah—traveling from Independence, Missouri, to Santa Fe—and were thus among the first to learn their brother was missing. "The party was in distress for water," Austin wrote, and Jedediah had gone in search of the Cimarron River when he was "attacked by fifteen or twenty [Indians]—they succeeded in alarming his animal not daring to fire on him so long as they kept face to face, so soon as his horse turned they fired, and wounded him in the shoulder he then fired his gun, and killed their head chief it is supposed they then rushed upon him, and despatched him—such . . . is the fate of him who you loved." Austin knew the report would grieve his father "much" but hoped Jedediah Sr. would not "take it to heart too sorely," for his lost son "trusted, and confided, in the Giver of all good and may we not hope, that his religion, was true, and will be rewarded—Come unto me all ye ends of the earth and ye shall be saved."[2]

Austin and Jedediah Jr.'s brother-in-law, Solomon Simons (married to their older sister Eunice), who lived in Ohio near Jedediah Sr., wrote, "I carried the letter to Father Smith last Thursday [October 19]. He seemed to be more resigned than I expected."[3] Jedediah Sr., who had not seen his namesake for ten years, was already a widower—his wife, Sally Strong, had died the previous year. In a letter to his brother Ralph, Jedediah Jr. wrote, "I received the mortifying intelligence of the Death of our much loved Mother, I had indulged the pleaseing hope of again Seeing and perhaps, administering to the necessities of Her to whoom we owe so much but he who had an undoubted right has called and She is gone——. We can See her no more here; therefore, let us prepare against the same Summons must be received by us."[4]

Like his predecessor Captain Lewis, Captain Smith died a violent death at a young age, the former at thirty-five, the latter at thirty-two. Unlike Lewis's steady decline in the last few years of his life, however, Smith had seen great feats and great tragedies in his. In July of 1826, two years and five months after he and Thomas Fitzpatrick led their men over South Pass, Smith and two other William Ashley men—David E. Jackson and William Lewis Sublette—organized the firm Smith, Jackson & Sublette and bought Ashley's company for $16,000. Ashley then returned to St. Louis, having made a net profit of approximately $70,000 since his first trip up the Missouri in 1822.[5]

From 1826 to 1830 Smith, Jackson & Sublette expanded Ashley's system, employing between 80 and 180 men each year and extending the trapping area north to Salish country, west to the Snake River, and east across the Continental Divide, into Crow and Blackfeet territory. The three partners complemented one another well and made a good profit.[6] In April 1830 Sublette organized a caravan to carry supplies and goods valued at close to $30,000 to the Wind River Rendezvous. Rather than relying on packhorses, however, Sublette arranged for ten wagons, each drawn by five mules; two Dearborn carriages, each drawn by one mule; a dozen cattle and one milk cow; and eighty-one recruits mounted on mules. This was the first wagon train to cross South Pass, another milestone in westward expansion and another bad omen for the Indian nations.[7]

The outlook for Smith, Jackson & Sublette looked bright, but Sublette had learned in St. Louis that the Astor-Chouteau American Fur Company, so successful in the Great Lakes area, was about to expand to the Rockies. It was understood that Astor, who seemed to have unlimited funds, wanted a monopoly on the American fur trade and nothing less. Whether that prompted Sublette to suggest selling is not clear, but in early August, at the rendezvous near the confluence of the Wind River and Popo Agie River, the future site of Riverton, Wyoming, he, Smith, and Jackson sold out to Thomas Fitzpatrick, Jim Bridger, Milton Sublette, Jean Baptiste Gervais, and Henry Fraeb, who founded the Rocky Mountain Fur Company. With the sale complete, the trio headed east, back to St. Louis, with seventy armed riders guarding the ten wagons loaded down with 170 packs of beaver pelts. They reached St. Louis safely on October 10.[8] Less than three weeks later, Smith, Jackson, and Sublette wrote a letter to Secretary of War John H. Eaton relating details of the journey from St. Louis to the Wind River and back: "Our men were all healthy during the whole time: we suffered nothing by Indians. . . . The usual weight in the wagons was about one thousand eight hundred pounds. The usual progress of the wagons was from fifteen to twenty-five miles per day. The country being almost all open, level, and prairie, the chief obstructions were ravines and creeks. . . . This is the first time that wagons ever went to the Rocky mountains; and the ease and safety with which it was done prove the facility of communicating over land with the Pacific ocean." The well-respected triad thus proposed what soon would follow—a trail to Oregon, even adding that in 1828 and 1829 Smith had spent several months at the "post of the Hudson's Bay Company, called Fort Vancouver, near the mouth of the Multnomah river," a bountiful area for growing wheat, barley, corn, apple orchards, and vineyards. Not only that, but the British Canadians were carrying on trade with local Indians, Mexico, the Sandwich Islands, and London: "The inequality of the convention with Great Britain in 1818 is most glaring and apparent, and its continuance is a great and manifest injury to the United States." The partners ended their lengthy missive with a request that Eaton lay "these *facts* . . . before President Jackson," a powerful portent of the flood of immigrants who would rush across the continent over the next several decades.[9]

By January 1831 Sublette and Jackson, still partners, agreed with Smith, who had just bought a spacious home in St. Louis, on a joint mission—a trading venture to New Mexico. There was money to be made, but that was a secondary concern for Smith—he wanted to add southwest geography to the maps he had labored on for years and also hoped to publish those maps with a narrative of his adventures, even hiring Samuel Parkman, a well-educated young man, to assist with the project as they traveled the Santa Fe Trail. Parkman had already gone west with Sublette in 1829. It also went without saying that Smith, as always, hankered to follow some unknown river to its source or its mouth, exploring for exploration's sake. So on April 10 twenty-two mule-drawn wagons pulled out of St. Louis. Jedediah owned eleven of them; Jackson and Sublette ten. The last wagon, jointly owned by all three, had a six-pound cannon mounted on the rear axle, ready for action. Two other men with wagons joined the caravan, bringing the total number of hands to eighty-three.[10]

"The most 'fashionable' prairie dress is the fustian frock of the city-bred merchant furnished with a multitude of pockets capable of accommodating a variety of 'extra tackling,'" wrote Josiah Gregg, an early historian of the Santa Fe Trail. "Then there is the backwoodsman with his leather hunting-shirt—the farmer with his blue jean coat—the wagoner with his flannel-sleeve vest. . . . The frontier hunter sticks to his rifle, as nothing could induce him to carry what he terms in derision 'the scatter-gun.' The sportsman from the interior flourishes his double-barrelled fowling piece. . . . A great many were furnished beside with a bountiful supply of pistols and knives of every description."[11]

Around the first of May, the convoy reached Independence, Missouri, the bustling fur-trade center founded just four years earlier, and spent a few days there. Also present in the area was a group of missionaries from the Church of Christ, organized in New York in 1830, whose disciples by that time were known as Mormonites. They had attempted to preach to the Delaware Indians in Kansas, but the local Indian agent forbade further contact. One of them, Oliver Cowdery, a close associate of Joseph Smith, apparently heard enthusiastic chatter among the frontiersmen about their upcoming trip. In a letter written on May 7—three days after the column of horsemen, mules, and wagons departed—Cowdery wrote, "I am informed of an other Tribe of Lamanites [Indians] lately who have abundance of flocks of the best kinds of sheep and cattle and manufacture blankets of superior quality the tribe is very numerous they live three hundred miles west of Santafee and are called navahoes."[12]

About this same time, Thomas Fitzpatrick arrived on the scene, reaching Missouri for the first time since he went upriver with Ashley in 1823 and no doubt surprised to see the new trading post of Independence. Jedediah and his former partners were also surprised—since neither Fitzpatrick nor any of his Rocky Mountain Fur Company partners had ordered goods for the 1831 season from Smith, Sublette, and Jackson by February, the deadline presumably agreed on when the two firms signed papers the previous August. After the sale, Fitzpatrick and others had traveled north to Three Forks and safely trapped beaver—despite the likely presence of Blackfeet Indians in the area. Fitzpatrick and a companion then descended the Missouri by boat all the way to Missouri. He now needed to obtain goods and get back to the Rockies as fast as possible, and Smith, Sublette, and Jackson agreed to provide him with the needed supplies when they reached Santa Fe: "This would make a long, roundabout route, but what alternative was there?"[13]

The leaders of the caravan were, of course, seasoned mountain men, but none had traveled the Santa Fe Trail. Gregg hardly minced words on that issue, writing that Smith and his fellows "set out without a single person in their company at all competent to guide them on the route."[14] At first it was not difficult to follow the path of other wagons, but after the group crossed the Arkansas River, they found themselves bewildered by a maze of buffalo tracks: "No discernable trace marked the course of the wagon road across this desert and Jedediah's party struck it at an especially bad time, when the country was parched by drought."[15]

"The party had been nearly three days without water, and as many as could be spared, were sent in different directions in search of it," read an 1832 account likely based on information from Fitzpatrick. "Smith, with Mr. Fitzpatrick, went forward in a south direction. . . . They came to a deep hollow, in which water had usually been found by former parties, but it was then dry. Smith left Fitzpatrick to wait till the party should come up, with directions to dig for water, while he would push on a few miles further south. . . . He was last seen, by a spy-glass, about three miles from Fitzpatrick." That was the last sure word of Jedediah Smith. Although his friends searched for him for two days, his body was never found. Austin Smith reported that "Spanish traders who trade with those Indians" told him fifteen or twenty Comanche

Indians killed Jedediah; the same traders gave Jedediah's gun and pistols to Austin. Austin's interaction with the traders, however, happened after the caravan reached Santa Fe, several weeks after Jedediah's death. There is no way of knowing how accurate that uncorroborated story was. As Kelly notes, "That [Smith] was killed on the Cimarron River by Comanche Indians . . . can never be substantiated. . . . Nevertheless, the tale persists, resisting, thus far, all attempts to dismantle the veracity of its intrinsic circumstances."[16]

The final sale of Smith, Jackson & Sublette assets took time, but when accounts were finally settled in 1831, each partner was due at least $17,500. By then, however, Jedediah had already vanished forever in the Cimarron Desert.[17] In a letter to his brother Ralph, written not quite a year and a half before his death, Jedediah acknowledged that two expeditions under his leadership suffered tragic losses: "In Augt. 1827 ten Men, who were in company with me, lost their lives, by the Amuchabas [Mohave] Indians on the Colorado River; & in July 1828 fifteen men, who were in Company with me lost their lives, by the Umpquah Indians, on the River of the Same name, one hundred miles South of the Mouth of the Columbia."[18] The mistreatment of Indians by Smith and his men likely triggered the second disaster.[19]

As for Smith's accomplishments, he understated the case when he wrote, "Since I left home I have passed throug[h] various vicissitudes of Fortune; I have been fortunate in some respects in others unfortunate—I have passed through the Country from St. Louis, Missouri, to the North Pacific Ocean, in different ways—through countrys of Barrennness & seldom one of the reverse."[20] A twentieth-century assessment called him "one of the nation's most important trapper-explorers," who "filled in many of the missing pieces of western geography and demonstrated that feasible routes existed across the West to northern and southern California and to Oregon. . . . A deeply religious person and literate and civilized man, he was admired and respected."[21]

"I Joined the Party under Fitzpatrick Bound for the Rocky Mountains"

As far as is known, no one in the caravan left a record of the desperate search for Jedediah Smith and at what point they decided to go on without him. Given his history of being presumed dead but then turning up alive more than once, they no doubt hoped for the best. Still, hope faded a little at a time, and in the midst of that uncertainty, Fitzpatrick, no doubt troubled by not being able to find Smith even though he had been the last to see him, was riding to the side of the wagons when he noticed a disturbance in the brush along the trail. He dismounted his horse to investigate and was shocked to see a small Indian boy on the verge of starvation. "The kind traveler picked up the waif," writes Fitzpatrick's biographer LeRoy R. Hafen, "soothed his fears, and carried him to the wagons, where with sympathetic ministrations the little fellow rapidly recovered strength and spirit."[22] With no sign of the boy's family or nation, Fitzpatrick adopted him, naming him Friday, after the day he was discovered.

"From the date of [Friday's rescue] he was ushered into a new state of existence, and soon acquired the language and habits of the whites," wrote frontiersman Rufus B. Sage. "Taken to St. Louis, he remained there for some five years, and received a partial education during the interval. So complete was the transformation, he even forgot the name and language of his nation, and became an adept in the customs of civilized life."[23]

At St. Louis in April 1833, as Charles Larpenteur was beginning his forty years as a trader on the upper Missouri, he met Fitzpatrick's friend Robert Campbell, who "arrived with a young man named James Lee, and a little Snake [Shoshone] Indian called Friday, who had been adopted by Mr. Fitzpatrick, a trapper in the mountains and afterwards an Indian agent."[24] A year and a half later, William M. Anderson traveled with Fitzpatrick and Friday from the Rocky Mountains to Missouri and offered a new perspective: "Mr. Fitzpatrick's little foundling, Friday, is becoming, every day, an object of greater & greater interest to me, his astonishing memory, his minute observation & amusing inquiries, interest me exceedingly. He has been from his band & kindred, 3 or 4 years, yet some scenes & incidents he describes with wonderful accuracy. He still remembers that he was called Warshinun which he tells me means 'black spot.[']"[25]

Sage was traveling the Santa Fe Trail in 1844 when his eastbound wagon train reached an Arapaho village. "Soon after this we were joined by a young Arapaho Indian named Friday, who was desirous of visiting the States," wrote Sage. "He had formerly lived in St. Louis, where he had acquired a knowledge of the English language, and still maintains a reputation for honesty, intelligence, and sobriety." As Sage and Friday traveled together, the latter told his story, which his friend published two years later, no doubt enhanced in the tradition of frontier yarn-telling. Friday was six years old when, after wandering "an unusual distance from camp" and passing "most of the day in a fruitless effort to catch prairie dogs" with his friends, he found himself lost in "a long reach of dry sand-prairie, eastward of the Cimarone, which was entirely destitute of water. . . . Another attempt to reach the village the day following was unsuccessful, and each repeated effort proved equally unavailing. At length . . . he laid himself down to die. . . . He thought himself a dweller of the Spirit Land and a ranger of the hunting ground of happy souls. . . . Strange voices greeted his ear, and sounds broke upon the stillness of solitude. . . . Thereupon he found himself in the firm grasp of two white men, who cut short his soliloquy by bearing him to their camp." As Friday remembered it, he had been rescued by Fitzpatrick and Sublette.[26]

Fitzpatrick thus had Friday with him when the caravan reached Santa Fe on July 4. As promised, Sublette and Jackson furnished Fitzpatrick with two-thirds of his goods and Parkman, now acting as Smith's agent, one-third. Forty of the men previously employed by Sublette and Jackson now hired on with Fitzpatrick, whose debt came to almost $6,000. He agreed to send to Taos, a trading town northwest of Santa Fe, "good clean, well handled mountain fur at the rate of $4.25 per pound" by the end of the year. Sublette exchanged the rest of his merchandise for fifty-five packs of beaver and eight hundred buffalo robes.[27]

At Taos, Fitzpatrick, already several weeks behind his hoped-for schedule, got his equipment and packhorses ready and hired the last of his recruits. One of them was a slightly built twenty-one-year-old Missouri runaway by the name of Christopher Houston Carson, "Kit" to his friends. Years later, Carson told Jessie Frémont, "I was a young boy in the school house when the cry came, 'Indians!' I jumped to my rifle and threw down my spelling book, and there it lies."[28] Fitzpatrick, however, was looking for someone literate in wilderness life, and young Carson, who had already trekked to Arizona and California with the veteran southwest frontiersman Ewing Young, fit the bill. "In 1831," Carson wrote in his autobiography, "I joined the party under Fitzpatrick bound for the Rocky Mountains. We traveled north"—crossing the Arkansas River near present Pueblo, Colorado—"till we struck the Platte River and then journeyed up the Sweetwater, a branch of the Platte."[29]

Meanwhile, Fitzpatrick's partners and hands in the Rocky Mountain Fur Company had already completed their spring hunt—bringing in an impressive fifty packs of beaver pelts—and were preparing for the summer rendezvous at Willow Valley, which straddles the northeastern Utah / southeastern Idaho border. According to trapper Joe Meek—on his way to becoming a prominent mountain man, law officer, and politician—"It was expected that Fitzpatrick would have arrived from St. Louis with the usual recruits and supplies of merchandise, in time for the summer rendezvous; but after waiting for some time in vain, Bridger and [Milton] Sublette determined to send out a small party to look for him."[30]

One of the Rocky Mountain Fur Company partners, Henry Fraeb, sought the assistance of a Crow shaman in finding Fitzpatrick. The prophet performed a days-long ceremony of chanting, singing, and dancing—all to the beating of drums—and finally proclaimed that Fitzpatrick was alive but coming on the wrong road. "The large number of men now employed, had exhausted the stock of goods on hand," continued Meek. "The camp was without blankets, and without ammunition; knives were not had; traps were scarce; but worse than all, the tobacco had given out, and alcohol was not! In such a case as this, what could a mountain man do?"[31]

Encouraged by the Crow elder, Fraeb and a few others set out in search of Fitzpatrick, going first in the direction of the Wind River but then going farther south to the Platte and the Sweetwater, where they somehow met the forty-odd men and train of packhorses. Fitzpatrick told Fraeb of how he ended up going to New Mexico and of Jedediah Smith's shocking disappearance, expressing his regrets and vowing to return with goods the next spring in time for the rendezvous. A sobered Fraeb took control of the supply party. "We trapped to the head of the Sweetwater, then on to Green River, and then to Jackson's Hole, on a fork of the Columbia River, and from there on to the head of the Salmon River," wrote Carson. "There we came upon the camp of a part of our band that we had been hunting for, and then went into winter quarters on the head of the Salmon River."[32]

Fraeb's meeting Milton Sublette, Bridger, and their men at Idaho's Salmon River shows the partners had agreed on a wintering spot and knew how to get there. Sublette and Bridger's group had followed a meandering path from Willow Valley to Bear River, then the Snake and Salmon, and then Montana's Deer Lodge and Flathead areas before circling back to the headwaters of the Salmon.[33] Their men were thrilled when they saw the pack train carrying the rendezvous goods. "Fraeb arrived," wrote Warren Ferris, "and camp presented a confused scene of rioting, and debauchery for several days, after which however the kegs of alcohol were again bunged, and all became tranquil. The men provided themselves with lodges, and made preparations for passing the winter as comfortable as possible."[34]

Friendly Flathead (Salish) and Nez Perce Indians wintered with the Rocky Mountain Fur Company men. When Insula, one of the Flathead chiefs, saw that Bridger's men had left valuables strewn about the camp, he ordered that none of his people take them.[35] Ferris had high praise for both nations, especially the Flatheads, "noted for humanity, courage, prudence, candour, forbearance, integrity, trustfulness, piety, and honesty. . . . They have been taught never to fight except in self defence, or at they express it, 'never to go out to hunt their own graves,' but to remain at home and defend manfully their wives and children when attacked."[36]

"He First Came to This Country with Lewis and Clark"

Not long after leaving Fraeb and the supply party, near the mouth of the Laramie River—at the future site of Fort Laramie—Fitzpatrick and his companions met a recently organized band of trappers under the leadership of John Gantt and Jefferson Blackwell, who had obtained a license from Superintendent William Clark about the same time that Fitzpatrick reached Missouri and found Smith, Sublette, and Jackson on their way to New Mexico.[37] "While at this place," wrote Zenas Leonard, one of the greenhorns, "four men (three whites and one Indian) came to our tent. This astonished us not a little, for a white man was the last of living beings that we expected to visit us in this vast wilderness. . . . The principal of these men was a Mr. Fitzpatrick . . . then on his way to St. Louis."[38]

The Indian, of course, was Friday, but Leonard said nothing else about him. Nor did he identify the other two white men with Fitzpatrick. He was too occupied with Fitzpatrick's flaws, saying the latter "was an old hand at the [fur] business and we expected to obtain some useful information from him, but we were disappointed. The selfishness of man is often disgraceful to human nature; and I never saw more striking evidence of this fact, than was presented in the conduct of this man Fitzpatrick. Notwithstanding we had treated him with great friendship and hospitality, merely because we were to engage in the same business with him, which he knew we never could exhaust or even impair—he refused to give us any information whatever, and appeared disposed to treat us as intruders."[39]

Leonard was young—about the same age as Carson—and hopeful. One can certainly empathize with his disillusionment, but he had no idea what a cutthroat business he had joined; no idea that Fitzpatrick's erstwhile pals Smith and Jackson, though not unkind, had conducted the recent transactions with their own profits in mind; no idea that even between brothers—or was it especially between brothers?—such as William and Milton, economic competition took on a harder edge. Nor could he know that because of circumstance, Fitzpatrick had just missed the good profits to be made at the rendezvous or that as a partner in the Rocky Mountain Fur Company, he was constantly competing with the likes of Hudson's Bay Company (which had merged with the North West Company in 1821) and Astor's American Fur Company.

Leonard concluded his comments on Fitzpatrick—at least for the present—by noting that "Captain Blackwell, with two others, joined Fitzpatrick, and started back to the state of Missouri, for an additional supply of merchandize, and were to return the [next] summer."[40]

Leonard would spend four years, four months, and five days in the wilderness and would meet a number of historic individuals, even though that was naturally not evident at the time. Luckily, he kept a good record of when and where he met these icons of the West, and just as he noted that he first met Fitzpatrick at the mouth of the Laramie, he added that in November 1832 he made another acquaintance at the mouth of a different stream. He and the other trappers were bold enough to be following seventy or eighty Crow warriors who "manifested the best of friendship" at first but then returned on the night of their departure and stole five of the trappers' best hunting horses. "We travelled for some days [down the Bighorn River]," wrote Leonard, "until we came to their village situated at the mouth of the Stinking river"[41]—now called the Shoshone River. Next came a series of passages in Leonard's memoir that have sparked a good deal of discussion and disagreement among historians:

> We found a negro man, who informed us that he first came to this country with Lewis and Clark—with whom he also returned to the State of Missouri, and in a few years returned with a Mr. Mackinney, a trader on the Missouri river, and has remained here ever since—which is about ten or twelve years. He has acquired a correct knowledge of their manner of living, and speaks their language fluently. He has rose to be quite a considerable character, or chief, in their village; at least he assumes all the dignities of a chief, for he has four wives with whom he lives alternately.[42]

When told about the missing horses, the negro said "the reason they were taken from us was because we were found in their enemies' country, and that they supposed we were going to trade them guns, &c." When the trappers gave the chiefs "some trifling presents," the horses were returned "in as good trim" as when they disappeared. Leonard and his comrades coexisted peacefully with the Crows for two months; then the Indians moved down the river.[43]

Several months later, Leonard met Joseph R. Walker and learned that he "was ordered to steer through an unknown country, towards the Pacific, and if he did not find bever, he should return to the Great S. L. [Salt Lake] in the following summer." Eager to see the Pacific coast, Leonard signed on with Walker, "kind and affable to his men, but at the same time at liberty to command without giving offence."[44] Walker, with Leonard and thirty-nine of Captain Benjamin Bonneville's other men and perhaps twenty free trappers, set out from Green River on July 24, 1833. Their harrowing journey took them from the Great Salt Lake to the barren deserts of Utah and Nevada and then across the terrible Sierra Nevadas to central California and finally to the coast. Their route "was to become the mainstream of migration and conquest for their countrymen who sought Manifest Destiny beyond western horizons."[45]

By the summer of 1834 Walker's men had reversed their route and reached a rendezvous along Ham's Fork of the Green River. A few months later they were back among their Crow friends along the Bighorn River, at the same village where they found their horses and "a negro man, in the winter of 1832–33." Walker and most of his band soon descended the Bighorn to build a trading post for the winter season, but Leonard and two others stayed with the Crows "for the purpose of instigating them in the business of catching beaver and buffaloe."[46]

In one of several asides, Leonard offered interesting observations on Crow culture, writing of the "Long Haired Chief, which name he derives from the extreme length of his hair, which is no less than nine feet eleven inches long." This "venerable looking old man," apparently seventy-five or eighty years old, took "every precaution to preserve his hair" and had never cut it since his infancy: "He worships it as the director or guide of his fate through life . . . adoring this talisman." Leonard knew that most of the Indian nations paid homage to sacred instruments or articles, but "no nation, I believe, are so devoutly attached to their talismans as the Crow nation. . . . Almost every individual of the Crow tribe has something of this kind, and which generally consists of a seed, a stone, a piece of wood, a bear or eagle's claw. . . . This magical thing, whatever it may be, is carefully enveloped in a piece of skin, and then tied around their neck or body."[47]

Such musings eventually found their way back to the main narrative, in which the Crows found themselves in conflict with their "implacable enemies, the Blackfeet tribe." Although the Crows attacked several times, they could not penetrate the rocky ledge where the Blackfeet held their ground, in a sort of "fort that might have done credit to an army of frontier regulars." As often as the Crows charged, they retreated with "severe loss." When "many appeared overwhelmed with despair . . . the negro . . . who had been in company with us . . . ascended a rock from which he addressed the Crow warriors in the most earnest and impressive manner," warning them they would be "laughed at, scorned, and treated with contempt by all nations" if they did not defeat the Blackfeet. Telling them "a black man . . . was not afraid to go amongst his enemy," the "old negro" leaped from the rock and made for the Blackfeet stronghold "as fast as he could run. The Indians, guessing his purpose, and inspired by his words and fearless example, followed close to his heels, and were in the fort dealing destruction to the right and left nearly as soon as the old man."[48]

The Crow nation celebrated their victory and mourned their dead, burying each fallen warrior "with his talisman, and any thing else to which he was attached." Each chief who lost his life in the battle was buried with his horse's shaved tail and mane, the Crows believing "that each of these hairs will turn into a beautiful horse in the land of spirits."[49] By the end of November 1834 Leonard and his two friends bade farewell to their Crow friends and joined Walker on the Wind River, never seeing the "old man" again.

When Hiram M. Chittenden published his monumental two-volume work *The American Fur Trade of the Far West* in 1902, he included a chapter entitled "Rose and Beckwourth, the Crow Chiefs," noting that Edward Rose and James P. Beckwourth, both of "mixed negro blood," were "recognized Crow leaders for many years." Beckwourth, reportedly born in 1798, "did not begin his career among the Crows until Rose was nearly done with them, and there are certain noted exploits related by Beckwourth in his autobiography which were probably performed by Rose."[50] As for the old man whom Leonard saw in 1832 and again in 1834 but never identified by name, Chittenden states unequivocally that it was Rose, not even considering the possibility that it was Beckwourth. Nor did Chittenden mention the one African American man who definitely "came to this country with Lewis and Clark"—York. Not only that, but Chittenden wrote that Leonard gave "a somewhat extended though inaccurate account" of Rose without explaining what he meant by that.[51] It seems that Chittenden could have addressed the issue of the identity of "the old negro" with considerably more depth and nuance. Indeed, in 1939, in her introduction to the publication of "The Five Scalps" (an 1829 biography of Rose), Stella M. Drumm threw everything into question when she mentioned a letter "written contemporaneously" with Rose's death that showed he was killed by an Arikara war party "some time during the winter of 1832–1833"—almost two years before Leonard saw the old man lead the Crows into battle.

If Rose really died then, the old man Leonard met must have been either York or Beckwourth. However, in his careful treatment of the issue in *In Search of York* (published in 1985), Robert B. Betts argued persuasively that after Rose was eliminated as a possibility, neither of the other two fit Leonard's description, thus leaving historians with what looked like an inscrutable mystery. Thirty years later, however, fur-trade researcher and writer Clay J. Landry went in search of primary documents that might shed light on the matter and struck gold at one of the quintessential archives of western Americana—the Missouri History Museum in St. Louis. Landry confirmed that an American Fur Company employee by the name of Rose was killed by Arikara Indians in the spring of 1833 but discovered the man's first name was *Colin*. That crucial detail, combined with a careful study of remarks made by Beckwourth, offers solid evidence that Edward Rose was not the man attacked and killed in 1833. Chittenden was thus proved correct: Zenas Leonard met Edward Rose among the Crows in 1832 and again in 1834. As far as we can reasonably speculate, Rose likely died while still with his Crow friends and relatives and was buried with his talismans. That is the final word on the man whose counterpart James P. Beckwourth called "one of the best interpreters ever known in the whole Indian country"—until, of course, another researcher turns up a document in an archive, an attic, a family Bible, or elsewhere.[52]

When Leonard published his memoir in 1839, he knew that his journey to California with Captain Walker had been historic. He also knew that Fitzpatrick had a certain status, but it was too early to see the big picture of a trader he disliked from the start. Leonard had a memorable experience with the Black man he met in Crow country and made it an interesting footnote in his narrative but had no idea who the old warrior really was. What Leonard could not realize was that he had encountered a unique pair of adventurers. Not only were they both veterans of the Arikara attack, the military campaign that followed, and the subsequent advance toward South Pass; between the two of them, they would eventually join in an incredible number of landmark explorations of the West, more so than any other frontiersman tandem. Rose—and Rose alone—ventured west with Manuel Lisa, Andrew Henry, Wilson Price Hunt, and Henry Atkinson. Fitzpatrick would eventually guide everyone from Father Pierre-Jean De Smet and Marcus and Narcissa Whitman to John C. Frémont, Stephen Watts Kearny, and Philip St. George Cooke.

7

"The Whirlwind Is Coming to Destroy My People!"

Indian Nations and the White Man's Fatal Maladies

On Monday, August 13, 1804, Lewis and Clark found themselves more than eight hundred miles upriver, along the northeast corner of Nebraska in Omaha Indian Country. Eager to meet the Omahas, the captains sent Sergeant John Ordway and four others to the main village "with a flag & Some Tobacco to invite the Nation to See & talke with us on tomorrow."[1]

When Ordway and his companions returned the next day, however, they said they had not found any Indians. The Omaha village, wrote Clark, was now in ruins, surrounded by innumerable hosts of graves; "the ravages of the Small Pox (4 years ago) . . . which Swept off 400 men & women & Children" had reduced the nation's population by more than half, leaving the survivors "to the insults of their weaker neighbors which before was glad to be on friendly terms with them." Clark also learned—apparently from Omahas who survived the epidemic—that when "this fatal malady was among them they Carried their franzey to verry extroadinary length, not only of burning their Village, but they put their *wives* & Children to *D[e]ath* with a view of their all going together to Some better Countrey—They burry their Dead on the tops of high hills and rais mounds on top of them." Clark further concluded that the Omahas likely caught smallpox "from Some other Nation by means of a warparty."[2]

Lewis and Clark were hardly the first outsiders to witness the aftermath of a smallpox outbreak among the Indians. In May of 1792 British captain George Vancouver—in his long but futile search for a northwest passage through North America—was exploring and mapping the Strait of Juan de Fuca, between Vancouver Island and Washington State's Olympic Peninsula, when he camped along Discovery Bay. "We landed not far from the largest rivulet, where we found a deserted village capable of containing an hundred inhabitants," he wrote. "The houses were built after the Nootka fashion, but did not seem to have been lately the residence of Indians. The habitations had now fallen into decay; their inside, as well as a small surrounding space that appeared to have been formerly occupied, were over-run with weeds; amongst which were found several human sculls and other bones, promiscuously scattered about."[3]

Vancouver was mystified by the scene, but as he and his crew used small seacraft such as pinnaces, cutters, and launches to explore inlets, the cause of the empty village became evident. Along Hood Canal, actually a fjord west of Puget Sound, the men met a group of about sixty Indians who greeted them with "great friendship and hospitality." As the sailors and Indians exchanged gifts, some of Vancouver's fellows recognized someone they had seen a few days earlier—a man "who had suffered very much from the small pox," a "deplorable disease" that was common and quite fatal among the Natives. "Its indelible marks were seen on many," continued Vancouver, "and several had lost the sight of one eye . . . owing most likely to the virulent effects of this baneful disorder."[4]

Virginia natives William Clark and Meriwether Lewis, born in 1770 and 1774, respectively, had heard of the terror of smallpox from their boyhood days. Indeed, as Elizabeth A. Fenn notes, from 1775 to 1782, smallpox, technically *variola major*, "ravaged the greater part of North America, from Mexico to Massachusetts, from Pensacola to Puget Sound . . . killing more than a hundred thousand people and maiming many more."[5]

In subsequent years, neither of the future captains was surprised by news of the dreaded sickness. In a letter written around 1789, young Lewis informed his mother that his brother-in-law, Edmund Anderson, would have started a business in Richmond, Virginia, "before this, had not the small-pox broke out in the City, which rages with great violence."[6] Four years later, at Fort Greenville (near present Greenville, Ohio), General Anthony Wayne ordered Lieutenant Billy Clark and his Chickasaw Indian scouts to escort Brigadier General James Wilkinson and a convoy of packhorses to Fort Washington (present Cincinnati). Clark and his Chickasaw allies spent a nervous few days at Fort Washington because of a smallpox eruption. Clark then left on a series of assignments, but when he returned in April of 1794, he received a smallpox "enocholation."[7] The inoculation (also called variolation) consisted of making a slight incision on Clark's hand or arm and then implanting smallpox sores or pustules into the wound. Clark likely developed a mild case of smallpox, but the inoculation also gave him permanent immunity to the disease.

Nor had the subject of smallpox been forgotten as Thomas Jefferson planned the expedition of the West. In April 1803 U.S. attorney general Levi Lincoln posed this question to Jefferson: "As Capt. Lewis may have in his company, some who have not had the small pox, would it not be best to carry some of the matter for the kine pox with him?"[8] Jefferson went a step further, advising Lewis to treat the Indians "in the most friendly & conciliatory manner which their own conduct will admit" and to "carry with you some matter of the kinepox" and inform the Indians "of it's efficacy as a preservative from the small pox; & instruct & encourage them in the use of it. This may be especially done wherever you winter."[9] Although Lewis obtained "some of the Vaxcine matter," he concluded by October 1803 that it was no longer effective. There is no evidence that he received an additional supply or that he provided inoculations to any Indians during the expedition.[10]

"Almost Entirely Destroyed by the Smallpox"

"Arikara Indian folklore is full of monsters: scalped men, cannibals, witches, water monsters, spirits, ghosts, and monstrous man-eating animals," writes Mark van de Logt. "But the most powerful monster of Arikara tradition was a devastating whirlwind." Prominent in several different versions of the Arikara creation story, this whirlwind annihilated and dispersed multitudes of people who had failed to offer sacrifices in its honor. In one version, Mother Corn implored the Great Chief Above directly, crying out, "I want help, for the Whirlwind is coming to destroy my people!" Van de Logt hypothesizes that the atrocious whirlwind, as well as such representations as snakes and bears, may have symbolized a series of epidemics among the Arikaras in the eighteenth century, meaning that "the Arikara creation account not merely tells the story of Arikara creation in the distant past but in fact covers Arikara history over an extended period of time, at least until the great smallpox epidemic of 1780–81."[11] Not only that, but Arikara oral tradition indicates that the whirlwind first shattered the Arikaras in the seventeenth century and then again in the eighteenth.[12]

Furthermore, historians have identified several epidemics that may have involved the Arikaras between 1750 and 1781, such as an outbreak of either smallpox or measles around 1750 or 1752. Interestingly, one Lakota winter count from Battiste Good names 1734–35 as the "used them up with belly ache winter," likely representing the Lakotas' first experience with smallpox.[13] In 1761 the Arikaras battled influenza, "followed by yet another smallpox or measles epidemic between 1762 and 1766. Although it is uncertain how these diseases reached Arikara settlements, it seems likely that germs traveled along the trade routes that connected the Arikaras to the various corners of the continent. The most devastating of the epidemics was the smallpox outbreak of 1780–81."[14]

Smallpox hit the New World as early as 1520 and 1562, with eruptions in Mexico and Brazil, respectively, each time on coastal regions and each time with the landing of ships from Europe or Africa. African slaves—first sent by Portugal to Brazil in 1526—were so vulnerable to smallpox "on the African coast, on shipboard, and in the New World, that a constant flow of new slaves was required to make up for losses due to smallpox among earlier arrivals." The malady usually started with chills, a high fever, malaise, prostration, cough, and headache. Within a few days it advanced to a skin eruption, which then went through its own stages, ending with pus-filled blisters. The later stages were conspicuous in terms of both sight and odor and were often accompanied by delirium or coma. Death normally ensued by the eighth to tenth day. If it did not, the fever would subside, and the pustules would dry. A long convalescence followed, but those who survived a bout with smallpox were left with lifelong immunity.[15]

"Even though smallpox was the leading cause of death in eighteenth-century Europe, accounting for between 5 and 10 percent of all deaths, it was more devastating still in the New World. In Europe, smallpox slowed population growth. In the Americas, it was the chief factor in the depopulation of the American Indians."[16] Indeed, the waves of pestilence that struck the Arikara nation between 1750 and 1781 possibly resulted in a population drop of almost 90 percent.[17] "In ancient times the Ricara nation was very large; it counted thirty-two populous villages, now depopulated and almost entirely destroyed by the smallpox, which broke out among them at three different times," wrote French fur trader Jean Baptiste Truteau, who visited the Arikaras in the mid-1790s. "This nation formerly so numerous, and which, according to their reports, could turn out four thousand warriors, is now reduced to about five hundred fighting men."[18]

The smallpox epidemic of the 1770s and '80s devastated many Indian nations, and no record reveals the calamity quite like the winter counts of the Arikaras' Missouri River neighbors to the south, the Lakotas. Among them, the chroniclers Battiste Good, American Horse, and Cloud Shield mentioned smallpox continuously:

1779–80: "Smallpox used them up winter."
1780–81: "Many died of small-pox; Smallpox used them up again winter."
1781–82: "Many died of small-pox; Many people died of smallpox."
1782–83: "Many people died of smallpox again."
1784–85: "A young man with small-pox shot himself."[19]

Of all the elements of European interaction with the Arikaras—including horses and guns—none was more dramatic than the "deadly germs" that caused "tremendous suffering, massive depopulation, social dislocation, and military decline."[20]

"My Youngest Son Died Today"

On April 17, 1837, the steamboat *St. Peters* departed St. Louis, making its annual trade voyage up the Missouri River for Pratte, Chouteau & Company (previously the Western Department of the American Fur Company). Joshua Pilcher, newly nominated agent for the Sioux, Cheyenne, and Ponca nations, and William N. Fulkerson, subagent for the upper Missouri Indians, were both onboard, along with $45,000 worth of trade goods, supplies for upriver posts, and annual government annuities in the form of provisions and products for the Omahas, Pawnees, and Sioux. Shortly before *St. Peters* reached Fort Leavenworth about April 29, a deckhand identified only as a "mulatto" fell sick with a fever, which could mean any of a variety of illnesses. A few days later, a "gentleman of the Indian Department"—probably Fulkerson—recognized the symptoms of smallpox and "suggested to the Capt. of the boat [Bernard Pratte Jr.] that it would be well to put the man ashore and leave him."[21] Leaving the sick man alone on the uninhabited shore, of course, likely meant leaving him to die. Pratte declined to do so.

By the time the steamboat reached the Council Bluffs Agency, north of the mouth of the Platte River, several other passengers were sick. While there, in late May, Pratte wrote, "I have small pox on board. We buried Vital Papin, and have 8 new cases, two since yesterday. I do not know where this will end."[22] Pratte understandably had no idea how to deal with the crisis—he proceeded upriver, predictably spreading smallpox at every stop, including the Sioux Agency, Fort Pierre, Fort Clark (just south of the Mandan villages), and Fort Union (near the mouth of the Yellowstone River), the final stop. Keelboats traveling west from Fort Union then carried the epidemic to Fort McKenzie (at the mouth of Marias River).[23]

"By July 1," writes Clyde D. Dollar, "the disease had spread among the Yankton and Santee at the Sioux agency where it reached epidemic proportions by mid-month. These bands suffered considerably from its ravages, but their exposure to the disease during the 1819–20 epidemic immunized them somewhat, thereby limiting the devastation in 1837. Also no doubt the ability of the Sioux to scatter into small family groups mitigated ravages among them by limiting contact." In the fall of 1837 the Skidi Pawnees attacked the Oglala Sioux and unknowingly took women and children afflicted with smallpox as hostages. The upshot was that as many as 2,500 Skidi Pawnees perished, perhaps a quarter of the entire nation.[24]

By the time *St. Peters* left Fort Union to return to St. Louis, a Pratte-Chouteau employee by the name of Jacob Halsey was already sick with smallpox. "I did not have the disease in its most malignant form though it was far from being light," he wrote, "however thank God I have escaped the disease but my condition has received a severe shock." Two weeks after Halsey took sick, "a second case of this detestable pest made its appearance in the fort, and a few days afterwards there was 27 persons ill with it in the fort out of which number 4 proved fatal." During this time, "the Assinboines were continually coming in. I sent our interpreter to meet them on every occasion, who represented our situation to them and requested them to return immediately from whence they came however all our endeavors proved fruitless, I could not prevent them from camping round the Fort—they have caught the disease, notwithstanding I have never allowed an Indian to enter the Fort, or any communication between them & the Sick." Among the Indians, he wrote, "it is raging with the greatest destruction imaginable at least 10 out of 12 died with it. I do not know how many Assiniboins have already died as they have long since given up counting but I presume at least 800 and of the Blackfeet at least 700."[25]

No trading post, however, was hit harder than Fort Clark, where a large group of Arikaras had settled in the spring, with 230 lodges camping with the Mandans and 20 with the Hidatsas. The three nations hoped their combined strength would prevent Sioux attacks. The trader in charge of the fort, Francis A. Chardon, was pleasantly surprised to find the Arikaras friendly and cooperative, contrary to their reputation in the fur business. Arikara chiefs Bloody Hand, Two Bulls, and Star regularly traded at the fort. The post and surrounding area were teeming with people, horses, and dogs. The future looked good.[26]

"The Steam Boat St Peters hove in sight at 2 P.M.," the careful journal keeper Chardon wrote on Sunday, June 18.[27] Unlike Chardon, the Indian agent Fulkerson was unhappy to see the Arikaras camped near the fort. "They make very fair promises . . . but no reliance can be placed in them," he wrote, based on what he had heard from others.[28] It was the Arikaras, however, who could rightfully mention broken promises because Fulkerson, for unknown reasons, had not brought the pledged annuities. The agent called a council with the chiefs but hardly inspired confidence when he "distributed out a few Presents to the Rees, and gave them a few words of good talk, and departed."[29]

When smallpox symptoms first became evident at Fort Clark is not clear, but in mid-July, two and a half weeks after *St. Peters* left for St. Louis, Chardon wrote, "A young Mandan died to day of the Small Pox—several others has caught it—the Indians all being out Makeing dried Meat had saved several of them." Chardon made similar entries later in July: "Indians all out for berries.

No News from any quarter. The small pox is Killing them up at the Village, four died to day" and "Several more Mandans died last night."[30]

By the first week of August, there was no doubt that the outbreak had reached epidemic status. Chardon learned that a "great many . . . Gros Ventres" (Hidatsas) had died, "several chiefs among them. They swear vengeance against all the Whites, as they say the small pox was brought here by the S. B. [steamboat]." Seven Arikaras died over the course of two days; several "left the Mandan Village, and Pitched their Lodges Out in the Prairie." Four more Indians died the next day. Chardon reported, "Two thirds of the Village are sick." Seven more succumbed the day after that.[31]

"All the Ree's that were encamped in the Mandan lodges, except for a few that are sick, Moved down to the Island hopeing to get rid of the small pox," Chardon wrote on August 10. "The Mandans talk of Moveing to the other side of the river, 12 or 15 died to day." The next day the Mandans did cross the river, "leaving all that were sick in the Village, I Keep no a/c of the dead, as they die so fast that it is impossible." One of Chardon's best friends in the Indian village died the next day; he also got news of a "war party of Gros Ventres and Rees (70) being used up by the [Sioux], quicker work than the small pox."[32]

Over the next few weeks Chardon frequently said that at least ten Indians were dying every day. Reports of suicide were frequent:

> A Mandan and his Wife Killed themselves yesterday to not Out live their relations that are dead. . . . A young Mandan . . . took up his gun and shot [his wife] dead, and with his Knife ripped open his own belly—two young men (Rees) Killed themselves to day, one of them stabbed himself with a Knife, and the other with an arrow. . . . News from the Little Village, that the disease is getting worse and worse every day. . . . Seven more died in the Village last Night, and Many More at the Rees camp at the Point of Woods below. . . . A young Mandan that died 4 days ago, his wife haveing the disease also—Killed her two children, one a fine Boy of eight years and the other six, to complete the affair she hung herself.[33]
>
> Month of August I bid you farewell with all my heart, after running twenty hair breadths escapes, threatened every instant to be all

> murdered, however it is the wish of humble servant that the Month of September will be More favorable, the Number of Deaths up to the Present is very near five hundred—The Mandans are all cut off, except 23 young and Old men.[34]

For Chardon, who had already lost an unidentified "best friend," things got much more personal. On Thursday, September 7, he wrote, "Started the canoe with two Men to Fort Pierre, sent My Boy down with them being afraid of the disease." The young son's name was Andrew Jackson Chardon, exact age unknown. Two weeks later, he added, "The Rees Crossed the river in quest of Buffaloe commenced tradeing Corn—Strong Wind from the South east Which Prevents my hauleing Wood—Entered into My Winter quarters, My youngest son [Andrew Jackson] died to day." A few days later, with the epidemic finally abated, he estimated that it had "distroyed the seven eights of the Mandans and one half of the Rees Nations."[35]

"The Smallpox Raged among Them for Many Years"

As discussed earlier, William Clark fully expected to meet the Crow Indians as he descended the Yellowstone River in July and August of 1806, but he never did. So while the captains returned with an impressive record of the history, culture, and language of the Arikara, Mandan, Hidatsa, Shoshone, Nez Perce, and Chinookan nations, they had no firsthand knowledge of the Crows. Almost a year before Clark started down the Yellowstone, however, another explorer visited the Crows and produced a detailed fifty-one page, day-by-day journal covering Crow life from weapons, dress, linguistics, warfare, and scalp dances to horsemanship, medicine practice, and belief in good and bad spirits. The compiler of this document, still a key primary source for the study of the Crows, was a twenty-one-year-old employee of the North West Company by the name of François-Antoine Laroque. Although he was born in Quebec to French-speaking parents, he was sent at a young age to the United States to learn English and kept his journals in that language. In early June 1805 he and two companions left a fort on Manitoba's Assiniboine River, traveled south to North Dakota's Mandan and Hidatsa country, then southwest into Wyoming's Big Horn Mountains, and finally, northwest to the

Yellowstone, which they followed (like Clark the next year) to its confluence with the Missouri, which they reached on October 8.[36]

Not surprisingly, the thorough Laroque wrote of disease among the Crows: "There are three principal tribes . . . & these tribes are again divided into many other small ones which at present consist but of a numerous people who were reduced to their present number by the ravage of the small Pox, which raged among them for many years successively & as late as three years ago [1802]. They told me they counted 2000 Lodges or tents in their Camp when all together before the small Pox had infected them. At present their whole number consists of about 2400 persons dwelling in 300 Tents and are able to raise 600 warriors."[37] As for the 1770s–80s epidemic, documentary evidence does not indicate what percentage of the Crow nation became infected with smallpox, but even if the number were 50 percent and less than half of that group died, approximately 3,500 Crows would have perished. If Laroque's statistics were applied to the earlier outbreak, however, the mortality rate would have been much higher.[38]

Edwin Thompson Denig, a fur trader on the upper Missouri from 1833 to 1856, told of an incident that happened his first year in the area. A victorious Crow war party returning to their village "rejoicing came suddenly upon a caravan of emigrants." The pioneers warned the Crows "not to approach the wagons as some of the Whites were then lying sick with smallpox. . . . It is but justice to these people to say that on this occasion they used their utmost endeavors to prevent the Indians from receiving the infection. They tried to deal with them at a distance from the sick, but all to no purpose." Before the Indians and emigrants parted, several Crows were sick: "In this case it was the same as with the other tribes—about one in six or seven recovered. . . . The camp broke up . . . in the hope of running away from the pestilence. All order was lost. . . . Terrible was the mourning on this occasion. . . . Out of the 800 lodges counted the previous summer but 360 remained, even these but thinly peopled. . . . [Chief] Rotten Belly had escaped the infection altogether. The Little White Bear had recovered, but the ranks of his once proud force of warriors were terribly thinned."[39] Charles Adrian Heidenreich writes that the chief "Arapooish pulled the tribe together in a remarkable stroke of leadership, but held the Whites responsible for the smallpox" and adds that in 1837 Chief Long Hair apparently died of smallpox.[40] Otherwise, losses from the 1837 smallpox epidemic were minor for the Crows. In 1845, however, writes Keith Algier, the Crows "suffered from an outbreak of scarlet fever, in 1848 from another smallpox epidemic, and in 1849 from an outbreak of influenza."[41]

Joe Medicine Crow agrees, concluding that by 1850 the epidemics had decreased the Crow population from more than eight thousand to less than one thousand. "About the time the colonists won their independence and became a new nation," he continues, "tribes of the Western Plains lived by the hunt for their subsistence and conducted intertribal warfare for their avocation. . . . To these nomads of the Plains, bravery was the highest of desired qualities. . . . It was through performing brave war deeds that a man attained chieftaincy." There lived among the Crows "a very brave man whose deeds were unparalleled to this day. He was called Plays With His Face. He was greatly respected . . . but he never acknowledged it. . . . His creed was to do the impossible and to succeed when others failed. He defied the prowess of men, scorned the dangers of animals, and challenged the powerful forces of nature. He ridiculed death itself!" His younger brother, Faces Opposite Direction, "was almost as accomplished. He duplicated many of his older brother's feats" and was also "invulnerable to enemy bullets and arrows. Their deaths, however, came in an unexpected way. They were old men when smallpox, the white man's disease, struck them and many of the Crow people. The older brother whispered to the younger, 'My throat is about to close, but I am not going to let the white man's cursed sickness kill me. I am going to kill myself with my gun.' The younger brother whispered back and said, 'As usual, I will follow you.'"[42]

8

“Major Fitzpatrick Was a Good Man”

Seeking the Road to Redemption

On June 20, 1834, the Rocky Mountain Fur Company was officially dissolved. Although the company’s returns had been satisfactory, they had not been sufficient to escape the stranglehold of their suppliers, William Lewis Sublette and Robert Campbell. As William Ashley had seen, it was the suppliers, not the trappers, who made the best profits. “The Rocky Mountain Fur Company was stuck with the fixed costs of engagés’ salaries and the standard rate of exchange for pelts,” writes one historian of the fur trade. “Indeed, the competition of the early 1830s produced a temporary inflation; at the 1833 rendezvous, the Rocky Mountain Fur Company was forced to pay $1500 a year for experienced mountain men and as much as $9 a pound for beaver.”[1] On behalf of the partners, Thomas Fitzpatrick signed a note to William Lewis Sublette for $1,258.66. The company founded by Fitzpatrick, Jim Bridger, Milton Sublette, Jean Baptiste Gervais, and Henry Fraeb had lasted not quite four years, ending as it begun—in debt, but not for lack of trying. The partners were skilled backwoodsmen, but their competitors had sharper market awareness, more financial backing, and better luck. All this had taken a toll. Milton Sublette’s health was failing, Bridger had somehow grown accustomed—since an autumn 1832 fight with Blackfeet Indians—to having an arrowhead embedded in his back, and Fitzpatrick had barely survived an escape from Gros Ventres Indians that eventually left him without a horse and without a firearm. None other than Zenas Leonard was on the scene at the 1832 rendezvous at Pierre’s Hole when friends of Fitzpatrick, alarmed because they saw an Indian riding his horse, went out to search for him. “He was completely exhausted, and so much wasted in flesh, and deformed in dress, that, under other circumstances, he would not have been recognized," wrote Leonard. "The poor man was reduced to a skeleton, and was almost senseless. . . . Although I was not much attached to the man . . . I can scarcely describe my feelings of joy on beholding him safely returned."[2] Fitzpatrick's hair reportedly turned white from the trauma; he was often called "White Hair" thereafter.

Shortly after the Rocky Mountain Fur Company closed down, Fitzpatrick formed a partnership with the experienced trader Lucien B. Fontenelle. During the following winter, the new partners applied to William Clark for a trading license and also purchased Fort William, on Wyoming's Laramie River. In the spring of 1835 Fitzpatrick and Friday joined a group headed for Fort William. Meanwhile, Fontenelle organized a caravan to travel from Liberty, Missouri, to Bellevue (near present Omaha, Nebraska) and then to the annual fur-trade rendezvous, this one on the Green River. Two missionaries, Samuel Parker and Dr. Marcus Whitman, sponsored by the American Board of Commissioners of Foreign Missions (ABCFM), arranged with Fontenelle to join the caravan. "They have between fifty and sixty men, six wagons, three yoke of oxen, and nearly two hundred horses and mules," wrote Whitman.[3]

Like Alexander Mackenzie, Lewis and Clark, and Wilson Price Hunt's Overland Astorians, Parker and Whitman had cast their eyes on the Pacific coast. The difference was this: rather than crossing the continent for commercial gain, they came to save souls, a zeal incited by an 1833 Christian newspaper article telling how four Indian chiefs from beyond the Rocky Mountains traveled to St. Louis to visit their great father William Clark and ask him about the "White Man's Book of Heaven." Clark reportedly confirmed that the Bible indeed revealed the truth, from man's "creation down to the advent of the Saviour . . . his life, precepts, his death, resurrection, ascension, and the relation he now stands to man as a mediator."[4]

The article was widely reprinted and "sparked religious zeal in the East and sounded a clarion call for action in nearly every proselyting religion. . . . Many, especially the Methodists and Catholics, responded immediately by preparing to send missionaries."[5] In 1834 Methodist missionaries Jason Lee, Daniel Lee, and Cyrus Shepard traveled west to the Oregon country with Nathaniel Wyeth's second expedition and became the first Americans to preach to Indians in the West. Jason was instrumental in the settlement of Oregon.[6]

In 1833, one month after reading the article about the Indians' interest in the Bible, fifty-four-year-old Parker volunteered to serve beyond the Rockies. The ABCFM first declined the offer because of Parker's age but reconsidered when he raised money for the journey. He left behind his wife and three children after the board promised to take care of them for at least a year if he perished on his mission. The board then appointed the thirty-one-year-old fellow Presbyterian Marcus Whitman to accompany Parker west as his assistant. Missionaries were expected to be married, and Whitman became engaged to twenty-five-year-old Narcissa Prentiss before departing.[7]

At Liberty, the two missionaries bought a horse for each of them and a pack mule to carry their supplies and belongings. The caravan left Liberty on May 14, and "Whitman quickly discovered that Parker was more of a liability than a help on the trail," wrote the Whitmans' biographer Clifford M. Drury. "Whitman was the practical type, eager to do his share of work and more." Parker was "tactless, fussy, and dogmatic," and the upshot was that Whitman did most of the packing, setting up camp, and cooking.[8] In subsequent years neither had much good to say about the other. Joe Meek, who met both men several weeks later, said that Parker "rebuked the sabbath-breakers quite severely . . . [but] Dr. Marcus Whitman was another style of man . . . preferring to teach by example rather than precept."[9]

Further complicating things, most of the traders made it clear that they weren't thrilled to be traveling with missionaries. Fontenelle's men especially resented the churchmen's holier-than-thou attitude of not joining in a friendly dram of whiskey and not traveling on the Sabbath (even though the caravan continued, and Parker and Whitman had to catch up the next day). "In order to remedy this," wrote Whitman, "I used to labor with extreme exertion with Mr. F's men in crossing rivers, making rafts & bridges, &c. . . . [But] I found I was very much exhausted in health, having been an invalid for some years previous."[10]

Whitman's presence was soon appreciated, however. On June 21, three weeks after arriving at the American Fur Company's fort at Bellevue, he wrote to Narcissa, "For the last twelve days have been attending upon

Mr. Fontenelle's men; the cholera has raged among them; three only have died. Mr. Fontenelle is sick with it himself, but now convalescent."[11] Fontenelle appreciated Whitman's care and followed his advice to move the men from the river bottom, where the water had apparently become polluted, to "a clean, healthy situation" on higher ground. There were no more deaths. Fontenelle "showed his gratitude," Whitman later wrote, "as well as all other persons concerned in the company, by bestowing upon us every favor in his power."[12]

"Dr. Whitman Has Been of Great Service to Us"

"While at Bellevue," wrote Parker, "a man by the name of Garrio, a half-blood Indian chief of the Arickara nation, was shot under very aggravated circumstances. Garrio and his family were residing in a log cabin on the Popillon river. Six or seven men went down to his house in the night, called him up, took him away half a mile, and shot him with six balls, scalped him, and left him unburied. The reason they assigned for doing so, was, that he was a bad man, and had killed white men. If he was guilty, who authorized them to take his life?"[13]

The murdered man's name was actually Antoine Garreau, an adopted son of the fur trader Joseph Garreau, who had interpreted for Lewis and Clark when they met the Arikaras. The thoughtful Parker added, "While we charge the Indians with inveterate ferociousness and inhuman brutality, we forget the too numerous wrongs and outrages committed upon them, which incite them to revenge."[14] Parker was more perceptive than he could have realized. In 1825 Joseph Garreau and his sons Pierre and Antoine had acted as interpreters in the treaty negotiations between Henry Atkinson and Benjamin O'Fallon and Arikara chiefs Bloody Hand, Little Bear, Skunk, Fool Chief, the Chief Who Is Afraid, and Bad Bear. (In this same series of treaties, Edward Rose was the interpreter for the Crow nation.) The treaty stated that from then on, "there shall be a firm and lasting peace between the United States and the Ricara tribe of Indians; and a friendly intercourse shall immediately take place between the parties."[15]

Although the Arikaras largely adhered to the conditions of the treaty, the government did not, acting quickly to punish Arikara maltreatment of whites but largely ignoring the opposite. Even more frustrating for the Arikaras was the government's failure to stop traders from providing guns and ammunition to the Sioux when they were at war with the Arikaras, as promised. Not only that, but while the American Fur Company built forts to trade with the Crees and Assiniboines (Fort Union), the Mandans and Hidatsas (Fort Clark), and the Sioux (Fort Pierre), no post was established in Arikara territory: "In fact, except for sporadic encounters, traders usually avoided the Arikaras altogether, effectively boycotting them while supplying surrounding tribes with goods. Consequently, the Arikaras either had to rely on Sioux middlemen or rob traders passing through their towns."[16]

Parker had it right: "When Indian offences are proclaimed, we hear only one side of the story, and the other will not be heard until the last great day." Shortly after Garreau's murder in mid-June, Fontenelle's wagon train departed Bellevue. By the first week of July they were following the north bank of the Platte westward. Whitman's health was not good, and he was battling dysentery when the group reached Fort William on July 26. On August 1 Parker wrote, "We recommenced our journey, and our next point is across the Rocky Mountains where the general rendezvous will be held. . . . Mr. Fontenelle stopped at the fort, and Mr. Fitz Patrick took his place in charge of the caravan. When we called for our bill, Mr. Fontenelle said he had none against us; for if any one was indebted, it was himself, for what Dr. Whitman had done for him and his men."[17] Fontenelle told his partners that Whitman "has been of great service to us," a sentiment that impressed Fitzpatrick and was not forgotten when he and Whitman met again a year later.[18]

Leaving the wagons at the fort, the caravan proceeded with pack mules and reached South Pass on August 10. "Though there are some elevations and depressions in this valley," wrote Parker, "yet, comparatively speaking, it is level. There would be no difficulty in the way of constructing a rail road from the Atlantic to the Pacific ocean; and probably the time may not be very far distant, when trips will be made across the continent, as they have been made to the Niagara falls, to see nature's wonders."[19] The cross-continental railroad was thirty-four years in the future, and the terrain between South Pass and the Pacific was more rugged than Parker imagined.

Arriving at the rendezvous on August 12, Parker and Whitman met a host of mountain men, but the latter took a special interest in one of them.

"I extracted an arrow point from the back of James Bridger, one of the partners of the company which had been shot in by the Blackfeet Indians near three years previous," wrote Whitman, who also removed an arrowhead from the back of an unnamed trader shot the year before. "These Indians and whites or trappers often fight and both seem mutually to exult in each others destruction."[20]

The 1835 rendezvous was also the site of another legendary event. "A hunter, who goes technically by the name of the great bully of the mountains, mounted his horse with a loaded rifle, and challenged any Frenchman, American, Spaniard, or Dutchman, to fight him in single combat. Kit Carson, an American, told him if he wished to die, he would accept the challenge," wrote Parker.[21]

> Shunar defied him—C. mounted his horse, and with a loaded pistol rushed into close contact, and both almost at the same instant fired. C.'s ball entered S.'s hand, came out at the wrist, and passed through the arm above the elbow. S.'s ball passed over the head of C. and while he went for another pistol, Shunar begged that his life might be spared. Such scenes . . . make the pastime of their wild and wandering life. They appear to have sought for a place where, as they would say, human nature is not oppressed by the tyranny of religion, and pleasure is not awed by the frown of virtue.[22]

On August 21 Whitman wrote, "Mr. Parker went on this morning, after we had unitedly sought the blessing and guidance of God."[23] Parker was on his way to Oregon, where, first with guidance from Bridger and then from Salish and Nez Perce Indians, he arrived on October 22. Whitman was returning east so that he and Narcissa and another missionary couple could make the journey to Oregon the next year. Based on his own experience and what he had heard from traders, he believed that white women could make the trip across the United States to the Pacific, something that had not happened before. The doctor thus accompanied Fitzpatrick, Friday, and the eastbound caravan—with its cargo of 120 packs of beaver and eighty bundles of buffalo robes—back to Fort William, where Fitzpatrick and Fontenelle once again traded places, with the latter escorting the caravan and the missionary back to Liberty.[24]

"Broken Hand"

Fitzpatrick never lacked a nickname. Close friends sometimes called him "Fitz," while others, as noted, dubbed him "White Hair." By the mid-1830s, however, Indians rechristened him "Broken Hand" because of an accident with a firearm that seriously injured his left hand. The only document from Fitzpatrick himself that possibly refers to the mishap is a vague statement in a March 1836 letter: "I need not undertake to give you a written account of our misfortunes, as you will too soon have a verbal one. . . . Our misfortunes in this expedition will be the cause of my making some extra expenses for horses."[25] Fitzpatrick was never more specific. Nor did anyone provide a detailed account of the injury until a Missouri newspaper did so in 1847, with information provided not by Fitzpatrick but by Peter A. Sarpy, reportedly with the former when the two traveled together in 1835 through "desert regions, and had occasion to separate, with an understanding of where they were again to meet." After they separated, a party of Blackfeet Indians discovered Fitzpatrick and pursued him in the direction of the Yellowstone River: "Captain Fitzpatrick . . . gained for a time on the Indians . . . [but] when within a short distance of the river . . . a steep bluff . . . suddenly presented itself. . . . With a firm hold of the bridle, he struck his heels in the horse's flanks, and horse and rider essayed a fearful plunge! That noble effort of the animal was succeeded by another.—and his last! He yet breasted the current of the river, and only reeled from exhaustion, when he had safely landed his rider on a sand bar on the opposite shore." As the horse vanished in the water, "the ruthless Indians, frantic with rage at the escape of their victim, took to the river." Fitzpatrick grabbed his rifle, "but in his haste to pull off the cover, by some mismanagement received the contents of his piece in the left wrist, which was frightfully shattered with the discharge." Despite his wound, Fitzpatrick reloaded the rifle and killed two of his pursuers. Then he fled into the woods, getting away even though the Blackfeet tracked him for several days. "Thirty days after this adventure, he got up with Mr. Sarpy, and gave him the details of this most extraordinary escape."[26]

Although the article—which has gone unconfirmed by a second source—states the accident occurred in 1835, LeRoy R. Hafen found early 1836 to be more likely, a date consistent with Fitzpatrick's March 1836 mention of "misfortunes."[27] Whenever Fitzpatrick injured his hand, he found ways to compensate and by all accounts was still capable in the use of a rifle.

"I Never Was So Contented and Happy Before"

On the evening of Sunday, May 15, 1836, Marcus Whitman and his missionary party were camped along the Missouri River when a messenger arrived from John Dougherty, Indian agent at Bellevue—and former associate of Andrew Henry, John Colter, and Edward Rose, to name a few—asking for Whitman's help in treating his seriously ill brother, Hannibal. Not hesitating, Whitman mounted his horse the next morning, rode eighteen miles north to Bellevue, and ministered to Hannibal, even though this meant further delaying the missionaries, already behind, in disarray, and desperate to catch Fitzpatrick's caravan.[28]

On May 17 Whitman rode west, found the train of wagons and animals, and asked Fitzpatrick if he could halt the caravan for a few days. Fitzpatrick said he would welcome Whitman's group but stopping was not possible, probably because he could not afford to miss another rendezvous. He provided the doctor with fresh mounts, however, by returning the horses left behind the previous fall and expressed confidence that Whitman's group could overtake the caravan before reaching hostile Indian Country.

It was not quite that easy. At the Platte River crossing he found that a second group of missionaries had not arrived as planned: "It did not arrive until the next day; the guide had got lost on the uninhabited prairie. This precipitated a new crisis; the caravan was moving further and further away with each passing day."[29] If they did not catch up by the time they reached the Pawnee Indian villages, they would have to turn back and quite likely lose the support of the mission board and thus lose any chance of fulfilling their divine calling of taking the gospel to the western Indians.

With their two wagons, twenty horses and mules, and seventeen head of cattle—including five milk cows—they pushed on, making an incredible sixty miles on May 24. Narcissa wrote that Marcus "had a cup tied to his saddle in which he milked what we wished to drink. This was our supper."[30] On May 26, at central Nebraska's Loup River, near the Pawnee villages, they finally caught the caravan, which had to stop to make axle grease from ox fat. "We then felt that we had been signally blessed, thanked God and took courage," Marcus wrote to Narcissa's parents, echoing the Apostle Paul.[31]

The caravan had about ninety men, 260 heavily laden mules, an unknown number of horses, seven wagons drawn by six mules each, and a two-mule cart for Milton Sublette, whose infected leg had finally been amputated. The missionary group consisted of Marcus and Narcissa Whitman, Henry and Eliza Spalding, William Gray, three Nez Perce boys (two of whom had traveled east with Marcus the previous year), a hired hand whose name has been lost, and a nineteen-year-old orphan—and future mountain man and founder of Ogden, Utah—by the name of Miles Morris Goodyear.[32] The Whitmans were scheduled to proselyte among the Cayuse Indians on the Walla Walla River, a tributary of the lower Columbia; the Spaldings among the Nez Perce on Idaho's Clearwater River. Interestingly enough, a few years earlier, Narcissa had refused Henry Spalding's marriage proposal, something he obviously resented because early in 1836 he had said in public, "I do not want to go into the same mission with Narcissa Prentiss as I question her judgment."[33] Narcissa was aware of the remark but nevertheless treated both Henry and Eliza respectfully.

The caravan followed the north bank of the Platte River, the same route taken by Brigham Young's company of Mormon pioneers eleven years later. Eliza was frequently ill from the diet of buffalo meat, but Narcissa thrived. "I wish I could describe to you how we live so that you can realize it," she wrote to her family. "I never was so contented and happy before. Neither have I enjoyed such health for years." At daybreak, "Arise, arise" was the first word heard: "Then the mules set up such noise as you never heard which puts the whole camp in motion. We encamp in a large ring—baggage and men, tents and wagons on the outside and all the animals, except the cows [which] are fastened to pickets, within the circle. This arrangement is to accommodate the guard who stands regularly every night and day. . . . We are ready to start, usually at six—travel till eleven, encamp, rest and feed, start again about two—travel until six or before if we come to a good tavern—then encamp for the night."[34]

The caravan reached Fort Laramie—previously called Fort William—on June 13 and stayed for eight days. Narcissa possibly became pregnant during the stay—her full-term baby daughter Alice Clarissa was born on the evening of her twenty-ninth birthday, March 13, 1837. The missionaries were not given rooms inside the fort, but Narcissa found it a welcome sight to see buildings again. Spalding preached at a fort worship service on June 19, and some of the caravan men attended. Narcissa and Eliza had their first of three opportunities to wash clothes (the others came at the rendezvous and at Fort Boise).[35]

Fitzpatrick, his men, and the missionaries left on June 21, now with one company wagon, one mission wagon, and an interminable mule pack train. "Our females endured the fatigues of the march remarkably well," wrote Spalding, "riding [sidesaddle] on horseback from morning till night day after day . . . at the rate of 25 and 30 miles a day, and at night have nothing to lie on but the hard ground."[36] The group crossed South Pass—which Fitzpatrick had first seen twelve years earlier—on July 4. Eliza made the only known contemporaneous account of the historic event: "Crossed a ridge of land today; called the divide, which separates the waters that flow into the Atlantic from those that flow into the Pacific, and camped for the night on the head waters of the Colorado."[37]

Both women would safely reach the Oregon country's Fort Vancouver with their husbands in September, making them the first European women to cross what became the continental United States. Fitzpatrick knew them well. In another parallel between him and Rose, the latter was acquainted with two Indian women known to have completed a long journey across the divide to the Pacific: Sacagawea, with Lewis and Clark from 1804 to 1805, and Marie Dorion, with the Overland Astorians from 1811 to 1812. Sacagawea was of the Shoshone nation; Marie, Iowa. Sacagawea made the trip with one young son; Marie with two. Both women rode horses at various times on their journeys, but neither had to ride sidesaddle.[38]

Fitzpatrick and his party reached the Green River rendezvous (near present Daniel, Wyoming) on July 6. The missionaries stayed for twelve days until they continued west with Hudson's Bay Company traders and Nez Perce and Salish Indians. As Marcus was preparing to leave, he asked Fitzpatrick for a bill to cover the caravan's costs for a variety of tasks, including shoeing the missionaries' horses and supplying buffalo meat. Fitzpatrick responded by asking Marcus for his bill for providing medical care to caravan men. "I have no bill," said Marcus. "Then," said Broken Hand Fitzpatrick, "neither have I."[39]

"The Starved Little Hero of the Cimarron"

Before leaving the rendezvous, Whitman recorded an important footnote to Fitzpatrick's career: "Major [Joshua] Pilcher joined us at Fort Williams and came to Rendezvous, as agent of Pratt, Choteau & Co. [American Fur Company], in whose behalf he bought out the 'mountain partners,' [Fontenelle, Fitzpatrick & Co.] so that the whole [fur] business now belongs to them."[40]

Fitzpatrick was thus an independent contractor when he led the 1837 caravan from western Missouri to another Green River rendezvous. The wealthy Scot Sir William Drummond Stewart was present, along with the artist Alfred Jacob Miller, who chronicled the trip with several paintings. "A party arrived from the States with supplies The cavalcade consisting of 45 men and 20 Carts drawn by Mules under the direction of Mr. Thomas Fitzpatrick," wrote trader Osborne Russell. "Joy now beamed in every countenance Some received letters from their friends and relatives Some received public papers and news of the day others consoled themselves with the idea of getting a blanket a Cotton Shirt or a few pints of Coffee."[41]

The year 1838 was reportedly when Fitzpatrick's adopted son Friday was returned to his Arapaho family. Again, Fitzpatrick left no record, but his friend Theodore Talbot wrote that on one of Fitzpatrick and Friday's journeys into Indian Country, Friday "accidentally entered an Arapaho village. He had not been there long when a woman rushing up clasped him fervently in her arms, claiming him as her lost son. An explanation ensued and what she said was proved true, great therefore were the rejoicings among his family on recovery of the promising boy." Although Friday was happy to see his family and friends, he "was still loathe to leave his ever kind friend and protector. It was only after oft repeated importunities & in fact vi et armis [with force and arms] that he could be induced to remain with them."[42]

Unmarried and otherwise childless, Fitzpatrick carried on.

On April 30, 1840, three frontiersmen Fitzpatrick knew well—Andrew Drips, Jim Bridger, and Henry Fraeb—guided a caravan of forty men and thirty carts to the sixteenth, and last, rendezvous. Father Pierre-Jean De Smet and the Reverends Harvey Clark, Philo B. Littlejohn, and Alvin T. Smith and their wives made up the missionary group. "Until the 17th of May," wrote De Smet, "we traveled over immense plains, destitute of trees or shrubs, except along the streams, and broken by deep ravines, where our voyageurs lowered and raised the carts by means of ropes."[43]

Fitzpatrick did not attend the rendezvous, but knowing this was the final gathering, trader Robert Newell reflected on the end of an era. "Come," he said to Joe Meek, "we are done with this life in the mountains—done with wading in beaver dams, a freezing or starving alternately—done with Indian trading and Indian fighting. The fur trade is dead in the Rocky Mountains, and it is no place for us now, if it ever was. . . . Let us go down to the Wallamet and take farms. . . . What do you say, Meek? Shall we turn American settlers?"[44]

Fitzpatrick, for one, did not turn settler but was back on the trail a year later, guiding Father De Smet—who either met or heard about Fitzpatrick on his 1840 journey—and an odd collection of others. Father De Smet was traveling to the Oregon territory with assistants Nicholas Point and Gregory Mengarini, five teamsters, and two trappers. They had been joined by several families of the Western Emigration Society, a group eager to see the oranges, grapes, and olive trees of the place called California. John Bartleson and John Bidwell were the leaders of the sixty-member contingent, and De Smet had convinced them they absolutely needed an experienced guide, something they did not consider at first.

If the society had not taken De Smet's advice, Bidwell wrote, "probably not one of us would ever have reached California, because of our inexperience. Afterwards when we came in contact with the Indians, our people were so easily excited that if we had not had with us an old mountaineer the result would certainly have been disastrous. The name of the guide was Captain Fitzpatrick; he had been at the head of trapping parties in the Rocky Mountains for many years."[45]

Fitzpatrick led the group west from Westport, Missouri, now a point of departure for both the Santa Fe and Oregon Trails, on May 10, 1841. Previous missionaries or settlers had always gone west with trading caravans on their way to the annual rendezvous, making this the first emigrant wagon train. Within days, they were overtaken by Joseph B. Chiles, with a wagon and five men, and a few days after that, by an outspoken Methodist preacher named Joseph Williams. The combined party numbered about eighty people.

Bidwell's mention of his people's getting easily excited proved true when a young man who had gone out to hunt ran into camp without his mule and his gun, declaring he had been attacked and robbed by Indians. The entire party panicked and ran their teams out of the camp. Fitzpatrick galloped his horse ahead and managed to get the carts and wagons gathered in a half-defensive position near the Platte. Then a band of at least fifty Indians appeared but hardly looked hostile—they began pitching their tepees. Fitzpatrick and another man carefully approached them, apparently communicating in sign language. Fitzpatrick soon recognized them as Cheyennes, who made it clear that they had disarmed the young man because his alarm at seeing them convinced them he was about to fire. They willingly returned the mule and the gun; Fitzpatrick thanked them, and the matter was closed.[46]

"Our leader, Fitzpatrick," wrote the preacher Williams, "is a wicked, worldly man, and is much opposed to missionaries going among the Indians. He has some intelligence, but is deistical in his principles." What was more likely was that Fitzpatrick was opposed to overzealous, self-righteous men like Williams going among the Indians. As he had with Whitman, Fitzpatrick developed a close friendship with De Smet. "I had the pleasure and happiness of traveling in his [Fitzpatrick's] company during the whole summer of 1842 [1841]," the priest wrote eight years later, "and every day I learned to appreciate him more."[47]

Fitzpatrick got the group of pioneers and preachers safely to Idaho, where one-half headed to California and the other to Oregon. The end of the rendezvous era had meant the beginning of Fitzpatrick's amazing career as a guide. In 1842 he led the White-Hastings party from Fort Laramie to Fort Hall. In the spring of 1843 John C. Frémont was organizing his second government-commissioned expedition, well funded by support from his powerful father-in-law, Senator Thomas Hart Benton. This would be Frémont's longest and most important exploration. "My party consisted principally of Creole and Canadian French and Americans, amounting in all to 39 men," he wrote. "Mr. Thomas Fitzpatrick, whom many years of hardship and exposure in the western territories had rendered familiar with a portion of the country it was designed to explore, had been selected as our guide."[48]

Intent on providing excellent maps of the area traveled, Frémont had hired cartographer Charles Preuss for the impressive sum of $2,000. The second-highest salary of the recruits went to Fitzpatrick, who signed on for $1,750.[49] The excursion began at Westport, Missouri, in June of 1843 and ended at Colorado's Fort Bent in July 1844: "During that time, they had explored the Great Salt Lake, traversed the Oregon Trail to Fort Vancouver, explored southeastern Oregon and northwestern Nevada, crossed the Sierra in winter to Sutter's Fort, visited the California towns . . . and followed a difficult desert route back to the Rocky Mountains of Colorado. . . . The crossing of the Sierras in winter was rather foolhardy and the party was lucky to come through as well as it did."[50] Kit Carson, who served as Frémont's chief guide in his first and third expeditions, joined the second one not long after it left Fort Bent. Although Fitzpatrick and Frémont never had the close friendship that the latter and Carson did, they shared a mutual respect.[51]

One of the most memorable scenes of Frémont's second expedition came on July 13, 1843, along the South Platte River above Bijou Creek. "A handsome young indian came dashing up to Fitz and cordially shaking his hand expressed in the best English kind interrogatories, as to his health, purpose, &c," wrote Theodore Talbot, one of Frémont's men. "We were much surprised at this unusual Indian salutation until we heard its cause explained." The handsome young Indian was Friday, then about nineteen years old and seeing "Fitz" for the first time in five years. The two of them had a few days to reminisce about their past adventures and what the future might hold. Then, remembered Talbot, "Friday, the starved little hero of the Cimarron, came to bid us good bye, as he accompanies the war party against the Youta [Ute] Indians, now just about leaving."[52]

Over the next decade Fitz and Friday would rejoice in each other's company several times.

"We Found Carson with an Express from California"

In the spring of 1845 Colonel Stephen Watts Kearny was ordered to reconnoiter the Oregon Trail from his own Kansas post of Fort Leavenworth to South Pass and determine the plausibility of establishing forts to protect pioneers from Indian attacks, which had increased with the explosion of westward expansion. Two years earlier, Marcus Whitman and others had led the first immigrant caravan that traveled all the way to Oregon by wagon. In 1845 alone nearly five thousand men, women, and children, with hundreds of wagons and thousands of horses, mules, and cattle, would traverse the trail.[53]

Kearny set out in late April with his orderly, chief bugler, and staff officers, followed by five fifty-man companies of the renowned 1st U.S. Dragoons—each soldier was armed with a saber, carbine, and pistol and mounted on a black, gray, bay, or sorrel horse, depending on the company. Next came two horse-drawn twelve-pound howitzers, then the teamsters with supply wagons, trailed by a drove of cattle and sheep. The main guard brought up the rear. Ahead of everyone, including the colonel, rode a lone scout: Thomas Fitzpatrick.[54]

Kearny completed the 2,200-mile expedition in fourteen weeks, returning by way of Bent's Fort and meeting with several groups of Indians in the process. Hundreds of Sioux, Cheyennes, and Arapahos were present at Fort Laramie, where Kearny smoked the pipe with the chiefs, gave them gifts, assured them that the great father in Washington—James K. Polk at the time—cared for them, and warned them to leave the westbound pioneers alone, adding an exclamation point by firing his howitzers. The last Indian council occurred on the Chugwater branch of the Laramie River, north of present Cheyenne, Wyoming, with Indians of the same name. Four Arapaho allies were present, one of them Friday, who stepped out of the crowd to greet the guide. The astonished soldiers then heard the tale of the little hero of the Cimarron.

Kearny had high praise for Fitzpatrick, calling him "an excellent woodsman—one who has been much west of the mountains, and has as good, if not a better, knowledge of that country than any other man in existence."[55] So on May 26, 1846, when General Kearny received a dispatch from

Washington informing him of the declaration of war with Mexico and ordering him to march the Army of the West on Santa Fe, it surprised no one that he summoned Fitzpatrick, then in St. Louis, to guide 1,600 soldiers more than eight hundred miles across plains, rivers, and mountains. Within weeks Fitz learned he had been appointed a federal Indian agent but would be allowed to continue with Kearny for the duration of the campaign.

Kearny took New Mexico without firing a shot, marching his troops into Santa Fe on August 18. Five weeks later, again guided by Fitzpatrick, Kearny and three hundred dragoons headed for California by way of the Gila River. By this time, Antoine Robidoux was present as an interpreter and Jean Baptiste Charbonneau, the forty-one-year-old mountain man and son of Sacagawea, as an additional guide. They had traveled about 140 miles southwest to the town of Socorro when, on October 6, they were shocked to meet several mountaineers on their way west. "Came into camp late and found Carson with an express from California," wrote one of Kearny's men, "bearing intelligence that the country had surrendered without a blow, and that the American flag floated in every port."[56]

Fitzpatrick's old friend Kit Carson had departed Bent's Fort in August 1845, leading Frémont's third expedition with the ostensible goal of exploring the upper Arkansas and Red Rivers, which meant a journey no farther west than Colorado. Frémont clearly intended to go to California, however, arriving there late in the year. The next nine months were so chaotic and unpredictable that they would require their own volume to be fully explained. What Kearney learned from Carson was that the U.S. naval commodore Robert F. Stockton had taken San Diego without violence and had employed sailors, marines, and Frémont's frontiersmen to also take Los Angeles. All of California was now U.S. territory, and Stockton had named Frémont the "Military Governor" of the entire area.

Upon hearing this news, Kearny made the unfortunate decision to send two-thirds of his men back to Santa Fe to be available for the war being waged with Mexico. He also had Carson and Fitzpatrick trade places, with Carson, who had just crossed the desert and could save time and supplies by reversing his route, leading the way, and Fitzpatrick, ready to assume his

Indian-agent duties, delivering Stockton and Frémont's letters to President Polk and Senator Benton. Fitzpatrick's days as a guide thus came to an end.[57]

"They Were Dying, One, Two, and Sometimes Five in a Day"

In December 1836, five months after bidding their friend Fitzpatrick farewell, Marcus and Narcissa Whitman got settled in a rude house Marcus built on Cayuse Indian land near present Walla Walla, Washington. Three months after that, Narcissa gave birth to a girl named Alice Clarissa, their only child. Rather than the peaceful, fulfilling venture they hoped for, a series of missteps or misfortunes followed. In August 1838 four other missionary couples arrived from the east, but the combined group frequently bickered over objectives, plans, and personal habits. On June 23, 1839, two-year-old Alice Clarissa drowned. Narcissa never healed from the tragedy, permanently giving up missionary labors. In 1842 the board ordered Whitman to close his mission; he made a hazardous journey to Boston and convinced them to change their minds. In 1844 Whitman was accused of causing the deaths of two Indian men under his care. In 1845 Cayuse chiefs unsuccessfully mandated that he pay for using their land and alleged that he would even poison them to take it.[58]

"It's hard to know why Whitman, in the face of so many warnings about the precariousness of his position, did not leave," writes Cassandra Tate, author of *Unsettled Ground: The Whitman Massacre and Its Shifting Legacy in the American West*. Perhaps it was a reluctance to admit failure, perhaps a conviction that God would protect him and Narcissa, perhaps because they refused to allow the mission to "fall into the hands of the Catholics."[59] Regardless, the convergence of two events in the autumn of 1847 sealed Marcus and Narcissa's fate.

First, more than a thousand wagons made their way past the Whitman mission, bringing some four thousand pioneers to Oregon, the largest migration yet, easily quadrupling—at least—the total population of Cayuse Indians. Although Marcus had been a great proponent of white settlement, even accompanying the first large wagon train on the Oregon Trail in 1843, he suddenly found himself in a bind, worried that needy emigrants would empty his warehouses. At his request, Henry Spalding, still stationed at his mission on the Clearwater River, brought a dozen and a half packhorses laden with corn, wheat, and other provisions.[60]

In a letter to her mother, Narcissa acknowledged the anxiety of the Cayuses: "The Indians are amazed at the overwhelming numbers of Americans coming into the country. They seem not to know what to make of it."[61] The word *overwhelming* was hardly an exaggeration. Although the Whitmans ostensibly established their mission for the sake of the Indians, they had largely become caretakers of white pioneers: "Seventy-five people lived at the mission, forty-five of them children. They had found places to sleep in the main mission house, in a nearby house for immigrants, in the blacksmith shop, in a sawmill cabin, and in a small Indian lodge. Narcissa had become the foster mother of eleven children who had lost their parents on the Oregon Trail."[62] Despite the mission administration duties that kept him exhausted, Marcus found time to ride to Indian villages to care for the sick—and sometimes help bury the deceased.

Second, an outbreak of measles, thought to be brought by American migrants, ravaged the Cayuses living near the Whitman mission.[63] The first fatalities in the area were recorded in late July, and it was soon evident that there were several Indian deaths and that many of those individuals perished after taking Dr. Whitman's medicine—an alarming omen given Whitman's 1843 report to the missionary board describing the Cayuse law that a shaman who lost his patients was worthy of death himself. At one Cayuse camp, seven people died, all most likely from measles, between October 30 and November 16. They ranged in age from one to sixty.[64] Spalding recorded the scene at the Whitman mission on November 22: "It was most distressing to go into a lodge of some ten fires and count twenty or twenty-five, some in the midst of measles, others in the last stage of dysentery. . . . They were dying . . . one, two, and sometimes five in a day, with the dysentery, which generally followed the measles."[65]

Into this tinderbox stepped a man by the name of Joe Lewis, son of a European father and Delaware mother and said to have fought under Frémont in California during the Mexican war. Lewis joined an 1847 pioneer caravan at Fort Hall but was left at the mission by emigrants who could no longer tolerate him. Whitman considered him "a worthless vagabond, not worth the food he eats," but gave him the benefit of the doubt by hiring him as a laborer.[66] The ungrateful Lewis apparently planned to do away with the Whitmans so he could plunder the mission. He went from one Cayuse lodge to another, pointing out that Indians treated by Whitman were dying but whites surviving—not mentioning that two children of an Osborne family died in November. He also claimed to have heard the Whitmans and Spaldings conspiring to murder the Cayuses and Nez Perces by treating them with poisoned medicine.[67]

On Sunday, November 28, Marcus and Spalding visited a friendly Indian by the name of Stickus, who warned the former that the Cayuses were planning on killing him and admonished him to leave. A somber Marcus listened attentively. Spalding, still hurting from his horse's falling on him the previous day, spent the night at Stickus's lodge; Marcus rode back to the mission, arriving around close to midnight. After checking on the sick children, he had a long talk with Narcissa, reportedly telling her of Stickus's caution and explaining he had decided not to leave. We have no record of how Narcissa responded.[68]

"In trying to understand Whitman's refusal to act on this warning," writes Whitman scholar Clifford M. Drury, "we must seek to appreciate his situation. Where could he go? He was responsible for the welfare and even the lives of more than seventy men, women, and children, some of whom were seriously ill. . . . These and many other problems were involved in any consideration of leaving [the mission]. The idea of Marcus and Narcissa deserting about seventy people while seeking only for themselves was unthinkable."[69] The perfect time for the Whitmans to leave would have been in 1842, when the board ordered the mission closed. The longer they stayed, the harder it got to leave. Nor did the sincere, well-intended Whitmans seem to recognize that this mission was never a good fit for them or that they never attempted to understand the Indians and accept them as they were.

November 29 dawned chilly and misty. "We saw nothing of Mother," remembered Catherine Sager. "She did not come out for breakfast. Elizabeth took some food on a plate and a cup of coffee and carried it to her. She was sitting with her face buried in her handkerchief, sobbing bitterly.

Taking the food she motioned the child to leave. The food was there, untouched, the next morning."[70]

The attack came shortly after the noon meal. "I was washing the dishes when I heard the report of a gun. It was the gun that killed Gillion [Gilliland], the tailor," Mary Marsh later wrote. "He was doing some sewing . . . when an Indian stood in the door and shot him. At the same time the horrible work was going on outside. I and some others went upstairs where we could look from a window and see a part of the conflict near the doctor's house. . . . Meanwhile Mrs. Whitman had barred the doors and windows to keep them out of the house—but they broke in anyway. I saw them break into the house, led by Joe Lewis, the instigator of the trouble. There they finished their bloody work for that day."[71]

The assailants, wielding guns or tomahawks, killed most of the victims, including Marcus and Narcissa, on November 29 and then held fifty-four women and children hostage until early February 1848.[72] In the week after the attack, others were killed—scholars do not agree on whether the final list included thirteen or fourteen individuals. David Dary lists the following fatalities of the "Whitman Massacre": Marcus and Narcissa Whitman; the teenage brothers John and Francis Sager (orphaned along with their five sisters when their parents died en route to Oregon, they were adopted by the Whitmans); mission sawmill operator Joseph Smith; mission schoolteacher Judge L. W. Saunders; Jacob Hoffman and Nathan S. Kimball, butchering a beef at the time of the attack; James Young, driving a wagonload of timber to the mission; Walter Marsh, mission gristmill operator and father of Mary Marsh; tailor Isaac Gilliland; Andrew Rogers, ministry student; and Crockett Bewley and Amos Sales, both patients of Dr. Whitman.[73]

"The key figures in this tale were neither heroes or villains but simply human beings, caught in a web not entirely of their making," writes Tate. "Their lives played out in ways that profoundly shaped the history of the Northwest and continue to influence it to this day. . . . It's a complex tale of arrogance, fortitude, naïveté, and misunderstandings. It can be seen as a singular American tragedy but also as representative of the tangle of cultural myopia and conflict that marked each wave of American incursion into the west."[74]

"I Believe I Have Found a Gold Mine"

One year and four months after Fitzpatrick and Carson parted—apparently for the last time—two events converged in what Elliott West has suggested could be "the most stunning coincidence in American history." On February 2, 1848, the United States and Mexico ended their war by signing the Treaty of Guadalupe Hidalgo, increasing the size of the former by 66 percent.[75] A mere nine days earlier at Sutters Fort, Henry Bigler, who crossed to the Pacific with a contingent of Kearny's Army of the West called the Mormon Battalion, wrote, "This day some kind of mettle was found in the tail race that looks like goald." The next morning, Bigler's boss, James W. Marshall, confirmed the find: "Boys, I believe I have found a gold mine."[76] He and his boss, John Augustus Sutter, tried to keep the discovery to themselves and their workers, but that was asking the impossible.

By June most of the men living in San Francisco had quit the area to search for gold along the American River. "My cook left me, like everybody else," wrote Sutter. "The merchants, doctors, lawyers, sea captains, . . . all left their wives and families in San Francisco and those which had none locked their doors, abandoned their houses [or] offered them for sale, cheap. . . . The recently opened school had to be closed; teacher and pupils had gone off to the mines."[77]

Eastern newspapers soon picked up the story. "THE GOLD DISCOVERY IN CALIFORNIA," read a headline in the November 30, 1849, issue of *The Brooklyn Daily Eagle*, adding that "Colonel Mason, for some months the military governor of California, writes to Washington, that with a sufficient number of men to aid, he would collect enough gold to pay off all the debt contracted for the war with Mexico, as well as our whole national debt besides, in less than a year. . . . He speaks of what he saw himself, and fears to write all he witnessed, lest he might not be credited."

Tens of thousands of folks afflicted with gold fever hastened to California in the next few years, initially from other parts of California and Oregon but eventually from South America, the Sandwich Islands, China, Australia, and Europe. Most, of course, came from the eastern United States, and the majority of them traveled on the Oregon Trail.[78] On May 18, 1849, a correspondent watching the parade at the Platte River's Fort Kearny offered this report:

> The ice is at last broken, and the inundation of gold diggers is upon us. The first specimen, with a large pick-axe over his shoulder, a long rifle in his hand, and two revolvers and a bowie knife stuck in his belt, made his appearance here a week ago last Sunday. He only had time to ask for a drink of buttermilk, a piece of ginger-bread and how "fur" it was to "Californy," and then hallooing to his long-legged, slab-sided cattle drawing a diminutive yellow-top wagon, he disappeared on the trail toward the gold "diggins." Since then wagons have been constantly passing. Up to this morning four hundred and seventy-six wagons have gone past this point; and this is but the advance guard.[79]

By June 10 the correspondent had counted 5,092 wagons, estimating that another 1,600 were on their way. The traffic finally subsided toward the end of June: "At a moderate calculation, there are 20,000 persons, and 60,000 animals now upon the road between this point and Fort Hall. This is below the actual number, as the numerous trains of pack mules are thrown in."[80]

Although the forty-niners traveling the Oregon Trail seldom encountered violence themselves, they found themselves in danger along the Platte River because the Pawnee and Cheyenne nations were carrying on a decades-long conflict. In June a gold seeker by the name of Cone wrote that "about three hundred 'Pawnee' Indians came down upon" the wagon train in "a most threatening attitude," demanding weapons, whiskey, and food. Although some of the pioneers "were anxious to have the first shot," the two groups somehow avoided violence. The Pawnees were content to leave with twenty papers of tobacco. The next day the wagon train met a Cheyenne war party searching for the Pawnees. "Their line extended nearly half a mile in length," wrote Cone, who estimated that the Cheyennes "numbered three hundred, and our numbers all told amounted to only forty three men, and one woman." Luckily, the Cheyenne band asked to trade, and the business ended with "the men cheating the Indians all they could, and the Indians in turn stealling whatever they could find that was not guarded. . . . Thus ended the whole affair without violence."[81]

"It is said by alarmists that different tribes intend opposing the emigrants," wrote another forty-niner. "They might as well oppose the whirlwind." Few Indians were seen, however, because they feared the cholera spread by the wagon trains. When a group of Cheyenne Indians met a wagon train and realized several of the pioneers were sick, they immediately fled, but "several had contracted the disease and died before they reached their villages. They called the sickness the Big Cramps. Several bands gathered for the sun dance on Smoky Hill River in Kansas in the summer of 1849—Cheyenne, Arapaho, Comanche, Kiowa, Osage, prairie Apache. On the last day of the ceremonies, a Kiowa sun dancer suddenly collapsed and died. Then an Osage fell to the ground. The Cheyenne fled for the Cimarron River but it was too late. Scores died."[82]

David A. White, editor of *News of the Plains and Rockies*, writes that "the scourge of the gold rush was the cholera epidemic of 1849–54," with the disease spreading from India to Europe and then crossing the Atlantic "in a packet ship from France to reach New York on December 1, 1848." Gold seekers subsequently "infected the continent, albeit with decreasing intensity westward. One tenth of the people in St. Louis and in the Rio Grande Valley died." No treatment seemed to work: "Unfortunate patients were vigorously bled, purged, puked, sweated, and immersed in ice water or rubbed with whiskey; they were given calomel (mercury), laudanum (opium), pepper, muster plasters, whiskey-soaked mean, sulfur pills, electric shocks, strychnine, and tobacco-smoke enemas." President Zachary Taylor declared a day of national prayer and fasting. "The miracle was that anybody survived," White writes. Cholera likely killed 1,500 forty-niners east of Fort Laramie, at least the same number of Pawnee Indians—a quarter of that nation—and unknown numbers of other Indians.[83]

"The more the gold rush energized the whites, the more it desolated the natives," White adds. "As some editors and others pointed out at the time, the genocide of the California Indians was the most sickening chapter in the conquest of the West." According to superintendent Edward F. Beale's estimate, approximately fifteen thousand Indians starved to death during the winter of 1851–52. "The intrusion of the white man upon the Indians' hunting grounds has driven off the game and destroyed their fisheries," claimed the

Sacramento Union on February 3, 1855. "The consequence is, the Indians suffer every winter for sustenance. Hunger and starvation follow them wherever they go. Is it, then, a matter of wonder that they become desperate and resort to stealing or killing?"[84]

One massacre of Indians followed another: Army forces slaughtered two hundred Pomos at Clear Lake and the Russian River in May 1850. After Indians killed a rancher and stole his cattle near Weaverville in May 1852, a sheriff and thirty-six armed men responded by making a surprise attack on an Indian village and killing more than 140 men, women, and children. In April 1859 a band of settlers along the Eel River tracked down and killed approximately 240 Yuki Indians. The leader of the settlers reportedly said that "he did not want any man to go with him to hunt Indians who would not kill all he could find, because a knit would make a louse."[85]

"In 1851–1852 three commissioners wrote out 18 treaties 'of friendship and peace,' promising reservations, beef, and flour, farming tools, clothes, and teachers, in exchange for [Indian] lands. The commissioners immediately defrauded the Indians on the beef contracts. Then, at the urging of the California Senator William M. Gwin, the Senate rejected the treaties and buried them in secrecy until 1905." The number of California Indians decreased from likely more than 300,000 in 1769, when the missions were founded, to approximately 150,000 in 1845, and then to about 30,000 in 1860: "Starvation and diseased took the greatest tolls, but whites murdered and massacred significant numbers."[86]

"You Will Get into Trouble with the Whites"

Although 1849 was dubbed the "rush" year, the traffic increased in 1850. By August 14 Fort Laramie's register tallied the year's statistics as follows: 39,506 men, 2,421 women, 609 children, 23,172 horses, 7,548 mules, 36,116 oxen, 7,323 cows, 2,106 sheep, 9,927 wagons, and 316 deaths en route. Because no more than 80 percent of pioneers registered, the total number was estimated at approximately 55,000, with 5,000 headed to Utah, 9,000 to Oregon, and 41,000 to California. As the representative for the Cheyenne, Arapaho, and Sioux nations and longtime explorer and guide on the Oregon Trail, Fitzpatrick knew as well as anyone that the horde of pioneers storming west had wreaked havoc on the buffalo range and reduced the herds, meaning that the Indian nations needed food, supplies, and trade goods from the Americans to counteract the loss of game.[87] He did not mince words in his 1850 report to federal officials: "This immense emigration traveling through that country for the past two years has desolated and impoverished it to an enormous extent. . . . Under these circumstances, would it not be just, as well as economical policy for the government at this time to show some little liberality, if not justice, to [the Indian nations'] passive submission?"[88]

Congress responded by appropriating $100,000 for the convening of a treaty council, with David D. Mitchell, superintendent of Indian Affairs at St. Louis, and Fitzpatrick designated as commissioners for the government. They chose to hold the council on September 1, 1851, at Fort Laramie. "By late August," notes Loretta Fowler, a leading authority on the Cheyenne and Arapaho nations, "there were about ten thousand Native people on Horse Creek (thirty-six miles from Fort Laramie), including almost all of the Southern and Northern Cheyennes, most of the Northern and Southern Arapahos, and many Lakota Sioux (mostly Brule and Oglala). . . . The treaty provided for peace between the tribes represented and the Americans. Tribal territories were recognized but with the understanding that hunting was not restricted to a particular territory. The Arapaho and Cheyenne Tribes jointly had the land between the North Platte and Arkansas Rivers, east to the upper Republican and west to the Rockies."[89]

The Indians and Americans both recognized that "depredations" such as theft or injury would likely occur, and the treaty stipulated how conflicts were to be resolved. Each nation would be accountable for depredations to Americans that happened in its territory. The violations would be paid for by reparations, usually by loss of some of the annuity goods, which "included guns and ammunition, cloth and blankets, kettles, knives, ornaments, and some provisions, all of which were important and became gradually more important as the buffalo decreased over time." The nations consented to the safe travel of pioneers and to the founding of military posts on the Platte and Santa Fe roads. Military troops were supposed to defend both Indians and migrants, but the treaty failed to specify such. From the perspective of the Arapahos and Cheyennes, speeches at the council after smoking the pipe were considered the actual "treaty."[90]

The Fort Laramie Treaty positively affected the Indians' interactions with the Americans. For the next five years, Arapahos and Cheyennes abstained from attacks and sent war parties against only the Pawnees and Utes, neither of which had signed the treaty. The Indian Office recounted that the Arapahos and Cheyennes were compliant and in 1853 displayed "increasing kindliness of disposition toward the whites."[91]

On February 8, 1854, the Washington DC *Evening Star* ran the following notice: "The veteran and venerable Thomas Fitzpatrick, Indian Agent for the Upper Arkansas, Platte, &c. Indians, who has been some weeks in Washington on business connected with his agency, died yesterday morning at Brown's Hotel of pneumonia. We presume his age must have been approaching seventy years. Mr. Fitzpatrick was a valued servant of the Indian Department, and possessed more influence with the wild denizens of the great plains than perhaps any other white man."

Because of Fitzpatrick's white hair or long list of accomplishments or both, this obituary and others exaggerated his actual age of fifty-five. Two months earlier, while in New York, Fitzpatrick discovered he had a sister, still an infant when he left Ireland, living there, Mrs. Mary Fitzpatrick Leonard. The two of them had a wonderful reunion. When he learned of her financial straits, he gave her $1,000 for her sons to launch a business. Typical Fitzpatrick. In 1849 he had married Margaret, daughter of the French Canadian trapper John Poisal and Snake Woman, the sister of the Arapaho chief Left Hand. Margaret, her son, Andrew Jackson, and her daughter, Virginia—born after Fitzpatrick's death—received an estate of about $8,500, two lots, and two houses.[92]

"Thomas Fitzpatrick was one of the greatest mountain men and one of the most capable Indian agents," writes David A. White. "He brushed death with Indians too often to trust them. They trusted him only as much as they could trust any white man. . . . Fitzpatrick's efforts as an Indian agent culminated in the treaties of 1851 and 1853. They were steps among many others leading to the end of Indian rule over the Great Plains."[93]

Fitzpatrick no doubt did his best to be fair in those treaties, but the Indians agreed to territorial boundaries that would become increasingly restricted. The Native nations were officially responsible for acts of warfare, but the white invasion continued unrestricted, and the U.S. government severely reduced the promised annuities.[94] Little wonder that trader Charles Larpenteur wrote in 1872, "It is plain to be seen that treaties made with Indians have never amounted to anything, and never will."[95]

At the same time, several of the chiefs who dealt with Fitzpatrick remembered him fondly. The Arapaho chief Little Raven said his nation "had but one fair agent; that was Major Fitzpatrick."[96] In 1865 the Cheyenne chief Black Kettle perhaps said it best: "Major Fitzpatrick was a good man; . . . he brought us our goods annually; he did not drive to forts and houses to unload them, but drove to our villages and threw them out, and our women were glad. Major Fitzpatrick said, 'My children, when I am dead and gone, you will get into trouble with the whites.'"[97]

Fitz was not mistaken. "In 1858 gold was discovered along streams flowing out of the Rockies," writes Elliott West, recipient of the 2024 Bancroft Prize, "and the next year more than 100,000 persons flooded across the plains to the new diggings. The Colorado gold rush attracted more than twice the number of persons who crossed to California in 1849."[98] A Missouri newspaper described the gold seekers: "Hoosiers, Suckers, Corn crackers, Buckeyes, Red-horses, Arabs and Egyptians, some with ox wagons, some with mules, but the greatest number on foot, with their knapsacks and old-fashioned rifles and shotguns. . . . Many have sold out all their homes, all their valuables, to furnish themselves with an outfit for Pike's Peak mines. . . . [They] blindly rush headlong into the wild delusion of glittering sands full of golden eggs."[99]

"Gold reconstructed the West and America, physically and mythically," argues West. "The strikes in California and Colorado drew floods of new population and spawned centers of Anglo-American power where none had been before." Unlike earlier images of the American West, which emphasized the values of rural life, "those of the gold rushes caught a new intoxicating spirit of plunge and grab. Mining camps, chugging locomotives, and throbbing smelters" were the symbols of the gold-rush world. But "that vision was as flawed as ever. Anyone who got in the way, notably Indian peoples and

Hispanics, at worst were assaulted as lower life-forms and at best patronized as anachronisms who were, as the commissioner of Indian Affairs told a delegation of Plains tribes in 1867, 'by the law of God, and the great law of nature, passing away.' In unstoppable numbers the newcomers rolled over everything before them."[100]

The gold-hungry newcomers built homes and opened stores, farms, and ranches on Arapaho and Cheyenne land. In 1859, with Fitzpatrick's foster son Friday likely interpreting for him, Medicine Man spoke for the Northern Arapahos: "Our country for hunting game has become very small. We see the white man everywhere. Their rifles kill some of the game, and the smoke of their camp fires scares the rest away, and we are no longer able to find any game. . . . Our old people and little children are hungry for many days, and some die, for our hunters can get no meat. . . . We wish to live."[101]

Also in 1859 Little Raven reportedly held a council with local American leaders who said they wanted to coexist with the Cheyennes and Arapahos and hoped the Indians would not harass or steal from them. Little Raven wanted the prospectors to realize they could take the gold but not the land. He also tried to understand the federal government and American society. At Fort Lyon he gave bolts of calico to the women and conducted tours of his camp.[102]

All this notwithstanding, Henry Villard, who compiled an 1860 guidebook for the Pike's Peak Gold Rush, rationalized that the arrival of prospectors "has inaugurated the era of civilization in a heretofore unbroken wilderness, and although the rights of the aborigines may seen to be encroached upon thereby, the apparent injustice of the act is but one of the inevitable contingencies of human progress, and must in the end prove beneficial to all." Ovando Hollister was more straightforward in 1867: "This is a life and death struggle, to be ended by the death of the savage—and the sooner it can be finished the better."[103]

Over the thirteen-year period from 1851 to 1864, the Cheyennes and Arapahos took "responsibility for maintaining peace with Americans, regardless of the great sacrifice, in order to remain in their homeland and subsist by a mixed economy of hunting, working for hire, and ranching," Fowler reports. "Without peace, they could not remain. Despite the tribes' efforts, the army (and most settlers) were not interested in peaceful coexistence. . . . Historical studies that minimize the tribes' commitment to economic adaptation and conclude that death or removal was inevitable due to Native resistance do so by not closely examining Cheyenne and Arapaho political activity and risk encouraging rationalization of the removal of Natives from Colorado."[104]

"Underneath That Hide of Christian Love"

On November 29, 1864, the former Christian minister Colonel John Milton Chivington and his Colorado Third Volunteer Regiment were on their way to a camp of Southern Cheyennes and Arapahos on Sand Creek when they stopped at Fort Lyon and made an unexpected request for additional men from the First Colorado Regiment, which had recently arranged a truce with the Indians. After spirited opposition by some of the Fort Lyon officers, the fort command sent the requested troops with Chivington. One of those opposing the attack on the Sand Creek camp was Captain Silas Soule.[105]

In February 1865 Soule wrote a letter to an army friend:

> Dear Walt,
>
> The Cheyennes didn't get their lands. Or food. Or justice. What they got was slaughtered. Last November 29th. The governor sent out Colonel Chivington and a regiment of Hundred Daysers just to kill the ones camped under our protection down at Sandy Creek. Along the way they managed to surround Fort Lyon, dragoon the Colorado First and me. The colonel cried for vengeance, said he'd string up any son-of-a-bitch who'd bury their bodies or their bones, quote unquote. It wasn't an army, it was a mob. I flat refused to order in my men or open fire. I soon found out what's underneath that hide of Christian love. That colonel-preacher went at me like I was 666 itself. But I stuck fast. Two days I testified before an Army board, the colonel shouting challenges, the works. I thought of you, and not without a smile. I mean, here I am a soldier hectored by a colonel just because I wouldn't fight. A preacher, who wanted to kill the innocent, up against an infidel who wouldn't. What do you make of that? Anyhow, about a half the population want to kill me. The other half

are getting there. But some Episcopals are showing signs of backbone and the Army's on my side. Do I know what Quakers must go through? Fraternal greetings.

Your friend,
Si[106]

"Evidence of Barriers Breached"

"Through the lenses of conquest, empire, ethnic cleansing, genocide, and settler colonialism," writes Stephen Aron in *Peace and Friendship*, "a generation of historical scholarship has exposed the destructive forces and eliminationist impulses that channeled the westward expansion of the United States and sculpted the West as it is today."[107] Certainly, it is hard to imagine an event more representative of conquest, genocide, and colonialism than the Sand Creek Massacre, in which Chivington and his men ambushed a peaceful camp of Cheyennes and Arapahos, killing at least 130 people, most of them women and children.[108]

No one made the case better than Chivington himself. In April 1865 he testified to federal investigators, claiming the Indians he attacked had been hostile, despite the common knowledge of both Indians and whites that the camp was led by peace chiefs like Black Kettle and Little Raven. "Give in detail the names of all Indians so believed to be hostile," said one of the officials, "with the dates and places of their hostile acts, so far as you may be able to do so." Chivington did not even feign to have such knowledge. "When a tribe of Indians is at war with the whites," he proclaimed, "it is impossible to determine what party or band of the tribe or the name of an Indian or Indians belonging to the tribe so at war are guilty of the acts of hostility." The Cheyennes and Arapahos at Sand Creek, he continued, "were of the same tribes with those who had murdered many persons and destroyed much valuable property on the Platte and Arkansas rivers during the previous spring, summer and fall."[109]

Chivington thus "stripped Native people of their individuality, suggesting that any given Indian was neither any better nor any worse than the next," buttressing that "contention by underscoring the essential fiendishness of all Indians, appealing to white racial solidarity, and invoking gender ideologies—the sanctity of white femininity—that structured Anglo-American society."[110] Chivington had no regrets.

While acknowledging that such acts of conquest and colonialism shaped the history of the West, Aron points out that the story of western expansion also includes episodes providing "evidence of barriers breached and accords reached, of erstwhile enemies overcoming their differences, of would-be combatants standing down." Illustrating this theme, Aron tells of a Shawnee chief named Blackfish, who captured Daniel Boone and several companions in February 1778. When asked if he were present at a previous skirmish in which Blackfish's son was killed, Boone admitted that he was and that he had fired at the Indians. However, he said, "many things happen in war that were best forgotten in peace." Rather than taking revenge, Blackfish followed the custom of Shawnees and other woodland Indians to "cover the dead" by adopting someone to take the place of the loved one. Blackfish's taking Boone as his surrogate son "showed how far Shawnees could go in forgetting what happened in war, since it left open the possibility that the particular dead in this instance was being covered by his slayer."[111]

Although Blackfish was just a few years older than Boone, he always called him "my son" after the adoption. The father would sometimes suck a chunk of sugar and then hand it to his son to finish. The two of them imagined what Kentuckians and Indians could gain from each other when they dwelled together as one people. Blackfish was open to adding farming and livestock to his settlement; Boone loved hunting with Shawnee companions and perfectly understood their need for elbow room. Boone's new mother loved him and took care to fix his favorite meals: "The ease with which Boone slipped into Shawnee ways and his easygoing manner soon gained him the trust of his family." William Hancock, one of Boone's fellow adoptees—and father of John Colter's partner Forrest Hancock—was suspicious and wondered how Boone could be "whistling and contented among a parcel of dirty Indians." As with other episodes of "erstwhile enemies overcoming their differences," this one did not last. Boone eventually "escaped," returned to his other family, and became his second father's enemy, later saying, however, that he "felt really sorry" to leave his Shawnee home.[112]

Aron's treatment of the enigmatic Boone transitions smoothly to mention of the Louisiana Purchase and, of course, Lewis and Clark, with a focus on their sojourn at Fort Clatsop. Not surprisingly, the captains are taken to task for stealing the canoe—they "could have continued to negotiate with the Clatsop party or found another group among the Clatsops or some other Indians in the vicinity with a canoe to sell." Aron also concedes that the corps' interactions with the coastal Indians were tense from the start and hardly changed the few months they were there. So where is the bright side? Aron answers that question by reminding us that "Clark came of age in Kentucky when it was still a dark and bloody ground and served in the United States Army in its campaigns to displace Ohio Indians in the 1790s." Ohio was where Clark met the junior officer Lewis, and during the expedition the two of them understandably remembered the Indian wars and, especially in their encounter with the Lakota Sioux, were given to strident talk and belligerent displays of their firepower. The farther west they traveled, however, the more they realized that "diplomacy, not militancy" was crucial to a safe return to St. Louis. Aron makes a valid and often neglected point: "The absence of violence was no small accomplishment, especially compared with the abundance of bloodshed on the Ohio Valley frontier where Lewis and Clark (and many in the Corps) had come of age." Moreover, "Any accounting should begin with the actions and inactions of Indians, who permitted the Lewis and Clark expedition to traverse their countries unharmed. . . . The captains deserve credit too."[113]

From the early 1840s to the late 1870s, there was no better example of a "would-be combatant standing down" than Fitzpatrick's foster son, Friday the Arapaho. Jedediah Smith vanished in the Cimarron Desert on Friday, May 27, 1831, and some historians, including Dale Morgan, believe "that same day [Fitzpatrick] found on the plains the Arapaho waif he named Friday, who shared many of his journeys over the next seven years."[114] Who better than Friday to fill Jedediah's big shoes? From all indications, he was, like Captain Smith, a gentle, sincere soul at home in the wilderness. "Few Indians or whites can compete with Friday as a buffalo hunter, either in the use of the bow or rifle," wrote Sage. "I have seen him kill five of these animals at a single chase, and am informed that he has not unfrequently exceeded that number." Sage also offered a glimpse of Friday's personality and intellect, calling him "agreeable and interesting. I am indebted to him for much valuable information relative to the habits and peculiarities of his own and various other Indian tribes, while his vast fund of ready anecdotes and amusing stories serves to beguile the weariness of camp hours."[115]

In 1843 Friday assisted Frémont in his efforts to meet with the Arapahos. The next year he acted in a similar capacity for Sage's party on the Arkansas River. In 1845 he and other Arapahos reassured Philip St. George Cooke and his troops of the peaceful objectives of a local Arapaho camp.[116] In 1851 Friday was one of the Arapaho delegates to the great Indian council at Fort Laramie, of course having both official and personal meetings with Commissioner Fitzpatrick. Friday and three other Arapaho representatives accompanied Fitzpatrick to the nation's capital. "The boy became the interpreter," wrote an Arapaho friend named Sun Road. "The boy with two chiefs to Washington went. This was the first delegation that went from the Arapahoes to Washington. They started in the fall on horseback. Took all winter and summer to go to Washington and come back."[117]

In 1857 Friday acted as a mediator when a band of Arapahos led by Black Bear encountered a Mormon settlement at Fort Bridger. By 1858 Friday had a wife and a son named Bill. At an 1859 peace council he represented the Arapahos with Little Owl, Cut Nose, Medicine Man, and Black Bear. "When Indian-white hostilities intensified in the 1860s, Friday continued to urge his tribesman to avoid military conflict with whites," states Fowler. "His conciliatory approach lost him the support of many Arapahoes. . . . After 1863 he became physically and socially isolated from the main body of Northern Arapahoes because he steadfastly refused to fight against whites despite tribal consensus on the issue."[118]

After the Sand Creek Massacre in 1864, in which several of Friday's friends were killed, he carried on his peace efforts. When the federal government called a council in the spring of 1868, Friday acted as interpreter for the Arapaho representatives, Sorrel Horse and Black Coal.[119] Several months later, on November 27, 1868, just two days short of the fourth anniversary of the Sand Creek Massacre, "Colonel George Custer led the men of the Seventh Calvary in an attack on the Cheyenne village led by Chief Black

Kettle," an old friend of both Fitzpatrick and Friday. Operating under orders from General Philip Sheridan, Custer's men were to move toward the Indian camps along the Washita River and "destroy their villages and ponies; to kill or hang all warriors, and bring back all women and children." Catching the 250 unsuspecting villagers almost entirely by surprise, the troopers swept into the camp, exchanging fire with fleeing Indians running for their lives. Despite Custer's orders to capture, not kill, the women and children, Captain Edward Myers's men shot some of them.[120] Black Kettle, who had survived Sand Creek, did not survive Washita River.

Enduring another agonizing instance of the legacy of conquest, the relentless Friday continued his mission to breach barriers and reach accords, representing his people at peace or reservation councils in 1869, 1870, 1875, and 1878. The most memorable meeting came in September 1877, when he acted as interpreter for the Arapaho delegates meeting with President Rutherford B. Hayes. The key objective of the trip was to convince Hayes and Secretary of the Interior Carl Schurz not to settle the Northern Arapahos on the Missouri River or in Indian Territory. Friday translated speeches given by Black Coal, Sharp Nose, Spotted Tail, Swift Bear, Touch the Clouds, Red Bear, White Tail, Red Cloud, and Little Bad Man. The government officials were convinced and agreed that the Arapahos could settle in Wyoming's Sweetwater country, the location they had hoped for.[121] That was where Friday, the extraordinary peacemaker, died of heart disease on May 13, 1881, at the probable age of fifty-six.

"No doubt, the collapses frustrate those seeking a sure, straight path to lasting peace and friendship. Seeing the demise of alternative relations only as dead ends, however, is too dark a view. . . . So, too, should we remember the imperfect arrangements that forestalled violence for a while," concludes Aron. "Better broken concord than no concord at all. And better to continue to seek out places and periods where people once (and not just once upon a time) overcame differences, for there lies our road to redemption."[122]

NOTES

Prologue

1. Moulton, *Journals*, 1:vii.
2. Thomas Jefferson to George Rogers Clark, December 4, 1783, and Clark to Jefferson, February 8, 1784, in Jackson, *Letters*, 2:654, 655. As James J. Holmberg writes, "Debts incurred in prosecuting the [Revolutionary War] that Virginia refused to honor led to [George Rogers Clark's] financial ruin and contributed to his political decline. He also slid into alcoholism during this period. One of the reasons that William Clark resigned from the army in 1796 was to help George with his financial and legal troubles" (Holmberg, *Dear Brother*, 24–25n).
3. Thomas Jefferson to Paul Allen, August 18, 1813, in Jackson, *Letters*, 2:588. As Jackson notes, "Here Jefferson claims to have originated the idea that Ledyard should attempt to walk across the continent from the Northwest coast. Actually it was Ledyard's own plan, probably conceived more than two years before he met Jefferson . . . and Ledyard, even if he had managed to cross the West with two dogs and an Indian pipe as he hoped, could have brought back little useful information" (Jackson, *Letters*, 2:593n2, 654). It hardly seems coincidental that Jefferson, well aware of Lewis's birth date, penned this letter to Allen (who had requested biographical information on Meriwether Lewis to include in the forthcoming *History of the Expedition under the Command of Lewis and Clark*) on what would have been Lewis's thirty-ninth birthday.
4. DeVoto, *Empire*, 299.
5. Thomas Jefferson to André Michaux, April 30, 1793, in Jackson, *Letters*, 2:669–70, brackets added. When Jefferson first proposed a western expedition to the American Philosophical Society in 1792, Meriwether Lewis, then a twenty-two-year-old army captain stationed at Charlottesville, Virginia, got word of the plan and volunteered his services. Although Jefferson chose the more experienced Michaux, he was impressed with Lewis's mettle: "I told [Lewis] it was proposed that the person engaged should be attended by a single companion only, to avoid exciting alarm among the Indians. This did not deter him" (Thomas Jefferson to Paul Allen, August 18, 1813, in Jackson, *Letters*, 2:589).
6. In his 1789 search for the Northwest Passage, Mackenzie departed Fort Chipewyan, on the south shore of Lake Athabasca (which straddles the northern border of Alberta

and Saskatchewan), and descended the Slave River to its mouth at Great Slave Lake. He then descended a west-flowing river (eventually named after him), convinced it would take him to the Pacific coast. The river then swung to the north, however, and Mackenzie correctly concluded his party was headed to the "Frozen," or Arctic, Ocean. "Although he had been the first to explore one of the world's great rivers, and in later years came to take pride in the fact, Mackenzie's first reaction was one of frustration." *Dictionary of Canadian Biography*, vol. 5, s.v. "Mackenzie, Sir Alexander (1764–1820)," by W. Kaye Lamb, accessed September 2, 2023, http://www.biographi.ca/en/bio/mackenzie_alexander_5e.html.

In May 1793 Mackenzie made a second attempt to cross to the coast, ascending the Peace and Parsnip Rivers and then crossing the Continental Divide and reaching a river later called the Fraser, correctly assuming it flowed to the Pacific but falsely believing it to be the Columbia. Indians warned him parts of the Fraser were impassable, however, and Mckenzie backtracked, eventually ascending the West Road (also called the Blackwater) River and then following well-used Indian trails to the Bella Coola River and then, in July, reaching an inlet of the Pacific called Dean Channel (missing what would have been a historic meeting with Vancouver, who had visited the same spot six weeks earlier). On the face of a large rock, McKenzie left this inscription: "Alexander Mackenzie, from Canada, by land, the twenty-second of July, one thousand seven hundred and ninety-three" (*Dictionary of Canadian Biography*, vol. 5, s.v. "Mackenzie, Sir Alexander").

In 1536 the Spanish explorer Álvar Núñez Cabeza de Vaca and three companions completed the first known continental crossing of North America when they reached the Pacific coast along the Gulf of California, in the present Mexican state of Sinaloa. Traveling on foot and often accompanied by Indians, they had departed present Florida in 1528. See Álvar Núñez Cabeza de Vaca, *The Narrative of Cabeza de Vaca*, edited, translated, and with an introduction by Rolena Adorno and Patrick Charles Pautz (Lincoln: University of Nebraska Press, 2003).

7. Jefferson's message to Congress, January 18, 1803, in Jackson, *Letters*, 1:13.
8. "Even as he was laying the groundwork for what became the Lewis and Clark Expedition . . . Jefferson gave his ambassador in Paris, Robert Livingston, instructions to . . . purchase for ten million dollars the Isle of Orleans, on which New Orleans was located, and 'the Floridas,' which ran along the coast from present-day Florida to Louisiana." On April 11, 1803, however, a French official surprised Livingston by offering to sell not only New Orleans but the entire Louisiana Territory. Convinced Jefferson would approve the agreement, Livingston and James Monroe signed the treaty on April 30 (De Cesar and Page, "Jefferson Buys Louisiana Territory").

Jefferson indeed approved the purchase and apparently received unofficial word of the agreement by mid-June. In Meriwether Lewis's June 19, 1803, letter inviting Clark to be coleader of the expedition, he wrote, "Expectations are at this time formed by our Government that the whole of that immense country watered by the Mississippi and it's tributary streams, Missourie inclusive, will be the property of the U. States in less than 12 Months from this date" (Jackson, *Letters*, 1:59). By the time the U.S. Senate authorized the purchase of Louisiana on October 20, the Lewis and Clark Expedition had already begun, with the captains and their recruits teaming up along the Ohio River in Clarksville, Indiana Territory. Lewis nevertheless handled political matters carefully, and on December 8, with John Hay and Nicholas Jarrot acting as interpreters, he met in St. Louis with the Spanish governor, Don Carlos Dehault Delassus, and obtained permission to proceed with his mission (Jackson, *Letters*, 1:146). Lewis was again present in St. Louis on March 9–10, 1804, for a "Three Flags" ceremony, in which ownership of Upper Louisiana was transferred from Spain to France and from France to the United States.

9. As Elliott West has noted, "Between February 19, 1846, and July 4, 1848, the United States acquired more than 1.2 million square miles of land"—773,510,680 acres—"far and away the greatest expansion in the nation's history, more than half again what had been added in the Louisiana Purchase" (West, *Continental Reckoning*, xix). The boundaries of the contiguous continental United States were essentially settled at that time, although the 1853 Gadsden Purchase added another 29,142,400 acres in present New Mexico and Arizona (*New Encyclopedia of the American West* [1988], s.v. "Gadsen Purchase," 417). In a remarkable coincidence, James W. Marshall discovered gold at Sutter's Mill nine days before the Treaty of Guadalupe Hidalgo brought California (as well as Nevada, Utah, New Mexico, most of Arizona and Colorado, and parts of Oklahoma, Kansas, and Wyoming) into the United States.
10. Thomas Jefferson to Meriwether Lewis, June 20, 1803, in Jackson, *Letters*, 1:61.
11. Moulton, *Journals*, 1:15n2, ix.
12. Jackson, review of *Passage through the Garden*, 309–10.
13. Moulton, *Journals*, 1:15n2.
14. DeVoto, *Empire*, back cover promotional copy.
15. Allen, *Image*, xv, brackets added.
16. Allen, *Image*, xix.
17. DeVoto, *Empire*, 488, 552–53.
18. Meriwether Lewis to Thomas Jefferson, September 23, 1806, in Jackson, *Letters*, 1:321, brackets added.
19. Cong. Globe, 30th Cong., 1 Sess., Senate, 916 (May 28, 1849), cited in Smith, *Virgin Land*, 28.
20. Whitman, *Two Rivulets*, 5n, cited in Smith, *Virgin Land*, 47.
21. Walt Whitman, "A Passage to India," Academy of American Poets, accessed April 30, 2025, https://poets.org/poem/passage-india.
22. Whitman, "Passage to India."
23. Smith, *Virgin Land*, 17, 21.
24. Baritz, "Idea of the West," 618, brackets added.
25. George Berkeley, "Verses on the Prospect of Planting Arts and Learning in America," America in Class, accessed on May 1, 2025, https://americainclass.org/wp-content/

uploads/2014/02/2_BERKELEY-VERSES-ON-THE-PROSPECT-OF-PLANTING-ARTS-AND-LEARNING-IN-AMERICA.pdf.

26. "From Thomas Jefferson to William Dunbar, 13 March 1804," Founders Online, National Archives, accessed May 1, 2025, https://founders.archives.gov/documents/Jefferson/01-43-02-0009.
27. Allen, *Image*, xix–xxvi, 2; Smith, *Virgin Land*, 19.

1. "A Passage to India"

1. Allen, *Image*, xx.
2. Aristotle, *On the Heavens*, II, cited in Baritz, "Idea of the West," 620, brackets added.
3. Strabo, *Geography*, book II, chapter 5, cited in Keay, *Spice Trade*, 12–13, brackets added.
4. Strabo, *Geography*, book I, chapter 4, brackets added, https://penelope.uchicago.edu/Thayer/e/roman/texts/strabo/1d*.html.
5. "Languages Jefferson Spoke or Read," Monticello, accessed May 2, 2025, https://www.monticello.org/research-education/thomas-jefferson-encyclopedia/languages-jefferson-spoke-or-read/.
6. Carman and Evans, "Two Earths of Eratosthenes," 1–2, brackets added.
7. Toscanelli to Fernam Martins, June 15, 1474, in Markham, *Journal*, 4–5, brackets added.
8. Ijoma, "Portuguese Activities," 137.
9. Lewis's journal entry, April 7, 1805, in Moulton, *Journals*, 4:9.
10. Vaseem Khan, "Inside India #11: A Brief History of Indian Spices," vaseemkhan.com, accessed May 2, 2025, https://vaseemkhan.com/2021/01/24/inside-india-11-a-brief-history-of-indian-spices/.
11. Lawton, *Silk, Scents, and Spice*, 75–76.
12. Exod. 30:22–24, 33, KJV, brackets added.
13. Julia Dubnoff, trans., "Poems of Sappho," University of Houston, accessed May 2, 2025, https://www.uh.edu/~cldue/texts/sappho.html.
14. Keay, *Spice Trade*, xi–xii.
15. 1 Kings 9:26–27 KJV.
16. 2 Chron. 9:21, KJV, brackets added.
17. John McClintock and James Strong, "Tarshish," Biblical Cyclopedia, accessed May 2, 2025, https://www.biblicalcyclopedia.com/T/tarshish.html.
18. Webb, "Alleged Phoenician Circumnavigation," 3, brackets added.
19. Strabo, *Geography*, 2.3.4, brackets added, https://www.perseus.tufts.edu/hopper/text?doc=Perseus%3atext%3a1999.01.0239%3abook%3d2%3achapter%3d3%3asection%3d4.
20. Strabo, *Geography*, 2.3.5, brackets added.
21. Hourani estimates that Eudoxus's voyages from Egypt to India took place between 120 and 110 BC (*Arab Seafaring*, 24).
22. Moreno, "Atlantic Seafaring," 5–8, brackets in original.
23. Turner, *History of a Temptation*, 60.
24. Huntingford, *Periplus of the Erythraean Sea*, 52.

25. Strabo, *Geography*, 2.5.12, brackets added.
26. Lawton, *Silk, Scents, and Spice*, 84; Turner, *History of a Temptation*, 65.
27. *World History Encyclopedia*, s.v. "Periplus of the Erythraean Sea," by James Hancock, last modified July 16, 2021, brackets added, https://www.worldhistory.org/Periplus_of_the_Erythraean_Sea/.
28. Huntingford, *Periplus of the Erythraean Sea*, 51–52, brackets added.
29. Keay, *Spice Trade*, 89, 105–6.
30. Lawton, *Silk, Scents, and Spice*, 11, brackets added.
31. "How the Radanite Traders Spiced Up Life in Dark-Ages Europe," Forward, accessed May 2, 2025, https://forward.com/news/8926/how-the-radanite-traders-spiced-up-life-in-the-dark-ag/; see also Gil, "Radhanite Merchants."
32. "Medieval Sourcebook: Urban II (1088–1099): Speech at Council of Clermont, 1095, Six Versions of the Speech," Fordham University, Fulcher of Chartres and Robert the Monk, accessed May 2, 2025, brackets added, https://sourcebooks.fordham.edu/source/urban2-5vers.asp.
33. Perry and Gabriele, "Myths of the Term 'Crusader.'"
34. Anna Comnena, *The Alexiad*, book X, https://sourcebooks.fordham.edu/basis/AnnaComnena-Alexiad10.asp.
35. William of Tyre, "The Capture of Jerusalem," History Muse, accessed May 2, 2025, brackets added, http://www.historymuse.net/readings/WilliamofTyrecaptureofjerusalem.htm (page no longer extant).
36. Nicol, *Byzantium and Venice*, 107, brackets added.
37. Madden, "Venetian Version," 311–13.
38. Madden, "Venetian Version," 313.
39. Geoffrey de Villehardouin, *Memoirs of the Fourth Crusade and the Conquest of Constantinople*, https://sourcebooks.fordham.edu/basis/villehardouin.asp.
40. Nicetas Choniates, "The Sack of Constantinople (1204)," Fordham University, Internet History Sourcebooks: Medieval Sourcebook, accessed May 2, 2025, https://sourcebooks.fordham.edu/source/choniates1.asp.
41. Cited in Larner, *Discovery of the World*, 47–48.
42. Larner, *Discovery of the World*, 153–55, brackets added.
43. Cited in Man, *Xanadu*, 282, 278–79.
44. Man, *Xanadu*, 12.
45. Andrew Holt, "Accounts of the Mongols in the Medieval Record," apholt.com, accessed on May 2, 2025, https://apholt.com/2020/06/08/accounts-of-the-mongols-in-the-medieval-record/.
46. Yule, *Book of Marco Polo*, prologue, 4, brackets added.
47. Yule, *Book of Marco Polo*, prologue, 10.
48. Yule, *Book of Marco Polo*, prologue, 18, brackets added.
49. Yule, *Book of Marco Polo*, prologue, 13.
50. Cited in Larner, *Discovery of the World*, 35.
51. Yule, *Book of Marco Polo*, prologue, 17, brackets added.

52. Larner, *Discovery of the World*, 40.
53. Yule, *Book of Marco Polo*, prologue, 20, 21–23, brackets added.
54. Yule, *Book of Marco Polo*, prologue, 77, 98, 110–11.
55. Yule, *Book of Marco Polo*, book I, 113, 127, 131, 155–56, 158.
56. Yule, *Book of Marco Polo*, book I, 190–91.
57. Yule, *Book of Marco Polo*, book I, 219, 221.
58. Man, *Xanadu*, 67.
59. Yule, *Book of Marco Polo*, prologue, 26; Yule, *Book of Marco Polo*, book 2, 420–21; Yule, *Book of Marco Polo*, prologue, 27.
60. Waldo, "Recollections," 92, brackets added.
61. Cliff, *Last Crusade*, 86.
62. Zurara, *Chronicle*, 55, 64, 66.
63. Zurara, *Chronicle*, 66.
64. Zurara, *Chronicle*, 83, 80.
65. Zurara, *Chronicle*, 82, brackets added.
66. Black, *Slavery*, 43, 2, 13–14, 17–18, 49, 41.
67. Black, *Slavery*, 2, 43, 209–11.
68. Massing, "Mapping the Malagueta Coast"; Ijoma, "Portuguese Activities," 136–39.
69. Delaney, "Columbus's Ultimate Goal," 261.
70. Morison, *Admiral of the Ocean Sea*, 102.
71. According to Samuel Eliot Morison, although Columbus knew of Eratosthenes's estimation of the earth's circumference, he argued from a "faulty premise [concluding] that the world was 25 per cent smaller than Eratosthenes . . . taught" (Morison, *Admiral of the Ocean Sea*, 65, brackets added).
72. *World History Encyclopedia*, s.v. "Treaty of Tordesillas," accessed May 2, 2025, brackets added, https://www.worldhistory.org/timeline/Treaty_of_Tordesillas/.
73. Cited in Cliff, *Last Crusade*, 166.
74. Cited in Cliff, *Last Crusade*, 217, brackets added.
75. Ravenstein, *Journal*, 87.
76. Cliff, *Last Crusade*, 237, 230.
77. Ravenstein, *Journal*, 44–45.
78. Ravenstein, *Journal*, 44–45, 76.
79. Cliff, *Last Crusade*, 271.
80. Account of Fernão Lopes de Castanheda (1500–1559), in Kerr, *Voyages*, 394.
81. Account of João de Barros (1496–1570), in Cliff, *Last Crusade*, 283, brackets added.
82. Cliff, *Last Crusade*, 284.
83. Account of Castanheda, in Kerr, *Voyages*, 398–400.
84. Account of Castanheda, in Kerr, *Voyages*, 408, 411–13; Cliff, *Last Crusade*, 285.
85. See Cliff, *Last Crusade*, 322–29.
86. Account of Castanheda, in Kerr, *Voyages*, 413–16.
87. Account of Castanheda, in Kerr, *Voyages*, 417–18; Cliff, *Last Crusade*, 286–87.
88. Stanley, *Three Voyages*, 313–15.

89. Maddy, "The Plunder and Massacre of 'The Meri,'" *Historic Alleys* (blog), accessed May 2, 2025, brackets added, https://historicalleys.blogspot.com/2011/04/plunder-and-massacre-of-meri.html.
90. Cited in "Plunder and Massacre," brackets added.
91. "Portuguese Establish Their Trade Empire in Asia," factsanddetails.com, accessed May 2, 2025, https://factsanddetails.com/india/History/sub7_1c/entry-4120.html.
92. Bergreen, *Edge of the World*, 21–24.
93. Bergreen, *Edge of the World*, 31.
94. Account of Bartolomé de las Casas, cited in Bergreen, *Edge of the World*, 32–33.
95. Cited in Bergreen, *Edge of the World*, 34.
96. "Pigafetta's Account," in Stanley of Alderley, *First Voyage*, 162.
97. Cano to Charles I, September 6, 1522, in Morison, *European Discovery*, 471–72, brackets added.
98. Cano to Charles I, in Morison, *European Discovery*, 471.
99. "Pigafetta's Account," in Stanley of Alderley, *First Voyage*, 35; Bergreen, *Edge of the World*, 404.
100. "Pigafetta's Account," in Stanley of Alderley, *First Voyage*, 37, 41 brackets added.
101. "Pigafetta's Account," in Stanley of Alderley, *First Voyage*, 44, 46.
102. Cited in Bergreen, *Edge of the World*, 49, brackets added.
103. "Maximilian's Letter," in Stanley of Alderley, *First Voyage*, 192; Joyner, *Magellan*, 136–37.
104. "Pigafetta's Account," in Stanley of Alderley, *First Voyage*, 55–56, brackets added.
105. Joyner, *Magellan*, 136–43; Bergreen, *Edge of the World*, 134–44.
106. Bergreen, *Edge of the World*, 160.
107. Cited in Joyner, *Magellan*, 163–64, brackets added.
108. Cited in Joyner, *Magellan*, 164.
109. "The Strait of Magellan: 250 Years of Maps (1520–1787)," Princeton University Library, accessed May 2, 2025, https://library.princeton.edu/visual_materials/maps/websites/pacific/magellan-strait/magellan-strait-maps.html.
110. "Pigafetta's Account," in Stanley of Alderley, *First Voyage*, 64–65, brackets added.
111. Joyner, *Magellan*, 170, 173.
112. "Pigafetta's Account," in Stanley of Alderley, *First Voyage*, 68–70, brackets added.
113. Joyner, *Magellan*, 180–91; Bergreen, *Edge of the World*, 244–45, 272.
114. "Pigafetta's Account," in Stanley of Alderley, *First Voyage*, 100–102, brackets added.
115. Joyner, *Magellan*, 167.

2. "That Wretched Portion"

1. Huser, *On the River*, 91.
2. Lewis's journal entry, August 12, 1805, in Moulton, *Journals*, 5:74.
3. Jefferson's instructions to Lewis, June 20, 1803, in Jackson, *Letters*, 1:62, 61.
4. Lewis's journal entry, August 12, 1805, in Moulton, *Journals*, 5:74.
5. Lewis's journal entry, August 13, 1805, in Moulton, *Journals*, 5:81.
6. Lang, "Lewis and Clark," 141.

7. Allen, *Image*, 72.
8. Clark's journal entry, September 2, 1805, in Moulton, *Journals*, 5:183.
9. Lewis's journal entry, September 9, 1805, in Moulton, *Journals*, 5:192, brackets added.
10. Lewis's journal entry, September 9, 1805, in Moulton, *Journals*, 5:192, italics in original, brackets added.
11. Ambrose, *Undaunted Courage*, 286, italics and brackets added.
12. Lewis's journal entry, September 10, 1805, in Moulton, *Journals*, 5:197.
13. Gass's journal entries, September 12, 16, and 17, 1805, in Moulton, *Journals*, 10:141, 143.
14. Clark's journal entries, September 14 and 16, 1805, in Moulton, *Journals*, 5:205, 209.
15. Nicandri, "Dissolution of Meriwether Lewis," 8.
16. Lewis to an unknown correspondent, October 14, 1806, in Jackson, *Letters*, 1:338.
17. Clark's journal entry, October 7, 1805, in Moulton, *Journals*, 5:249.
18. Lewis to an unknown correspondent, October 14, 1806, in Jackson, *Letters*, 1:338.
19. "In the fall of 1805, hurrying to reach the Pacific before winter arrived, the expedition experienced real whitewater for the first time. They ran rapids they should have scouted and bashed boats on rocks, splitting them and perching them on sleepers. They sank boats, soaked the baggage, and swamped canoes in big waves," writes Huser (*On the River*, 44).
20. Jefferson to Lewis, June 20, 1803, in Jackson, *Letters*, 1:61.
21. Clark's journal entry, November 7, 1805, in Moulton, *Journals*, 6:33. As Moulton says, Clark's celebration was premature because he actually saw the Columbia estuary rather than the Pacific.
22. Moulton, *Journals*, 6:2.
23. Clark's journal entries, November 12, 22, and 28 and December 8, 9, 20, and 24, 1805, in Moulton, *Journals*, 6:43, 79, 91, 117, 118, 133–34, 137, respectively.
24. Lewis's journal entry, January 1, 1806, in Moulton, *Journals*, 6:151–52, italics added.
25. Lewis's journal entry, April 17, 1806, in Moulton, *Journals*, 7:131.
26. Lewis's journal entries, March 18 and March 22, 1806, in Moulton, *Journals*, 6:425, 444, respectively.
27. Ordway's journal entry, March 18, 1806, in Moulton, *Journals*, 9:278.
28. Jefferson to Lewis, January 22, 1804, in Jackson, *Letters*, 1:166.
29. Ronda, *Lewis and Clark among the Indians*, 211, brackets added.
30. Nicandri, "Dissolution of Meriwether Lewis," 17.
31. Lewis's journal entry, April 11, 1806, in Moulton, *Journals*, 7:105.
32. Lewis's journal entry, April 11, 1806, in Moulton, *Journals*, 7:105.
33. Lewis's journal entries, April 18 and 19, 1806, in Moulton, *Journals*, 7:136, 143, respectively.
34. Lewis's journal entry, April 20, 1806, in Moulton, *Journals*, 7:146. Clark, still upstream trading for horses, took a more hopeful view of the Indians, saying, "Those people are Pore and Kind durty & indolt" (Clark's journal entry, April 20, 1806, in Moulton, *Journals*, 7:147).
35. Lewis's journal entry, April 21, 1806, in Moulton, *Journals*, 7:152, italics and brackets added.

36. Nicandri, "Dissolution of Meriwether Lewis," 16.
37. Lewis's journal entry, April 21, 1806, in Moulton, *Journals*, 7:152.
38. Gass's journal entry, April 21, 1806, in Moulton, *Journals*, 10:213.
39. Lewis's journal entry, March 18, 1806, in Moulton, *Journals*, 6:430.
40. Huser, *On the River*, 154.
41. Clark's journal entries, May 18 and 19, 1806, in Moulton, *Journals*, 7:271, 272–73, respectively, italics in original, brackets added. See Paton, *Lewis and Clark*, 169.
42. Lewis's journal entry, June 2, 1806, in Moulton, *Journals*, 7:325.
43. Lewis's journal entries, June 9 and 10, 1806, in Moulton, *Journals*, 7:349, 8:7, respectively.
44. Lewis's journal entry, June 14, 1806, in Moulton, *Journals*, 8:24.
45. Lewis's journal entry, June 16, 1806, in Moulton, *Journals*, 8:27–28.
46. Lewis's journal entry, June 17, 1806, in Moulton, *Journals*, 8:31–32, brackets added.
47. Gass's journal entry, June 17, 1806, in Moulton, *Journals*, 10:241.
48. Lewis's journal entry, June 17, 1806, in Moulton, *Journals*, 8:32; Ambrose, *Undaunted Courage*, 362.
49. Lewis's journal entry, June 18, 1806, in Moulton, *Journals*, 8:34–35.
50. "When Lewis struck the mark twice from a range of 220 yards, those warriors could not help but be impressed with the weapons that might soon be in their hands," writes Ronda (*Lewis and Clark among the Indians*, 227).
51. Lewis's journal entry, June 20, 1806, in Moulton, *Journals*, 8:39–40, brackets added.
52. Lewis's journal entries, June 21 and 22, 1806, in Moulton, *Journals*, 8:43–44, 45, respectively, brackets added.
53. Lewis's journal entry, June 23, 1806, in Moulton, *Journals*, 8:46–47, brackets added.
54. Lewis's journal entries, June 24 and 25, 1806, in Moulton, *Journals*, 8:48, 50, respectively, brackets added.
55. Lewis's journal entry, June 26, 1806, in Moulton, *Journals*, 8:52–53, brackets added.
56. Lewis's journal entry, June 27, 1806, in Moulton, *Journals*, 8:56.
57. Lewis's journal entry, June 29, 1806, in Moulton, *Journals*, 8:62–63.
58. Lewis's journal entry, June 30, 1806, in Moulton, *Journals*, 8:65–66.
59. Ambrose, *Undaunted Courage*, 369.
60. Clark's journal entry, July 3, 1806, in Moulton, *Journals*, 8:161. Clark was also accompanied by Sergeants Ordway and Pryor, William Bratton, Collins, Colter, Cruzatte, Gibson, Hall, Howard, Francois Labiche, Lepage, Potts, Shannon, Shields, Weiser, Whitehouse, Willard, Windsor, and York.
61. Clark's journal entry, November 12, 1804, in Moulton, *Journals*, 3:234, brackets added. "The Crows . . . had been driven from the Black Hills of South Dakota by the Sioux some time before this. However, the captains understood the term 'Black Hills' as covering all the eastern outlying ranges of the Rockies which include the Laramie range as well," writes Moulton (*Journals*, 3:26n3).
62. "Estimate of the Eastern Indians," undated document in William Clark's hand, in Moulton, *Journals*, 3:333–35, 386–87, 427–29.
63. See Moulton, *Journals*, 3:386–450, for Clark's complete "Estimate of the Eastern Indians."

64. "Affluents of the Missouri River," undated document in Meriwether Lewis's hand, "prepared at Fort Mandan," in Moulton, *Journals*, 3:364, brackets added.
65. Lewis's journal entry, June 8, 1805, in Moulton, *Journals*, 4:266, italics added.
66. Lewis's journal entry, July 3, 1806, in Moulton, *Journals*, 8:83.
67. Lewis's journal entries, July 8, 9, and 10, 1806, in Moulton, *Journals*, 8:97–99.
68. Lewis's journal entries, July 11, 12, and 13, 1806, in Moulton, *Journals*, 8:106, 107–8.
69. Lewis's journal entries, July 14 and 15, 1806, in Moulton, *Journals*, 8:108, 109–10.
70. Lewis's journal entry, July 15, 1806, in Moulton, *Journals*, 8:110–11.
71. Gass's journal entry, July 16, 1806, in Moulton, *Journals*, 10:254.
72. Clark's journal entries, July 3 and 4, 1806, in Moulton, *Journals*, 8:162, 63.
73. Clark's journal entry, July 5, 1806, in Moulton, *Journals*, 8:165, brackets added.
74. Clark, "Estimated Distances," undated document, in Moulton, *Journals*, 8:393.
75. Clark's journal entry, July 6, 1806, in Moulton, *Journals*, 8:167, brackets added.
76. Clark's journal entry, July 8, 1806, in Moulton, *Journals*, 8:171, brackets added. The site of Camp Fortunate is now under Clark Canyon Reservoir, southwest of present Dillon, Montana.
77. Clark's journal entries, July 8, 9, and 10, 1806, in Moulton, *Journals*, 8:172–76, brackets added.
78. Clark's journal entry, July 13, 1806, in Moulton, *Journals*, 8:179–80, brackets added. Ordway was accompanied by Collins, Colter, Cruzatte, Howard, Lepage, Potts, Weiser, Whitehouse, and Willard. The following individuals went overland with Clark: Sergeant Pryor, Bratton, Gibson, Hall, Labiche, Shannon, Shields, Windsor, York, Charbonneau, Sacagawea, and Jean Baptiste.
79. Clark's journal entry, July 15, 1806, in Moulton, *Journals*, 8:185.
80. Jenkinson, *Explorer in the Wilderness*, 166.
81. Lewis's journal entry, July 1, 1806, in Moulton, *Journals*, 8:74.
82. Kukla, *Wilderness So Immense*, 286.
83. Kukla, *Wilderness So Immense*, 286–87. Jefferson made his estimate in a July 5, 1803, letter to Thomas Mann Randolf (his son-in-law), Jefferson Papers, Library of Congress.
84. Allen, *Image*, 135–36.
85. Lewis's journal entry, July 17, 1806, in Moulton, *Journals*, 8:112–13.
86. Lewis's journal entry, July 18, 1806, in Moulton, *Journals*, 8:115–16.
87. Lewis's journal entry, July 21, 1806, in Moulton, *Journals*, 8:121, 122n3, italics added.
88. Lewis's journal entry, July 22, 1806, in Moulton, *Journals*, 8:122–23, brackets added.
89. Lewis's journal entry, July 23, 1806, in Moulton, *Journals*, 8:125.
90. Lewis's journal entries, July 24 and 25, 1806, in Moulton, *Journals*, 8:126–27, brackets added.
91. Lewis's journal entry, July 26, 1806, in Moulton, *Journals*, 8:127–28.
92. Lewis's journal entry, July 26, 1806, in Moulton, *Journals*, 8:129–32, brackets in original.
93. Lewis's journal entries, July 27 and 28, 1806, in Moulton, *Journals*, 8:136–38.
94. Ordway's journal entry, July 28, 1806, in Moulton, *Journals*, 9:341.
95. Ambrose, *Undaunted Courage*, 378.

96. Lewis's journal entries, July 29, 30, and 31, 1806, in Moulton, *Journals*, 8:140–41.
97. Lewis's journal entry, August 2, 1806, in Moulton, *Journals*, 8:146.
98. Lewis's journal entry, August 3, 1806, in Moulton, *Journals*, 8:146, brackets added.
99. Lewis's journal entry, August 7, 1806, in Moulton, *Journals*, 8:149.
100. Lewis's journal entry, August 7, 1806, in Moulton, *Journals*, 8:149–50.
101. Lewis's journal entry, August 7, 1806, in Moulton, *Journals*, 8:150–51, brackets added.
102. Lewis's journal entry, April 25, 1805, in Moulton, *Journals*, 4:67.
103. Lewis's journal entry, August 8, 1806, in Moulton, *Journals*, 8:152.
104. Lewis's journal entry, April 25, 1805, in Moulton, *Journals*, 4:67.
105. Jenkinson, *Explorer in the Wilderness*, 176. Thanks to Clay Jenkinson for his profound insights into the character of Meriwether Lewis, drawn on in no small degree here.
106. Lewis's journal entry, August 8, 1806, in Moulton, *Journals*, 8:152.
107. Nicandri, "Dissolution of Meriwether Lewis," 8.
108. Jefferson's message to Congress, January 18, 1803, in Jackson, *Letters*, 1:12, 13.
109. Lewis to Clark, June 19, 1803, in Jackson, *Letters*, 1:60.
110. Lewis's journal entry, April 7, 1805, in Moulton, *Journals*, 4:10, brackets and angle brackets in original.
111. Jenkinson, *Explorer in the Wilderness*, 178–79, 182.
112. Lewis's journal entry, August 9, 1806, in Moulton, *Journals*, 8:153.
113. Lewis' journal entry, August 10, 1806, in Moulton, *Journals*, 8:152.
114. Jenkinson, *Explorer in the Wilderness*, 188.
115. Lewis's journal entry, August 11, 1806, in Moulton, *Journals*, 8:154.
116. Paton, *Lewis and Clark*, 189.
117. Lewis's journal entry, August 11, 1806, in Moulton, *Journals*, 8:155.
118. Lewis's journal entry, August 11, 1806, in Moulton, *Journals*, 8:155.
119. Lewis's journal entry, August 11, 1806, in Moulton, *Journals*, 8:155–56, brackets added.
120. Gass's journal entry, August 12, 1806, in Moulton, *Journals*, 10:266.
121. Lewis's journal entry, August 12, 1806, in Moulton, *Journals*, 8:157, brackets added.
122. Gass's journal entry, August 12, 1806, in Moulton, *Journals*, 10:266.
123. Lewis's journal entry, August 12, 1806, in Moulton, *Journals*, 8:157–58.
124. Ordway's journal entry, August 12, 1806, in Moulton, *Journals*, 9:348, brackets added.
125. Clark's journal entry, August 12, 1806, in Moulton, *Journals*, 8:290.
126. Gass's journal entry, August 12, 1806, in Moulton, *Journals*, 10:266.
127. Ordway's journal entry, August 14, 1806, in Moulton, *Journals*, 9:350.
128. Clark's journal entries, August 19 and 28 and September 9, 1806, in Moulton, *Journals*, 8:309, 326, 354, respectively.

3. "He Draws a Line"

1. James Wilkinson to Henry Dearborn, October 8, 1805, in Jackson, *Letters*, 1:261–62. Wilkinson, writes Ambrose, "was secretly a Spanish spy, code name 'Agent 13.' As an officer in the revolution, he had entered into the Conway Cabel (a group trying to

supplant General Washington), and from then on until his death in 1825 he never met a conspiracy he didn't embrace" (*Undaunted Courage*, 334).

2. Clark's journal entry, October 10, 1804, in Moulton, *Journals*, 3:156. Clark initially called the chief in question "*Pia he to* (or Eagles Feather)," but there have also been other attempts to transcribe his name. Jefferson settled on "Arketarnawhar" after crossing out "Piaketa" and "Toone." Two variations of Jefferson's spelling were "Ankedoucharo" and "Arketarnashar." See Moulton, *Journals*, 3:155, 156n5; and "What's in a Name?"
3. Lewis and Clark to the Oto Indians, August 4, 1804, in Jackson, *Letters*, 1:203–8, italics in original.
4. Miller, *Native America Discovered*, 1.
5. Ronda, *Lewis and Clark among the Indians*, 57.
6. Moulton, *Journals*, 3:157n2.
7. Clark's field notes, October 10, 1804, in Moulton, *Journals*, 3:156–57.
8. Clark's undated record, likely created on October 12, 1804, in Moulton, *Journals*, 3:166.
9. Van de Logt, *Between the Floods*, 118–21.
10. Lewis to Jefferson, April 7, 1805, in Jackson, *Letters*, 1:234–36.
11. Rather than sending twenty-two men to escort the chiefs, "Wilkinson assigned all of two soldiers to conduct them home in a boat. Just before the soldiers and Indian delegates reached the mouth of the Kansas River, they encountered a group of Kansa Indians who, after strong words from both sides, readied their weapons. . . . Unable to proceed upriver against the current without facing a barrage of fire, the soldiers turned the boat around and . . . [returned] to St. Louis" (Steinke, "Too Né's Map," 597), brackets added.
12. Wilkinson to Jefferson, December 23, 1805, in Jackson, *Letters*, 1:272–73, italics in original.
13. Steinke, "Too Né's Map," 597–98.
14. Steinke, "Too Né's Map," 597–98.
15. "William Dunlap's Meeting with Too Né," 16–17—citing *Diary of William Dunlap*, 2:389–93, brackets added. As Jenkinson points out, Indian maps "generally follow a different set of cartographical protocols and conventions than Euro-American maps. While there is clearly some directional orientation on Too Né's map, scale, distances, and even placement do not conform to non-native standards. Native maps often seem impressionistic or even directionally vague to non-natives" ("Maney Extroadenary Stories," 30n28).
16. Clark's journal entry, October 17, 1804, in Moulton, *Journals*, 3:180.
17. Van de Logt, *Between the Floods*, 122–23.
18. Steinke, "Too Né's Map," 591–92. The entire May 2018 (volume 44, no. 2) issue of the Lewis and Clark quarterly, *We Proceeded On*, is devoted to the map and its importance and includes a pullout color copy of the map. Copies of the map are also available in Steinke, "Too Né's Map," and van de Logt, *Between the Floods*.
19. Henry Dearborn to James Wilkinson, April 9, 1806, in Jackson, *Letters*, 1:303.
20. Dearborn to Wilkinson, April 9, 1806, in Jackson, *Letters*, 1:303–5.
21. Jefferson to the Arikaras, in Jackson, *Letters*, 1:306.

22. Clark's journal entry, August 21, 1806, in Moulton, *Journals*, 8:311, brackets added.
23. Clark's journal entry, August 21, 1806, in Moulton, *Journals*, 8:312–13, brackets added.
24. Ronda, *Lewis and Clark among the Indians*, 249–50.
25. Clark's journal entry, August 21, 1806, in Moulton, *Journals*, 8:315–16, brackets added.
26. Clark's journal entries, August 22–23, 1806, in Moulton, *Journals*, 8:317–20.
27. Irving, *Astoria*, 138. Irving never met McClellan, who died in 1815, but he interviewed several men who knew him well, including Clark.
28. Ordway's journal entry, September 12, 1806, in Moulton, *Journals*, 9:361.
29. Clark's journal entry, September 12, 1806, in Moulton, *Journals*, 8:357–58, brackets added.
30. Majors, "John McClellan," 582–83.
31. Robert McClellan to Meriwether Lewis, April 5, 1807, William Clark Papers, Clark Family Collection, Missouri History Museum, brackets added.
32. McClellan to Lewis, April 5, 1807, brackets added.
33. Lewis to Jefferson, September 23, 1806, in Jackson, *Letters*, 1:321.
34. Morris, "Mysterious Charles Courtin," 21–23.
35. Charles Courtin to "Gentlemen," June 22, 1807, entry 18, Letters Received, 1801–70, Records of the Office of the Secretary of War, Record Group 107, National Archives, College Park, MD.
36. Courtin to "Gentlemen," June 22, 1807, brackets added.
37. Foley and Rice, "Return of the Mandan Chief," 7.
38. Courtin to "Gentlemen," June 22, 1807.
39. Anglin and Morris, *Mystery of John Colter*, 62–63.
40. Courtin to "Gentlemen," June 22, 1807.
41. Anglin and Morris, *Mystery of John Colter*, 62–65; see 75–98 for a discussion of Colter's probable route from Montana's Pryor Creek to the Yellowstone area and back.
42. Brackenridge, *Views of Louisiana*, 141–42, brackets added.
43. Nathaniel Pryor to William Clark, October 16, 1807, in Jackson, *Letters*, 2:433, brackets added.
44. Pryor to Clark, October 16, 1807, in Jackson, *Letters*, 2:432.
45. Pryor to Clark, October 16, 1807, in Jackson, *Letters*, 2:433–35, 432–33.
46. Pryor to Clark, October 16, 1807, in Jackson, *Letters*, 2:435, italics in original.
47. Pryor to Clark, October 16, 1807, in Jackson, *Letters*, 2:436.
48. For more on what we know about Joseph Field's final days, see Holmberg, *Dear Brother*, 93–96.
49. Pryor to Clark, October 16, 1807, in Jackson, *Letters*, 2:437.
50. Thomas Biddle to Henry Atkinson, October 29, 1819, American State Papers, Library of Congress, 202.
51. Jackson, "Journey to the Mandans," 184.
52. Jefferson to Lewis, July 17, 1808, in Jackson, *Letters*, 2:444–45.
53. Buckley, *William Clark*, 66–69.
54. See Lewis to Jefferson, June 27, 1807, in Jackson, *Letters*, 2:418.

55. Jefferson wrote to Lewis, "Since I parted with you in Albemarle in Sep. last I have never had a line from you" (Jefferson to Lewis, July 17, 1808, in Jackson, *Letters*, 2:444).
56. Ambrose, *Courage Undaunted*, xx.
57. Agreement for return of the Mandan chief, February 24, 1809, in Jackson, *Letters*, 2:446–50.
58. License issued to Manuel Lisa, June 7, 1809, Lisa Papers, Missouri History Museum.
59. Cited in Jackson, *Letters*, 2:445n1.
60. Lewis to Pierre Chouteau, June 8, 1809, in Jackson, *Letters*, 2:452–55, brackets added.
61. Christian, *Before Lewis and Clark*, 5–6.
62. Agreement for return of the Mandan chief, in Jackson, *Letters*, 2:448; Oglesby, *Manuel Lisa*, 75–76; Morris, *Perilous West*, 31–33.
63. James, *Three Years*, 11, brackets added. There is good evidence that the "old chief" who rode out at high speed was Edward Rose, who had left the Crows and was now living with the Arikaras. He joined Henry's group and went with them to the Yellowstone River and then to Three Forks. See Morris, *Perilous West*, 38–39.
64. Pierre Chouteau to William Eustis, December 14, 1809, in Jackson, *Letters*, 2:481, brackets added.
65. Chouteau to Eustis, December 14, 1809, in Jackson, *Letters*, 2:481–82.
66. Pierre Chouteau to William Simmon, November 23, 1809, Pierre Chouteau Letterbook, Missouri History Museum.

4. "Mr. Rose Came Running"

1. Camp, *James Clyman*, 15, brackets in original.
2. Holmes, "Five Scalps," 8.
3. *Missouri Republican*, January 15, 1823, cited in Morgan, *West of William H. Ashley*, 19, italics and capital letters in the original.
4. Wishart, *Fur Trade*, 27, brackets added.
5. Ashley and Henry likely founded their company in the summer of 1821 (Clokey, *William H. Ashley*, 63).
6. William H. Ashley to *Missouri Republican*, June 4, 1823, in Morgan, *West of William H. Ashley*, 24.
7. Ashley to *Missouri Republican*, in Morgan, *West of William H. Ashley*, 26.
8. Letter by one of Ashley's men to a friend in the District of Columbia, June 17, 1823, in Morgan, *West of William H. Ashley*, 32.
9. Richard Graham to the Senate Committee on Indian Affairs, February 10, 1824 (18th Congress, 1st Session, *Senate Document 56* [Serial 91], p. 6), cited in Morgan, *West of William H. Ashley*, 236n102, brackets added. Although Ashley claimed that Rose's warning came around 3:30 a.m., Clyman and an unidentified boatman both said it came shortly after midnight.
10. Camp, *James Clyman*, 15.
11. Camp, *James Clyman*, 15, brackets added. Rather than enlisting in the regular militia when the War of 1812 broke out, Ashley formed his own company of volunteer mounted

rangers, who elected him their captain and eventually their general. See Clokey, *William H. Ashley*, 27.

12. Camp, *James Clyman*, 15.
13. Report of Colonel Henry Leavenworth, October 20, 1823, cited in Morgan, *West of William H. Ashley*, 234n80. Leavenworth did not identify the source of this information.
14. William H. Ashley to a gentleman in Franklin, Missouri, June 7, 1823, in Morgan, *West of William H. Ashley*, 30.
15. Camp, *James Clyman*, 16.
16. Letter by one of Ashley's men, in Morgan, *West of William H. Ashley*, 32.
17. Ashley to *Missouri Republican*, in Morgan, *West of William H. Ashley*, 27.
18. Holmes, "Five Scalps," 55.
19. "Jedediah Strong Smith," 398.
20. Waldo, "Recollections," 82, brackets added.
21. Camp, *James Clyman*, 16, brackets in original.
22. Camp, *James Clyman*, 16.
23. Ashley to *Missouri Republican*, in Morgan, *West of William H. Ashley*, 26.
24. Letter by one of Ashley's men, in Morgan, *West of William H. Ashley*, 32–33.
25. Camp, *James Clyman*, 16, brackets in original.
26. Camp, *James Clyman*, 16, brackets added.
27. Camp, *James Clyman*, 16–17.
28. Camp, *James Clyman*, 17.
29. Camp, *James Clyman*, 17, brackets added.
30. Camp, *James Clyman*, 17–18, brackets in original.
31. Camp, *James Clyman*, 18, brackets in original.
32. Hugh Glass to the parents of John S. Gardner, June 1823, in Morgan, *West of William H. Ashley*, 31. Morgan adds, "Jedediah Smith's prayer has been described as the first act of public worship in what is now South Dakota. The scene is fancifully portrayed in a mural in the State Capitol at Pierre" (*West of William H. Ashley*, 236n96).
33. Nester, *Arikara War*, 2–3.
34. Ashley to Benjamin O'Fallon and the commanding officer at Council Bluffs, June 4, 1823, in Morgan, *West of William H. Ashley*, 28–29.
35. Morgan, *Jedediah Smith*, 380–81n22; Morgan, *West of William H. Ashley*, 235n92.
36. Waldo, "Recollections," 83.
37. Ashley to Benjamin O'Fallon and the commanding officer at Council Bluffs, in Morgan, *West of William H. Ashley*, 29.
38. While horses—and smallpox—reached the Missouri River Indian nations from the south, especially from Mexico, guns came from the north by way of Hudson's Bay Company and the North West Company, which merged in 1821. The Arikaras, like their Sioux, Mandan, and Hidatsa neighbors, were well supplied with flintlocks by the time the French Canadian explorer and trader Jean Baptiste Truteau visited the area in 1794–96. "The trade gun," writes Charles E. Hanson Jr., "was a sound, dependable arm. . . . The Indian lived by hunting and he demanded a gun just large enough to kill

big game at close range and still light enough to carry all day with comfort." The guns ranged in length from forty-six to sixty-four inches, the barrels part octagon, usually twenty-four gauge (about .58 caliber), "and smooth-bored for using either shot or a 30 gauge ball." Indians and traders used these guns from about 1775 to 1875. "Probably no other model of gun in American history had such widespread use for so long a period" (*Northwest Gun*, 1–2).

39. Orser, "Understanding Arikara Trading Behavior," in Buckley, *Rendezvous*, 106.
40. Calloway, *One Vast Winter Count*, 302.
41. Journal of Truteau on the Missouri River, 1794–95, in Nasatir, *Before Lewis and Clark*, 299.
42. Ubelaker and Bass, "Arikara Glassworking Techniques," 467.
43. Parks, *Traditional Narratives*, 3:vii–xiii.
44. Van de Logt, *Between the Floods*, 9–10.
45. Henry Leavenworth to Henry Atkinson, June 18, 1823, in Robinson, "Official Correspondence," 181–82.
46. Van de Logt, *Between the Floods*, 135.
47. Potter, *Sheheke*, 179.
48. Morris, *Fate of the Corps*, 114.
49. Van de Logt, *Between the Floods*, 132–34.
50. Benjamin O'Fallon to William Clark, June 24, 1823, in Morgan, *West of William H. Ashley*, 37.
51. "Mr. Pilcher's Answers," March 18, 1824, cited in Sunder, *Joshua Pilcher*, 39; Joshua Pilcher to Benjamin O'Fallon, July 23, 1823, in Morgan, *West of William H. Ashley*, 48.
52. Leavenworth to Atkinson, in Robinson, "Official Correspondence," 206–8, brackets added. Accidental deaths were so common in nineteenth-century life—and especially frontier life—that William Clark reported the demise of Leavenworth's soldiers to Secretary of War John C. Calhoun in this casual manner: "The Expedition under Col Levenworth has proceeded on very [well] except for the Loss of a Boat and Seven of his men drowned" (Clark to Calhoun, July 18, 1823, in Morgan, *West of William H. Ashley*, 47, brackets in original).
53. Leavenworth to Atkinson, in Robinson, "Official Correspondence," 210–11.
54. Cited in Morgan, *West of William H. Ashley*, 52.
55. Cited in Morgan, *West of William H. Ashley*, 52.
56. Leavenworth to Atkinson, in Robinson, "Official Correspondence," 213, brackets added.
57. Leavenworth to Atkinson, in Robinson, "Official Correspondence," 213–14, brackets added.
58. Camp, *James Clyman*, 20, brackets in original.
59. Leavenworth to Atkinson, in Robinson, "Official Correspondence," 216.
60. Leavenworth to Atkinson, in Robinson, "Official Correspondence," 216, brackets added.
61. Camp, *James Clyman*, 21, brackets in original.
62. Leavenworth to Atkinson, in Robinson, "Official Correspondence," 217.
63. Van de Logt, *Between the Floods*, 137.

64. Leavenworth to Atkinson, in Robinson, "Official Correspondence," 217–18.
65. Camp, *James Clyman*, 21.
66. Leavenworth to Atkinson, in Robinson, "Official Correspondence," 220–22.
67. Leavenworth to Atkinson, in Robinson, "Official Correspondence," 222.
68. Leavenworth to Atkinson, in Robinson, "Official Correspondence," 222.
69. Leavenworth to Atkinson, in Robinson, "Official Correspondence," 223.
70. Leavenworth to Atkinson, in Robinson, "Official Correspondence," 223–24.
71. Leavenworth to Atkinson, in Robinson, "Official Correspondence," 225.
72. Leavenworth to Atkinson, in Robinson, "Official Correspondence," 225–26.
73. Leavenworth to Atkinson, in Robinson, "Official Correspondence," 226.
74. Leavenworth to Atkinson, in Robinson, "Official Correspondence," 228, brackets added.
75. Leavenworth to Atkinson, in Robinson, "Official Correspondence," 228–29.
76. Leavenworth to Atkinson, in Robinson, "Official Correspondence," 229, brackets added.
77. Leavenworth to Atkinson, in Robinson, "Official Correspondence," 230–31.
78. Colonel Abram R. Wooley took command of Fort Atkinson when Leavenworth was transferred to Green Bay, Wisconsin, on December 9, 1825 (Kelly, *Lost Voices*, 275).
79. Leavenworth to Atkinson, in Robinson, "Official Correspondence," 231.
80. Leavenworth to Atkinson, in Robinson, "Official Correspondence," 231.
81. Leavenworth to Atkinson, August 30, 1823, in Niles, *Niles Weekly Register*, 25:86.
82. Cited in van de Logt, *Between the Floods*, 139.
83. Morgan, *West of William H. Ashley*, 56, brackets in original.
84. Leavenworth to Atkinson, August 30, 1823, in Niles, *Niles Weekly Register*, 25:86, brackets added.
85. Joshua Pilcher to Henry Leavenworth, August 26, 1823, in Morgan, *West of William H. Ashley*, 57–58.
86. Morgan, *Jedediah Smith*, 78.
87. *New Encyclopedia of the American West* (1988), s.v. "Fur Trade, in the United States," 414–15.
88. "The farm upon which James Clyman was born . . . was owned by President George Washington and . . . young James grew up there, obtaining a 'smattering of education,' which doubtless included many a glimpse of the old General. . . . Clyman [was] engaged in the Black Hawk War in the same company with Abraham Lincoln," writes Camp (*James Clyman*, 11). John Quincy Adams was another of the rare individuals who met both Washington and Lincoln.
89. See Coleman, *Here Lies Hugh Glass*, for an interesting take on Glass's legacy.
90. William Lewis Sublette was the eldest of the five Sublette brothers. The others were Milton Green (1801–37), Pinckney W. (1812–28), Andrew Whitley (1814–53), and Solomon Perry (1816–57). In her extensive discussion of the Sublette family, Anne F. Hyde writes, "None of them survived into old age, but the five Sublette brothers touched every aspect of the fur and hide trades and participated in the most important cultural and political revolutions of the Far West before the Civil War as we see them marry, run for office, speculate in land, and head west" (*Empires, Nations, and Families*, 57).

91. Mattes, "Hiram Scott," in Hafen, *Mountain Men*, 1:355.
92. Confer, "Beginning and the End," 11.

5. "Captain Smith"

1. Rollins, *Discovery*, 281.
2. Chittenden, *American Fur Trade*, 1:169.
3. Irving, *Astoria*, 36, 134; Morris, *Perilous West*, 67, 97, 178, 181.
4. *Missouri Gazette*, April 12, 1809.
5. Morris, *Perilous West*, 13–18, 29–36, 44.
6. Irving, *Astoria*, 39.
7. Ross, *First Settlers*, 43.
8. James Cook, one of Lewis's idols, circumnavigated the globe twice, from 1768 to 1771 and 1772 to 1775. The first American to accomplish the feat was Robert Gray, from 1787 to 1790.
9. Irving, *Astoria*, 39–40n.
10. Clark to Eustis, September 12, 1810, in Carter, *Territorial Papers*, 14:412, brackets added.
11. John Jacob Astor to Albert Gallatin, May 26, 1810, in Lavender, *Fist in the Wilderness*, 444n10.
12. Rollins, *Discovery*, 303.
13. *Louisiana Gazette*, July 26, 1810, brackets added.
14. Bradbury, *Travels*, 35; Jefferson to Lewis, August 16, 1809, in Jackson, *Letters*, 2:458.
15. Jefferson to Lewis, August 16, 1809, in Jackson, *Letters*, 2:458.
16. Bradbury, *Travels*, 35.
17. John Bradbury to William Roscoe, July 24, 1810, in Jackson, *Letters*, 2:458–59n1.
18. Bradbury, *Travels*, 35–36.
19. Bradbury, *Travels*, 39, 43. The site of La Charette, near present Marthasville, Missouri, is now covered by the encroaching Missouri River. Boone, born November 2, 1734, was actually seventy-six when he met Bradbury.
20. Bradbury, *Travels*, 45–46. Bradbury told the story of Colter's Run in a long footnote (44–47n).
21. Bradbury, *Travels*, 60, 70, italics in original.
22. Bradbury, *Travels*, 96–97, brackets added.
23. "We had on board a Frenchman named Charboneau, with his wife, an Indian woman of the Snake nation, both of whom had accompanied Lewis and Clark to the Pacific, and were of great service," wrote Brackenridge. "The woman, a good creature, of a mild and gentle disposition, greatly attached to the whites, whose manners and dress she tries to imitate, but she had become sickly, and longed to revisit her native country; her husband, also, who had spent many years among the Indians, had become weary of civilized life" (*Journal of a Voyage*, 10). Charbonneau, Sacagawea, and their son Baptiste (called "Pomp" or "Pompey" by Clark) had remained at the Mandan villages as the captains returned home in 1806, but in 1809, after Chouteau's expedition safely escorted Sheheke to that area and several in that group turned back for St. Louis, the

Charbonneau family went with them, arriving late in the autumn, just as news of Lewis's death also reached the city. With help from Clark, the Charbonneaus thus spent a year and a half in St. Louis before joining Lisa in the spring of 1811. Baptiste then remained in St. Louis and attended school, supported by Clark (Morris, *Fate of the Corps*, 15–16, 107–8, 115, 117).

24. Brackenridge, *Journal of a Voyage*, 58–60.
25. Brackenridge, *Journal of a Voyage*, 72–73.
26. Bradbury, *Travels*, 97.
27. Brackenridge, *Journal of a Voyage*, 102.
28. Brackenridge, *Journal of a Voyage*, 107–9, brackets added.
29. Bradbury, *Travels*, 98, italics in original.
30. Bradbury, *Travels*, 98–100, brackets added.
31. Irving, *Astoria*, 178.
32. Bradbury, *Travels*, 103–6, brackets added.
33. Bradbury, *Travels*, 108, brackets added.
34. Bradbury, *Travels*, 113, 117, brackets added.
35. Bradbury, *Travels*, 119, brackets added.
36. Brackenridge, *Journal of a Voyage*, 128.
37. Bradbury, *Travels*, 122.
38. Brackenridge, *Journal of a Voyage*, 138–39, brackets added.
39. Irving, *Astoria*, 213–14.
40. Clark's journal entry, August 8, 1806, in Moulton, *Journals*, 8:284, brackets added.
41. Rollins, *Discovery*, 134.
42. Irving, *Astoria*, 214–15.
43. Chittenden, *American Fur Trade*, 2:676.
44. Papers of John Jacob Astor, Prairie du Chien Journal, vol. 1B, February 19, 1811–February 20, 1812, Baker Library, Harvard University Graduate School of Business; Irving, *Astoria*, 214–15n11.
45. Holmes, "Five Scalps," 8.
46. See Heidenreich, *Smoke Signals*, 48, for the sites of several Crow villages or camps established before 1855 in both Montana and Wyoming, most of them near a tributary of the Yellowstone River.
47. Holmes, "Five Scalps," 8.
48. Lowie, *Crow Indians*, 87. "Tepee-making was a woman's task. At least over a dozen buffalo pelts had to be tanned and properly weather-cured and sewn together into a large covering. The poles were also cut and cured by women. In the making of a new lodge many women contributed labor, such as tanning hides, and sewing them together," writes Medicine Crow ("Effects of European Culture," 1).
49. Holmes, "Five Scalps," 9, brackets added.
50. Holmes, "Five Scalps," 10.
51. James, *Three Years*, 35, italics and deleted letters in original.

52. Coyner, *Lost Trappers*, 58. See David J. Weber's introduction (v–xxvii) for a discussion of the value of Coyner's original work as a source.
53. Holmes, "Five Scalps," 11.
54. Bradbury, *Travels*, 183.
55. Rollins, *Discovery*, 281.
56. Rollins, *Discovery*, 282–83.
57. Rollins, *Discovery*, 284.
58. Rollins, *Discovery*, 284–85, italics in original.
59. Questions revolving around Hunt's so-called journal complicate the picture. While the authorship and provenance of Reed's financial record are not in question, it's a different story with the Hunt document. The "original" was published in French in Paris in 1821. How it got to Paris and from whom is unknown. Rollins published an English translation in the 1935 edition of *The Discovery of the Oregon Trail*. Not only does the document not include a byline; the first part of the account refers to Hunt in the third person and puts his words in quotation marks. The narrative eventually transitions to the first-person exclusively, not using quotation marks. From that point on, the narrator, who never identifies himself, certainly seems to be Hunt. In addition, the document is rich with names and places and many other details consistent with what is known about the Astorians from other sources. Irving did not question its authenticity—nor have the multitude of historians following him, including Rollins and Todd.
60. Irving, *Astoria*, 227, brackets added.
61. Rollins, *Discovery*, 285, brackets added.
62. Irving, *Astoria*, 276.
63. Rollins, *Discovery*, 292.
64. Irving, *Astoria*, 292.
65. Rollins, *Discovery*, 299.
66. Irving, *Astoria*, 301.
67. Rollins, *Discovery*, 301–2.
68. Irving, *Astoria*, 322–23, brackets added. Irving got most of his information on this part of the Astorians' journey from the writings of three Astor employees who talked to McClellan and the other ten men on their arrival at the fort: Gabriel Franchere, Ross Cox, and Alexander Ross. The same is true for Irving's account of what happened to Crooks and Day after they separated from Hunt. For the possible routes of McClellan, Mackenzie, and Reed, see Josephy, *Nez Perce Indians*, 663.
69. Rollins, *Discovery*, 308.
70. *Missouri Gazette*, May 15, 1813; Ross, *First Settlers*, 192–93. Alexander Ross, who kept a list of "the number of casualties or disasters which befell the Pacific Fur Company during its short existence," offered these statistics:

Lost on the bar	8
Land expedition	5
Tonquin	27

Astoria	3
Lark	8
Snake country	9
Final departure	1
Total	61

Ross, *First Settlers*, 270, italics in original. The ship *Lark* was carrying a number of Astorians when it foundered near the Sandwich Islands in August 1813. Among those killed by Indians in the Snake country in January 1814 were John Reed, Pierre Dorion, and Hoback, Reznor, and Robinson. For more on the amazing story of the Astorians, see Rollins, *Discovery*; Irving, *Astoria*; Ronda, *Astoria and Empire*; and Morris, *Perilous West*.

71. Rollins, *Discovery*, 84, brackets added.
72. Rollins, *Discovery*, 134, brackets and italics in original.
73. Rollins, *Discovery*, 152, 156, 163–64, italics added.
74. *Missouri Gazette* (St. Louis), May 15, 1813, reprinted in Morris, *Perilous West*, 187–93.
75. Lavender, *Fist in the Wilderness*, 177.
76. Ronda, *Astoria and Empire*, 288.
77. *New-York Gazette and General Advertiser*, November 12, 1814.
78. Morgan, *West of William H. Ashley*, xlviii.
79. Report of Thomas Biddle, October 29, 1819, in Morgan, *West of William H. Ashley*, l.
80. Bagley, *South Pass*, 54, brackets added.
81. Camp, *James Clyman*, 22, brackets added. For Fitzpatrick's likely role as coleader of the group, see Hafen, *Broken Hand*, 34–35.
82. "Missouri Trapper," 215–16.
83. "Missouri Trapper," 216.
84. "Missouri Trapper," 216–17.
85. "Missouri Trapper," 217. The earliest documentary evidence for Glass's survival of a grizzly attack comes from an 1824 letter written by Daniel T. Potts, who signed on with Ashley and Henry in 1822. As Henry and his men made their way along the Grand River in the fall of 1823, Potts was at Henry's Fort at the mouth of the Yellowstone—he apparently heard of Glass's experience by the winter of 1823–24. In the letter, Potts wrote, "One man was allso tore nearly to peases by a White Bear and was left by the way without any gun who afterwards recovered" (Daniel T. Potts to "Dear and respected friend," July 7, 1824, Hugh Glass: An Unforgettable Man, https://hughglass.org/wp-content/uploads/2016/05/Potts-Letter-July-7th-1824-2.pdf, original document held at the Yellowstone National Park Museum).
86. Morgan, *Jedediah Smith*, 391n2.
87. Enzler, *Jim Bridger*, 24–30.
88. Camp, *James Clyman*, 25–26.
89. Camp, *James Clyman*, 26.
90. Camp, *James Clyman*, 25–26.
91. Camp, *James Clyman*, 27, brackets added.

92. Ronda, *Lewis and Clark among the Indians*, 50.
93. Wishart, *Great Plains Indians*, 48, 75.
94. Camp, *James Clyman*, 25–27.
95. Wishart, *Great Plains Indians*, 47.
96. Camp, *James Clyman*, 27–28.
97. Camp, *James Clyman*, 28.
98. Hoxie, *Parading through History*, 56.
99. Irving, *Captain Bonneville*, 164–65. Joe Medicine Crow reprints the entire speech as an epigraph in *From the Heart of the Crow Country*, xxi–xxii.
100. Atkinson-Kearny journal, 1824–26, in Jensen and Hutchins, *Wheel Boats on the Missouri*, 91, 90.
101. Camp, *James Clyman*, 29, brackets added.
102. Solitaire, "Major Fitzpatrick: The Discoverer of South Pass," *Weekly Reville* (St. Louis), March 1, 1847, reprinted in Hafen, *Broken Hand*, 338–42, brackets added. "Solitaire" was the pseudonym of Charles S. Robb, who apparently interviewed Fitzpatrick.
103. Montgomery, *Biographical Sketch*, Bancroft Library, CA, MS, cited in Camp, *James Clyman*, 42, brackets added.
104. Camp, *James Clyman*, 29–33, brackets in original.
105. Barbour, *Jedediah Smith*, 54.
106. *St. Louis Enquirer*, June 7, 1824, in Morgan, *West of William H. Ashley*, 76.
107. Clokey, *William H. Ashley*, 132.
108. Solitaire, "Major Fitzpatrick," in Hafen, *Broken Hand*, 341, brackets added. Fitzpatrick's original letter to Ashley has been lost.
109. Ashley was now acting on his own. Henry had returned at the end of August 1824 and had ended his partnership with Ashley (Clokey, *William H. Ashley*, 139).
110. Utley, *Life Wild and Perilous*, 79.
111. Ashley's narrative, cited in Morgan, *West of William H. Ashley*, 269n105.
112. *New Encyclopedia of the American West* (1988), s.v. "Fur Trade, in the United States," 415.

6. "A Young Arapaho Indian"

1. Austin Smith to Jedediah Smith Sr., September 24, 1831, in Morgan, *Jedediah Smith*, 362, brackets added.
2. Austin Smith to Jedediah Smith Sr., in Morgan, *Jedediah Smith*, 362–63, brackets added.
3. Solomon A. Simons to Ralph Smith, October 23, 1831, in Morgan, *Jedediah Smith*, 365–66, brackets in original.
4. Jedediah S. Smith to Ralph Smith, September 10, 1830, in Morgan, *Jedediah Smith*, 355–56.
5. Wishart, *Fur Trade*, 126–27.
6. Wishart, *Fur Trade*, 132.
7. Gowans, *Rocky Mountain Rendezvous*, 56–57.
8. Barbour, *Jedediah Smith*, 248.

9. Jedediah S. Smith, David E. Jackson, and W. L. Sublette to the Honorable John H. Eaton, secretary of war, October 29, 1830, Morgan, *Jedediah Smith*, 346, 48, italics in original.
10. Barbour, *Jedediah Smith*, 251–53; Morgan, *Jedediah Smith*, 325–26.
11. Gregg, *Commerce of the Prairies*, 33, 39, cited in Hafen, *Broken Hand*, 95–96.
12. Oliver Cowdery to our dearly beloved brethren, May 7, 1831, Joseph Smith Letterbook, Church Archives, The Church of Jesus Christ of Latter-day Saints, Salt Lake City, brackets added. Cowdery and Richard Cummins, the local Indian agent, both contacted William Clark about the matter. Cowdery requested permission to teach the Indians "the Christian religion without intruding . . . with any other Mission now established." Cummins called the Mormons strange and said they claimed to have a new revelation from God. Clark is not known to have responded to either Cowdery or Cummins (Buckley, *William Clark*, 221–23).
13. Hafen, *Broken Hand*, 95, background from 93–95.
14. Cited in Kelly, "Hallowed Death Tale of Jedediah Strong Smith," 7.
15. Morgan, *Jedediah Smith*, 329.
16. Kelly, "Hallowed Death Tale of Jedediah Strong Smith," 11. In his well-researched article, Mark Kelly raises several questions surrounding Smith's death, such as the following: Was Smith competent in his management of the mule-drawn freight wagons? Which crossing of the Arkansas River did Smith utilize to access the "water scrape"? How did the otherwise capable leadership of Smith result in the extreme deprivation of water for men and mules prior to reaching the low or Wagon Bed Spring? When and where did Smith make his departure to the south in search of water? Where on the Cimarron River was Smith killed? What role did the Spanish traders play in Smith's death? Did Comanche Indians kill Smith? Most of these questions go unasked by Smith's biographers Dale Morgan and Barton H. Barbour. In regard to possible mismanagement by Smith, Jackson, and Sublette, it should be noted that one week before Smith disappeared, a clerk in the company by the name of Minter was killed—reportedly by Pawnee Indians—while hunting antelope. According to Gregg, more than three hundred traders transported a quarter of a million dollars' worth of merchandise over the Santa Fe Trail in 1831, but only two men—Minter and Smith—perished (Barbour, *Jedediah Smith*, 258).
17. Barbour, *Jedediah Smith*, 249. In accordance with Jedediah Jr.'s 1831 will, lifetime annuities were issued "to his father, brothers and sisters, and dear friends. . . . In 1834, for example, Smith's father and siblings received $4,500 from Jedediah's estate" (272). In 1829, the generous Jedediah Smith, after informing his brother Ralph that Ashley would be sending $2,200 to the family on Jedediah's behalf, wrote, "It is, that I may be able to help those that stand in need, that I face every danger—it is for this, that I traverse the Mountains covered with eternal Snow—it is for this that I pass over the Sandy Plains, in the heat of Summer . . . but I shall count all this pleasure, if I am at last allowed by the Alwise Ruler the privilege of Joining my Friends—Oh My Brother let us render

to him to whoom all things belongs, a proper proportion of what is his due" (Jedediah Smith to Ralph Smith, December 24, 1829, in Morgan, *Jedediah Smith*, 353).

18. Jedediah Smith to Ralph Smith, December 24, 1829, in Morgan, *Jedediah Smith*, 352, brackets added.
19. See Barbour, *Jedediah Smith*, 233–35.
20. Jedediah Smith to Ralph Smith, December 24, 1829, in Morgan, *Jedediah Smith*, 352, brackets in original.
21. *New Encyclopedia of the American West* (1988), s.v. "Smith, Jedediah Strong (1798–1831)," 1058.
22. Hafen, *Broken Hand*, 97.
23. Sage, *Scenes in the Rocky Mountains*, 298, brackets added.
24. Larpenteur, *Personal Narrative*, 12, brackets added.
25. Anderson's diary entry, September 25, 1834, in Anderson, *Rocky Mountain Journals*, 222, brackets in original.
26. Sage, *Scenes in the Rocky Mountains*, 294, 297–98.
27. Hafen, *Broken Hand*, 97–98.
28. Roberts, *Newer World*, 55.
29. Carson, *Autobiography*, 22.
30. Victor, *River of the West*, 99.
31. Victor, *River of the West*, 99.
32. Carson, *Autobiography*, 22.
33. Enzler, *Jim Bridger*, 61.
34. Ferris, *Life in the Rocky Mountains*, 70.
35. Enzler, *Jim Bridger*, 61.
36. Ferris, *Life in the Rocky Mountains*, 50.
37. Hafen, *Broken Hand*, 100–101.
38. Leonard, *Narrative of Zenas Leonard*, 12.
39. Leonard, *Narrative of Zenas Leonard*, 12–13, brackets added.
40. Leonard, *Narrative of Zenas Leonard*, 13.
41. Leonard, *Narrative of Zenas Leonard*, 83–84.
42. Leonard, *Narrative of Zenas Leonard*, 84.
43. Leonard, *Narrative of Zenas Leonard*, 84–85.
44. Leonard, *Narrative of Zenas Leonard*, 104–5, brackets added.
45. Walker, "Joseph R. Walker," 366.
46. Leonard, *Narrative of Zenas Leonard*, 226–28.
47. Leonard, *Narrative of Zenas Leonard*, 228–29.
48. Leonard, *Narrative of Zenas Leonard*, 237–38, 241–43.
49. Leonard, *Narrative of Zenas Leonard*, 248.
50. Chittenden, *American Fur Trade*, 2:675.
51. Chittenden, *American Fur Trade*, 2:678.
52. The letter mentioned, but not reproduced, by Stella M. Drumm (Holmes, "Five Scalps," 4) stated,

> During the last winter a war party belonging to that [Arikara] nation came on the Yellowstone [River] below the Big Horn [River] where they fell in with three men belonging to A. Fur Co. [American Fur Company] who they treacherously killed. Two of these men had been dispatched from Fort Cass (a new Fort mouth of Big Horn) in the morning with the express to go on to Fort Union; (mouth of Yellowstone) The third was a free man, a veteran Trapper who was accompanying the others as far as a camp of White Hunters some short distance below the Fort. They scalped them and left part of the Scalps of each tied to poles on the grounds of the Murder . . . The Names of the men killed are Rose, Menard & Glass (John F. A. Sanford to William Clark, July 26, 1833, Records of the Department of the Interior, Office of Indian Affairs, Letters Received 1824–81, Record Group 75, cited in Landry, "Hugh Glass," 11, underlining in original, brackets added).

Although Sanford did not provide the first names of the men killed, given the familiar and prominent names *Rose* and *Glass*, historians naturally assumed that two of the men were Edward Rose and Hugh Glass, a conclusion no one seemed to question (including the current author, who speculated that the old man whom Leonard met was Beckwourth posing as Rose—see Morris, *Fate of the Corps*, 145–48). The assumption about Glass was correct, but the one about Rose incorrect. Landry found that detailed American Fur Company ledgers prove that "Colin Rose, Hilain Menard, and Hugh Glass were killed by Arikara Indians near Fort Cass within the first six months of 1833" (Landry, "Hugh Glass," 10). The ledgers are thus consistent with Sanford's letter but clarify the first names of the men killed. As to whether Rose ever used a different first name, Landry points out that he was "uniformly listed in the records of the Missouri Fur Company, the Pacific Fur Company (Astorians) and the Henry/Ashley Company as Edward Rose" (Landry, "Hugh Glass," 9).

As for the evidence that Leonard met Edward Rose rather than someone else, consider Leonard's details that "the negro man . . . informed us that he first came to this country with Lewis and Clark . . . and in a few years returned with Mr. Mackinney, a trader on the Missouri river, and has remained here ever since—which is about ten or twelve years." Of course, York did go west with Lewis and Clark, but there is no evidence that he ever returned west. Nor did he have any contact with Crow Indians during the expedition. Beckwourth was much too young to have come west with Lewis and Clark or anyone associated with them before the 1820s. True, Rose was not a member of the expedition, but he did travel up the Missouri in 1807 with several Lewis and Clark veterans, including John Colter and George Drouillard. It was thus true that Rose first went west with Lewis and Clark's men. The mention of "Mackinney" is more problematic. Some have suggested it was a reference to Kenneth Mckenzie, prominent in the American Fur Company, who had dealings with Beckwourth but not until the early 1830s. Rose had no known connection with Kenneth Mckenzie but was definitely involved with Astorian Donald Mckenzie and traveled across South Dakota and into Wyoming with Mckenzie, Hunt, Crooks, and McClellan in 1811. Rose thus had a Mckenzie connection four years after his Lewis and Clark association. Moreover, by the time Rose met Leonard, he had stayed in the West for more than ten or twelve years. The timeline hardly matches Leonard's exact words, but either Leonard or Rose himself may have garbled the details. The general description of the old negro fits Rose much better than either Beckwourth or York—see Betts, *In Search of York*, 135–43.

Lastly, Beckwourth's two mentions of Rose support the claim that Edward Rose and Colin Rose were not the same person. Early in the narrative Beckwourth dictated to Bonner, the former mentioned Rose's service with the Atkinson-O'Fallon Expedition in 1825 and said, without giving a first name, that Rose "was one of the best interpreters ever known in the whole Indian country" (Bonner, *Life and Adventures*, 84)—clearly a reference to Edward. Later, in discussing the three men killed on the Yellowstone River, Beckwourth said Glass's body was found near the fort and added, "I then set the men to work in building boats, to carry our peltry down to Fort Union. . . . I forwarded orders for such goods as were wanted, and also word for another *clerk* in the place of poor Rose, who had lost his life in the service of the company" (Bonner, *Life and Adventures*, 259, italics added)—a reference to Colin. Edward was an interpreter, scout, hunter, trapper, and warrior. A "poor" clerk was the last thing he was.

7. "The Whirlwind Is Coming"

1. Clark's journal entry, August 13, 1804, in Moulton, *Journals*, 2:477.
2. Clark's field notes and journal entry, August 14, 1804, in Moulton, *Journals*, 2:478–79. "By the mid-eighteenth century . . . the contagious nature of smallpox was widely understood," writes Fenn (*Pox Americana*, 29).
3. Vancouver, *Voyage of Discovery*, 2:516–17. Thanks to Elizabeth Fenn for pointing out Vancouver's discussion of smallpox (*Pox Americana*, 9–11). A few days before exploring the Strait of Juan de Fuca, Vancouver was sailing north along Oregon's Cape Flattery—the northwesternmost point of the contiguous United States—when he saw a ship with an American flag making its way southward, the *Columbia Rediviva*. Vancouver sent two of his officers to talk to the captain, Robert Gray, an American merchant seaman involved in the lucrative sea otter trade. About two weeks after meeting with Vancouver's men, Gray experienced the "climax of his career, the discovery of the Columbia River, which he named after his ship. Others [including Vancouver] had suspected the existence of the river, but Gray was the first who dared to take his ship through the forbidding breakers and shoals that stretched across its mouth. By so doing he gave the United States one of its strongest claims to the Oregon country" (*Dictionary of Canadian Biography*, vol. 5, s.v. "Gray, Robert [1755–1806]," by W. Kaye Lamb, accessed August 27, 2023, brackets added http://www.biographi.ca/en/bio/gray_robert_1755_1806_5e.html).
4. Vancouver, *Voyage of Discovery*, 2:528.
5. Fenn, *Pox Americana*, 3.

6. Meriwether Lewis to Lucy Marks, n.d., Lewis Papers, Missouri Historical Society, cited in Ambrose, *Undaunted Courage*, 26.
7. William Clark journal, 1792–94, Missouri Historical Society, cited in Jones, *William Clark*, 74. Inoculation was quite risky—and controversial—because many of those inoculated died from smallpox. "Nowhere was inoculation more restricted and unpopular than in New England. Most New Englnd cities imposed very strict quarantines and banned all smallpox inoculation except when epidemics broke out," writes Fenn. In 1798, four years after Clark was inoculated, the English physician Edward Jenner announced that he had developed a vaccination for smallpox by infecting people with cowpox, a disease related to but much milder than smallpox (Fenn, *Pox Americana*, 39, 33).
8. Levi Lincoln to Thomas Jefferson, April 17, 1803, in Jackson, *Letters*, 1:35. "Jefferson did not need to be reminded of this; he had administered the vaccine himself in 1801" (Jackson, *Letters*, 1:36n1).
9. Thomas Jefferson to Meriwether Lewis, June 20, 1803, in Jackson, *Letters*, 1:60.
10. Lewis to Jefferson, October 3, 1803, in Jackson, *Letters*, 1:130; Pearson, "Medical Diplomacy," 112. "Reports indicate that as early as 1780, Catholic missionaries used live smallpox virus to inoculate nearly seven thousand Native Americans near Valladolid, Guatemala, and that another sixty to seventy thousand were inoculated in southern Mexico," writes Pearson ("Medical Diplomacy," 106). Such efforts offer a sharp contrast to the actions of British official Lord Jeffrey Amherst and others, who, during the siege of Fort Pitt in June and July of 1763, distributed blankets infected with smallpox among the Pontiac Indians as a form of biological warfare (Peter d'Errico, "Jeffrey Amherst and Smallpox Blankets," people.umass.edu/derrico/, accessed May 14, 2025, http://people.umass.edu/derrico/amherst/lord_jeff.html).
11. Van de Logt, "Epidemics in Arikara Oral Tradition," 52, 61.
12. Van de Logt, *Between the Floods*, 57.
13. Greene and Thornton, *Lakota Winter Counts*, 81.
14. Van de Logt, *Between the Floods*, 89. "Horses had reached virtually every tribe on the plains by the second half of the eighteenth century, and the routes of exchange by which horses spread continued to pulse with activity. When smallpox broke out in 1779 it raced across the plains along roughly the same lines by which horses spread across the West," writes Calloway (*One Vast Winter Count*, 419).
15. Dollar, "High Plains Smallpox Epidemic," 17–18.
16. Riley, "Smallpox and American Indians Revisited," 45–46.
17. Van de Logt, *Between the Floods*, 90.
18. Journal of Truteau on the Missouri River, 1794–95, in Nasatir, *Before Lewis and Clark*, 299. As to whether the Native nations had an inherent vulnerability to smallpox, historian James C. Riley answers in the negative: "American Indians are known to have responded to vaccination with vaccina in the same way as Europeans. That makes it unlikely that American Indians harbored any generalized orthopox-virus immune response deficiency, . . . Smallpox's failure until about 1800 to establish an endemic presence in the Americas means that many outbreaks were spaced far enough apart for

mothers and infants alike to have no immune protection. The pattern in America meant episodic catastrophe in place of the heavy year-to-year toll in Europe" ("Smallpox and American Indians Revisited," 467, 477).

19. Greene and Thornton, *Lakota Winter Counts*, 101–3, 106.
20. Van de Logt, *Between the Floods*, 70.
21. Joshua Pilcher to William Clark, February 5, 1838, in Casler, "Larpenteur's Observations of the Smallpox Epidemic," 20, brackets added.
22. Bernard Pratte Jr. to Pierre Chouteau Jr., May 29, 1837, in Casler, "Larpenteur's Observations of the Smallpox Epidemic," 21.
23. Casler notes that some have blamed Pratte for "not stopping the boat to let the disease burn itself out. However, a number of mitigating factors pressed Captain Pratte upriver, among them the rigors of commerce, as well as ignorance of effective ways to deal with smallpox. The steamer was already struggling in the river's low water level. Waiting for the disease to run its course could have stranded the boat for the winter, leaving the trade goods and Indian annuities undelivered. The Indian agents on board would not have tolerated that" ("Larpenteur's Observations of the Smallpox Epidemic," 31–32).
24. Dollar, "High Plains Smallpox Epidemic," 23–24.
25. Jacob Halsey to Mess. Pratte Chouteau & Co., November 2, 1837, in Abel, *Chardon's Journal*, 394–95.
26. Van de Logt, *Between the Floods*, 153, 54.
27. Abel, *Chardon's Journal*, June 28, 1837, 118.
28. Cited in van de Logt, *Between the Floods*, 153.
29. Abel, *Chardon's Journal*, June 18, 1837, 118.
30. Abel, *Chardon's Journal*, July 14, 27, and 29, 1837, 121, 123, 124, respectively.
31. Abel, *Chardon's Journal*, August 5–9, 1837, 126, brackets added.
32. Abel, *Chardon's Journal*, August 10–13, 1837, 126–27, brackets added.
33. Abel, *Chardon's Journal*, August 19, 20, 22, 24, and 31, 129, 130, 131, 131–33, and 133, respectively, brackets added.
34. Abel, *Chardon's Journal*, August 31, 1837, 133.
35. Abel, *Chardon's Journal*, September 7, 22, and 30, 22, 24, and 31, respectively, brackets added.
36. Wood and Thiessen, *Early Fur Trade*, 129, 156–57, 161.
37. Laroque's Yellowstone journal, in Wood and Thiessen, *Early Fur Trade*, 206, brackets added.
38. Fenn, *Pox Americana*, 271.
39. Denig, *Five Indian Tribes*, 169–70, brackets added.
40. Heidenreich, "Crow Indians of Montana," 68, 70.
41. Algier, *Crow and the Eagle*, 123.
42. Crow, *From the Heart of the Crow Country*, 14, 25–29.

8. "Major Fitzpatrick"

1. Wishart, *Fur Trade*, 146–47.
2. Leonard, *Narrative of Zenas Leonard*, 44.
3. Cited in White, *News of the Plains and Rockies*, 3:94.
4. William Walker to "Dear Friend," January 19, 1833, in "The Flathead Indians," *Christian Advocate and Journal and Zion's Herald*, March 1, 1833, reprinted in Furtwangler, *Bringing Indians to the Book*, 194–97.
5. Buckley, *William Clark*, 221. Clark's meeting with the four chiefs took place in either 1830 or 1831. He confirmed that the meeting took place but left no written record of it. As Furtwangler writes, "Did Clark then foster Christianity as well as American settlement beyond the Rockies? The records do not quite provide a straight answer. . . . The missions set off with convictions based on complicated misinformation. The remaining certainty is that Clark was in the middle of it and much cited as its source" (*Bringing Indians to the Book*, 15).
6. Hardee, *Hope Maintains Her Throne*, 2:12–16.
7. White, *News of the Plains and Rockies*, 3:93, 113.
8. Drury, *Marcus and Narcissa Whitman*, 1:122.
9. Cited in White, *News of the Plains and Rockies*, 3:95, brackets added.
10. Cited in Drury, *Marcus and Narcissa Whitman*, 1:119, brackets added.
11. Marcus Whitman to Narcissa Prentiss, June 21, 1835, in Drury, *Marcus and Narcissa Whitman*, 1:123–24.
12. Marcus Whitman to David Greene, May 10, 1839, in Drury, *Marcus and Narcissa Whitman*, 1:124.
13. Parker, *Journal of an Exploring Tour*, 44.
14. Parker, *Journal of an Exploring Tour*, 44. Van de Logt identifies the murdered man as Antoine Garreau (*Between the Floods*, 147).
15. Cited in van de Logt, *Between the Floods*, 145.
16. Van de Logt, *Between the Floods*, 145.
17. Parker, *Journal of an Exploring Tour*, 45, 69.
18. Drury, *Marcus and Narcissa Whitman*, 1:129.
19. Parker, *Journal of an Exploring Tour*, 73.
20. Cited in Gowans, *Rocky Mountain Rendezvous*, 122. Parker wrote that Whitman "extracted an iron arrow, three inches long, from the back of Capt. Bridger. . . . It was a difficult operation in consequence of the arrow being hooked at the point by striking a large bone, and a cartilaginous substance had grown around it. The doctor pursued the operation with great self-possession and perseverance; and Capt. Bridger"—enduring the ordeal without anesthesia—"manifested equal firmness" (*Journal of an Exploring Tour*, 76).
21. Parker, *Journal of an Exploring Tour*, 79.
22. Parker, *Journal of an Exploring Tour*, 79–80. Kit Carson gave a similar account of the duel and added, "During the remainder of our stay in camp we had no more bother with this

French bully" (Carson, *Autobiography*, 44). Carson's biographers believe "Shunar" is an anglicized version of the French name "Chouinard" and that the duel may have been fought over the affections of an Indian girl (see, for example, Roberts, *Newer World*, 70–72).

23. Cited in Drury, *Marcus and Narcissa Whitman*, 1:139.
24. Hafen, *Broken Hand*, 149.
25. Thomas Fitzpatrick to Pierre Chouteau, March 18, 1836, in Hafen, *Broken Hand*, 152.
26. "A Rocky Mountain Adventure," *Jefferson Inquirer*, December 25, 1847, reprinted, with minor changes in punctuation, in Hafen, *Broken Hand*, 151–52, brackets added.
27. Hafen, *Broken Hand*, 152.
28. Drury, *Marcus and Narcissa Whitman*, 1:178–79. Hannibal Dougherty, who served as an agriculturalist to the Oto Indians, died on June 25. "It is with much sorrow and regret that I . . . report the death of Mr. Hannibal Dougherty," John Dougherty wrote to William Clark. "He was highly esteemed by [the Indians] and was conducting their domestic affairs to great advantage for them" (John Dougherty to William Clark, July 5, 1836, in Kelly, *Lost Voices*, 523, brackets added).
29. Drury, *Marcus and Narcissa Whitman*, 1:179.
30. Narcissa Whitman to Augustus Whitman, June 27, 1836, in Drury, *Marcus and Narcissa Whitman*, 1:180.
31. Marcus Whitman to Stephen and Clarissa Prentiss, June 4, 1836, in Drury, *Marcus and Narcissa Whitman*, 1:180.
32. White, *News of the Plains and Rockies*, 3:119.
33. Cited in Drury, *Marcus and Narcissa Whitman*, 1:155–56. Referring to Henry Spalding in an 1840 letter to her father, Narcissa wrote, "*The man who came with us is one who never ought to have come.* My dear husband has suffered more from him in consequence of his wicked jealousy, and his great pique towards me, than can be known in this world" (Narcissa Whitman to Stephen Prentiss, October 10, 1840, in Drury, *Marcus and Narcissa Whitman*, 1:376–77, italics in original).
34. Cited in Drury, *Marcus and Narcissa Whitman*, 1:183, brackets in original.
35. Drury, *Marcus and Narcissa Whitman*, 1:186, 244; White, *News of the Plains and Rockies*, 3:120.
36. Cited in White, *News of the Plains and Rockies*, 3:120, brackets in original.
37. Cited in Drury, *Marcus and Narcissa Whitman*, 1:187.
38. Marie Dorion and her husband Pierre Jr. were already traveling with Hunt when Rose joined the party on the Missouri in 1811 and went with them into Wyoming's Bighorn Mountains. In 1812, Rose and Charbonneau (later known to have worked together) and Sacagawea were all with Lisa at Fort Manuel, where Sacagawea died on December 20, 1812. For more on Marie Dorion, see Irving, *Astoria*; and Morris, *Perilous West*. For more on Sacagawea, see the entire issue of *We Proceeded On* 49, no. 3 (August 2023), especially the article by Maren C. Burgess and Jay H. Buckley "Seeking Sacagawea: A Comparison of the Principal Accounts of the Birth, Life, and Death of Bird Woman" (4–30), which offers an incredibly thorough and balanced discussion of the multitude of controversies surrounding Sacagawea.

39. Marcus Whitman to David Greene, July 16, 1836, in Drury, *Marcus and Narcissa Whitman*, 1:196.
40. Cited in Hafen, *Broken Hand*, 159, brackets added.
41. Russell, *Journal of a Trapper*, 60.
42. Cited in Anderson, *Rocky Mountain Journals*, 316, brackets added. See Hafen, *Broken Hand*, 187–88, for Rufus B. Sage's version of how Friday was reunited with his family.
43. Cited in Gowans, *Rocky Mountain Rendezvous*, 194.
44. Cited in Gowans, *Rocky Mountain Rendezvous*, 198.
45. Cited in Hafen, *Broken Hand*, 175.
46. Hafen, *Broken Hand*, 177.
47. Cited in White, *News of the Plains and Rockies*, 3:376, brackets added.
48. Cited in Hafen, *Broken Hand*, 186.
49. Egan, *Frémont*, 125–26.
50. Carter, *Historical Christopher Carson*, 117–18.
51. Frémont's fourth expedition, a private venture undertaken without the help of Fitzpatrick or Carson, was a failure, to put it mildly. As Hafen writes, when Frémont and Fitzpatrick saw each other at Fort Bent in November of 1848, "little did [Frémont] divine that before two months had passed all of his 120 pack animals and a third of his gallant company would lie dead beneath the powdery, shifting snows of the Colorado Rockies" (*Broken Hand*, 267, brackets added).
52. Cited in Anderson, *Rocky Mountain Journals*, 316, brackets added.
53. Hafen, *Broken Hand*, 212.
54. Morris, "Taking of California," 95–96.
55. Cited in Hafen, *Broken Hand*, 217.
56. W. H. Emory, *Notes*, cited in Morris, "Taking of California," 107.
57. Kearny soon regretted leaving two hundred dragoons behind. On November 23, as his company approached the mouth of Rio Gila, they learned "that the Mexicans about the Pueblo de Los Angeles, had revolted and were in possession of that part of the country" (Henry Smith Turner's diary entry, in Morris, "Taking of California," 108). On December 6, at the Battle of San Pasqual, Kearny led his hundred dragoons and forty of Stockton's marines in a poorly executed attack on a similar number of Californio lancers. Bested initially, the Americans eventually gained the upper hand, and the Californios retreated. Kearny's "victory" was hollow because he lost twenty-three men, more than the enemy. By mid-January 1847, however, the combined forces of Kearny and Stockton won crucial battles, and the war in California ended. The junior army officer Frémont continually defied General Kearny and in November of 1847 was charged in a court-martial with mutiny, disobedience of the lawful command of his superior officer, and conduct to the prejudice of good order and military discipline. He was found guilty on all three charges, declined the offer of a pardon from President Polk, and was dismissed from the army. As Ferol Egan writes, Frémont's "glory years were all behind" (*Frémont*, 463). He died in 1890 at age seventy-seven. Ten months after Frémont's court-martial, in October 1848, Kearny died of yellow fever at age fifty-four.

58. Tate, *Unsettled Ground*, xi.
59. Tate, *Unsettled Ground*, 162.
60. Harden, *Murder at the Mission*, 80; Tate, *Unsettled Ground*, 163.
61. Narcissa Whitman to Clarissa Prentiss, August 23, 1847, in Harden, *Murder at the Mission*, 81.
62. Harden, *Murder at the Mission*, 80–81.
63. Boyd argues convincingly that "Indians themselves probably brought measles to the Pacific Northwest [from California], and were likely the main agents of its spread through the Columbia Plateau. The immigrant trains, however, carried the disease down the Columbia to Vancouver, and whites were apparently the main agents of its diffusion up the Pacific coast" ("Pacific Northwest Measles," 7).
64. Boyd, "Pacific Northwest Measles," 13–17; Harden, *Murder at the Mission*, 83.
65. Cited in Boyd, "Pacific Northwest Measles," 17. Boyd adds, "A major . . . factor in accounting for different mortality rates appears to have been variations in treatment of the disease. In areas where Indians persisted in exposing themselves to cold water (either through drinking or bathing), or where (as in the Columbia River drainage) Natives treated the disease by placing infected individuals in sweat lodges, mortality appears to have been higher" ("Pacific Northwest Measles," 41).
66. Marcus Whitman to Alanson Hinman, November 8, 1847, in Tate, *Unsettled Ground*, 12.
67. Dary, *Oregon Trail*, 179; Tate, *Unsettled Ground*, 164–65.
68. Dary, *Oregon Trail*, 179; Tate, *Unsettled Ground*, 166.
69. Drury, *Marcus and Narcissa Whitman*, 2:217, brackets added.
70. Cited in Drury, *Marcus and Narcissa Whitman*, 2:223.
71. Undated letter written by Mary Marsh Carson, in Dary, *Oregon Trail*, 181.
72. The Whitmans had essentially adopted the daughters of famed mountain men Joe Meek and Jim Bridger, each of whom asked them to raise and educate their girls. In 1840 Meek brought his daughter, two-year-old Helen Mar Meek, whose mother was a Nez Perce woman. A year later Bridger left his daughter, six-year-old Mary Ann Bridger, whose mother, Cora, a Salish Indian, was Bridger's first wife. The girls soon became surrogate daughters to Narcissa, who called them "my two little half-breed girls," kept them away from other Indian children at the mission, and did not allow them to learn or speak the Nez Perce language. At the time of the massacre, Helen, nine, and Mary Ann, twelve, were both among those taken hostage. "Hudson's Bay Company's Peter Skene Ogden finally bartered the release of the captives, buying their freedom by giving the Cayuse Indians fifty blankets, fifty shirts, ten guns, ten fathoms of tobacco, ten handkerchiefs, one hundred lead balls, and gun powder," writes Enzler. Both girls died, apparently from disease and exposure, either during their confinement or shortly thereafter (Enzler, *Jim Bridger*, 154–58; Tate, *Unsettled Ground*, 127, 155).
73. Dary, *Oregon Trail*, 180–81.
74. Tate, *Unsettled Ground*, xx.

75. West, "Golden Dreams," 4. The huge area ceded by Mexico included all of New Mexico, Nevada, Utah, and California, most of Colorado and Arizona, and parts of Wyoming, Oklahoma, and Kansas. Adding another crucial event to the mix, on August 14, 1848, the U.S. Congress approved the formation of the Oregon Territory, which included all of Oregon, Washington, and Idaho, as well as sections of Wyoming and Montana.
76. Cited in Bagley, *So Rugged and Mountainous*, 373.
77. Cited in Ward, *West*, 120–21.
78. West, "Golden Dreams," 4–5; Hafen and Young, *Fort Laramie*, 145.
79. Correspondence from "Pawnee," in *Missouri Republican*, June 14, 1849, cited in Hafen and Young, *Fort Laramie*, 146.
80. Correspondence from "Pawnee," in *Missouri Republican*, July 6, 1849, cited in Hafen and Young, *Fort Laramie*, 18.
81. Cited in Bagley, *With Golden Visions*, 70.
82. Ward, *West*, 125, 153.
83. White, *News of the Plains and Rockies*, 6:20.
84. White, *News of the Plains and Rockies* 6:23–24.
85. White, *News of the Plains and Rockies* 6:24–25.
86. White, *News of the Plains and Rockies* 6:26.
87. Fowler, "Arapaho and Cheyenne Perspectives," 364.
88. Annual report of the commissioner of Indian Affairs for 1850, cited in Hafen and Young, *Fort Laramie*, 178, brackets added.
89. Fowler, "Arapaho and Cheyenne Perspectives," 365, 66.
90. Fowler, "Arapaho and Cheyenne Perspectives," 366.
91. Annual report of the commissioner of Indian Affairs for 1853, cited in Fowler, "Arapaho and Cheyenne Perspectives," 368.
92. Hafen, *Broken Hand*, 319, 274.
93. White, *News of the Plains and Rockies*, 3:376, 78.
94. White, *News of the Plains and Rockies*, 3:395–96.
95. Larpenteur, *Personal Narrative*, 422.
96. Cited in Hafen, *Broken Hand*, 321.
97. Cited in White, *News of the Plains and Rockies*, 3:379.
98. West, *Contested Plains*, xv.
99. *Missouri Republican*, March 27, 1859, cited in West, "Golden Dreams," 8.
100. West, "Golden Dreams," 10–11.
101. Cited in Fowler, "Arapaho and Cheyenne Perspectives," 372.
102. Fowler, "Arapaho and Cheyenne Perspectives," 385–86.
103. Cited in White, *News of the Plains and Rockies*, 7:221.
104. Fowler, "Arapaho and Cheyenne Perspectives," 373.
105. Cutler, *Massacre at Sand Creek*, vii–ix.
106. Silas Soule to Walter Whitman, February 12, 1865, in Cutler, *Massacre at Sand Creek*, 114–15. On April 23, 1865, two months after he testified against Chivington, Soule was

killed in a gunfight, possibly ambushed by Chivington supporters. For more information, see Kelman, *Misplaced Massacre*, 175–76.

107. Aron, *Peace and Friendship*, 205. Aron introduces his discussion of recent historical scholarship thus: "The 1987 publication of Patricia Nelson Limerick's *The Legacy of Conquest: The Unbroken Past of the American West* heralded the dawning of the 'New Western History.' . . . In this book and other writings, Limerick dismissed the construct of 'frontier' as outmoded and ethnocentric and did away with the divide that cleaved the West after the supposed closing of the frontier from its earlier history. In place of longtime shibboleths, she argued for a history in which conquest and its legacy were the defining experiences of the region across its colonialist past and present" (*Peace and Friendship*, 205).

108. Fowler, *Arapaho*, 52.

109. Cited in Kelman, *Misplaced Massacre*, 14.

110. Kelman, *Misplaced Massacre*, 14–15.

111. Aron, *Peace and Friendship*, 4, 14.

112. Aron, *Peace and Friendship*, 27, 36. In October 1778 a military tribunal charged Boone with conspiring with the Shawnees and found him innocent. Two of his fellow prisoners—Richard Calloway and Benjamin Logan—were never convinced he did not betray them. Blackfish died in the spring of 1779 from gunshot wounds suffered when three hundred militiamen under the command of John Bowman attacked his village (*Peace and Friendship*, 30–31, 36).

113. Aron, *Peace and Friendship*, 98, 207, 75, 109. Aron properly calls the death of the two Blackfeet "the exception and not the rule of encounters between Indians and explorers" (*Peace and Friendship*, 109). Ironically, it was partly because of the goodwill experienced by Lewis and his companions and the young Blackfeet that Lewis lapsed into shortsightedness and failed to post a guard.

114. Anderson, *Rocky Mountain Journals*, 315–16, brackets added.

115. Cited in Anderson, *Rocky Mountain Journals*, 317.

116. Fowler, *Arapahoe Politics*, 41.

117. Cited in Fowler, *Arapahoe Politics*, 41.

118. Fowler, *Arapahoe Politics*, 42.

119. Fowler, *Arapahoe Politics*, 45.

120. Nichols, *Massacring Indians*, 87.

121. Fowler, *Arapahoe Politics*, 47–49, 55, 63–64, 70–71.

122. Aron, *Peace and Friendship*, 210.

BIBLIOGRAPHY

Abel, Annie Heloise, ed. *Chardon's Journal at Fort Clark, 1834–1839: Descriptive of Life on the Upper Missouri; of a Fur Trader's Experiences among the Mandans, Gros Ventres, and Their Neighbors; of the Ravages of the Smallpox Epidemic of 1837*. Lincoln: University of Nebraska Press, 1997.

———. *Tabeau's Narrative of Loisel's Expedition to the Upper Missouri*. Norman: University of Oklahoma Press, 1939.

Abridgement of the Debates of Congress, from 1789 to 1856. Vol. 3. New York: D. Appleton, 1858.

Algier, Keith. *The Crow and the Eagle: A Tribal History from Lewis and Clark to Custer*. Caldwell ID: Caxton Printers, 1993.

Allen, Gay. "Walt Whitman: Passage to India." *Indian Literature* 2, no. 2 (April–September 1959): 38–44. https://www.jstor.org/stable/23329322.

Allen, John L. "Another Way of Reading the Land." *We Proceeded On* 44, no. 2 (May 2018): 32–33.

———. "The Forgotten Explorers." In Hardee, *Selected Papers*, 26–39.

———. *Lewis and Clark and the Image of the American Northwest*. New York: Dover, 1991. First published as *Passage through the Garden: Lewis and Clark and the Image of the American Northwest*. Urbana: University of Illinois Press, 1975.

———. "'So Fine a Country': The Early Exploration of Louisiana Territory, 1540–1802." *We Proceeded On* 49, no. 4 (November 2023): 4–39.

Ambrose, Stephen E. *Undaunted Courage: Meriwether Lewis, Thomas Jefferson, and the Opening of the American West*. New York: Simon and Schuster, 1996.

Anderson, William M. *The Rocky Mountain Journals of William Marshall Anderson: The West in 1834*. Edited by Dale L. Morgan and Eleanor Towles Harris. Lincoln: University of Nebraska Press, 1987.

Anglin, Ronald M., and Larry E. Morris. *The Mystery of John Colter: The Man Who Discovered Yellowstone*. Lanham MD: Rowman & Littlefield, 2016. First published as *Gloomy Terrors and Hidden Fires: The Mystery of John Colter and Yellowstone*. Lanham MD: Rowman & Littlefield, 2014.

Aron, Stephen. *Peace and Friendship: An Alternative History of the American West*. New York: Oxford University Press, 2022.

Bagley, Will. *So Rugged and Mountainous: Blazing the Trails to Oregon and California, 1812–1848*. Norman: University of Oklahoma Press, 2010.

———. *South Pass: Gateway to a Continent*. Norman: University of Oklahoma Press, 2014.

———. *With Golden Visions Bright before Them: Trails to the Mining West, 1849–1852*. Norman: University of Oklahoma Press, 2012.

Barbour, Barton H. *Jedediah Smith: No Ordinary Mountain Man*. Norman: University of Oklahoma Press, 2009.

Baritz, Loren. "The Idea of the West." *American Historical Review* 66, no. 3 (April 1961): 618–40. https://www.jstor.org/stable/1846967.

Benton, Thomas Hart. *Thirty Years' View; or, A History of the Working of the American Government for Thirty Years, from 1820 to 1850*. New York: Appleton, 1858.

Bergreen, Laurence. *Over the Edge of the World: Magellan's Terrifying Circumnavigation of the Globe*. New York: HarperCollins, 2019.

Berry, Don. *A Majority of Scoundrels: The Western Frontier, 1822–1834*. New York: Ballantine, 1971.

Betts, Robert B. *In Search of York: The Slave Who Went West to the Pacific with Lewis and Clark*. Denver: University Press of Colorado, 2000.

Black, Jeremy. *Slavery: A New Global History*. Philadelphia: Robinson, 2011.

Blenkinsop, Willis. "Edward Rose." In Hafen, *Mountain Men*, 9:335–45.

Bongard-Levin, Gregory. "India as Seen from Ancient Europe." *World Affairs: The Journal of International Issues* 8, no. 1 (January–March 2004): 1118–26. https://www.jstor.org/stable/10.2307/48504975.

Bonner, Thomas D. *The Life and Adventures of James P. Beckwourth*. New York: Harper & Brothers, 1856.

Boorstin, Daniel J. *The Americans: The National Experience*. New York: Vintage Books, 1965.

Bosworth, A. B. "The Historical Setting of Megasthenes' Indica." *Classical Philology* 91, no. 2 (April 1996): 113–27. https://www.jstor.org/stable/270500.

Boyd, Robert. "The Pacific Northwest Measles Epidemic of 1847–1848." *Oregon Historical Quarterly* 95, no. 1 (Spring 1994): 6–47. https://www.jstor.org/stable/20614558.

Brackenridge, Henry Marie. *Journal of a Voyage up the River Missouri; Performed in Eighteen Hundred and Eleven*. Baltimore: Coale and Maxwell, 1816.

———. *Views of Louisiana, Together with a Journal of a Voyage up the Missouri River, in 1811*. Pittsburgh: Cramer, Spear, and Schaeffer and Eichbaum, 1814.

Bradbury, John. *Travels in the Interior Parts of America, in the Years 1809, 1810, and 1811*. Liverpool: Smith and Galway, 1817.

Branigan, Ciaran. "The Circumnavigation of Africa." *Classics Ireland* 1 (1994): 42–46. https://www.jstor.org/stable/25528263.

Buckley, Jay H. *William Clark: Indian Diplomat*. Norman: University of Oklahoma Press, 2008.

Buckley, Thomas C., ed. *Rendezvous: Selected Papers of the Fourth North American Fur Trade Conference, 1981*. St. Paul MN: North American Fur Trade Conference, 1984.

Calloway, Colin G. *One Vast Winter Count: The Native American West before Lewis and Clark*. Lincoln: University of Nebraska Press, 2003.

Camp, Charles L. "George C. Yount." In Hafen, *Mountain Men,* 9:411–20.

———. "James Clyman." In Hafen, *Mountain Men,* 1:233–52.

———, ed. *James Clyman: American Frontiersman, 1792–1881*. San Francisco: California Historical Society, 1928.

Carman, Christián Carlos, and James Evans. "The Two Earths of Eratosthenes." *History of Science Society* 106, no. 1 (March 2015): 1–16. https://www.jstor.org/stable/10.1086.681034.

Carson, Christopher. *Kit's Carson's Autobiography*. Lincoln: University of Nebraska Press, 1966.

Carter, Clarence, comp. and ed. *The Territorial Papers of the United States*. 25 vols. Washington DC: Government Printing Office, 1943–60.

Carter, Harvey Lewis. "Caleb Greenwood." In Hafen, *Mountain Men,* 9:187–92.

———. *"Dear Old Kit": The Historical Christopher Carson*. Norman: University of Oklahoma Press, 1968.

———. "John Hoback, Jacob Reznor, and Edward Robinson." In Hafen, *Mountain Men,* 9:211–14.

———. "Ramsay Crooks." In Hafen, *Mountain Men,* 9:125–31.

Casler, Michael M. "'This Outrageous Disease': Charles Larpenteur's Observations of the 1837 Smallpox Epidemic." *Rocky Mountain Fur Trade Journal* 10 (2016): 18–36.

Chittenden, Hiram M. *The American Fur Trade of the Far West*. 2 vols. Lincoln: University of Nebraska Press, 1986.

Christian, Shirley. *Before Lewis and Clark: The Story of the Chouteaus, the French Dynasty That Ruled America's Frontier*. New York: Farrar, Straus and Giroux, 2004.

Chuinard, E. G. *Only One Man Died: The Medical Aspects of the Lewis and Clark Expedition*. Fairfield WA: Ye Galleon, 1999.

Clarke, Charles G. *The Men of the Lewis and Clark Expedition*. Lincoln: University of Nebraska Press, 2002.

Clarke, Dwight L., ed. *The Original Journals of Henry Smith Turner: With Stephen Watts Kearny to New Mexico and California, 1846–1847*. Norman: University of Oklahoma Press, 1966.

———. *Stephen Watts Kearny: Soldier of the West*. Norman: University of Oklahoma Press, 1961.

Cliff, Nigel. *The Last Crusade: The Epic Voyages of Vasco da Gama*. New York: HarperCollins, 2011.

Clokey, Richard M. *William H. Ashley: Enterprise and Politics in the Trans-Mississippi West*. Norman: University of Oklahoma Press, 1980.

Coleman, Jon T. *Here Lies Hugh Glass: A Mountain Man, a Bear, and the Rise of the American Nation (an American Portrait)*. New York: Hill and Wang, 2013.

Confer, Clarissa. "The Beginning and the End: Lewis and Clark among the Upper Missouri River People." *Wicazo Sa Review* 19, no. 1 (Spring 2004): 11–19.

Connors, Catherine. "Eratosthenes, Strabo, and the Geographer's Gaze." *Pacific Coast Philology* 46, no. 2 (2011): 139–52. https://www.jstor.org/stable/41851022.

Cortada, James W. "Myths, Facts, and Debates: Christopher Columbus and the New World before 1492." *Renaissance and Reformation* 12, no. 2 (1976): 89–95. https://www.jstor.org/stable/43464992.

Coues, Elliott, ed. *The History of the Lewis and Clark Expedition*. 3 vols. New York: Dover, 1964.

Cutler, Bruce. *The Massacre at Sand Creek: Narrative Voices*. Norman: University of Oklahoma Press, 1995.

Darby, John F. *Personal Recollections*. St. Louis: C. I. Jones, 1880.

Dary, David. *The Oregon Trail: An American Saga*. New York: Oxford University Press, 2004.

Debates and Proceedings in the Congress of the United States: Thirteenth Congress—First and Second Sessions. Washington: Gales and Seaton, 1854.

De Cesar, Wayne T., and Susan Page. "Jefferson Buys Louisiana Territory, and the Nation Moves Westward." *Prologue Magazine* 35, no. 1 (Spring 2003). https://www.archives.gov/publications/prologue/2003/spring/louisiana-purchase.html.

Delaney, Carol. "Columbus's Ultimate Goal: Jerusalem." *Comparative Studies in Society and History* 48 no. 2 (April 2006): 260–92.

Denig, Edwin Thompson. *Five Indian Tribes of the Upper Missouri: Sioux, Arickaras, Assiniboines, Crees, Crows*. Norman: University of Oklahoma Press, 1961.

DeVoto, Bernard. *The Course of Empire*. Boston: Houghton Mifflin, 1980.

Diary of William Dunlap (1766–1839): The Memoirs of a Dramatist, Theatrical Manager, Painter, Critic, Novelist, and Historian. 3 vols. New York: New York Historical Society, 1930.

Dickson, Frank H. "Joseph Dickson." In Hafen, *Mountain Men*, 3:71–79.

Dillon, Richard. *Meriwether Lewis: A Biography*. Santa Cruz CA: Western Tanager, 1988.

Dolin, Eric Jay. *Fur, Fortune, and Empire: The Epic History of the Fur Trade in America*. New York: W. W. Norton, 2010.

Dollar, Clyde D. "The High Plains Smallpox Epidemic of 1837–38." *Western Historical Quarterly* 8, no. 1 (January 1977): 15–38. https://www.jstor.org/stable/967216.

Douglas, Walter B. *Manuel Lisa*. Edited by Abraham P. Nasatir. New York: Argosy-Antiquarian, 1964.

Drury, Clifford M. *Marcus and Narcissa Whitman and the Opening of Old Oregon*. 2 vols. Seattle: Northwest Interpretive Association, 1986, 1994.

Egan, Ferol. *Frémont: Explorer for a Restless Nation*. Reno: University of Nevada Press, 1977.

Emory, W. H. *Notes of a Military Reconnoissance*. Albuquerque: University of New Mexico Press, 1951.

Engels, Donald. "The Length of Eratosthenes' Stade." *American Journal of Philology* 106, no. 3 (Autumn 1985): 298–311. https://www.jstor.org/stable/295030.

Enzler, Jerry. *Jim Bridger: Trailblazer of the American West*. Norman: University of Oklahoma Press, 2021.

Felton, Harold W. *Edward Rose: Negro Trail Blazer*. New York: Dodd, Mead, 1967.

Fenn, Elizabeth A. *Pox Americana: The Great Smallpox Epidemic of 1775–82*. New York: Hill and Wang, 2001.

Ferris, Warren Angus. *Life in the Rocky Mountains: A Diary of Wanderings on the Sources of the Rivers Missouri, Columbia, and Colorado, 1830–1835*. Las Vegas: Pantianos Classics, 2021.

Fleek, Sherman L. *History May Be Searched in Vain: A Military History of the Mormon Battalion*. Spokane WA: Arthur H. Clark, 2006.

———. "The Kearny/Stockton/Frémont Feud: The Mormon Battalion's Most Significant Contribution in California." *Journal of Mormon History* 37, no. 2 (Summer 2011): 229–57.

Foley, William E. *Wilderness Journey: The Life of William Clark*. Columbia: University of Missouri Press, 2004.

Foley, William E., and Charles David Rice. "The Return of the Mandan Chief." *Montana: The Magazine of Western History* 29, no. 3 (Summer 1979): 2–15.

Fowler, Loretta. *The Arapaho*. New York: Chelsea House, 1989.

———. "Arapaho and Cheyenne Perspectives: From the 1851 Treaty to the Sand Creek Massacre." *American Indian Quarterly* 39, no. 4 (Fall 2015): 364–90.

———. *Arapahoe Politics, 1851–1978: Symbols in Crises of Authority*. Lincoln: University of Nebraska Press, 1982.

———. *The Columbia Guide to American Indians of the Great Plains*. New York: Columbia University Press, 2003.

———. *Shared Symbols, Contested Meanings: Gros Ventre Culture and History, 1778–1984*. Ithaca NY: Cornell University Press, 1987.

Furtwangler, Albert. *Acts of Discovery: Visions of America in the Lewis and Clark Journals*. Urbana: University of Illinois Press, 1993.

———. *Bringing Indians to the Book*. Seattle: University of Washington Press, 2005.

Gil, Moshe. "The Radhanite Merchants and the Land of Radhan." *Journal of the Economic and Social History of the Orient* 17, no. 3 (September 1974): 299–328. https://www.jstor.org/stable/3632174.

Gowans, Fred R. *Rocky Mountain Rendezvous: A History of the Fur Trade Rendezvous 1825–1840*. Layton UT: Gibbs Smith, 2005.

Greene, Candace S., and Russell Thornton, eds. *The Year the Stars Fell: Lakota Winter Counts at the Smithsonian*. Washington DC: Smithsonian Institution; Lincoln: University of Nebraska Press, 2007.

Gregg, Josiah. *Commerce of the Prairies*. Norman: University of Oklahoma Press, 1954.

Grinnell, George Bird. *The Cheyenne Indians: Their History and Lifeways*. Bloomington IN: World Wisdom, 2008.

Gudde, Erwin G. *Bigler's Chronicle of the West*. Berkeley: University of California Press, 1962.

Hafen, Ann W. "Jean Baptiste Charbonneau." In Hafen, *Mountain Men*, 1:205–24.

Hafen, LeRoy R. *Broken Hand: The Life of Thomas Fitzpatrick: Mountain Man, Guide and Indian Agent*. Lincoln: University of Nebraska Press, 1981.

———, ed. *The Mountain Men and the Fur Trade of the Far West*. 10 vols. Glendale CA: Arthur H. Clark, 1965–72.

———. "Toussaint Charbonneau." In Hafen, *Mountain Men*, 9:53–62.

Hafen, LeRoy R., and Francis Marion Young. *Fort Laramie and the Pageant of the West, 1834–1890*. Lincoln: University of Nebraska Press, 1984.

Hämäläinen, Pekka. "The Rise and Fall of Plains Indian Horse Cultures." *Journal of American History* 90, no. 3 (December 2003): 833–62. https://www.jstor.org/stable/3660878.

Hanson, Charles E., Jr. *The Northwest Gun*. Lincoln: Nebraska State Historical Society, 1955.

Hardee, Jim. *Hope Maintains Her Throne: The Western Expeditions of Nathaniel J. Wyeth*. Vol. 2, *1834–1836*. Pinedale WY: Sublette County Historical Society, 2018.

———. *Pierre's Hole! The Fur Trade History of Teton Valley, Idaho*. Pinedale WY: Sublette County Historical Society, 2010.

———, ed. *Selected Papers of the 2010 Fur Trade Symposium at the Three Forks*. Three Forks MT: Three Forks Historical Society, 2011.

Harden, Blaine. *Murder at the Mission: A Frontier Killing, Its Legacy and Lies, and the Taking of the American West*. New York: Penguin, 2022.

Hasselstrom, Linda M. *Journal of a Mountain Man: James Clyman*. Boise ID: Tamarack, 1998.

Hassrick, Royal B. *The Sioux*. Norman: University of Oklahoma Press, 1989.

Hatcher, Scott. "The Birth of the Monsoon Winds: On the Existence and Understanding of Hippalus, and the 'Discovery' of the Apogeous Trade Winds." *Terrae Incognitae* 45, no. 1 (April 2013): 19–29.

Hayes, Derek. *First Crossing: Alexander Mackenzie, His Expedition across North America, and the Opening of the Continent*. Seattle: Sasquatch Books, 2001.

Hays, Carl D. W. "David E. Jackson." In Hafen, *Mountain Men*, 9:215–44.

Hebard, Grace Raymond. "The First White Woman in Wyoming." *Washington Historical Quarterly* 8, no. 1 (January 1917): 29–31.

Heidenreich, Charles Adrian. "Ethno-Documentary of the Crow Indians of Montana, 1824–1862." PhD diss., University of Oregon, 1971. https://media.proquest.com/cdn/media/hms/ORIG/2/ytohH?_tm=1690817076183&_cfs=FyPylirvgcWkphn0zhFt%2Bw4qFNsm66M0brBmfiGNY4Q%3D.

———. "The Native Americans' Yellowstone." *Montana: The Magazine of Western History* 35, no. 4 (Autumn 1985): 2–17.

———. *Smoke Signals in Crow (Apsáalooke) Country: Beyond the Capture of Horses from the Lewis and Clark Expedition*. Billings MT: Self-published, 2006.

Holmberg, James J., ed. *Dear Brother: Letters of William Clark to Jonathan Clark*. New Haven CT: Yale University Press, 2002.

Holmes, Reuben. "The Five Scalps." *Missouri Historical Society Glimpses of the Past* 5 (January–March 1938): 1–54.

Hourani, George F. *Arab Seafaring in the Indian Ocean in Ancient and Early Medieval Times*. Revised and expanded by John Carswell. Princeton: Princeton University Press, 1995.

Hoxie, Frederick E. *Parading through History: The Making of the Crow Nation in America*. Cambridge: Cambridge University Press, 1995.

Huntingford, G. W. B., trans. and ed. *The Periplus of the Erythraean Sea, by an Unknown Author: With Some Extracts from Agatharkhides "On the Erythraean Sea."* New York: Routledge, 2016.

Huser, Verne. *On the River with Lewis and Clark*. College Station: Texas A&M University Press, 2004.

Hyde, Anne F. *Empires, Nations, and Families: A New History of the North American West, 1800–1860*. Lincoln: University of Nebraska Press, 2011.

Ijoma, J. O. "Portuguese Activities in West Africa before 1600: The Consequences." *Transafrican Journal of History* 11 (1982): 136–46. https://jstor.org/stable/24328537.

Irving, Washington. *The Adventures of Captain Bonneville, U.S.A., in the Rocky Mountains and the Far West*. Edited by Edgeley W. Todd. Norman: University of Oklahoma Press, 1961.

———. *Astoria*. 1836. Edited by Edgeley W. Todd. Norman: University of Oklahoma Press, 1964.

Isenberg, Andrew C. "An Empire of Remedy: Vaccination, Natives, and Narratives in the North American West." *Pacific Historical Review* 86, no. 1 (February 2017): 84–113. https://www.jstor.org/stable/10.2307/26419728.

Isenberg, Andrew C., and Thomas Richards Jr. "Alternative Wests: Rethinking Manifest Destiny." *Pacific Historical Review* 86, no. 1 (February 2017): 4–17. https://www.jstor.org/stable/10.2307/26419725.

Jablow, Joseph. *The Cheyenne in Plains Indian Trade Relations, 1795–1840*. Lincoln: University of Nebraska Press, 1994.

Jackson, Donald. "Journey to the Mandans, 1809; the Lost Narrative of Dr. Thomas." *Bulletin of the Missouri Historical Society* 20 (April 1964): 179–92.

———. *Letters of the Lewis and Clark Expedition, with Related Documents, 1783–1854*. 2 vols. Urbana: University of Illinois Press, 1978.

———. Review of *Passage through the Garden: Lewis and Clark and the Image of the American Northwest*, by John L. Allen. *Western Historical Quarterly* 7, no. 3 (July 1976): 309–10. https://www.jstor.org/stable/967086.

———. *Thomas Jefferson and the Stony Mountains: Exploring the West from Monticello*. Norman: University of Oklahoma Press, 1993.

James, Thomas. *Three Years among the Indians and Mexicans*. Philadelphia: J. B. Lippincott, 1962.

"Jedediah Strong Smith." *Illinois Monthly Magazine*, no. 21 (June 1832): 393–98.

Jenkinson, Clay S. *Becoming Jefferson's People: Re-inventing the American Republic in the Twenty-First Century*. Reno NV: Marmarth, 2004.

———. *The Character of Meriwether Lewis: "Completely Metamorphosed" in the American West*. Reno NV: Marmarth, 2000.

———. *The Character of Meriwether Lewis: Explorer in the Wilderness*. Washburn ND: Dakota Institute Press, 2011.

———. "'Maney Extroadenary Stories': The Significance of the Arikara To Né's Map." *We Proceeded On* 44, no. 2 (May 2018): 23–30.

———. "On the Future of the Doctrine of Discovery." *We Proceeded On* 49, no. 4 (November 2023): inside front and back covers.

———. "Six Metaphors in Search of an Epic." *Oregon Historical Quarterly* 107, no. 4 (Winter 2006): 553–60. https://www.jstor.org/stable/20615687.

———. "Thomas Slaughter's Expedition: Exploring (and Deploring) Lewis and Clark." *Oregon Historical Quarterly* 105, no. 4 (Winter 2004): 624–31. https://www.jstor.org/stable/20615479.

———. *A Vast and Open Plain: The Writings of the Lewis and Clark Expedition in North Dakota, 1804–1806*. Bismarck: State Historical Society of North Dakota, 2003.

———. "The WPO Interview." *We Proceeded On* 44, no. 2 (May 2018): 35–36.

Jensen, Richard E., and James S. Hutchins. *Wheel Boats on the Missouri: The Journals and Documents of the Atkinson-O'Fallon Expedition, 1824–26*. Helena: Montana Historical Society Press; Lincoln: Nebraska State Historical Society, 2001.

Jones, Landon Y. *William Clark and the Shaping of the West*. New York: Hill and Wang, 2004.

"Joseph Gravelines." *We Proceeded On* 44, no. 2 (May 2018): 19.

Josephy, Alvin M., Jr. "David Thompson." In Hafen, *Mountain Men*, 3:309–37.

———. *The Nez Perce Indians and the Opening of the Northwest*. Boston: Houghton Mifflin, 1965.

Joyner, Tim. *Magellan*. Camden ME: International Marine, 1992.

Keay, John. *The Spice Trade: A History*. Berkeley: University of California Press, 2006.

Kelly, Mark William. "The Hallowed Death Tale of Jedediah Strong Smith: Circumstances, Fact and Fabrication." *Castor Canadensis: Newsletter of the Jedediah Smith Society*, Spring–Summer 2019, 1–12.

———. *Lost Voices on the Missouri: John Dougherty and the Indian Frontier*. Leavenworth KS: Sam Clark, 2013.

Kelman, Ari. *A Misplaced Massacre: Struggling over the Memory of Sand Creek*. Cambridge MA: Harvard University Press, 2013.

———. "Remembering Sand Creek on the Eve of Its Sesquicentennial." *Journal of the Civil War Era* 5, no. 2 (June 2015): 195–203.

Kerr, Robert. *General History and Collection of Voyages and Travels*. Edinburgh: William Blackwood, 1824. https://ia804709.us.archive.org/34/items/cihm_47795/cihm_47795.pdf.

Kolbaba, Tia M. "Fighting for Christianity: Holy War in the Byzantine Empire." *Byzantion* 68, no. 1 (1998): 194–221. https://www.jstor.org/stable/44172480.

Kraft, Louis. *Sandcreek and the Tragic End of a Lifeway*. Norman: University of Oklahoma Press, 2020.

Kukla, Jon. *A Wilderness So Immense: The Louisiana Purchase and the Destiny of America*. New York: Alfred A. Knopf, 2003.

Landry, Clay J. "Hugh Glass: The Rest of the Story." *Rocky Mountain Fur Trade Journal* 10 (2016): 1–17.

Lang, William L. "Lewis and Clark on the Columbia: The Power of Landscape in the Exploration Experience." *Pacific Northwest Quarterly* 87, no. 3 (Summer 1996): 141–48. https://www.jstor.org/stable/40491641.

Large, Arlen J. "Expedition Specialists: The Talented Helpers of Lewis and Clark." *We Proceeded On* 9, no. 1 (February 1994): 4–10.

Larner, John. *Marco Polo and the Discovery of the World*. New Haven: Yale University Press, 1999.

Larpenteur, Charles. *Forty Years a Fur Trader on the Upper Missouri: The Personal Narrative of Charles Larpenteur, 1833–1872*. Edited by Elliott Coues. 2 vols. New York: Francis P. Harper, 1898.

Lass, William E. *Navigating the Missouri: Steamboating on Nature's Highway, 1819–1935*. Norman OK: Arthur H. Clark, 2008.

———. "The Northern Boundary of the Louisiana Purchase." *Great Plains Quarterly* 35, no. 1 (Winter 2015): 27–50. https://www.jstor.org/stable/24465560.

Lavender, David. *Bent's Fort*. Lincoln: University of Nebraska Press, 1972.

———. *The Fist in the Wilderness*. Lincoln: University of Nebraska Press, 1998.

Lawton, John. *Silk, Scents, and Spice*. Paris: UNESCO Publishing, Economica, 2004.

Leonard, Zenas. *Adventures of a Mountain Man: The Narrative of Zenas Leonard*. Edited by Milo Milton Quaife. Lincoln: University of Nebraska Press, 1978.

Limerick, Patricia Nelson. *The Legacy of Conquest: The Unbroken Past of the American West*. New York: W. W. Norton, 1987.

Lloyd, Alan B. "Necho and the Red Sea: Some Considerations." *Journal of Egyptian Archaeology* 63 (1977): 142–55. https://www.jstor.org/stable/3856314.

Lowie, Robert H. *The Crow Indians*. Lincoln: University of Nebraska Press, 1983.

———. *Indians of the Plains*. Lincoln: University of Nebraska Press, 1972.

———. *Myths and Traditions of the Crow Indians*. New York: American Museum of Natural History, 1918. Facsimile of the first edition. Forgotten Books, 2012.

Luttig, John. *Journal of a Fur-Trading Expedition on the Upper Missouri, 1812–1813*. Edited by Stella M. Drumm. St. Louis: Missouri Historical Society, 1920.

Madden, Thomas F. "The Fires of the Fourth Crusade." *International History Review* 17, no. 4 (November 1995): 726–43.

———. "The Venetian Version of the Fourth Crusade: Memory and the Conquest of Constantinople in Medieval Venice." *Spectrum* 87, no. 2 (April 2012): 311–44. https://www.jstor.org/stable/23488041.

Majors, Harry M. "John McClellan in the Montana Rockies, 1807: The First Americans after Lewis and Clark." *Northwest Discovery* 2 (November–December 1981): 554–630.

Man, John. *Xanadu: Marco Polo and Europe's Discovery of the East*. New York: Bantam, 2009.

Markham, Clements R., trans. *The Journal of Christopher Columbus and Documents Relating to the Voyages of John Cabot and Gaspar Corte Real*. New York: Burt Franklin, 1893.

Massing, Andreas. "Mapping the Malagueta Coast: A History of the Lower Guinea Coast, 1460–1510 through Portuguese Maps and Accounts." *History in Africa* 36 (2009): 331–65. https://www.jstor.org/stable/40864524.

Mattes, Merrill J. "Hiram Scott." In Hafen, *Mountain Men*, 1:355–66.

Mattison, Ray H. "Joshua Pilcher." In Hafen, *Mountain Men*, 4:251–60.

McGinnis, Anthony R. *Counting Coup and Cutting Horses: Intertribal Warfare on the Northern Plains, 1738–1889*. Lincoln: University of Nebraska Press, 1990.

Medicine Crow, Joseph. "The Effects of European Culture Contacts upon the Economic, Social, and Religious Life of the Crow Indians." Master's thesis, University of Southern

California, 1939. https://media.proquest.com/cdn/media/hms/ORIG/2/qO5iH?_tm=1690844243605&_cfs=qeYDAeJMkzFHe8rTFd2y59DKZSfJBLvt1ghJ2BgHXy4%3D.

———. *From the Heart of the Crow Country: The Crow Indians' Own Stories.* New York: Crown Trade Paperbacks, 1992.

Merk, Frederick. *Manifest Destiny and Mission in American History: A Reinterpretation.* Cambridge MA: Harvard University Press, 1963.

Meyer, Roy W. *The Village Indians of the Upper Missouri: The Mandans, Hidatsas, and Arikaras.* Lincoln: University of Nebraska Press, 1977.

Michino, Gregory F. *Encyclopedia of Indian Wars: Western Battles and Skirmishes, 1850–1890.* Missoula MT: Mountain Press, 2003.

Miller, Robert J. *Native America Discovered and Conquered: Thomas Jefferson, Lewis and Clark, and Manifest Destiny.* Lincoln: University of Nebraska Press, 2008.

"The Missouri Trapper." *Port Folio* (Philadelphia), January–July 1825.

Moreno, Luis A. Garcia. "Atlantic Seafaring and the Iberian Peninsula in Antiquity." *Mediterranean Studies* 8 (1999): 1–13.

Morgan, Dale L. *Jedediah Smith and the Opening of the West.* Lincoln: University of Nebraska Press, 1964.

———, ed. *The West of William H. Ashley.* Denver: Old West, 1964.

Morison, Samuel Eliot. *Admiral of the Ocean Sea: A Life of Christopher Columbus.* Boston: Little, Brown, 1970.

———. *The European Discovery of American: The Southern Voyages, 1492–1616.* New York: Oxford University Press, 1974.

Morris, Larry E. *The Fate of the Corps: What Became of the Lewis and Clark Explorers after the Expedition.* New Haven CT: Yale University Press, 2004.

———. *In the Wake of Lewis and Clark: The Expedition and the Making of Antebellum America.* Lanham MD: Rowman & Littlefield, 2019.

———. "The Life of John Colter." *We Proceeded On* 34, no. 4 (November 2008): 6–15.

———. "Mountain Men and the Taking of California, 1845–1847." *Rocky Mountain Fur Trade Journal* 10 (2016): 94–121.

———. "The Mysterious Charles Courtin and the Early Missouri Fur Trade." *Missouri Historical Review* 104, no. 1 (October 2009): 21–39.

———. "'Natural Born Indian': The Apprenticeship of Edward Rose." *Rocky Mountain Fur Trade Journal* 16 (2022): 22–49.

———. *The Perilous West: Seven Amazing Explorers and the Founding of the Oregon Trail.* Lanham MD: Rowman & Littlefield, 2013.

———. "The War and the Corps: An Expedition Roster, 1812." *We Proceeded On* 44, no. 1 (February 2018): 6–15.

Moulton, Gary E., ed. *The Journals of the Lewis and Clark Expedition.* 13 vols. Lincoln: University of Nebraska Press, 1986–97.

Myers, John Myers. *The Saga of Hugh Glass: Pirate, Pawnee, and Mountain Man.* Lincoln: University of Nebraska Press, 1976.

Nasatir, A. P., ed. *Before Lewis and Clark: Documents Illustrating the History of the Missouri, 1785–1804*. Norman: University of Oklahoma Press, 2002.

———. "Jean Baptiste Truteau." In Hafen, *Mountain Men*, 4:381–97.

Nathan, Lord, Eva Taylor, Armando Cortesão, and Alan Burns. "Prince Henry the Navigator and the Discovery of the Sea Route to India: Discussion." *Geographical Journal* 127, no. 2 (June 1961): 155–58. https://www.jstor.org/stable/1792891.

Nell, Donald F., and Anthony Demetriades. "The True Utmost Reaches of the Missouri: Were Lewis and Clark Wrong When They Identified the Source of This Great River?" *Montana Outdoors*, July–August 2005. https://web.archive.org/web/20120118010715/http://fwp.mt.gov/mtoutdoors/HTML/articles/2005/MissouriSource.htm.

Nester, William R. *The Arikara War: The First Plains Indian War*. Missoula MT: Mountain Press, 2001.

Nicandri, David L. "The Columbia Country and the Dissolution of Meriwether Lewis: Speculation and Interpretation." *Oregon Historical Quarterly* 106, no. 1 (Spring 2005): 6–33. https://www.jstor.org/stable/20615502.

———. *River of Promise: Lewis and Clark on the Columbia*. Washburn ND: Dakota Institute Press, 2009.

Nichols, Roger L. "The Arikara Indians and the Missouri River Trade: A Quest for Survival." *Great Plains Quarterly* 2, no. 2 (Spring 1982): 77–93.

———. "The Army and the Indians, 1800–1830: A Reappraisal: The Missouri Valley Example." *Pacific Historical Review* 41, no. 2 (May 1972): 152–68.

———. "Backdrop for Disaster: Causes of the Arikara War of 1823." *South Dakota History* 14, no. 2 (Summer 1989): 93–113.

———. *General Henry Atkinson: A Western Military Career*. Norman: University of Oklahoma Press, 1965.

———. *Massacring Indians: From Horseshoe Bend to Wounded Knee*. Norman: University of Oklahoma Press, 2021.

Nicol, Donald M. *Byzantium and Venice: A Study in Diplomatic and Cultural Relations*. Cambridge: University of Cambridge Press, 1988.

Niles, N., ed. *Niles Weekly Register*. Vol. 25. Baltimore: Franklin Press, 1824.

O'Briant, Kevin. "Too Né's World: The Arikara Map and Native American Cartography." *We Proceeded On* 44, no. 2 (May 2018): 6–35.

Oglesby, Richard Edward. "Manuel Lisa." In Hafen, *Mountain Men*, 5:179–201.

———. *Manuel Lisa and the Opening of the Missouri Fur Trade*. Norman: University of Oklahoma Press, 1963.

———. "William Morrison." In Hafen, *Mountain Men*, 3:197–203.

Orser, Charles E. "Understanding Arikara Trading Behavior: A Cultural Case Study of the Ashley-Leavenworth Episode of 1823." In Buckley, *Rendezvous*, 101–8.

Parker, Samuel. *Journal of an Exploring Tour beyond the Rocky Mountains, under the Direction of the A. B. C. F. M. Performed in the Years 1835, '36, and '37*. Minneapolis: Ross & Haines, 1967.

Parkman, Francis, Jr. *The Oregon Trail*. New York: Oxford University Press, 2008.

Parks, Douglas R. *Myths and Traditions of the Arikara Indians*. Lincoln: University of Nebraska Press, 1994.

———. *Traditional Narratives of the Arikara Indians*. Vol. 3, *Stories of Alfred Morsette: English Translations*. Lincoln: University of Nebraska Press, 1991.

Paton, Bruce E. *Lewis and Clark: Doctors in the Wilderness*. Golden CO: Fulcrum, 2001.

Pearson, J. Diane. "Lewis Cass and the Politics of Disease: The Indian Vaccination Act of 1832." *Wicazo Sa Review* 18, no. 2 (Autumn 2003): 9–35. https://www.jstor.org/stable/1409535.

———. "Medical Diplomacy and the American Indian: Thomas Jefferson, the Lewis and Clark Expedition, and the Subsequent Effects on American Indian Health and Public Policy." *Wicazo Sa Review* 19, no. 1 (Spring 2004): 105–30. https://www.jstor.org/stable/1409489.

Perry, David M., and Matthew Gebriele. "The Many Myths of the Term 'Crusader,'" *Smithsonian Magazine*, November 2021. https://www.smithsonianmag.com/history/the-many-myths-of-the-term-crusader-180979107/.

Phillips, Jonathan. *The Fourth Crusade and the Sack of Constantinople*. New York: Penguin, 2004.

Pigafetta, Antonio. *Magellan's Voyage around the World*. Translated and edited by James Alexander Robertson. 3 vols. Cleveland: Arthur H. Clark, 1906.

Porter, Kenneth W. *John Jacob Astor, Business Man*. 2 vols. Cambridge MA: Harvard University Press, 1931.

———. "Roll of Overland Astorians, 1810–1812." *Oregon Historical Quarterly* 34 (June 1933): 103–12.

Potter, Tracy. *Sheheke, Mandan Indian Diplomat: The Story of White Coyote, Thomas Jefferson, and Lewis and Clark*. Helena MT: Farcountry Press and Fort Mandan Press, 2003.

Ravenstein, E. G., trans. and ed. *A Journal of the First Voyage of Vasco da Gama*. New York: Burt Franklin, 1898. https://www.gutenberg.org/files/46440/46440-h/46440-h.htm#Page_xxxvii.

Remley, David. *Kit Carson: The Life of an American Border Man*. Norman: University of Oklahoma Press, 2011.

Ricketts, Norma Baldwin. *The Mormon Battalion: US Army of the West*. Logan: Utah State University Press, 1996.

Riley, James C. "Smallpox and American Indians Revisited." *Journal of the History of Medicine and Allied Sciences*. 65, no. 4 (October 2010): 445–77. https://www.jstor.org/stable/24631803.

Roberts, David. *A Newer World: Kit Carson, John C. Frémont, and the Claiming of the American West*. New York: Simon & Schuster, 2000.

Robinson, Doane. "Official Correspondence of the Leavenworth Expedition into South Dakota in 1823." *South Dakota Historical Collections* 1, no. 7 (1902): 181–256.

Rollins, Philip Ashton, ed. *The Discovery of the Oregon Trail: Robert Stuart's Narratives of His Overland Trip Eastward from Astoria in 1812–13*. New York: Charles Scribner's Sons, 1935.

Ronda, James P. *Astoria and Empire*. Lincoln: University of Nebraska Press, 1990.

———. *Beyond Lewis and Clark: The Army Explores the West.* Tacoma: Washington Historical Society, 2003.

———. *Finding the West: Explorations with Lewis and Clark.* Albuquerque: University of New Mexico Press, 2001.

———. *Lewis and Clark among the Indians.* Lincoln: University of Nebraska Press, 1984.

———. "A Moment in Time: The West—September 1806." In Ronda, *Finding the West,* 77–95.

———, ed. *Thomas Jefferson and the Changing West.* St. Louis: Missouri Historical Society Press, 1997.

———, ed. *Voyages of Discovery: Essays on the Lewis and Clark Expedition.* Helena: Montana Historical Society Press, 1998.

Ross, Alexander. *Adventures of the First Settlers on the Columbia River, 1810–1813.* Corvallis: Oregon State University Press, 2000.

Russell, Carl P. "Duncan McDougal." In Hafen, *Mountain Men,* 5:217–26.

———. *Firearms, Traps, and Tools of the Mountain Men.* Albuquerque: University of New Mexico Press, 1977.

———. *Guns on the Early Frontiers: From Colonial Times to the Years of the Western Fur Trade.* Mineola NY: Dover, 2005.

Russell, Osborne. *Journal of a Trapper.* Edited by Aubrey L. Haines. Lincoln: University of Nebraska Press, 1965.

Sage, Rufus B. *Scenes in the Rocky Mountains, and in Oregon, California, New Mexico, Texas, and the Grand Prairies.* London: Wentworth, 2016.

Schreurs, Peter. "The Voyage of Fernão de Magalhães: Three Little-Known Eyewitness Accounts." *Philippine Quarterly of Culture and Society* 28, no. 1 (March 2000): 90–109.

Sheehan, Bernard W. "Jefferson and the West." *Virginia Quarterly Review* 58, no. 2 (Spring 1982): 345–52. https://www.jstor.org/stable/26436871.

———. *Seeds of Extinction: Jeffersonian Philanthropy and the American Indian.* Chapel Hill: University of North Carolina Press, 1973.

Sides, Hampton. *Blood and Thunder: The Epic Story of Kit Carson and the Conquest of the American West.* New York: Anchor, 2006.

Skarsten, M. O. "George Drouillard." In Hafen, *Mountain Men,* 4:69–82.

———. *George Drouillard: Hunter and Interpreter for Lewis and Clark & Fur Trader, 1807–1810.* Lincoln: University of Nebraska Press, 1995.

Slaughter, Thomas P. *Exploring Lewis and Clark: Reflections on Men and Wilderness.* New York: Alfred A. Knopf, 2003.

Smith, Henry Nash. *Virgin Land: The American West as Symbol and Myth.* Cambridge MA: Harvard University Press, 1970.

Spence, Mary Lee, and Donald Jackson, eds. *The Expeditions of John Charles Fremont.* Vol. 2, *The Bear Flag Revolt and the Court-Martial.* Urbana: University of Illinois Press, 1973.

Stands in Timber, John, and Margot Liberty. *Cheyenne Memories.* 2nd ed. New Haven CT: Yale University Press, 1998.

Stanley, Henry E. J., trans. and ed. *The Three Voyages of Vasco da Gama and His Viceroyalty from the Lendas da India of Gaspar Correa: Accompanied by Original Documents*. New York: Burt Franklin, 1869.

Stanley of Alderley, ed. *The First Voyage round the World, by Magellan*. London: Hakluyt Society, 1874.

Steiger, John W. "Benjamin O'Fallon." In Hafen, *Mountain Men*, 5:255–81.

Steinke, Christopher. "'Here Is My Country': Too Né's Map of Lewis and Clark in the Great Plains." *William and Mary Quarterly* 71, no. 4 (October 2014): 589–610.

Stewart, Edgar L. "Donald MacKenzie." In Hafen, *Mountain Men*, 5:227–38.

Stieglitz, Robert R. "Long-Distance Seafaring in the Ancient Near East." *Biblical Archaeologist*, 47 (September 1984): 134–42. https://www.jstor.org/stable/3209914.

Stone, B. G. "The Spice Trade." *Journal of the Royal Society of Arts* 112, no. 5097 (August 1964): 703–13. https://www.jstor.org/stable/41367670.

Sunder, John E. *Bill Sublette: Mountain Man*. Norman: University of Oklahoma Press, 1959.

———. *Joshua Pilcher: Fur Trader and Indian Agent*. Norman: University of Oklahoma Press, 1968.

———. "William L. Sublette." In Hafen, *Mountain Men*, 5:347–59.

Tarn, W. W. "Ptolemy II." *Journal of Egyptian Archaeology* 14, nos. 3–4 (November 1928): 246–60. https://www.jstor.org/stable/3854301.

Tate, Cassandra. *Unsettled Ground: The Whitman Massacre and Its Shifting Legacy in the American West*. Seattle: Sasquatch Books, 2020.

Tubbs, Stephenie Ambrose, with Clay S. Jenkinson. *The Lewis and Clark Companion: An Encyclopedic Guide to the Voyage of Discovery*. New York: Henry Holt, 2003.

Turner, Jack. *The History of a Temptation: Spice*. New York: Vintage Books, 2004.

———. "The Spice That Built Venice." *Smithsonian Magazine, Smithsonian Journeys Travel Quarterly*, November 2015. https://www.smithsonianmag.com/travel/spice-trade-pepper-venice-180956856/.

Ubelaker, Douglas H., and William M. Bass. "Arikara Glassworking Techniques at Leavenworth and Sully Sites." *American Antiquity* 35, no. 4 (1970): 467–75.

Utley, Robert M. *A Life Wild and Perilous: Mountain Men and the Paths to the Pacific*. New York: Henry Holt, 1997.

Vancouver, George. *A Voyage of Discovery to the North Pacific Ocean and round the World, 1791–1795*. Edited by William Kaye Lamb. 4 vols. London: Hakluyt Society, 1984.

Van de Logt, Mark. *Between the Floods: A History of the Arikaras*. Norman: University of Oklahoma Press, 2023.

———. "'The Whirlwind Is Coming to Destroy My People!' Symbolic Representations of Epidemics in Arikara Oral Tradition." *American Indian Quarterly* 39, no. 1 (Winter 2015): 52–72.

Victor, Frances Fuller. *The River of the West: Life and Adventure in the Rocky Mountains and Oregon*. Hartford CT: Columbian Book Company, 1871.

Voelker, Frederic E. "Ezekiel Williams." In Hafen, *Mountain Men*, 9:393–409.

———. "Ezekiel Williams of Boon's Lick." *Bulletin of the Missouri Historical Society* 8, no. 1 (October 1951): 17–51.

———. "Thomas Eddie." In Hafen, *Mountain Men*, 1:273–80.

———. "Thomas James." In Hafen, *Mountain Men*, 4:153–67.

Waldo, William. "Recollections of a Septuagenarian." *Missouri Historical Society Glimpses of the Past* 4–6 (April–June 1938): 59–94.

Walker, Ardis M. "Joseph R. Walker." In Hafen, *Mountain Men*, 5:361–80.

Ward, Geoffrey C. *The West: An Illustrated History*. Boston: Little, Brown, 1996.

Waugh, Teresa, trans. *The Travels of Marco Polo*. New York: Facts on File, 1984.

Weatherford, Jack. *Genghis Khan and the Making of the Modern World*. New York: Broadway Books, 2004.

Webb, E. J. "The Alleged Phoenician Circumnavigation of Africa: Considered in Relation to the Theory of a South African Ophir." *English Historical Review* 22 (January 1907): 1–14. https://www.jstor.org/stable/549751.

West, Elliott. *Contested Plains: Indians, Goldseekers, and the Rush to Colorado*. Lawrence: University Press of Kansas, 1998.

———. *Continental Reckoning: The American West in the Age of Expansion*. Lincoln: University of Nebraska Press, 2023.

———. "Golden Dreams: Colorado, California, and the Reimagining of America." *Montana: The Magazine of Western History* 49, no. 3 (Autumn 1999): 2–11.

"What's in a Name?" *We Proceeded On* 44, no. 2 (May 2018): 22.

White, David A., ed. *News of the Plains and Rockies, 1803–1865*. 9 vols. Spokane WA: Arthur H. Clark, 1996–2001.

Whitman, Walt. *Two Rivulets*. Camden NJ: W. Whitman, 1876.

"William Dunlap's Meeting with Too Né in Washington, DC, February 25–28, 1806." *We Proceeded On* 44, no. 2 (May 2018): 16–17.

Wishart, David J., ed. *Encyclopedia of the Great Plains Indians*. Lincoln: University of Nebraska Press, 2007.

———. *The Fur Trade of the American West, 1807–1840*. Lincoln: University of Nebraska Press, 1992.

Wood, W. Raymond, William J. Hunt, and Randy H. Williams. *Fort Clark and Its Indian Neighbors: A Trading Post on the Upper Missouri*. Norman: University of Oklahoma Press, 2013.

Wood, W. Raymond, and Thomas D. Thiessen, eds. *Early Fur Trade on the Northern Plains: Canadian Traders Among the Mandan and Hidatsa Indians, 1738–1818*. Norman: University of Oklahoma Press, 1985.

Woodger, Elin, and Brandon Toropov. *Encyclopedia of the Lewis and Clark Expedition*. New York: Checkmark, 2004.

Yule, Henry, ed. *The Book of Ser Marco Polo, the Venetian: Concerning the Kingdoms and Marvels of the East*. 2nd ed. London: John Murray, 1875.

Zurara, Gomes Eanes de. *The Chronicle of the Discovery and Conquest of Guinea*. Vol. 1. New York: Burt Franklin, 1896.

INDEX